READING SIDONIUS' *EPISTLES*

Sidonius Apollinaris' letters offer a vivid series of glimpses into an otherwise sparsely documented period. His rich anecdotes feature the events, characters, and moments that defined his life, ranging from the treason trial of Arvandus to the Visigothic raiding of Clermont, from the corrupt and vile Seronatus to the holy widow Eutropia, and the day-to-day incidents that confronted a Gallo-Roman poet, aristocrat, and bishop as the Late Roman West transitioned into the barbarian successor kingdoms. Like any good storyteller, Sidonius exploited a wide array of narratological tools, manipulating temporality for dramatic effect, sketching his heroes and villains in vivid detail, and recreating witty dialogue in a collection that is highly organised and carefully strategised. This book provides a fuller understanding of his contribution to Latin literature, as a careful arranger of his self-image, a perceptive exploiter of narrative dynamics, and an influential figure in Late Antique Gaul.

M. P. HANAGHAN is Research Fellow (Latin Christianity in Late Antiquity) at the Institute for Religion and Critical Inquiry, Australian Catholic University. His research is principally focused on epistolography, panegyric, and historiography, especially intertextuality, narratology, visuality, and reader response.

READING SIDONIUS'
EPISTLES

M. P. HANAGHAN

Australian Catholic University, Melbourne

CAMBRIDGE
UNIVERSITY PRESS

CAMBRIDGE
UNIVERSITY PRESS

University Printing House, Cambridge CB2 8BS, United Kingdom

One Liberty Plaza, 20th Floor, New York, NY 10006, USA

477 Williamstown Road, Port Melbourne, VIC 3207, Australia

314–321, 3rd Floor, Plot 3, Splendor Forum, Jasola District Centre, New Delhi – 110025, India

79 Anson Road, #06-04/06, Singapore 079906

Cambridge University Press is part of the University of Cambridge.

It furthers the University's mission by disseminating knowledge in the pursuit of education, learning, and research at the highest international levels of excellence.

www.cambridge.org
Information on this title: www.cambridge.org/9781108429214
DOI: 10.1017/9781108554305

© M. P. Hanaghan 2019

First published 2019

Printed and bound in Great Britain by Clays Ltd, Elcograf S.p.A.

A catalogue record for this publication is available from the British Library.

Library of Congress Cataloging-in-Publication Data
Names: Hanaghan, M. P., author.
Title: Reading Sidonius' epistles / M. P. Hanaghan.
Description: Cambridge: Cambridge University Press, 2019. |
Includes bibliographical references and index.
Identifiers: LCCN 2018039113 | ISBN 9781108429214 (Hardback) |
ISBN 9781108453349 (Paperback)
Subjects: LCSH: Sidonius Apollinaris, Saint, 431 or 432 – approximately 487. Correspondence. |
Sidonius Apollinaris, Saint, 431 or 432 – approximately 487 – Criticism and interpretation.
Classification: LCC PA6694.S8H36 2018 | DDC 876/.01–dc23
LC record available at https://lccn.loc.gov/2018039113

ISBN 978-1-108-42921-4 Hardback

Contents

Maps

vi

Preface

Sidonius' epistles offer a vivid series of glimpses into a sparsely documented period. Their exciting anecdotes draw on the characters and moments that defined his age and filled his life. Barbarians rub shoulders with clergy, vile and corrupt aristocrats exploit the turbulence of his age, as Roman Gaul transitioned into the successor kingdoms, and Sidonius and his friends try to make the best of their situation.

Chapter 1 offers an overview of Sidonius and his world and reviews current scholarship. Chapter 2 analyses Sidonius' self-presentation, in line with similar scholarly treatments of Cicero, Seneca, and Pliny. The remaining chapters consider how Sidonius exploited a rich array of narratological tools (like any good story teller), manipulating temporal aspects for dramatic effect (Chapter 3), sketching his heroes and villains in exacting and vivid detail (Chapter 4), recalling and recreating witty dialogue (Chapter 5), and bringing it all together with considered arrangement (Chapter 6). The epistles are highly organised, strategised, with elements artificially fine-tuned and dressed up as efforts made on the spur of the moment. This book aims to move consideration away from the limited historical value of Sidonius' letters towards a fuller understanding of their contribution to Latin literature. Each chapter of this book, like each epistle, is ultimately about Sidonius, who emerges as a careful arranger of his self-image, a perceptive exploiter of narrative dynamics, and an influential figure in Late Antique Gaul.

Acknowledgements

This book was begun at the University of Sydney, continued at the University of Exeter, and completed at University College Cork and the Institute for Religion and Critical Inquiry at ACU, Melbourne. Along the way many colleagues and friends generously read drafts and offered suggestions. I am especially grateful to Catherine Ware whose criticism, encouragement, and good humour were a constant source of inspiration. I would like to thank Richard Miles and Paul Roche for their encouragement, and Richard Flower, Gavin Kelly, Rebecca Langlands, Andrew Pettinger, Deborah Roberts, Joop Van Waarden, and Jeroen Wijnendaele for reading and commenting on my ideas. I am very appreciative to Michael Sharp for his wonderful guidance, and to the two reviewers who offered many insightful suggestions and corrections, Roy Gibson and an anonymous colleague.

My research has profited from many audiences including at the SCS, Celtic Classics conference, International Society for Late Antique Literary Studies, and in seminars at Exeter and Cork.

This book would not have been possible without the seemingly endless support of my wife, Diana Withnall. I would especially like to thank the Irish Research Council for the funding that directly supported this research. Thanks are also due to Daniel Ogden, Lynette Mitchell, Sharon Marshall, Nicolo' D'Alconzo, Jason Harris, Diarmuid Scully, David Woods, James Uden, Scott McGill, and David Bright.

North
Sea

ATLANTIC

OCEAN

DIOCESE
OF BRITAIN

Trier

D I O C E S E
OF
G A U L
Clermont°
Lyon
Vienne
Bordeaux

D I O C E S E
OF ITALY

Apt
Toulouse
Riez
Marseilles

Ravenna°

WESTERN ROMAN EMPIRE
Rome
DIOCESE OF
THE CITY
OF ROME

D I O C E S E
OF
S P A I N

Mediterranean

DIOCESE
OF SPAIN

D I O C E S E   O F   A F R I C A

Carthage
PROCONSULATE
OF AFRICA

Sea

| 0 | 200 | 400 | 600 km |
| 0 | 100 | 200 | 300 miles |

Prefecture of Gaul
Prefecture of Italy
Prefecture of Illyricum (Eastern Roman Empire)

Map 1 Map of the Western Roman Empire, twenty years before Sidonius' birth

Map 2 Map of the barbarian successor kingdoms, in the final years of Sidonius' life

xi

CHAPTER I

Sidonius' World

As a young man in the 440s and 450s Sidonius enjoyed all the traditional markers of the Roman elite: a noble birth, a classical education, a good marriage, privilege, and wealth.[1] By his death in the mid to late 480s the great secular Gallo-Roman aristocrat of his age was a bishop.[2] Barbarians likely lodged in his villa.[3] They certainly occupied his see, Clermont. His wife's father had been murdered shortly after becoming emperor.[4] The last Roman emperor in the West was dead, and the next generation inspired Sidonius with little confidence that his belletrism would continue in the family, or even the Gallo-Roman aristocracy. Documenting accurately this fascinating period was not Sidonius' aim – he checked himself from writing history.[5] If he was, as McLynn claims "Fifth Century Gaul's … great historian *manqué*," this miss is of his own making.[6] Events during the

---

[1] The exact date of Sidonius' marriage to Papianilla, the daughter of Fl. Eparchius Avitus is unclear. Loyen (1970a: x) suggested that Sidonius was twenty, Stevens (1933: 19) proposes a slightly later date. For two later assessments of Sidonius' life see Gregory of Tours 2.22 and Gennadius of Marseilles 92, neither of which may be relied upon with any certainity; Gregory manipulates Sidonius as a source when it suits him and on occasion misreads his meaning, for an example of which see Moorhead (2007: 331), and for detailed analysis Furbetta (2015c). Gennadius' account may be a later insertion as it does not feature in the earlier manuscript tradition, for which see Schaff and Wace (1892: 401) and more recently Chronopoulos (2010: 242).

[2] For the date range for Sidonius' death see pp. 7–8.

[3] The term "barbarian" is used throughout when a more specific name is unsuitable or as (as here) to maintain Sidonius' focalisation.

[4] Avitus' exact cause of death is unclear, see pp. 4–5.

[5] Sidonius explicitly rules out writing history in *Ep.* 4.22.1, 5 which was addressed to Leo, a Visigothic adviser. In that epistle, as elsewhere, he cites Pliny the Younger (henceforth Pliny) as his major epistolary model and compares Leo to Tacitus by using Pliny's remarks in *Ep.* 6.16.21–22, which was addressed to Tacitus; for an analysis see Ash (2003: 211–215), for the influence of Pliny on Sidonius see especially pp. 14–15, 176–178. Rousseau (1976: 360) argues that Sidonius considered writing generally more dangerous than reading.

[6] McLynn (1993: 354). According to Matthews (2000: 34) "Sidonius is never easy to use. On the one hand, there is the risk of over-literal interpretation of what he intends metaphorically; on the other hand, his metaphorical language is precise if one can find the key to it."

last decades of Roman power in the West demanded that Sidonius control meticulously how he presented himself to the outside world.

The struggle for survival and relevancy consumes Sidonius' epistles as they respond to specific circumstances.[7] Barbarians are both condemned and praised, and secular literature is depicted as a key part of his daily life, even after he became a bishop who could not quite keep his promises to stop writing poetry.[8] At every point the complexity of Sidonius' persona is enhanced, as the political pragmatist who deals with barbarians as the situation demands or allows, and as the bishop who never jettisoned his classical *paideia*.[9]

Sidonius' fascinating life, with all its ups and downs, becomes the raw material which he develops into rich and engaging narratives; characters are brought to life, dramatic events heightened, moments reworked, and dialogue condensed. Ultimately his epistles' pseudo-biographical treatment of his life draws to an end as the death of his persona matches his own. The epistles draw the reader into his world which is filtered by his repeated concerns for Latin literary culture and the Roman governance of Gaul.

Vita

In the late fourth century large numbers of barbarian groups began to migrate west. In 407, in response to the growing threat of these groups and Roman disengagement from the north-western sphere of the Empire, the usurper Constantine III tried to wrestle control from the imperial authorities.[10] Sidonius' grandfather Apollinaris followed Constantine III's son and general Constans II into Spain as a prefect.[11] Prior to the siege of Arles in 411 Apollinaris was demoted, and was either put to death or returned to his native Lyon.[12]

---

[7] Harries (1994: 11).

[8] Hebert (1988) and Overwien (2009: 93–113). See p. 55.

[9] In *Ep.* 9.6.2, for example, Sidonius includes references to Charbydis and Ulysses in his remarks to Ambrosius, another bishop, in praise of newlyweds.

[10] Drinkwater (1998) offers a detailed assessment of the evidence and events. See also Fanning (1992: 288).

[11] *Prosopography of the Later Roman Empire* (1971–1992; henceforth PLRE) "Apollinaris 1." Zosimus *Nova Historia* 6.4: See Drinkwater (1998: 288) and Mascoli (2002: 184). Sidonius had many relatives with the name Apollinaris, including an uncle (PLRE "Apollinaris 2") and son (PLRE "Apollinaris 3").

[12] Zosimus *Nova Historia* 6.13. Drinkwater (1998: 288) suggests that Apollinaris could have been executed after joining Jovinus' revolt. Dalton (1915: clxi) offers that Apollinaris returned to Lyon

There some twenty years later Apollinaris' grandson Gaius Sollius Modestus Sidonius Apollinaris was born.[13] Throughout the 440s, as Roman and barbarian forces clashed with one another, Sidonius received a traditional Roman education.[14] At about twenty years of age he married Papianilla, the daughter of the Gallo-Roman noble and general Eparchius Avitus.[15] In 451 a coalition of Roman and barbarian forces, made up primarily of Visigoths and Alamanni, defeated Attila's Hunnic horde at the battle of the Catalaunian Plains. At around this time Sidonius attended the Visigothic court as a Roman envoy.

In 454 the influential Roman general Aëtius was murdered by the Emperor Valentinian III.[16] In response Valentinian was himself killed.[17] His death marked the end of the Theodosian dynasty's rule in the West.[18] The new emperor, an ambitious senator named Petronius Maximus then married one

although this is not explicit in any primary source. For this claim he cites Fauriel who merely mentions that Apollinaris was from Lyon, Fauriel (1836: 67, 99). In the absence of any clear evidence, Apollinaris' return to Lyon must remain a mere probability; see Mascoli (2001: 131) and (2010: 13–17). For a clear account of these events see Kulikowski (2000: 332–340).

[13] The month was November, but the exact year is unknown. Sidonius indicates the month in *Carm.* 20.1–2. His date of birth can be approximated by *Ep.* 8.6 v.5 where Sidonius refers to himself as an *adulescens* when describing events that took place in 449: Stevens (1933: 1), Anderson (1936: xxxii), Dill (1910: 187), and Harries (1994: 36).

[14] The educational system in Gaul was eventually affected by the collapse of Roman rule but this happened well and truly after Sidonius had already achieved his education, see Mohrmann (1955: 13), Mathisen (2005: 6–9), and Judge (2010: 260). Sidonius' education was based on the key classical and secular texts which had formed the mainstay of the Roman education system from the first century. Sidonius *Ep.* 6.1, Dill (1910: 188), and Hooper and Schwartz (1991: 287). Van Dam (1998: 151) argues that this education system fostered "reverence for the past." See also Anderson (1936: xxxiv) and Kaster (1997: 89–92). Gaul was renowned for the quality of education on offer in its major cities; see Borius (1965: 17). Mathisen (1999: 29) argues that an author's use of classical allusions can be considered evidence of their education, but Sidonius also alludes to authors he is unlikely to have studied, such as Sallust; for which see Engelbrecht (1890: 495). As Max (1979: 227) argues, Sidonius was certainly familiar with the *Bellum Catilinae*.

[15] Loyen (1970a: x–xi). Stevens (1933: 19) dates the marriage to 452 or later. Krause (1991: 543) provides multiple examples of aristocratic men marrying in their early twenties in Late Antique Gaul. In *Ep.* 9.6 Sidonius approves of the behaviour of a young man who left his lover and married (*Ep.* 9.6.2) "intactam … tam moribus natalibusque summatem quam facultatis principalis" (a chaste woman … foremost in character and birth and with a princely fortune). Sidonius hardly fits the unnamed protagonist, but his approval of the man's wife resonates with his marriage to Papianilla, whose birth was impeccable and wealth considerable. Translations are largely my own except where noted otherwise and with the exception of Anderson and Warmington's loeb editions which I have borrowed from and adapted freely.

[16] For a detailed assessment of this period see Stickler (2002: 70–83); see also Twyman (1970: 480ff); for Valentinian's likely motivation see Oost (1964: 25).

[17] Moss (1973: 771) and Roberto (2017: 776). For Aëtius' early career see Wijnendaele (2017: 468–482).

[18] Kulikowksi (2012: 46) notes the problems this then caused for subsequent emperors to assert their legitimacy. See also Gillet (2003: 94–95) and Szidat (2010: 239).

of Valentinian's daughters, probably Eudocia, to his own son.[19] This act likely cancelled the agreement that Valentinian had struck with the Vandal king Geiseric to marry Eudocia to his heir Hunneric. Partly as a consequence the Vandals sacked Rome in May 455 in the lead up to which Petronius Maximus was himself killed.[20]

On 9 July 455 Sidonius' father-in-law Avitus was proclaimed emperor in Gaul after securing the support of the Visigothic king, Theodoric II, whereupon he marched to Rome accompanied by Visigothic bodyguards.[21] On 1 January of the following year Sidonius delivered a panegyric for Avitus. At its end Sidonius optimistically asserted (*Carm.* 7.600–601): "felix tempus nevere sorores / imperiis, Auguste" (the Fates have spun a fortunate span for your rule, Emperor). Events thwarted this panegyrical longing for stability. The Eastern Emperor Leo never recognised Avitus as Augustus in the West. Precisely what happened next is unknown; John of Antioch claims that Rome's bankruptcy prevented Avitus from paying his Visigothic guards who in turn left Rome to pursue their interests in Spain.[22] The barbarian potentate Ricimer forced Avitus to flee the city after which he died in circumstances which are unclear in the sources – although his successor Majorian may well have also been involved.[23]

---

[19] O'Flynn (1983: 92–94) argues that there may have been some hesitancy to follow through on the promise to Geiseric to marry Eudocia to his son. Szidat (2010: 34) claims that Petronius' ascension was not considered an usurpation at the time. The situation is clouded somewhat by the fact that Valentinian had another daughter, Placidia, and the sources are unclear as to whether she was already married to Olybrius by 455, for discussion of which see Connant (2012: 27–28).

[20] Merrills and Miles (2010: 116–119) and Roberto (2017: 779). See pp. 22, 113–114, 187–188.

[21] For a detailed consideration of the evidence for Avitus' reign see Mathisen (1985: 326–335) and Burgess (1987: 336–340). The sources differ as to the precise date of Avitus' acclamation as Emperor; see *Monumenta Germaniae Historica*, 15 vols (1877–1919; repr. 1961), AA Auctores Antiquissimi 9. 304; Loyen (1970a: xi) and (1942: 54), Burgess (1987: 336), and Kulikowski (2008: 336) all favour 9 July.

[22] John of Antioch fr. 202, to which may be added support from later sources including Zosimus and John Lydus, for discussion of which see Roberto (2017: 775–801) who argues that Avitus' decision to melt down Roman statues was critical to his removal from office. Stroheker (1970: 53–54) puts the blame on Avitus' inability to rule rather than the trying circumstances.

[23] Avitus died in either 456 or 457, after which Sidonius never again mentioned him by name in any of his works. For a considered analysis of subtle references to Avitus in the remainder of Sidonius' corpus see Mathisen (1979: 165–171) and Rousseau (2000: 253). MacGeorge (2002: 188–197) offers a careful and considered analysis of the evidence. Hydatius 176 (183) focused on the removal of Avitus' Visigothic guards but does not explicitly blame Ricimer or Majorian for his death. Victoris Tonnennsis a. 456 and the *Continuatio Haunensis Prosperi* 1383 maintain that Ricimer defeated Avitus, who was then ordained as a bishop. The Anonymous *Gallic Chronicle of 511* states that Majorian killed Avitus. The most detailed account is John of Antioch fr. 202: "Ἐπιθέμενοι δὲ αὐτῷ κατὰ τὴν ὁδόν, Μαιουρῖνός τε καὶ Ῥεκίμερ, εἰς τέμενος φυγεῖν κατηνάγκασαν,

Sidonius somehow managed to extricate himself to the relative safety of Gaul, where he next appears in the historical record in 459 delivering a panegyric to the Emperor Majorian who had journeyed to Gaul to placate unrest among the Gallo-Roman nobility.[24] The panegyric did enough to spare Sidonius' life, and even, so it seems, to spare Gaul from the worst of its tax burden.[25] For the next decade Sidonius lived in Gaul and likely held local office; very little is known about this period of his life.[26]

In 461 Ricimer had Majorian killed.[27] His replacement Libius Severus ruled until his own death in 465 whereupon an interregnum existed until the Eastern Roman Emperor Leo appointed Anthemius as the Emperor in the West in 467.[28] Sidonius journeyed from Gaul to Rome to make some sort of representation to the new emperor, the specifics of which cannot be determined from our extant sources.[29] There his efforts at Anthemius' court won him the honour of delivering a panegyric on 1 January 468

ἀπαγορεύοντα τῇ ἀρχῇ, καὶ τὴν βασίλεον ἀποδυσάμενον στολήν. Ἔνθα οἱ περὶ Μαιουρῖνον οὐ πρότερον τῆς πολιορκίας ἀπέστησαν, πρὶν ἢ λιμῷ πιεσθεὶς τὸν βίον ἀπέλιπε ... οἱ δέ φασι ὅτι ἀπεπνίγη" (When Majorian and Ricimer attacked him on the road, they forced him to flee to sanctuary, give up his rule, and remove his imperial robe. Then Majorian's men did not withdraw from the siege until drained by hunger he lost his life ... others say that he was strangled). Max (1979: 225) notes "there is so much obscurity in the history immediately following the deposition [of Avitus] ... that scarcely anything certain can be advanced concerning it." Börm (2013: 102) considers both Ricimer and Majorian to have been involved but notes the lack of clarity regarding the specifics of Avitus' demise. Accounts that assert a single version of events, such as Loyen's (1970a: xiii) must be treated with scepticism. Oost (1964: 23–4) ascribes Majorians' rise in part to his connections to Aëtius.

[24] During the intervening period the shadowy Marcellan conspiracy occurred about which little can be deduced with any certainty from our sources. Sidonius mentions it briefly in *Ep.* 1.11.6. Mathisen (1985: 333–334), Courcelle (1948: 168), and Köhler (1995: 308–309). See also Jiménez Sánchez (2003: 119–125).

[25] Harries (1994: 5, 86). For the significant expenditure problems Majorian faced see Oost (1970: 232). Sidonius may have exaggerated the danger that he faced. See *Carm.* 4.11–12.

[26] Some, such as Loyen (1970a: xvii), Styka (2011: 303), and Mratschek (2013: 253–254), have sought to characterise this period as Sidonius' "retirement" or "withdrawl" from politics, but Sidonius likely remained involved in local political activities.

[27] Loyen (1970a: xvi–xvii), for which see Hydatius 205 (210): "Maiorianum de Gallis Romam redeuntem ... [Rechimer] fraude interfecit" (Ricimer deceitfully killed Majorian as he was returning to Rome from Gaul) and Marius, Bishop of Aventicensis, *Chronica* 461: "deiectus est Mariorianus de imperio in civitate Dertona a Recemere patricio, et interfectus" (Majorian was removed from power in the city of Dertona by the patrician Ricimer, and then killed).

[28] Harries (1994: 142–145), MacGeorge (2002: 235–236), and O'Flynn (1991: 125).

[29] *Ep.* 1.9.5: "[dum] aliquid de legationis Arvernae petitionibus elaboramus" (When I will detail the particulars of the Arvernian embassy's petitions). If Sidonius has been sent by the *concilium septem Galliarum* one would expect to see *Arelate* rather than *Arvernae*. Zeller (1905: 15) argues that Sidonius went to Rome both as an ambassador of the *Arverni* and as he was summoned by the emperor, and probably, as a representative of the *concilium septem provinciarum*.

to mark the new emperor's first consulship.[30] Sidonius' performance was rewarded with the office of prefect of Rome.[31]

That year was a turning point in Sidonius' life: his friend Arvandus was tried and convicted on charges of treason.[32] Sidonius managed to avoid presiding over the case (which as urban prefect should have been his responsibility) but could not avoid his close ties to Arvandus irrevocably damaging his standing in Rome.[33] He returned to Gaul and there took up ecclesiastical office as the bishop of Clermont in late 469 or early 470. It is difficult to know what to make of Sidonius' election as the bishop of Clermont; he himself has very little to say about it, other than it was forced upon him, but scholarship should be very wary of taking that claim at face value. Augustine said as much about his own episcopacy, and by Sidonius' time it had become de rigueur to disavow any worldly ambition to become a bishop.[34] At the same time, opportunities for further advancement in his secular career had surely become very limited.[35] A bishopric, even of a relatively unimportant see like Clermont, offered an enduring status and some level of protection.

A year or so after Sidonius took up his episcopacy the Visigothic king Euric I began to harry Clermont each summer.[36] Euric had murdered his older brother Theodoric II (453–466) for the Visigothic throne.[37] Theodoric

---

[30] Sidonius *Carm.* 2. Lynette Watson (1998: 179–180) favours Harries' interpretation (1994: 144) that the panegyric was delivered as part of a Gallic diplomatic mission to ascertain Anthemius' intended policy towards the defence of Gaul, over Sivan's assertion (1989: 92) that they sought a reduction in sentence for their fellow Gallo-Roman noble Arvandus, who had been found guilty of treason. Sidonius was the last Gaul to hold this office, and the first to do so in over fifty years, Wickham (2005: 160–161).

[31] *Ep.* 1.9.6. Loyen (1970a: xvii–xix)

[32] For a detailed analysis of the likely process see Pietrini (2015: 304–322).

[33] Stevens (1933: 103), Loyen (1970a: xxi), Teitler (1992: 309–312), and Harries (1994: 158–166). Arvandus' trial is described by Sidonius in *Ep.* 1.7 for which see pp. 10, 67, 76, 143–147.

[34] Augustine *Ser.* 355.1.2. See for example Sidonius' remarks at *Ep.* 3.1.1 and 6.1.1.

[35] *Ep.* 3.1; 5.3. Harries (1992b: 169–173). Mathisen (1993a: 103–104) argues that movement into the church "offered Gallic aristocrats the opportunity to pursue local interests, to maintain their class consciousness and collegiality and to satisfy their desire for public office ... [while preserving] their won *Romanitas* in the face of the ever more conspicuous barbarian presence." The advancement of Sidonius' secular career through the 460s was far from certain. Episcopal office on the other hand offered far more stability and, if used judiciously, significant influence.

[36] The term "besieged" is often used to cover the initial period of skirmishes between 471 and 472, followed by the famine of 473–474; for this and the influence of modern French historiography on understanding Euric's confrontation with the Arverni see Delaplace (2012: 278).

[37] *Chronicorum Caesaraugustanorum Reliquae* 466: "His diebus Theodoricus rex Gotthorum a suis interfectus est et Euricus frater eius Gotthorum rex efficitur" (In those days Theodoric king of the Goths [Theodoric II] was killed by his own and Euric, his brother, was made king of the Goths). According to the *Chronica* of Marius the Bishop of Aventicensis, in 455 the Gothic regal brothers had broken out into war: 455.2 "Et ingressus est Theodoricus rex Gothorum Arelatum cum fratribus suis in pace." Marius himself ascribes the murder of Theodoric II by Euric to 467: "Eo anno interfectus

had himself only become king after killing Thorismund (451–453), their father's heir and their older brother.[38] As Anthemius' position deteoriated in the early 470s Euric aggressively sought to expand the Visigothic kingdom of Toulouse into the last remnants of Roman Gaul.[39]

Sidonius and his brother-in-law Ecdicius led the response, ultimately to no avail. In 475 a treaty, negotiated without Sidonius' involvement or approval, ceded Clermont to Euric.[40] Sidonius was arrested and imprisoned by the king, perhaps because of his refusal to temper his condemnation of the treaty and his political support for the Burgundians who had acted as a check against Visigothic expansion.[41] In time, however, Sidonius altered his behaviour towards Euric. He wrote to Leo, a Gallo-Roman adviser of the king, and included in the letter strong statements in praise of Euric.[42] With Leo's intervention Sidonius was released to return to his see. There he died at some point during the reign of Zeno (476–491) probably in the mid 480s.[43]

est Theodoricus rex Gothorum a fratre suo Euthorico Tholosa" (In that year Theodoric king of Visigoths was killed by his brother Euric in Tolosa). See Kulikowski's (2008: 339–342) detailed analysis of Sidonius' depiction of Avitus and diplomatic mission in *Carm.* 7, which argues that a dispute had arisen between Frederic (another son of Theodoric I), who had been in command of Visigothic forces in Spain, and Theodoric in Gaul. King (1972: 3) offers that Euric murdered Theodoric in part owing to their different attitudes towards the Romans arguing that the latter was prepared to work with them while the former was not.

[38] See Hydatius 148 (156). Their father was Theodoric I.

[39] Gillet (1999: 33–35) shows that Euric's aggression towards Roman Gaul only really began in the 470s; see also Delaplace (2015: 241–247). Kulikowski (2012: 31–34) rightly maintains that barbarian groups had *reges* well before they established clear kingdoms in Western Europe which only really began in the late fifth century. Ferreolus, the praetorian prefect of Gaul managed to come to terms with Thorismund in 451 after the defeat of Attila, for which see pp. 3, 120, 129. Theodoric seems to have largely continued Thorismund's approach.

[40] For Ecdicius' role see Sarti (2011: 109) and Drinkwater (2013: 60–61), who elsewhere (2001: 143) shows that few Gallic nobility took up arms. Dill (1926: 5) took this as an indication of the "absence of military virtue" among the Gallo-Roman population. Whittaker (1993: 1996) claims that Sidonius "led the defence of the town." Harries (1994: 227) offers that Sidonius was "the leader of the Clermont resistance." Sarti (2011: 91) states that Sidonius "assumed a military command himself." Barcellona (2013: 15) notes that "[assunse] la difesa della sua diocesi" ([he assumed] the defence of his diocese). Similar claims appear in Dewar (2013: 93). These claims rely solely on Sidonius' own evidence, which is our only source for his involvement. Gregory of Tours (2.22) does not mention Sidonius' role in the defence against the Visigothic attack, but instead focuses on Ecdicius' command of the town's defences. This could be however because of Gregory's concerted effort to focus on Sidonius' holy acts over his more mundane and pragmatic activities, for which see Furbetta (2015c: 1–12). The Auvergne was the last place of Roman power in "middle Gaul," see Stroheker (1965: 199). It had only resisted Visigothic expansion, if Sidonius can be believed, because the Burgundians acted as a counterbalance, see *Ep.* 3.4.1, 7.1.1. For a critical treatment of Sidonius' evidence for this period, see Delaplace (2012: 272–274).

[41] Allen and Neil (2013: 46).

[42] *Ep.* 8.3.3. Harries (1996: 43).

[43] Sidonius' epitaph is housed in the *Musée Bargoin*. For its discovery and analysis of the incomplete text see Prévot (1993: 229–233) and (1999: 77–79). A more complete text of the epitaph survived in

In his early adult years Sidonius served the Roman state and Gaul as an ambassador. In time his political career led to higher offices and eventually transitioned into his episcopacy.[44] Sidonius carefully positioned himself as Roman control of the Auvergne became part of the Visigothic kingdom of Toulouse. While it was feasible, he looked to enlist the Visigoths under Theodoric II as allies for the Roman state, but as the situation changed under Euric, his role as a bishop provided ongoing position and rank.

Sidonius' Epistolography

Through his correspondence and position in Gallo-Roman society Sidonius knew a wide range of important people.[45] He wrote to monks, other bishops, laymen, fellow aristocrats, priests, and political advisers.[46] His acquaintance with this wide and eclectic mix of people was not the product of some haphazard endeavour. Rather, Sidonius understood the importance and utility of *amicitia*.[47] His literary output, especially his letters, developed and promoted a carefully construed persona, as a learned, sophisticated and influential Gallo-Roman aristocrat, and later, as the pious and humble bishop of Clermont.[48]

The theorist L. Stanley considered epistolary exchange a form of gift exchange:

> There is the gift of the letter itself, but more importantly there is what it metonymically stands for and symbolised about the ongoing social bond between writer-giver and addressee-reciever … the letter as gift always has … obligatory and constraining reciprocity.[49]

the margin of one manuscript and was printed in Luetjohann's 1887 edition (1887: 6). The last line of that text stated that his death occurred during the reign of the Emperor Zeno, which ended in 491. Recently another version of the epitaph has come to light in a privately held manuscript, for which see Furbetta (2014: 135–157). The text of that version may limit Sidonius' death to Zeno's consulship (479) rather than reign. Mathisen (2013: 223) dates Sidonius' death to approximately 485.

[44] The role of bishop was political as well as religious. Sirks (2013: 88) compares the behaviour of bishops as mediators to that of Roman patricians.

[45] Sidonius' period saw intense political and military activity, as a procession of emperors, generals, office holders, and kings paraded across the historical stage. Some of these feature in the rich character sketches and detailed anecdotes of his epistles, for which see Chapter 3.

[46] Dalton (1915: clx–clxxxiii).

[47] Wood (1992: 9–10): "Gaul as seen through the letter collections of Sidonius Apollinaris and his acolytes of the following generation is dominated by the exercise of *amicitia*." Mathisen (1989: 1): "In late Roman Gaul, the bonds of friendship were extremely important."

[48] Daly (2000: 19–29), Frye (2003: 191), and Russell (1994: 150), who says, "The Gallo-Roman episcopacy was the last operative administrative remnant of Roman dominion in Gaul." Rousseau (1976) is a detailed study of the effect of Sidonius' episcopal role on his self-fashioning.

[49] Stanley (2011: 140). Conybeare (2000: 19–30) includes gift giving as part of "a wider nexus of communication" (19) that also included Late Antique epistolary exchange, but Stanley (2011) goes

Sidonius collated and circulated his letters.[50] This irrevocably changed their impact, enhancing the socio-cultural value of the "letter as gift," memorialising the addressee for posterity, and turning each addressee into the public reader, not as in private unpublished communication, the sole intended reader.[51] Collectively the epistles constructed a literary circle of like-minded Gallo-Roman aristocrats and clergy drawn around Sidonius' persona, who appears well connected and at ease among the rich, powerful, and learned. This circle was focused on Sidonius, whose self is fashioned in some way or another by every epistle, but it also linked and promoted each addressee to Sidonius' contemporary readership and posterity.[52]

Knowing who the addressee was and when the epistle was written may allow the reader to complete the hermeneutic journey from text to context and back. This context is often obfuscated by Sidonius who tells us just enough so that we may follow along but not enough that we may easily interrogate his narratives. Our ignorance is not necessarily our fault, but it is certainly our problem if we expect Sidonius' epistles to tell us more about his world than he is willing to disclose.

Sidonius' *Epistles* and Their Scholarship

Sidonius' contemporaries looked to him as a leading figure in the literary landscape of Late Antique Gaul (which flourished despite its self-deprecation), his epistles were admired in the middle ages as literary models worthy of emulation, and were widely read and taught by leading humanists.[53] Much of the vitriol levelled at Sidonius' works in the twentieth century may tell us far more about trends in literary criticism than it can about Sidonius' literature.[54]

---

further in thinking about the epistolary communication as the actual gift exchange, rather than the epistle itself as the gift. For consideration of epistolary exchange by Cicero and Seneca as a gift exchange see Wilcox (2012: 10–12).

[50] See Appendix II. For a full discussion of which see pp. 170–184.

[51] Despite his affected disregard for what posterity may think about his epistles *Ep.* 8.4, 10, 13; 9.6, 9, 14, 16.

[52] On the hierarchy of epistolary exchanges see Stanley (2011: 14).

[53] For a detailed study of Sidonius' influence on certain humanists see Hernández Lobato (2014). Juan Vives, tutor to Mary Tudor, for example, listed Sidonius as one of only eighteen authors suitable for her to read. See F. Watson (1912: 245), and Perkins (2007: 21).

[54] For a representative example one may point to the introduction of the Loeb edition "[Sidonius] succeeds in writing three "poems" [the panegyrics] which for prolonged insipidity, absurdity, and futility would be hard to beat. It is often very difficult to see what he means – all the more difficult because he means so very little … It is pathetic to think that such mouldy antiquarianism was considered a worthy tribute:" Anderson (1936: liii–liv). Cf. Champomier (1938: 52).

The characters, times, and events of his world are innately bound up in the epistles and their narratives. Historical and literary approaches are interdependent; neither can complete the hermeneutic journey on their own, nor should they try.[55] This is a problem that confronts the genre. The epistolary theorist Reinhard Nickisch asserted:

> Für den Literaturwissenschaftler … ist die Beachtung der » historischen Dimension « unverzichtbar wenn seine Interpretationen nicht essentielle Elemente und Aspekte eines solchen [literarischen] Briefes verfehlen sollen.
>
> For the literary scholar … observance of the 'historical dimension' is indispensable if his interpretations are not to miss the essential elements and aspects of such (literary) letters.[56]

The "historical dimension" is critical to reading the rich literary dynamics and context of Sidonius' ornate Latinity. *Ep.* 1.7, for example, provides an account of the trial of Arvandus, who as the Praetorian Prefect of Gaul tried to negotiate with the Visigoths independently of Rome ca. 468, and was subsequently arrested and brought to Rome for trial.[57] Sidonius does not provide extensive details of the case.[58] If Sidonius had wanted to do so, he most surely would have – the suggestion that he was incapable of communicating clearly no longer enjoys the acceptance it once did.[59] So we are left with an account that does not aspire towards historical veracity; the events were in any case all too recent and still politically sensitive.[60] Instead Sidonius makes the story of Arvandus all the more exciting by narrating the present as the moment when Arvandus had been sentenced to death but was yet to be executed (see chapter 3) manipulates the climax of the story to focus on his own involvement (chapter 5), and creates a rich character sketch of Arvandus (chapter 4), all the while appearing as a reliable and wise friend (chapter 2) The readers' knowledge that Arvandus was subsequently spared the death penalty is a spoiler that is otherwise forgotten.[61]

---

[55] A similar trend is discernible in Plinian scholarship. Marchesi (2015: 4) notes "the wider reorientation of Pliny studies that has been underway for the last fifteen years and has seen the shift in focus from (crudely put) socio-historical data-mining campaigns to a more explicitly literary engagement with Pliny's texts." The parentheses are original. Harries (1994: 2) clearly outlines the importance to the historian in analysing "the political aspects of Sidonius' literary technique."

[56] Nickisch (1991: 238).

[57] Köhler (1995: 231–232).

[58] Stevens (1933: 106); Teitler (1992: 312) is more forgiving, noting "Sidonius' letter leaves many questions unanswered."

[59] Van Waarden (2013a: 5) calls rightly for "relegating the case against Sidonius to the archives of the history of scholarship."

[60] See pp. 65–66.

[61] Sivan (1989: 93n51) and Teitler (1992: 310–311).

Far too often scholarship has focused on the "where" and "when" of an epistle when that has no bearing on the story Sidonius is telling. When the "where" and "when" do matter Sidonius mentions them, and then their narratological importance is made all the more significant coming from an author who is generally vague on such details. We are stuck then in an awkward middle ground, scrounging to find out more about Sidonius and his world but invariably in vain. His epistles are not a great source for an account of the fall of Roman Gaul (which he uniquely records), they *are* the account told as Sidonius wanted to tell it: detailed when he deemed it necessary and scattered with rich anecdotes. At every point this account asserts Sidonius' enduring relevancy in a rapidly changing world where status could no longer be defined simply by traditional means.

Modern approaches to Sidonius' literature began with studies in nineteenth-century Europe that focused on reconstructing his text, his use of Latin syntax and vocabulary, and his sources.[62] The approach of these studies was to subject Sidonius' text to an exacting analysis in an attempt to deduce facts beyond those immediately apparent. Duckett, writing in 1930, and Stevens, in 1933, introduced Sidonius' life and work to a wider Anglophone audience, but both of their works suffer from value-based criticisms of Sidonius' literature and actions.[63] In 1955 Chadwick offered some understanding of Sidonius' literature that was not influenced by subjective assessments of its relative worth.[64] In the twentieth century various works also used Sidonius' corpus as evidence in their focus on the fifth century and Gaul.[65] This interest developed as the field of Late Antiquity received new levels of scholarly attention.[66] In 1994 Harries published a monograph on Sidonius' life, which showed the value of carefully interpreting Sidonius' literature alongside our other evidence for his period.[67] She carefully mapped Sidonius' writings, especially his epistles, against his life and showed how the politics of his age permeated his work.

---

[62] The majority of scholarship on Sidonius during this period was in French or German, for the former see Amherdt (2013: 27–29) for the latter see Köhler (2013: 39–40).

[63] Stevens (1933: ix, 1–2, 17, 19, 33, 35 *et alibi*). Duckett (1930: 8, 53). López Kindler (2003: 837) carefully rejects similar out-dated criticisms made in Sidonian scholarship in the early to mid-twentieth century.

[64] Chadwick (1955: 296, 301, 305).

[65] The most influential were Courcelle (1948, repr. 1964), Stein (1959), Stroheker (1970), Reydellet (1981), Drinkwater and Elton (1992), and Mathisen and Sivan (1996).

[66] This attention has been spurred on by Brown's influential *The World of Late Antiquity* (1971). In the Anglophone world other notable contributors include Averil Cameron (1993), Bowersock, Brown, and Grabar (1999), and Ward-Perkins (2006). For a more extensive list see Hernández Lobato (2012: 28n4).

[67] Harries (1994) – see Mathisen's review (1996: 246–250).

Two significant edited volumes have recently been published, one in English, commentaries are forthcoming, and Sidonius' literature is being translated and retranslated in many different languages.[68]

Sidonius' epistles are highly stylised,[69] which affects their evidentiary value.[70] Cloppet, Percival, and Hutchings, for example, examined Sidonius' description of travel and hospitality in fifth-century Gaul with a view to linking his remarks to accounts in other sources or the archaeological record.[71] Others have examined Sidonius' description of barbarians to try to read a continuum into his beliefs and infer broad generalisations regarding the interaction between barbarians and Romans during Sidonius' era.[72] This approach invariably fails to appreciate the significance of the specific context of Sidonius' remarks, such as whether he was writing to advisers at the Visigothic court while wallowing away under imprisonment.[73]

Traditional literary approaches to Sidonius' corpus focused on defining and locating "classical" features at the expense of considering the diverse features of Late Antique Latin whether archaic or mannerist.[74] In 1979 Gualandri published the first major modern study of Sidonius' corpus to focus on the literary value of his work in which she argued that Sidonius' unique use of Latin was worthy of an exacting and careful analysis.[75] Just over a decade later Roberts' seminal work *The Jeweled Style* showed that the literary appreciation of Late Antique texts must consider the very different literary aesthetics which existed during this period.[76] Hernández Lobato followed in 2012 with a detailed study of the aesthetics of Sidonius' literature that included taking this exploration in important new directions especially for Sidonius' poetry; and in 2015 Schwitter published a detailed study of the importance of *obscuritas* to Late Antique epistolography which

---

[68] See G. Kelly and Van Waarden (eds), *New Approaches to Sidonius Apollinaris* (2013) and Poignault and Stoehr-Monjou (eds), *Présence de Sidoine Apollinaire* (2014).

[69] Allen and Neil (2013: 25) cite Sidonius as an example of "the bias of stylized letter-collections."

[70] This is not to say that Sidonius' literature can or should be discarded as evidence but rather that it should be used with exceptional care. Goffart (2006: 164), for example, identifies the prevalence of Sidonius as a source for assessments of the Burgundian settlement in northern Gaul despite the limited utility of his evidence.

[71] All of whom express some concern regarding Sidonius' historical credibility: Cloppet (1989: 859), Percival (1999: 279–287), and Hutchings (2009: 65–67).

[72] Schuster (1940: 119–126), Bonjour (1981: 109–118), Staubach (1983: 1–16), Sivonen (1997: 430–432), and F-M. Kaufmann (1995). Castellanos (2013: 202) rightly cautions against extrapolating and generalising from Sidonius' remarks.

[73] *Ep.* 8.9 for which see pp. 97–98.

[74] Auerbach (1958, repr. 1965: 152) and Curtius (1953: 368). For this trend in the study of Late Antique literature see G. Kelly (2008: 162).

[75] Gualandri (1979). Consolino's (1974) article remains influential for the study of Sidonius' poetry.

[76] M. Roberts (1989: 148–155).

includes extensive and innovative analysis of several of Sidonius' epistles. To date no study has focused on the literary value of Sidonius' epistles.

Sidonius' Epistolarity

More epistles have been handed down to posterity from Late Antiquity than any earlier epoch. This fact reflects that later texts are more likely to have been available for copying, but also a marked increase in the production of epistles, evident in Latin in the tremendous output of fourth- and fifth-century writers like Symmachus, Augustine, and Jerome. This literary phenomenon has been understood in socio-historical terms as the product of the decline in public rhetoric, and the increased dangers posed by physical travel, which the sending of letters could in part address by bridging the communicative gap between author and addressee.[77] Aristocrats, who once may have travelled but dared not risk the dangers of the road, instead sent letters.[78] The socio-historical explanation however is only part of the picture; in the East, where the dangers and difficulties posed by travelling were far less, letters gained favour as a critically important literary genre, which could readily and frequently display the authors' *paideia* by invoking the classical tradition.

Scholarship once tried to distinguish the "real" documentary letter from the embellished literary epistle.[79] This distinction has proved difficult to sustain.[80] "Fictional" letters pose a similar methodological problem.[81] One

---

[77] Gillet (2012: 816).

[78] Mathisen (1993a: 23) and (2001: 106), and Salzman (2004: 94). Abram (1994: 5) argues that after Augustine epistolary collections in the West from the fifth century were largely confined to Gaul.

[79] Deißmann (1908: 158–159): "Der Brief ist etwas unliterarisches: er dient dem Verkehr der Getrennten … Die Epistel ist eine literarische Kunstform, die Gattung der Literatur …" (The letter is something unliterary: it provides communication to the isolated … The epistle is a literary art form, a type of literature). Rosén (1980: 28) infers that the suitability of narratology to studying epistolography. See also Conring (2001: 18–19). Some, such as Sivonen (2006: 41) inferred that epistles may be relied upon to validate or interrogate other more embellished texts, but the literary dynamics of letters like Sidonius' largely invalidates that methodology.

[80] For consideration of the problems and limitation of Deißmann's dichotomy see Hodkinson and Rosenmeyer (2013: 1–2, 9), and for its impact on scholarly approaches to Pliny's tenth book see Noreña (2007: 240–241). This dichotomy has largely come to replace "public" and "private," and so the distinctions made between "public" and "private," and "literary" and "non-literary" can be almost equated, although not always, as "private" is determined in part by the editing process rather than publication (Potter 1999: 23), while "literary" letters are also defined by topic and language (White 2010: 90–99). As Abram (1994: 86) indicates Sidonius is one of the few authors to provide evidence for the compilation of his letter collection such as in *Ep.* 1.1.1. De Pretis' (2003: 128) study of three of Pliny's epistles usefully circumvents this issue by focusing on epistolarity rather than their relation to fiction or reality.

[81] Ebbeler (2001: 14).

may, for instance, write a letter that describes immediate events but then not send it straight away, but the next day. By then the claims made in the epistle about what was happening "now" have become fictional but they were not when the epistle was written. Equally one may write an entirely fictitious letter only for it to be read as an assertion of fact. Separating epistolary fact from fiction is wholly reliant on the reader's interpretation of the writer's conception of what was written. Ultimately, this division is unhelpful for texts that manifest their epistolarity, their identifying epistolary features, as an inherent part of their composition.[82]

When an epistle is compiled and arranged in a collection (as was the case for every one of Sidonius' epistles) a second moment of composition is created that invites the reader to consider the epistle on fictional terms, whether as an example of what once was, but now is not, or simply as a perspective on reality, prone like any perspective to errors of bias, emphasis, embellishment, and even deceit.[83] As Ebbeler notes:

> Late antique letters which survive because they were collected and frequently copied are sophisticated textual performances intended to advertise their author's literary skill to their contemporaries and posterity ... [such letters are] a reflective lens designed to distort as much to reveal.[84]

All of Sidonius' epistles are thus to some degree fictional, even if they were not at the moment of composition, because they portray a "reality" that must be temporally removed from the act of reading.

Sidonius' epistles are closest to Pliny's, whose example he consciously followed as an epistolary model.[85] Comparison to other Latin epistolary authors is less intrinsic. Cicero's epistles hardly constitute a single collection, nor were they all arranged by him and circulated while he was alive. Indeed, as Beard has shown, they have been edited so extensively that the "original" order may never be known.[86] Sidonius tellingly puts Cicero aside as an epistolary model, humbly asserting that perfection cannot be bested, but his own awareness of the impracticality of following Cicero's model may also have informed this decision.[87] Still inadvertent similarities

---

[82] Gamberini (1983: 123–125).
[83] Wood (1992: 12).
[84] Ebbeler (2009: 272–273); see also Gerth (2012: 159), and for Sidonius, Harries (1994: 10–11).
[85] See pp. 15–16, 170–178.
[86] Beard (2002: 107–115) and Gibson (2012: 59ff); see also McCutcheon's (2016: 41–45) assessment of Beard's approach. Sogno (2014) argues that Sidonius invokes Cicero, Pliny, and Symmachus to assert the "genealogy" of the "senatorial letter collection." This suggestion is undermined by Sidonius' emphatic claim that he does not follow Cicero as a model and problematised by Sidonius' clear identification as a bishop at the beginning of book three (and for the remainder of the collection).
[87] *Ep.* 1.1.2.

may perhaps be found in Cicero's ultimately doomed attempt to save the Republic and Sidonius' struggle to prop up Roman Gaul, both surviving long enough to see their failure play out. Sidonius' disavowal of Cicero as a model is undermined somewhat by his repeated mention of the republican orator by name.[88]

Seneca's epistles are useful as a point of contrast; the single addressee, the sustained philosophical content and the prolonged (imagined) dialogues clearly set them apart.[89] Nevertheless they remain connected to the genre by their form, quotidian diction and ubiquitous self-fashioning. Fronto's epistles are equally useful for their sustained self-fashioning, yet the peculiarity of the epistolary exchange between emperor and tutor limits the extent to which comparisons with Sidonius' collection may be usefully made.

Sidonius explicitly claims Pliny and Symmachus as his epistolary models in his opening programmatic epistle[90] (1.1.1): "Quinti Symmachi rotunditatem, Gai Plinii disciplinam maturitatemque vestigiis praesumptuosis insecuturus" (I will follow with presumptuous footsteps the rotundity of Quintus Symmachus, the *disciplina* and maturity of Gaius Pliny).[91] In *Ep.* 4.22.2 Sidonius preferences Pliny.

It is unclear how influential a model Symmachus was, if at all; "following Symmachus' *rotunditas*" could in its narrowest sense simply mean publishing a single volume of letters.[92] Occasional connections between Symmachus and Sidonius may be considered more usefully a product of

---

[88] Contra Sogno (2014: 203) and Furbetta (2015b: 349). Köhler (1995: 106–107) notes that despite Sidonius' claim here that he does not follow Cicero as a model and the almost complete absence of allusions to Cicero's corpus, Cicero is frequently mentioned in the collection. Gualandri (1979: 80) does not list Cicero as one of Sidonius' epistolary models. Damon's (2010: 375) remark regarding Cicero is equally apt for Sidonius in Late Antique Gaul "[friendship] retained and indeed increased its importance when everything in his world was reorientating itself to new political and social constellations."

[89] Altman (1982: 89) places the possibility of exchange (which is largely or perhaps even wholly absent from Seneca's epistles) as a key tenet of epistolography "if there is no desire for exchange, the writing does not differ significantly from a journal, even if it assumes the outer form of the letter."

[90] Sidonius' decision to put Cicero aside at *Ep.* 1.1.3 follows Pliny at *Ep.* 9.26.8.

[91] Salzman and Roberts (2011: lvii–lviiin215) argue that Sidonius is imitating Pliny and Symmachus' publication of a single book rather than their epistolarity more broadly. Their interpretation does not account for *rotunditatem* as the direct object of *insecturus*, nor that the terms applied to Pliny – *disciplina* and *maturitas* – certainly reference style. Conybeare's (2012: 414) assertion, in support of Salzman and Roberts, that Sidonius uses *rotunditas* to describe Symmachus' "well-roundedness" as "aplomb in diverse circumstances" relies on a specific meaning of *rotunditas* unattested in any earlier literature.

[92] The use of *rotunditas* may allude to Symmachus' use of obscure and archaic words for novel concepts, see Haverling (1988: 205, 231, 251). Kröner's (1989: 640) explanation of *rotunditas* is overly limited by his focus of its presence in only one letter of Symmachus, see also Hanaghan (2017a: 260) and Mratschek (2016: 313) who renders *rotunditas* as "harmonious balance."

their broad generic compatibility than the more deep and meaningful textual relationship that Sidonius develops between his epistles and Pliny's. The same may be said of other Latin epistolary authors, especially Jerome and Augustine, who may at times be usefully compared to Sidonius, but who likely exhibited minimal influence on his epistolary undertaking.[93]

Gibson has recently analysed in depth Sidonius' literary allusions to Pliny and his structural engagement with Pliny's epistolary arrangement.[94] Like Pliny Sidonius exploits the narrative potential of epistles. But Sidonius' world is vastly different to Pliny's, so the characters and events of his age clearly tie his epistolary project to his Gallo-Roman circle of the mid to late fifth century. Unlike Pliny Sidonius had a clear epistolary model with which to interact. This allowed Sidonius to position his work in response to Pliny's, by invoking sustained intertextuality to Pliny in individual epistles and throughout the collection as whole. Pliny's collection, like his world, enjoyed a greater degree of continuity than Sidonius'. Inevitably its instability affected his epistolary project; his move from secular aristocrat to episcopal office, for example, struggles to parallel Pliny's move to consular office.

Following the first chapter's socio-historical approach to Sidonius' world, the remaining chapters focus on literary dynamics within the epistles. Chapter 2 analyses how the epistles assert, promote and (where needed) make compatible different aspects of Sidonius' status as a wealthy aristocrat, pious bishop, learned author, and Gallo-Roman. It reveals how Sidonius carefully manipulates his reader by offering implied comparisons between himself and others in which he always comes out better off: wealthier, humbler, more learned, more sophisticated, and more important. This chapter shows the benefits of a linear (rather than chronological) reading of the epistles, as Sidonius invites his audience to read continuities, inconsistencies, contrasts, and comparisons.

Time is a constant of every narrative, but it is especially central to epistles, which assert a clearly defined moment of composition and reading.[95] Chapter 3 examines how Sidonius manipulates time in the epistles by deconstructing the assumption that the epistolary present – his "time of writing" – is inherently accurate. Instead it posits that Sidonius

---

[93] For Jerome's influence see Pricoco (1965: 95, 129, 148–150). On the influence of Augustine in fifth-Century Gaul see Mathisen (1993b: 29–41) and for Jerome see Mathisen (2009b).

[94] See especially Gibson (2013c: 198–200), and also pp. 176–178. Sidonius' assertion of the lightness of sense and structure in his second key programmatic epistle (*Ep.* 7.18) follows similar claims by Pliny that scholarship has successfully read through for which see Bodel (2015: 18–30, 54–60).

[95] Ricœur (1980: 169–170).

carefully chose the precise moment of the epistolary present to accentuate aspects of certain epistles' narratives.

Gallo-Roman aristocrats, clergy, barbarian kings, and emperors fill the pages of Sidonius' epistles, interacting with his persona in a wide array of exciting contexts. These depictions create an array of narratives set within the last decades of fifth-century Gaul. Chapter 4 identifies how these character depictions sustain narratives which drive wider plots forward, ranging in scale from the collapse of Roman Gaul and the rise of the Visigothic kingdom of Toulouse to the legal problems that confronted a widow in Sidonius' parish.

An epistle is written and read in the voice of the author; as a genre, epistolography is thus highly mimetic of direct speech. The fifth chapter analyses how Sidonius uses direct, indirect and implied speech to vary his narrative speed and shift focalisation. These dialogues are critical to the ebb and flow of the epistolary narratives, foreshadowing plot movements, creating climaxes, and facilitating the interaction of Sidonius' persona with the other epistolary characters.

The last chapter assesses Sidonius' arrangement of the collection, attempts to follow Pliny as his model, and use of closural dynamics for narrative effect, subverting some plot lines, creating others, and invoking specific structural connections within and between epistles and across the collection as a whole.

CHAPTER 2

Self and Status: Reading "Sidonius" in the Epistles

commendo igitur varios iudicio tuo nostri pectoris motus, minime
ignarus, quod ita mens pateat in libro velut vultus in speculo. (*Ep.* 7.18.2)

And so I commend the various movements of my heart to your
judgement, not unaware that the mind reveals itself in a book just
like a face in a mirror.[1]

Sidonius employs an epistolary convention and literary conceit "the mirror
of the soul," which had gathered popularity in Late Antiquity.[2] The simile
is apt to the rigours of self-fashioning in his epistles.[3] While the mirror
may appear to reflect reality, in fact it reflects the reality that the user of the
mirror wants to display, by providing the user with the chance to correct
or change their image.[4] The contrast falls between the corporality and aesthetic quality of the *vultus in speculo* and the incorporeity and indetermin-
able thoughts and feelings of an author.[5]

---

[1] See Squillante (2008: 35).

[2] Gualandri (1979: 28), Köhler (1998: 333–340), and Schröder (2007: 8). Thraede (1970: 74) traces
this convention to Pliny's letter collection. Its earliest appearance is in the pre-socratic philosopher Democritus *Sententiae Pythagoreorum* 119A1: ἐν μὲν τοῖς ἐσόπτροις ὁ τῆς ὄψεως, ἐν δὲ ταῖς
ὁμιλίαις ὁ τῆς ψυχῆς χαρακτὴρ βλέπεται. "In mirrors, the quality of the appearance reveals itself,
in exchanges the quality of the soul." For a detailed list of the deployment of this trope in epistolary
collections see Abram (1994: 116–120), for discussion see Howland (1991: 101), and Hodkinson and
Rosenmeyer (2013: 15).

[3] Gualandri (1979: 28).

[4] Altman offers a similar analysis of Mitsou's behaviour with a mirror in Collette's novel *Mitsou* "[she]
discovers the disparity between the self as seen from the outside (in the physical mirror) and the
self as seen from the inside (in the letters as mirror)." See also Creese (2007: 17–18, 180). Ebbeler
(2009: 272–273) rightly warns against reading letters as an accurate account of the author's self rather
than merely as an indication of how the author wanted that self portrayed, for which see p. 14. See
also Gerth (2013: 159).

[5] Both his contemporary and modern readers should be considered targets for his self-fashioning,
despite the occasional disingenuous claim to the contrary. In his insightful book on Pliny's self-
fashioning Henderson (2002a: x) described the unique ability of letters to present a refined version
of self as "emphatic egomorphism," and credited renewed interest in this facet of epistolarity to "the
revaluation of rhetorical creation of the self."

Every epistle involves Sidonius' persona in augmenting and safeguarding his reputation among his readers. This persona distorts our knowledge of Sidonius the historical figure in ways we can recognise but struggle to avoid.[6] His frequent protestation of his own scriptural ignorance, for example, as Daly has shown, ought to be read critically as the profession of *humilitas* rather than as actual evidence of Sidonius' unfamiliarity with the Bible.[7] Yet little can be said definitively about the extent to which he knew the Bible; he surely did, but how well is unclear. Similarly, claims that he wrote quickly offer little to no insight into Sidonius' method, but are instead a literary strategy intended to lure the reader to appreciate his style all the more (but he may well have also preferred to write quickly).[8]

We cannot know Sidonius from reading his letters, but we can try to tease out the rhetoric of his self, the multiple complex strands of his persona as a father, son, grandson, husband, brother-in-law, son-in-law, bishop, secular office holder, Gallo-Roman, Lyon native, adopted *Arvernus*, letter writer, poet, friend, adviser, advocate, and aristocrat. These strands combine to form his epistolary self-image which is a long-term project that must respond and develop dynamically to the dramatic changes that took place to his world over the course of his life. Sidonius cannot project the constancy of Seneca's self or Pliny's post-Domitian relief from a time of crisis. The self-fashioning in his epistles focuses instead on asserting his ongoing relevancy and status: the two elements which ensured his survival through the tumultuous final decades of the Roman empire in the West as the barbarians conquered his native Gaul. This is a high stakes and intricate endeavour at the very heart of his epistolary output that must be read against his world.

While specific studies have added much to our understanding of the complexity of aspects of Sidonius' self-fashioning, such as his episcopal rank or satirical prowess, limiting an analysis to individual strands risks devaluing their interdependence and thus losing awareness of the broader

---

[6] The temptation to conflate Sidonius' persona and personality has been acutely felt by classical scholarship, for an example of which see Stroheker (1970: 58). Others, such as Van Dam (1985: 159–161) have similarly felt that Sidonius betrays his real attitudes in his epistles.

[7] Daly (2000: 20–24) and for examples *Ep.* 6.1.4-5, 6.3.1, 6.6.2, 6.7.1, 7.4.1, 7.4.3, 7.6.1.

[8] Mathisen (2013: 234–235) posits (in part) that Sidonius may have used dossiers of letters to aid him in his hasty compilation of the collection, but as Pagán (2010: 196) shows the speed of writing is a trope in prefaces and programmatic works. Cf. Statius' remarks at *Silvae* 4.26 on the slowness of composition of the *Thebaid* "Thebais multa cruciata lima"; see Nauta (2006: 35). The speediness that Statius claims for the composition of the *Silvae* is likely linked to his humble aspirations for the work, see Pavlovskis (1962: 1), Vessey (1972: 174), and Newlands (1991: 438). Cf. Lucan *Pharsalia* 1.1-7, concerning which Tarrant (1997: 67) notes: "Lucan gives the impression of having written at furious speed."

endeavour to promote and safeguard his reputation in a rapidly changing world.[9] Sidonius' self-fashioning has a clear, desperate agenda that goes well beyond massaging his ego; bishops are harder to kill and literati are best unprovoked.

Four aspects are particularly critical to his battle for relevancy and survival: his wealth and office, *paideia*, identification as a Gallo-Roman, and claims regarding his literary style.[10] The changes to his self-presentation will be loosely mapped to two pivotal changes that take place outside of the epistolary collection, but are referenced by that collection, and so occur and exist both within and outside of the text, namely Sidonius' episcopal promotion and the fall of Roman Gaul.[11] Ultimately, Sidonius' self-image may provide very little reliable and verifiable information about Sidonius the historical figure but much about the perceptions, ideas, and Zeitgeist of Sidonius and his literary circle.

Mapping the Wealth and Offices of Sidonius' Self

The first two books of the epistles depict Sidonius as a wealthy public office holder and successful Gallo-Roman aristocrat. His secular career advancement thematically unites the first book; as a diplomat in *Ep.* 2, an ambassador in *Ep.* 5, and the prefect of Rome in *Ep.* 7, 8, and 10.[12] The book's other letters, which do not focus on Sidonius' career, may still be read in light of it given their close proximity in the collection.[13] Sidonius records his own ambition in *Ep.* 1.3, for example, and then in *Ep.* 1.4 praises the Gallo-Roman aristocrat Gaudentius for attaining office, praise which the

[9] Rousseau (1976: 356ff) examined the influence of Sidonius' episcopacy on his letter wrting. Bonjour (1981: 109–118) analysed Sidonius' persona as it interacts with barbarians. Henke (2008: 155–173) assessed Sidonius' image as a writer of satire. Van Waarden (2011a: 555–561) studies Sidonius' episcopal self through *Ep.* 7.5, 8, and 9. Obermaier (1999: 59) analyses how Sidonius criticised himself. For the concept of self-fashioning in Latin epistolography see Riggsby (1995: 123–135).

[10] None of which have received studies in their own right, although significant attention has been paid to Sidonius' identity rather than *presentation* as a Gallo-Roman, for an example of which see Heather (1999: 245–247) who focuses on Sidonius' distinction between himself and barbarians. Others have made efforts to deduce what Sidonius read (and thus how he was educated), for an example of which see Horvath (2000).

[11] Küppers (2005: 251–277); see also Liebeschuetz (2004: 98), Wood (1992: 13), and Teitler (1992: 310). Castellanos (2013: 289) applies this methodological to the depiction of barbarians in the collection, but this is problematic owing to the difficulty in dating precisely key epistles for discussion of which see pp. 59–60.

[12] Harries (1994: 9–17), Whitby (1995: 42), Gibson (2012: 62), and Wolff (2017: 74). The first letter is the exception, as its concerns are programmatic. See Köhler (1995: 99), Gibson (2013a), and (2013b).

[13] Mathisen (2013: 235–237) and (2014: 207–209) dates these epistles to the 450s and proposes that they were inserted into this book as a dossier of letters, but it is equally possible that their insertion into book 1 (not in chronological order) was designed to manipulate the reader's response.

reader is induced by the book's arrangement to project onto Sidonius in
Ep. 1.10 as the prefect of Rome.[14] The final letter of that book, *Ep.* 1.11,
signs off on Sidonius' secular career. The thematic unity of this book may
be read in different ways; historically – since the events detailed occurred
prior to his episcopacy circa 470 and so evidently the first book covered
this period; or intertextually – Gibson noted a clear parallel in Pliny and
Sidonius' first books in their temporally focused treatment of a period of
political intrigue.[15] We may also map Sidonius' description of his secular
career onto his representation of self, however.

Sidonius claims the status that a secular career offers; he has rubbed
shoulders with Visigothic kings, made representations to the emperor, and
secured the grain supply for Rome as the last Gallo-Roman prefect of the
city.[16] As Drinkwater argues:

> [For] integrated late Roman Gauls … [like] Sidonius Apollinaris … the
> holding of Roman office was more than just a matter of *noblesse oblige*, or
> the price of ambition. Rather such office made them part of a living legend
> that ran from oldest Antiquity and would last forever.[17]

By the time the first book of epistles was circulated in the late 460s, these
feats had become more difficult for other Gallo-Romans to replicate, as the
Burgundian and Visigothic kingdoms expanded into the ever-shrinking
territory of Roman Gaul.[18] Thus Sidonius claims the accentuated status of
his early career, augmented by the relative rarity of individuals who had
held similar offices and the even rarer number of those who would go on
to hold similar office. In a way some still did – Sidonius mentions several
Gallo-Romans who held office as advisers in the successor kingdoms, such
as Leo, the Visigothic adviser, and Syagrius, whom Sidonius styles as a
Burgundian Solon.[19]

In the final letter of book 1 Sidonius describes how he defended himself
in front of the Emperor Majorian on the charge of authoring a satire.[20]

---

[14] Gaudentius was the *vicarius septem provincarum per Gallias*. See PLRE "Gaudentius 8." See Sivonen (2006: 58–59).

[15] Gibson (2013b: 343). Mathisen (2013: 235–237) argues that *Ep.* 1.3, 1.4, and 1.6 dated to a trip Sidonius took to Rome in 455, but the structural connection between these epistles is not simply reliant on their shared dating.

[16] *Ep.* 1.2, 6, 7, 9.

[17] Drinkwater (2013: 69).

[18] Mathisen (1984: 168) and (1993a: ii).

[19] Kulikowski (2013: 88). For Sygarius see *Ep.* 5.5 and Castellanos (2013: 283). He is also presented as Amphio, for which see Giuletti (2014: 99–100). For Leo see *Ep.* 4.22, 8.3, 9.13. Mathisen (1984: 168n28) lists some more examples.

[20] See pp. 108–111.

Sidonius manages his own defence adeptly, nevertheless the epistle offers a word of warning to political aspirants regarding the dangers inherent in a career that is involved in imperial politics[21] (*Ep.* 1.11): "quod iuvenem militantemque dictasse praesumptiosum fuisset, publicasse autem periculosum" (this [work, i.e the satire] would have been audacious for me to compose and dangerous to publish when I was a young man serving the government). His self thus adopts a new dimension, as the wiser, older, political survivor, who has tried his hand and avoided getting burnt by the fire of imperial politics.

Ep. 2.13 underscores his retirement from secular politics.[22] Sidonius takes Serranus, his addressee, to task for his praise of Petronius Maximus who reigned for a few months after Valentinian III was murdered but was subsequently killed, probably stoned to death by the mob.[23] Early on Petronius Maximus was doing well for himself (*Ep.* 2.13.4): "cuius anterius epulae mores, pecuniae pompae, litterae fasces, patrimonia patrocinia florebant" (earlier [in his life] his banquets, character, wealth, display, writing, offices, estate, and clients were flourishing). But then, like a scorpion, fortune struck him down.[24] The letter segues into discussion of Damocles, concluding with a gnomic assertion about the dangers of imperial power (*Ep.* 2.13.8):

> unde post mixtas fletibus preces atque multimoda suspiria vix absolutus emicatimque prosiliens illa refugit [Damocles] celeritate divitias deliciasque regales, qua solent appeti, reductus ad desideria mediocrium timore summorum et satis cavens, ne beatum ultra diceret duceretque qui

---

[21] The danger of secular politics is referenced elsewhere in the collection, such as in *Ep.* 5.9.1 which links Aquilinus to Sidonius through their grandfathers' connection, both of whom served the usurper Constantine III "quos laudabili familaritate coniunxerat litterarum dignitatum, periculorum conscientiarum similitudo" "whom the similarity of their education, honours, dangers and consciences joined together in praiseworthy closeness." For discussion of the circumstances of *Ep.* 1.11 see Köhler (1995: 288–292) and Styka (2008: 64–65); see also pp. 108–111.

[22] *Ep.* 2.13 is the penulimate epistle in the second book, which was also circulated prior to Sidonius' episcopacy, for which see p. 6. As Furbetta (2014–2015a: 15) argues, this epistle's philosophical reflections on the nature of power is an exception to Sidonius' normally pragmatic approach. For an analysis of the remainder of the epistle see the Epilogue.

[23] See for example, Hydatius 154 (162): "tumultu populi et seditione occiditur miliari" ([Petronius] was killed by a mob of the people and a military conspiracy) and *Gallic Chronicle of 511*, 623: "tumultu vulgi occisus est" ([Petronius] was killed by a mob of the people). For a complete list of primary sources see Henning (1999: 31). Wessel (2008: 47) favours Prosper's account (*Epit. Chron.* a455, 1375) that Petronius was killed by his royal servants. For a description of these events see Heather (2005: 375ff), Mitchell (2006: 109ff), Börm (2013: 94–96).

[24] *Ep.* 2.13.4. Furbetta (2014-15a: 150–151) draws out the contrast between Petronius' earlier successful life and his disastrous reign.

saeptus armis ac satellitibus et per hoc raptis incubans opibus ferro pressus premeret aurum.

so after prayers had been mixed with tears and after many sighs scarcely had he been freed when leaping forward in a flash he [Damocles] fled the wealth and royal pleasures with the speed with which they are customarily sought, drawn back to desire middling positions out of fear of the highest, and suitably warned not to remark or think that he is happy who is enclosed by weapons and guards and pressed down by this [i.e Damocles'] sword touches his gold.

Sidonius' version draws upon Damocles' depiction in earlier Latin literature.[25] Damocles looms as an example not just for Petronius Maximus' brief and disastrous reign, but also resonates more broadly with the dangers Sidonius faced in the aftermath of Avitus' reign which he avoided by writing a panegyric in favour of Avitus' successor Majorian, who may well have conspired with Ricimer to murder or at least do away with Avitus.[26]

Sidonius thus makes the high status of political office essential to his self-representation but also indicates that opportunities to serve in such offices are rapidly dwindling. By the time the first epistles were circulated in the late 460s his readers could not reasonably expect to match these achievements.[27] The last celebration of public office occurs in *Ep*. 3.6, in which Sidonius praises Eutropius for his promotion to the praetorian prefecture of Gaul.[28] Sidonius credits him with (finally) abandoning his contempt for public service, which so turns him into a model for others. The optimistic tone with which this epistle ends, hoping for better times ahead under good governance, does not last long in the collection.[29] A mere two epistles later Sidonius bemoans the limited rewards for public service (*Ep*. 3.8.1):

> Veneror antiquos, non tamen ita, ut qui aequaevorum meorum virtutes aut merita postponam. neque si Romana respublica in haec miseriarum extrema defluxit, ut studiosos sui numquam remuneretur

---

[25] Geisler (1887: 360) notes a verbal similarity to Cicero's description of Damocles at *Tusc.* 5.21.61. Van Wageningen (1905: 321) also deduces Sidonius' borrowing of phrasing from Horace's *Epod.* 12.21 and *Ep.* 2.1.207, and Juvenal *Sat.* 3.81. See also Squillante (2007–08: 254–255) and Montone (2017: 26). Sidonius' version subsequently influenced others, such as Avitus of Vienne's, for which see M. Roberts (1995: 95). For Sidonius' characterisation of Petronius Maximus in this epistle see pp. 113–114.

[26] See Furbetta (2014–2015a: 152–153). For Avitus' death see p. 4.

[27] For the details of this process see p. 173.

[28] *Ep.* 3.6.2–3.

[29] *Ep.* 3.6.3: "animorum spebus erectis fas est de cetero sperare meliora" (and indeed since the hopes of our hearts have risen it is right to hope for better things to come).

> I respect the ancients, but not so that I put down the virtues and qualities
> of my contemporaries. Even though the Roman state has descended to the
> very worst of wretchedness, such that it no longer rewards those who are
> devoted to it

Sidonius keeps the status he derived from his public offices.[30] The state
ought to be rewarding public service, Sidonius asserts, but alas can no
longer, rendering his achievements rarer and thus of greater value. A clear
contrast is drawn between his own secular advancement and that of his
contemporaries, but a more direct implication for Sidonius is also clearly
felt: if the state is no longer able to reward those who are devoted to it, like
Sidonius, episcopal office presents as a suitable alternative. His example
stands as a clear articulation of the kind of career that was once achievable
but is no longer so.

Sidonius' promotion of his secular career advancement, which reached
its pinnacle when he was the urban praetor of Rome in 468, may be usefully
compared to similar efforts by Latin epistolographers. Both Cicero and
Pliny trumpeted their consulships regularly.[31] Whereas Pliny makes himself
out to be quite the critic of Domitian (only after the latter was dead), and
Seneca's silence is unsurprising given the disasters of the Neronian court
continued unabated after his retirement, Sidonius' criticism of imperial
politics is systemic.[32] His achievements in Roman public office were among
the last performed by Gallo-Romans – they could not be repeated – and
when the system of aristocratic attainment ended, he promptly adapted to
his new political climate as the bishop of Clermont. Sidonius' transition
to the clergy is clearly marked at the beginning of book 3 and supported
by clear references to the superiority of clerical rank to secular rank. In *Ep.*
3.10, for example, Sidonius' praise of Theodorus is not based on his senatorial rank (*vir clarissimus*) but on his modest demeanour (*modestissimae
conversationis*).[33] In a similar vein, in book 7 Sidonius emphatically puts
Ferreolus in his place by including an epistle addressed to him only after

---

[30] *Ep.* 3.1.1. "[isdem] princibus evecti stipendiis perfuncti sumus" (we were promoted by the same
emperors, performed the same state service). Barnes (1983: 265) rightly notes that the phrase
isdem principis must refer to Majorian and Avitus. Giannotti (2016: 112) highlights the emphatic
placement of these remarks at the opening of book three.

[31] These comments are particularly prolific in his epistles to those he knew well, featuring for example
in four epistles in book 1 of the letters to Atticus at Cic. *Att.* 1.14, 1.16, 1.19, and 1.20.

[32] For Pliny see for example *Ep.* 1.12.6, 8 for which see p. 109, and *Ep.* 4.11, for discussion of which see
Traub (1955: 214–215). For a recent summary of approaches to Pliny's relationship to Domitian see
Strunk (2013: 89–90). The absence of any reference to Nero in Seneca's epistles led Murray (1965: 50)
to infer that Seneca's epistolary aim was to distance himself from Nero's court.

[33] *Ep.* 3.10.1. Cf. *Ep.* 4.9.5, for which see pp. 133–134.

letters to Sidonius' fellow clergy, a fact he explicitly defends by explaining to Ferreolus that their ecclesiastical achievements automatically outweigh Ferreolus' own extensive political successes.[34]

Wealth and political rank were important to the status of a Roman aristocrat. In Late Antique Gaul *paideia* and *amicitia* became more important, but wealth and political rank nevertheless remained as the traditional markers of the elite.[35] An aristocrat's villa was paramount to the display of wealth. Two epistles describe villas in Sidonius' second book: *Ep.* 2.2 details his own estate Avitacum, and *Ep.* 2.9 depicts Sidonius' visit to the estates of Ferreolus and Apollinaris.[36] Both letters describe baths, which together with their arrangement in close proximity to one another in the collection, encourages the reader to read one description against the other.[37]

In *Ep.* 2.2 Sidonius' description of the bath complex at Avitacum interweaves modest and ostentatious elements. Either his description is incomplete or the baths themselves are, as they lack the normal array of rooms, having only the hot room (§4), the cold room and hall (§5–7), and the swimming pool (§8–9).[38] Nevertheless the bathing complex exhibits impressive features, such as the swimming pool (*piscina*), which Sidonius notes has a capacity of twenty-thousand *modii*, roughly two thirds the capacity of a modern Olympic swimming pool.[39]

Sidonius' description of the baths at the villas of Ferreolus and Apollinaris in *Ep.* 2.9 pales in comparison. Neither of their baths works (*Ep.* 2.9.8):

> Balneas habebat in opera uterque hospes, in usu neuter … vicina fonti aut fluvio raptim scrobis fodiebatur, in quam forte cum lapidum cumulus ambustus demitteretur, antro in hemisphaerii formam corylis flexibilibus intexto fossa inardescens operiebatur … qui [vapor] undae ferventis aspergine flammatis silicibus excuditur.

---

[34] *Ep.* 7.12.1, for discussion of which see pp. 119–121.

[35] Mathisen (1989: 1–4) and Sivan (1993: 9–10). Damon's (2010: 375) remark regarding Cicero is equally apt for Sidonius in Late Antique Gaul "[friendship] retained and indeed increased its importance when everything in his world was reorientating itself to new political and social constellations."

[36] See pp. 25–26, 56.

[37] For this methodology see p. 20.

[38] Thébert (2003: 108n100).

[39] Fagan (1999: 176n2) argues that Sidonius' description of the baths reveals his Christian modesty. This must be juxtaposed with his other comments, Sidonius not only "vaunt[s] the pleasures that awaits [the bath's] users" but also notes its considerable size. Analysis of Sidonius' bath complex is problematised by its apparent lack of completeness, for which see Balmelle (2001: 178) who notes that Sidonius' claim is consistent with the archaeological record of other examples of large *piscinae* in south-east Gaul. Babic (2015: 89) argues that the bath is comparable in size to ancient public baths. Whitton (2013a: 236) notes that Sidonius' use of the phrase *piscina forinsecus seu, si graecari mavis, baptisterium* affects "linguistic pretention" to heighten the status of such display.

> Both my hosts had baths under construction, but neither were in use …
> nearby to a spring and river a ditch was quickly dug, in which a heated pile
> of stones would be casually dropped, then the ditch, starting to get hot, was
> covered by a woven cave in the shape of a semi-sphere, made out of pliable
> hazel … the steam of the hot water was fomented by pouring water onto
> the burning rocks.

This bath forms a stark contrast to Sidonius' complex. The phrase *neuter
in usu* (neither were in use) ought to be read as a criticism.[40] Aristocrats
could reasonably expect better from the hospitality of others, especially
since baths were the defining feature of a villa.[41] Ferreolus and Apollinaris'
inability to provide proper baths is suggested by Sidonius' use of passive
verbs in this description; the ditch is dug (*fodiebatur*), the pile of hot rocks
is dropped (*demitteretur*), the hole is covered (*operiebatur*), and the steam
is shut in (*excuditur*). Sidonius invites the comparison between these two
descriptions by their arrangement in the collection and their similar shape,
both of the baths are domed.[42] Clearly the comparison favours Sidonius,
whose baths work and are a permanent structure and an impressive size.
Ferreolus and Apollinaris' failure to match his baths indicates the high level
of hospitality offered by him at Avitacum, especially relative to comparable
estates in south-west Gaul, and thus promotes his status at their expense.
This reading is consistent with Sidonius' friendly relationship with them
both; the slur is slight – Ferreolus and Apollinaris do the best they can
given the circumstances to make a bath of sorts for their guests, but their
aristocratic hospitality remains clearly inferior to Sidonius'. Perhaps at

---

[40] Percival (1997: 286) argues that this expression is either an "attempt to laugh away problems" or "gives a positive impression of a flourishing establishment" depending upon how *in opera uterque ... in usu neuter* is read. If the establishments were flourishing they certainly would have been able to afford some sort of alternative bathing complex more sophisticated than rocks in a pit, or even ensured that the renovations happened at separate times given the proximity of their villas. Sidonius does not want to laugh away the problem, but rather, draws attention to the failure of their baths compared to the (relatively) impressive bath complex at Avitacum.

[41] Hutchings (2009: 71) claims that Sidonius' apparent enjoyment of these "makeshift" baths indicates that they were an acceptable alternative. Sidonius' comments slight his hosts – not only did they not have baths in operation, but Sidonius had written and circulated(!) an epistle to that effect. Pavlovskis' (1973: 51) labelling of the setup as a "crude steambath" hints at an awareness of this slight. Lucht (2011: 71–72) refuses to rule out the alternative that this passage should be read positively, as it indicates that Apollinaris and Ferreolus could afford to renovate their baths. If Sidonius had intended such a reading, one would expect some remark in the *Ep.* 2.9 or elsewhere in his corpus about the successful progression or completion of the baths. Cf. the description of baths in the *Anthologia Latina* for an indication of their enduring importance in Late Antiquity for which see Miles (2005: 305ff) and Chalon et al. (1985: 207ff).

[42] *Ep.* 2.2.5 and 9.8. Sidonius was particularly proud of his villa, especially the baths' domed roof see *Carm.* 18.3–4: "aemula Baiano tolluntur culmina cono / parque cothurnato vertice fulget apex" (The roof rises, a rival to the cone of Baiae, And the apex shines equally with an elevated tip).

some unspecified point in the future their baths may be in a position to rival his but Sidonius never returns to them in the collection.

Other elements of Sidonius' villa description complement the baths' emphatic display of wealth. Local marble rather than foreign imports keep the house cool in summer.[43] Some fourteen rooms are described, including seasonal dining rooms.[44] A large colonnade leads out into the grounds that overlook the nearby lake. Towards the end of the epistle Sidonius briefly mentions the wealth generated by the estate (*Ep.* 2.2.19): "Iam vero ager ipse, quamquam hoc supra debitum, diffusus in silvis pictus in pratis, pecorosus in pascuis in pastoribus peculiosus" (Now truly that land, although this is beyond what is required, is spread out through woodlands, coloured by its flowers, stocked with cattle in its fields and wealth for its shepherds). This final statement is heavily stylised by its sustained alliteration (*debitum, diffusus, pictus, pratis, pecorosus, pascuis, pastoribus, peculiosus*), sibilance, the repetitive phrasing through four adjectives each followed by the preposition *in* governing a part of the landscape, and at its end the chiasmus *pecorosus … peculiosus*. It stands out as Sidonius' only statement regarding the productivity of Avitacum, and draws attention to the wealth that ultimately underpins Sidonius' enjoyment of *otium* at his estate.

Describing a villa afforded authors the opportunity to record and preserve this act of display, whether for a patron, such as Martial or Statius, or for themselves (and by extension their patron) such as in the case of Horace's Sabine estate.[45] Sidonius' villa ecphrasis places him in the elite company of other Latin epistolographers whose depictions of their own estates are extant. Seneca's bemused reaction to the aging of his estate, for example, cleverly reflects on the aging of his persona, but not badly, the estate may be crumbling, as it happens, but this is not down to any mismanagement.[46] Instead Seneca's wealth appears as a constant from his childhood, when he played in the villa as a boy, to his old age when he returned for a visit. Pliny's villa epistles similarly display his vast wealth as the owner of large estates.[47] Villa ecphrases thus affect the permanency

---

[43] *Ep.* 2.2.7, for discussion of which see pp. 46–47.

[44] *Matronale triclinium, textrinum, cella penaria, porticus, vestibulum, cryptoporticus, frigidum, cubiculum, hiemale triclinium, diaeta/cenatiunculam, deversorium, consistorio, area virenti, nemus,* and not counting the seemingly temporary *aleatorium.*

[45] See for example Martial 3.58, 4.64, 10.30; Statius *Silvae* 1 prf. 29–31 and 1.5; Horace *Carm.* 1.17; 2.13; 3.16, 29; 4.11. Newlands (2013: 69): "Roman rhetorical discourse frequently correlated a person's literary style with his character; in turn, architectural ecphrasis correlated a resplendent style with a resplendent house."

[46] Seneca *Ep.* 12 see Loretto (1977: 77n2) and Schirok (2005: 244n36).

[47] Pliny *Ep.* 2.17 and 5.6 for an assessment of which see Myers (2005: 103–111).

of their owner's status even more so than the structures themselves, which may fall into disrepair or be sold.

An epistolary author may indicate their wealth in other ways. Pliny, for example, regularly details his acts of generosity to others, often recording precise sums lest there be any doubt as to the scale involved.[48] For Sidonius, however, displays of wealth became undoubtedly more difficult after he became a bishop. This is not to say that they cannot be found. In *Ep.* 3.12, for example, Sidonius makes it very clear to his second cousin Secundus (and to his readers by circulating the epistle without redacting these statements) that he had covered the cost of repairing their ancestor's grave.[49] Still such efforts are closer to a display of *pietas* than of wealth itself. Consequently Sidonius' villa epistle is the single most evident example in the collection of his display of aristocratic wealth.

We may imagine Sidonius wallowing in the cool waters of Avitacum's baths in the boiling summers of the mid to late 460s, and perhaps even later. At no point in the epistolary collection does anything really ever repudiate his position as the master of Avitacum; there is no downsizing epistle as a corollary to the grandiose description of *Ep.* 2.2, instead the status he derives as the master of such an estate, like the status from his early secular office holding, continues to augment the status of his self.[50] Playing the Roman aristocrat of old in a villa imbued with the classical tradition is an assertion of status made all the stronger by the political and social unrest of Late Antique Gaul.

Paideia

The difficulty of gaining elite recognition pervades the material culture and texts of the ancient world. The specific ways may vary: clothes, speech, wealth, rank, appearance, gait, familial connections, but the struggle remains largely constant. Education (*paideia*) could not be removed, burnt, or lost once it was bestowed, but it still needed to be displayed to enhance and assert the status that it conveyed. As Brown has clearly shown, powerful elites and *paideia* were intricately connected.[51] In Late

---

[48] See for example Pliny *Ep.* 5.7.4 in which he describes his transfer of a bequest to the town of Comum while clearly advertising that he had the legal right to keep the bequest. Similarly in *Ep.* 9.23.1–2 Pliny includes specific details of his contributions to Calpurnia's dowry, to bring his generosity and wealth into focus, for which see Gibson (2003: 235). Manuwald (2003: 204–205) contextualises the importance of generosity to Pliny's self-fashioning by comparison to Cicero's.

[49] See pp. 69–72.

[50] In *Ep.* 8.12 Sidonius describes himself as a guest at another villa which may have been a permanent or temporary arrangement.

[51] Brown (1992). For the specific importance of reading see Johnson (2010: 39).

Antique Gaul *paideia* became increasingly important as a way of defining the elite, especially as the more traditional markers of that elite, wealth and public office, became harder to obtain and display. Mathisen notes that "[Gallo-Roman aristocrats] become increasingly dependent on the sense of superiority they derived from the appreciation of a classical literary culture that they shared with their fellow aristocrats."[52] When Sidonius and his peers were in their formative years the same traditional classical education of centuries past was still available to them, so Sidonius could rely on his contemporary readers' ability to recognise the nuances of his language and support his promotion of *paideia*.[53]

Sidonius wrote his epistles in an ornate style that prioritised the social and cultural importance of *paideia* by promoting the exclusivity and rarity of his audience who could read and appreciate his literature. He represents his readership in his epistolary corpus as the special few who could understand his literary endeavours, appreciate them, and in turn, receive recognition as class equals. When Sidonius discusses the decline of learning in his age, his comments are exclusively restricted to those outside of his literary circle, far removed from the epistolary I/you discourse.[54] Others lack *paideia* but these are not people with whom Sidonius corresponds.

Sidonius' assertions of the cultural importance of *paideia* are innately entwined with his concerns for the perceived (future) decline of Latin and Roman culture. In *Ep.* 2.10 Sidonius links his praise of the addressee Hesperius to his concern about the future (§1, 5):

> Amo in te quod litteras amas et usquequaque praeconiis cumulatissimis excolere contendo tantae diligentiae generositatem ... tantum increbruit multitudo desidiosorum ut nisi vel paucissimi quique meram linguae Latiaris proprietatem de trivialium barbarismorum robigine vindicaveritis eam brevi abolitam defleamus interemptamque: sic omnes nobilium sermonum purpurae per incuriam vulgi decolorabuntur ... neque apud te litterariam curam turba depretiet imperitorum, quia natura comparatum est ut in omnibus artibus hoc sit scientiae pretiosior pompa, quo rarior. Vale.
>
> I love in you that you love literature and I try to extol everywhere with abundant cries the excellence of such attentiveness ... the crowd of disengaged men has grown so great that unless there are (what one might call) the very few to defend the true use of the Latin language from the rust

---

[52] Mathisen (1988: 50).

[53] The educational system in Gaul was eventually affected by the collapse of Roman rule but this happened well and truly after Sidonius had already achieved his education, see Mohrmann (1955: 13), Mathisen (2005: 6–9), and Judge (2010: 260).

[54] Mathisen (1988: 46–52).

of trite barbarisms, soon we will mourn its destruction and removal: thus all the adornments of noble speech will be discoloured by the neglect of the mob... do not let the crowd of unskilled men cheapen your love of literature, since it is determined by nature that in all the arts the display of knowledge is more valuable as it becomes rarer. Goodbye.[55]

Sidonius' affection for Hesperius is emphatically linked (*amo, amas*) to their shared interest in literature. He contrasts the crowd (*multitudo, vulgi, turba*) with the very few (*paucissimi*) who use ornate Latin, which clearly included Sidonius and Hesperius. Sidonius displays this ornate Latinity as he describes it using the purple phrase *omnes nobilium sermonum purpurae*. This is of course only a concern for the right sort of people. The uneducated mob simply do not care (*incuriam, desidiosorum*). Instead it is up to the very few to defend the real use of Latin.[56] This "very few" is clearly defined: it is Hesperius, as identified by the personal pronoun *te*, it is Sidonius' audience, as evidenced by the second personal plural *vindicaveritis* and the pronoun *quique*. Ultimately it is all of "us," Sidonius' audience, contained within the first person plural *defleamus*.[57] At the end of the letter Sidonius returns to his initial premise for the epistle by praising Hesperius for his *cura*. Again, it is the unskilled crowd who cheapen their pursuits. Sidonius' final point asserts a rule of nature that as something becomes rarer (*rarior*) it increases in value. This assertion provides the intellectual context of Sidonius' ornate style. Simply put, Sidonius is cultivating an audience of the "right people," the value of which is inversely proportional to their number. In a circular way, we the few have increased the importance and worth of reading Sidonius, owing to our paucity, and our paucity in turn has increased the value of Sidonius' letters.

In *Ep.* 2.10 Sidonius characterises his position as "anti-populist" and equally characterises the "populist position" by its alterity – it is cheap, uneducated, unskilled, and inactive. The class dimension to Sidonius' assertion of the importance of *paideia* is evident again at the end of *Ep.* 3.13 in which he praises his son for avoiding the company of people who do not act properly (*Ep.* 3.13.11):

---

[55] This approach follows Mathisen's (1988: 46ff) analysis of *Ep.* 2.10; see also Postel (2011: 177) and Squillante (2014: 278).

[56] The social dimension to this discourse is critical. Denecker (2015: 410) links Sidonius' criticism of contemporary Latin to his supposed dislike of innovation, but this is inconsistent with Sidonius' own innovative use of Latin and reuse of classical phrases and tropes. Castellanos (2013: 246) rightly distinguishes Sidonius' projection and dissemination of his concerns about literary decline in this epistle from whatever genuine concerns he may have had.

[57] Denecker (2015: 411) draws attention to Sidonius' use of first person plural pronouns in the passage which distinguishes the "others" from Sidonius' side.

Nam quibus citra honestatis nitorem iactitabundis loquacis faece petulantiae lingua polluitur infrenis, his conscientia quoque sordidatissima est. denique facilius obtingit ut quispiam seria loquens vivat obscene quam valeat ostendi qui pariter existat improbus dictis et probus moribus. Vale.

Indeed, those boasters fall short of the sheen of virtue. Their unrestrained language is soiled by the filth of their wanton prattle – their conscience is so very spoiled. Lastly, it is easier to find someone talking seriously who lives obscenely than it is possible for someone to be pointed out who is immoral in his speech but moral in his ways.[58]

Sidonius contrasts the dirt and filth of such people with the honour of proper behaviour.[59] His exhortation to his son is to associate with people who speak well and appreciate the cultural and social value of *paideia*. Their inability to speak properly is evidence of their flawed character. Sidonius' didactic assertion warns his son that it is far better to associate with those who can at least speak well, and who are probably therefore virtuous. The alternative is too risky: those who cannot speak well in all likelihood lack the kind of desirable traits that he should look for in his friends.

In the next epistle in the collection Sidonius asserts how *docti* ought to engage with texts (*Ep.* 3.14.2):

Nam qui maxume doctus sibi videtur, dictionem sanam et insanam ferme appetitu pari revolvit, non amplius corrupiscens erecta quae laudet quam despecta quae ridet. Atque in hunc modum scientia pompa proprietas linguae Latinae iudiciis otiosorum maximo spretui est quorum scurrilitati neglegentia comes hoc volens tantum legere, quod carpat, sic non utitur litteris quod abutitur.

For he who seems to himself greatly learned, he generally examines with equal interest good and bad expression, desiring lofty efforts to praise no more than woeful ones to ridicule. And so in this way, skill, pomp and the proper use of the Latin language is despised greatly in the judgment of these idle men, with their contempt and folly the scholar wants to read only to criticise, thus he does not make use of literature but abuses it.[60]

Sidonius bemoans the critics' failure to appreciate three qualities in Latin: *scientia*, *pompa*, and *proprietas*, which he uses in their specific sense regarding style: *scientia* refers to the correct application of knowledge; *pompa* to display; *proprietas* to the correct use of words, suitable

---

[58] Condorelli (2012: 409ff) clearly details the comedic elements which underpin this serious message.

[59] Giannotti (2016: 259).

[60] For Sidonius' syntax at "sic … abutitur" see Gianotti (2016: 267). For his sentiment see Van Dam (1992: 330). Gibson (2013b: 347) links the position and content of this epistle to Pliny's *Ep.* 3.21 which ends his third book.

to the task at hand.[61] He argues that the enjoyment of texts requires an approach without criticism that is not focused on ridiculing others' efforts. Throughout his corpus, Sidonius often responds to would-be critics. This prompted Loyen to call him "very sensitive."[62] The basis of this claim is not so much Sidonius' own proclivities but rather the social importance of *paideia* – according to Sidonius, critics fall into the group of people who do not understand his work and appreciate his style. Such displays of *paideia* are commonly found among Latin epistolographers. Pliny's literary circle, for example may not have liked his poetry but his description of their meetings and criticism asserts and displays the value they place on *paideia*.[63]

Sidonius' polemical discourse against the unlearned and thus uncultured at times targets specific others. In *Ep.* 4.7, addressed to Simplicius, Sidonius enters into a prolonged invective against the carrier of the epistle, who had asked Sidonius whether he could take an epistle on his behalf, unaware of the *amicitia* between author and addressee.[64] For the aristocracy of fifth-century Gaul misreading the social connection between two individuals was a significant faux pas (*Ep.* 4.7.2):

> Videre mihi videor, ut homini non usque ad invidiam perfaceto nova erunt omnia cum invitabitur peregrinus ad domicilium, trepidus ad conloquium, rusticus ad laetitiam, pauper ad mensam et cum apud crudos caeparumque crapulis esculentos hic agat vulgus, illic ea comitate retractabitur ac si inter Apicios epulones et Byzantinos chironumantas hucusque ructaverit.

> I imagine[65] that everything will be new to this man, who is not enviably witty, when he is welcomed into your home as a stranger, as a nervous man for a chat, as a country bumpkin to gaiety, as a poor man to table, especially since among those who crudely gorge themselves on onions[66] and drink, he leads the crowd, but at your house will be treated by such kindness, as if he had belched at Apicius' dinners and there among Byzantine carvers.[67]

---

[61] Giannotti (2016: 266). *Thesaurus Linguae Latinae: pompa* s.v 2.B.b. See Quintilian 8.2.1–11 on the concept of *proprietas* in literature, and Denecker (2015: 412).

[62] Loyen (1970a: 3) "Sidoine était sensible très à la critique; il se plaint souvent de ses détracteurs" (Sidonius was very sensitive to criticism; he often complains about his detractors). Cf. Castellanos (2013: 144) whose assertion that Sidonius enjoyed talking about himself belittles the important role that self-presentation played in his political survival.

[63] For a detailed assessment of Pliny's depiction as a poet see Hershkowitz (1995: 176–180).

[64] Allen (2015a: 211) uses this epistle as evidence that low status letter bearers were sometimes used.

[65] Amherdt (2001: 215) cites Cic. *Fam* 14.3.5 as a precedent for the epistolary formula "videre mihi videor."

[66] Sidonius' cites onions owing to their low culinary status drawn from their capacity to sate the diner in a very cost effective manner, for which see Amherdt (2001: 217–218).

[67] For the reference to dining see Cabouret (2012: 161) and Amherdt (2001: 219).

Sidonius thus invites us the audience to laugh along with him at the carrier's cultural inferiority. He will be completely out of his depth and unable to adapt his habits to his new environment, unable to increase his cultural standing. Sidonius' *paideia* is here effortlessly displayed by the contrast in tone between his description of the crude hypothetical behaviour of the letter carrier, belching and gorging, and the sophistication of his allusion to Apicius and Byzantine carvers which would surely go over the carrier's head.[68] Sidonius controls and defines what it means to be unlearned and uncultured. The letter carrier may well have been literate, and probably upwardly mobile if he was rubbing shoulders with Sidonius and Simplicius but that is not enough on its own to be part of Sidonius' literary clique.[69]

The same discourse is evident in a less targeted way in *Ep.* 4.17, addressed to Arbogastes who was a *comes* in Trier. Sidonius encourages Arbogastes to keep up his reading especially as he interacts with barbarian groups (*Ep.* 4.17.1): "sic barbarorum familiaris, quod tamen nescius barbarismorum" (thus you are familiar with barbarians, but still do not know barbarisms). Sidonius' praise of Arbogastes focuses on the fine line between barbarian interaction and influence.[70] Inevitably this praise reflects on Sidonius' own interaction with barbarians.[71] His advice draws attention to his role as a worthwhile *exemplum* for Arbogastes of how a Gallo-Roman may engage with barbarians without falling under their sway. Reading is Sidonius' cure for literary and cultural decline, the answer for elites struggling to receive the recognition of their status.

In a letter to Syagrius, another Gallo-Roman aristocrat extensively involved with barbarians, Sidonius depicts him getting the better of barbarians in their own language (*Ep.* 5.5.3):

> aestimari minime potest, quanto mihi ceteris sit risui, quotiens audio, quod te praesente formidet linguae suae facere barbarus barbarismum.

---

[68] As Amherdt (2001: 214) notes, an antithesis is clearly formed between the correct behaviour, as modelled by Sidonius, and the incorrect behaviour as demonstrated by the letter carrier.

[69] Allen (2015a: 211) argues that the letter carrier to whom Sidonius refers was of "lowly status" but the carrier of *Ep.* 4.7 does not seem to have done so in a paid capacity, which means he may well not have been of lowly status, but simply not high enough for Sidonius and Simplicius' social rank.

[70] Denecker (2015: 417–418) limits the applicability of these remarks to Arbogastes' language, although for Sidonius and his circle, language and behaviour were intricately connected, see *Ep.* 3.13.11 for which see pp. 30–31. Arbogastes was of Frankish descent (PLRE II "Arbogastes") through his ancestor Arbogastes (PLRE I "Arbogastes"), a *magister militum* during the reign of Theodosius for which see Castellanos (2013: 247), who notes the literary effect of Arbogastes' Frankish name. Heinzelmann (1976: 82) cites the occurrence of another Arbogastes (unlisted in the PLRE) who features in a fifth century episcopal list from Chartres.

[71] See, for example pp. 101–102, 142 for Sidonius' diplomatic efforts at the Visigothic court as depicted in *Ep.* 1.2.

it is inestimable how amusing it is to me and the others, whenever I hear, that in your presence the barbarian fears to make a barbarism in his own language."[72]

The letter ends on a more serious note, reminding Syagrius to continue his reading of Latin (*Ep.* 5.5.4:): "restat hoc unum, vir facetissime, ut nihilo segnius, vel cum vacabit, aliquid lectioni operis impendas custodiasque hoc, prout es elegantissimus, temperamentum, ut ista tibi lingua teneatur, ne ridearis, illa exerceatur, ut rideas" (this one point remains, most charming sir, to spend some time on reading (not at all lazily) even when the opportunity for leisure time presents, and protect this balance, as a very stylish man, so that this language is still yours, so you are not laughed at, and practice the other, so that you may laugh at them). Regular reading is the only way Syagrius can maintain his Latin literary culture while engaging and speaking with barbarians.[73] Sidonius thus constructs a hierarchy of cultural value: at the moment Sygarius and he both laugh at the barbarians; but if Syagrius slips up with his reading, he will become the target of laughter from Sidonius and his literary circle.[74] Syagrius may still be able to laugh at the barbarians for making solecisms in their own language, but he will not be able to do so from the same cultural vantage point as Sidonius and other Gallo-Roman literati.[75] There is no room in Sidonius' conception of *paideia* for behaviours which do not draw their cultural valency from the continuance of the classical tradition.[76] Barbarians learn Latin, not the other way around.

---

[72] Laes (2013: 22) considers Arbogastes' example in *Ep.* 4.17 the one to be followed, and Syagrius "a rather funny exception" as a Roman capable of speaking a barbarian language. Becker (2014a: 296) suggests that Syagrius' position was not yet acceptable for an aristocrat whereas Geary (2009: 866) posits that Syagrius represented a new trend. Amherdt (2001: 389) points out the difference in Sidonius' almost critical tone towards Syagrius and his more gentle tone towards Arbogastes. Becker (2014a: 296ff) explains this difference by drawing attention to the different political situations: by 476 the Visigoths had become a daily political reality for Sidonius while the Burgundians remained further north. Sidonius may have felt compelled to relax his criticism of the Visigoths after Leo had secured his release from prison following the fall of Clermont, for which see Harries (1996: 43). Squillante (2009: 149) suggests that Syagrius' bilingualism may have contributed to the Burgundians improving their understanding of Roman cultural practice. Ovid's *Ex Ponto* 4.19.23 records his shame at writing in a barbarian language, but there are no clear verbal similarities in this epistle to preference Ovid as Sidonius' model.

[73] Squillante (2014: 283).

[74] Denecker (2015: 413–415). Wolff (2017: 79) points out that genuine criticism of Syagrius underpins Sidonius' jest.

[75] B. Ward-Perkins (2005: 80) perhaps picks up on Sidonius' tone – "[laughing] at Syagrius" – as does Giuletti (2014: 97). Squillante (2014: 283) labels the situation "grotesque" and sees hostility underpinning Sidonius' remarks.

[76] See Denecker (2017: 255–256) for a summary of Sidonius' remarks regarding barbarian languages.

Sidonius' friends could end up the target of this discourse if their behaviour did not correlate with what he expected from his literary circle. A doctrinal controversy began in Gaul around 469 with the anonymous publication of a treatise "Quaeris a me," which argued that the soul was corporeal.[77] Claudianus Mamertus, a priest, wrote *De statu animae* as a response to this treatise, dedicating it to his friend Sidonius Apollinaris. In this work Claudianus employed Neoplatonist and Neopythagorean ideas to defend the incorporeity of the soul while launching a fierce invective against the anonymous author of that treatise.[78] The anonymity of Faustus of Riez as the author of this controversial work was dispelled shortly after, or perhaps even before, Claudianus' publication.[79] This put Sidonius in a difficult situation, as he was friends with both Claudianus and Faustus.[80]

Sidonius wrote *Ep.* 4.3 as a direct reply to Claudianus, whose initial letter Sidonius included in his collection as the previous epistle (*Ep.* 4.2). Claudianus' letter accused him of not doing his duty; he had dedicated

---

[77] The corporeal status of the soul was an ongoing concern to early Christian thinkers, such as Tertullian *De Carne Christi* 11; Augustine *Ep.* 166 and Jerome, recorded in Augustine's collection as *Ep.* 172, John Cassian *Coll.* 7.13. See Lievestro (1956: 266), Simonetti (1976: 416), Tibiletti (1979: 281), Daly (1987: 21–23, 29–31), Ganz (1995: 780), and Teske (2001: 118–122). For a list including Greek authors see De La Broise (1890: xvii). For details pertaining to the circumstances of this controversy in southern Gaul see Mathisen (1989: 235–244) and Brittain (2001: 240–243). Koch (1895: 17) suggests Claudianus' views were favoured, as Faustus never revisited the issue. Augustine's views exerted significant influence on Claudianus: Zimmerman (1914: 493–494) and Gilson (1955: 97). He also drew on a range of sources, for a recent study see Militello (2005: 146–149).

[78] Bömer (1936: 61–69, 127–128) and Beutler (1937: 552–558).

[79] Gennadius Massiliensis attributed the work to Faustus in his *Liber de scriptoribus ecclesiasticis* I.85.j. "legi … alium [opus] adversus eos qui dicunt esse in creaturis aliquid incorporeum, in quo et divinis testimoniis et Patrum confirmat sententiis, nihil credendum incorporeum praeter Deum" (I have read another of Faustus' work against those who say that there is something incorporeal in created beings. In this work he proves by divine testimony and the opinions of the fathers that nothing ought to be thought of as incorporeal except God). Fortin (1959: 44–45) argues that Claudianus already knew that Faustus was the author when he wrote the *De statu animae*, see also Mathisen (1989: 237) and (2009b: 201–202). Rehling (1898: 44) disagrees. It seems probable that Claudianus did not know Faustus was the author at the time of composition, particularly if, as Elg (1937: 114) notes, "Ac nonnumquam Claudianus locos Faustianos disputationi suae inseruit atque laudavit" (Claudianus incorporated serveral of Faustus' points into his argument and even praised them). Weigel (1938: 80) argues that Claudianus suspected that Faustus was the author, without knowing definitively. Alciati (2009b: 203–204) following De La Broise (1890: 31n3) argues that *De statu animae* 2.9 alludes to Faustus specifically at "Cedo mihi nunc illos … damnari."

[80] Shanzer and Wood (2002: 193) argue that *Ep.* 9.3 shows that Sidonius was Faustus' "spiritual protégé." While *Carm.* 16 indicates that Faustus had a significant influence on Sidonius' early development, and *Ep.* 9.3.5 that Sidonius enjoyed Faustus' sermons – see Engelbrecht (1889: 47) – *Ep.* 9.3.1 suggests this influence had waned. Both Claudianus and Faustus influenced Sidonius' spiritual development: Van Waarden (2011b: 111). It is possible, albeit speculative, that Claudianus' brother Mamertus, the bishop of Vienne, bore ill will towards Faustus from the events of 464, when Pope Hilary pursued Mamertus for consecrating a bishop outside of his diocese, for which see Weigel (1938: 80). Faustus was part of the council that resulted in Hilary's decision against Mamertus.

his treatise to Sidonius but had not received any acknowledgement of his publication. Sidonius' failure to do so, particularly as the dedicatee, was anathema to the Gallic elite's social and literary mores, given their concern regarding perceived literary decline, which the publication of new works was understood to redress.[81] In *Ep.* 4.3 Sidonius uses hyperbole to undermine his praise of Claudianus. At the end of a detailed catalogue of comparison between Claudianus and other authors, generals, and poets, Sidonius' hyperbole reaches fever pitch, beginning with an alliterative run (*tuam tubam totus*) of dentals (*Ep.* 4.3.10):

> tuam tubam totus qua patet orbis iure venerabitur, quam constat geminata felicitate cecinisse, quando nec aemulum repperit nec aequalem, cum pridem aures et ora populorum me etiam circumferente pervageretur. Nobis autem grandis audacia, si vel apud municipales et cathedrarios oratores aut forenses rabulas garriamus, qui etiam cum perorant – salva pace potiorum turba numerosior – illitteratissimis litteris vacant. Nam te, cui seu liberum seu ligatum placeat alternare sermonem, intonare ambifariam suppetit, pauci, quos aequus amavit, imitabuntur.

> the entire earth, as far as it extends, justly honours your trumpet. It is agreed that it has sounded with twin success, as it has found no rival nor equal, since even as I spread it around, it reached some time ago the ears and faces of the people. But for me it would be an act of great audacity, if I were to chatter among the locally appointed orators or the court room pleaders who even when they are making a case – with the exception of a few of the more capable ones, but for the most part – waste their time on unliterary letters.[82]

Sidonius freely acknowledges the popularity of Claudianus' treatise and refutes Claudianus' accusations that he has not done enough to publicise the work. His tone affects apparent surprise at his own involvement in popularising the work – Sidonius was (probably) barely involved in distributing it – he asks for a copy of it back from another aristocrat in *Ep.* 5. 2, but that epistle is probably included in the collection to provide evidence against Claudianus' remarks in *Ep.* 4.2 that Sidonius has not done anything to promote the work. The controversy on the soul was worth avoiding for Sidonius especially as its main protagonists were both friends of his.[83] If Sidonius sided with one or the other he risked losing his ties of *amicitia*, indeed this may have happened anyway if *Ep.* 9.3 (addressed to Faustus) is evidence of their estrangement.[84]

---

[81] Germain (1840: 10), Mathisen (1988: 45–47).
[82] Squillante (2009: 142).
[83] See p. 86.
[84] See p. 161.

Sidonius carefully chooses the terms he uses to display Claudianus' popularity. Claudianus "has no rival nor equal." Few have attempted to do what he has done, principally take a position on the corporality of the soul which was a controversial issue for the Church (as it was yet to acknowledge a doctrinal position) and hence inherently dangerous. The people that enjoy Claudianus' work are the *rabulas*, the *turba numerosior* who waste their time on texts that are not literary.[85] Allusions to Pliny and Symmachus sit behind these comments, as Sidonius chastises Claudianus for writing a popular work, he asserts his own *paideia*.[86]

In some respects Sidonius' display of *paideia* is similar to other Latin epistolographers. Fronto's didactic responses to Marcus Aurelius clearly remind the reader of his role as the emperor's tutor. Pliny appears as the centre of an active literary circle. The difference for Sidonius is that dramatic changes to his society increased exponentially the relative importance of *paideia* as an intangible marker of elite status that cannot be removed.

Sidonius readily uses ridicule to define and assert what norms and behaviour he expects from his social circle. Syagrius better be careful or others will be laughing at him. The letter carrier clearly is not one of Sidonius' clique; he does not get the joke because he is the joke. The importance of *paideia* for Sidonius and other aristocrats in Late Antique Gaul is evident in the sophisticated and highly ornate style that he employs and his preparedness to preclude others from his social circle, or at least, to imply that they risk social exclusion.

Sidonius Transalpinus

Julius Caesar's conquest (58–52 BCE) marked the beginning of direct Roman control over Gaul.[87] Over time Gaul's importance grew. By the middle of the first century CE leading figures from Gaul had become directly involved in Roman politics; some had been admitted to the senate, and had other honours and advantages bestowed.[88] By the end of the first century this

---

[85] Their literacy is not in doubt. Sidonius' criticism focuses on their reading of texts devoid of literary value which by implication includes Claudianus' treatise. Banniard (1992: 422) takes this part of the letter to indicate that "une catégorie culturelle moyenne" (middle cultural category) existed in Gaul between the elite senatorial class and common people. Sidonius places Claudianus' work below his aristocratic literary circle.

[86] See Symmachus *Ep.* 3.23: *forenses rabulas*, and Pliny *Ep.* 1.10.9: *illitteratissimas litteras*, for the listing of which see Geisler (1887: 363). For brief discussion see Amherdt (2001: 163–164).

[87] Drinkwater (1983: 5–19).

[88] Levick (1978: 91–92, 98–99) links Claudius' policies to Caesar's. For the opposition to these moves see Griffin (1982: 414–415), see also Woolf (1998: 65–66).

trend seems largely to have petered out, although as long as the interests of Gaul and Italy were compatible political tension remained largely in check. From 260 to 274 a series of self-proclaimed emperors, beginning with Postumus, sought to govern Gaul removed from the destabilising politics of Rome.[89] By the late third century threats to the north-western provinces prompted ongoing political instability. The concentration of soldiers needed to deter these threats and protect the frontier represented a potentially volatile polity that at times appointed their commanders as emperors. Through the fourth century more Gallic senatorial families rose to prominence.[90] Trier, the major city of Gaul, grew in size, and became an imperial residence, and important cities throughout Gaul developed into prominent centres of learning.[91] Gallic aristocrats who served in the imperial administration in the fourth century maintained close ties of affection towards Gaul.[92] This was compatible with their service to the Roman state because Gallic interests were still well accommodated; there were no barbarians in their midst, no Visigothic settlement in Aquitania, and no Vandal armada threatening Rome.

Towards the end of the fourth century and into the early fifth century it was becoming increasingly clear that Rome could not maintain the Rhine frontier nor guarantee the Gallo-Roman aristocracy that it would serve Gaul's best interests.[93] Political unrest in Gaul largely manifested not in separatist movements but rather in attempts to usurp and grab power in Rome. Most of these attempts failed, such as Constantine III's efforts from 407–411, in which Sidonius' grandfather Apollinaris was involved.[94] Some met initial success. Sidonius' father-in-law, Avitus, for example, was proclaimed emperor in Gaul, marched to Rome, and promptly made

---

[89] For a detailed analysis of Gaul during this period see Drinkwater (1987).

[90] Stroheker (1970: 17–36).

[91] Sivan (1993: 5–10, 14).

[92] Matthews (1971: 1088–1089).

[93] Harries (1994: 243) cites the crossing of the Rhine by Germanic groups at the end of 406 as a defining moment. For a detailed assessment of the possible reasons for this movement of people see Heather (2009: 3–29); for an assessment of preceeding barbarian movements that have been overshadowed somewhat by the events of the end of 406 see Wijnendaele (2016: 267–280).

[94] Orosius 8.42 and Sozomen 9.15, Kulikowski (2000: 325–330. Prior to the siege of Arles in which Constantine III was killed, Apollinaris was demoted and so managed to avoid death, perhaps by returning to Lyon. See pp. 2–3. Zosimus *Nova Historia* 6.4. See Mascoli (2002: 184). After Constantine III was murdered Jovinus also launched an usurpation from Gaul, see Stroheker (1965: 54). Muhlberger (1990: 190) argues that many of the Gallic aristocrats who followed Avitus to Rome in 455 were sons of those who had supported Jovinus. Drinkwater (2013: 62–64) carefully deconstructs assumptions that Gauls sought to separate from the Roman state. According to Sidonius Avitus managed to repeal the tax penalty placed on Gaul following Jovinus' failed usurpation, see *Carm.* 7.207–213, Drinkwater (1998: 287–290), and Leppin (2013: 347). For the political context to these usurpations see Heather (2009: 4–6).

Sidonius his panegyrist. Sidonius described the acclamation in his panegyric to Avitus (*Carm.* 7.577–579):[95]

> concurrunt proceres et milite circumfuso
> aggere composito statuunt ac torque coronant
> castrensi maestum donantque insignia regni.[96]

> the chiefs rush together and with the soldiery gathered around they place him on an assembled mound and crown him, saddened, with a military torc and give him the insignia of sovereignty.

Avitus may have used the torc as an expression of Gallic identity.[97]

Sidonius was an integral member of the active and extensive Gallo-Roman aristocracy that strove to assert itself in the rapidly changing geopolitical environment as Roman imperial power in Europe waned.[98] Sidonius' self is consistently presented as Gallo-Roman in his epistolary collection, which was read throughout Roman Gaul and included epistles addressed to individuals well beyond Sidonius' *civitas*, which may partly account for why his claims extend beyond his role as an adopted *Arvernus* to his identification as a proud Gallo-Roman.[99] This is most evident in two epistles (*Ep.* 1.5 and 8) which offer an agonistic comparison between Gaul and Italy, and their inhabitants; and two which describe the hospitality on offer by Sidonius in Gaul (*Ep.* 2.2 and 8.12).

In the autumn of 467 Sidonius travelled to Rome. He describes this journey in *Ep.* 1.5 which is a very literary and political travelogue.[100]

---

[95] Sidonius uses several literary strategies in his *Panegyric to Avitus* in an effort to legitimise his ascension – see Brocca (2003–2004: 291–292) – and characterise Avitus as the ideal candidate to respond to recent destabilising events, such as the sack of Rome in 455, Bonjour (1982: 11–12).

[96] The adjective *maestum* depicts Avitus as not wanting the role of emperor which is a traditional refusal that may have been enhanced by the dire circumstances of May–June 455, for which see pp. 3–4.

[97] Santos (2011: 287) places this revolt in the context of the Rhine frontier's political instability owing to barbarian attacks. Castellanos (2013: 115) sees Avitus' rise as a powerplay from both the Gallic aristocracy and the Visigoths. For its circumstances see Grotowski (2010: 294) and Henning (1999: 41, 133). Ammianus Marcellinus (20.4.17–18) notes that Julian did this because a diadem could not be found. If Sidonius' account is an embellishment, then the expression of Gallic identity is his, rather than Avitus', and so is still significant. Torcs had multivalent symbolism, for which see Rowan and Swan (2015: 82–89), so it could simply indicate Avitus' military identity, which could be considered reactionary to the imperial legacy of Honorius and Valentinian III, neither of which identified particularly as military men.

[98] Mathisen (1993a: xi).

[99] Sidonius' self-fashioning as a Gallo-Roman should not be conflated with his identity. The point of this assessment is not how he thought about himself but rather how he projected his self. These may be related but are not necessarily so. For the importance of the *civitas* to Gallic identity during this period, and to Sidonius in particular, see Lewis (2000: 69–77), Sivonen (2006: 16–17), and Drinkwater (2013: 61–69).

[100] Hanaghan (2017c: 631–649).

Sidonius arrived in the city as the nuptial celebrations of Ricimer and Alypia, Anthemius' daughter, were ongoing (*Ep.* 1.5.10): "igitur nunc in ista non modo personarum sed etiam ordinum partiumque laetitia Transalpino tuo latere conducibilius visum" (And so now, amid the rejoicing not only of individuals but even classes and parties, it seemed quite advantageous to your *Transalpinus* [Sidonius] to lie low). Sidonius arrives in the city as an outsider. He is so unconnected to the Roman aristocratic families that he is forced initially to find private lodgings.[101] The contrast with the first stages of his journey is acute; Sidonius is met by a group of friends whose affection slows him down.[102] He describes his departure from Lyon (*Ep.* 1.5.2): "Egresso mihi Rhodanusiae nostrae moenibus" (After I had gone out of the gates of our Rhodanusia). Sidonius' use of the toponym *Rhodanusia* is a hapax.[103] Its etymology can be traced to the noun *Rhodanus*.[104] Sidonius uses *Rhodanusia* however to refer to a city, he leaves *moenia* (battlements) behind as he sets out on his journey. One may detect a degree of pride in the use of this toponym to refer to Lyon, his city of birth, by its relation to the Rhone, the impressive river that runs past the city.[105] These Gallic peripheral elements, specifically Sidonius' identification as a *tranalpinus* and pride in his native Lyon, must be considered in conjunction with the more manifestly Roman (core) elements of the epistle; Sidonius is summoned by imperial post-horses and interacts with the landscape as a keen reader of Latin literature.[106] Sidonius describes a Rome in chaos, overrun by the excessive wedding celebrations.[107]

His praise of Rome in the next epistle is nostalgic for what the city once was (*Ep.* 1.6.2): "[in iuventa] domicilium legum, gymnasium litterarum, curiam dignitatum, verticem mundi, patriam libertatis, in qua unica totius orbis civitate soli barbari et servi peregrinantur" ([in its youth] the home of laws, the grammar school of literature, the court of honours, the top of the world, the native land of freedom, in this one city in the entire world

101 *Ep.* 1.5.9. For the particulars of the political deal between Anthemius, Ricimer, and Leo see MacGeorge (2002: 235).
102 Fournier and Stoehr-Monjou (2013: 7).
103 A *hapax legomenon* is a word that has only a single attested use.
104 *Lewis and Short: Rhodanus*, I.
105 Arnold (2014: 88) argues that the poetry of Ausonius, Sidonius, and Venantius Fortunatus closely connected "the rivers of Gaul to their concerns over political and cultural identity." The same could be said of Sidonius' epistles.
106 *Ep.* 1.5.1–10. Hanaghan (2017c: 631–642).
107 *Ep.* 1.5.10.

only barbarians and slaves may be said to be foreign).[108] Not even that is now secure; Ricimer, a barbarian of mixed Suevian and Gothic ancestry, has just married into the imperial house.[109]

Sidonius' Gallo-Roman self responds in part to Italian influences. In *Ep.* 1.5 he is unable to lodge with friends in Rome, not because of his cultural alterity but rather because he simply lacked friends among the Italian senatorial aristocracy in residence. This distinction between Gaul and Italy is central to *Ep.* 1.8, a witty riposte to Candidianus, in which Sidonius strongly defends his Gallic roots with an intricate display of *paideia*. He refutes Candidianus' criticisms of Gaul with a stinging rebuke of Ariminum, Candidianus' birthplace (*Ep.* 1.8.1–2): "nebulas ergo mihi meorum Lugdunensium exprobras et diem quereris nobis matutina caligine obstructum vix meridiano fervore reserari. et tu istaec mihi Caesenatis furni potius quam oppidi verna deblateras?" (therefore you offer up against me the fogs of my Lyon and complain that the daylight hidden by morning mist is scarcely revealed in the midday heat. And do you blabber this rubbish to me, you a native of Caesena, an oven rather than a town?). Sidonius' offence at Candidianus' comments is clear. His withering tone (*istaec, deblateras*) belittles Candidianus' complaint and ridicules his native city, which Sidonius implies Candidianus did not like and so moved to Ravenna.[110] Sidonius' proceeds to mock Ravenna for its notorious difficulties with mosquitos, owing to the nearby Padus river, and the swampy ground that surrounded the city.[111] Everything is upside down (*Ep.* 1.8.2):

> turres fluunt naves sedent, aegri deambulant medici iacent, algent balnea domicilia conflagrant, sitiunt vivi natant sepulti, vigilant fures dormiunt potestates

> walls fall and water is stagnant, towers float and ships sit, the sick walk about and doctors lie down, baths freeze and residences burn, the living thirst, the buried swim, thieves are on watch and the powers that be sleep[112]

---

[108] Cf. *Carm.* 7.45–49 where Rome is depicted as old and broken, for which see Hanaghan (2017b: 269–272). For *Roma* as an aged deity in pre-Sidonius fifth century literature see M. Roberts (2001: 533–541).

[109] For Ricimer's birth see Gillet (1995: 380–384).

[110] *Ep.* 1.8.2: "cuius natalis tibi soli vel iucunditate vel commodo quid etiam ipse sentires, dum migras, indicavisti" (You have indicated what you in fact feel about the charm and convenience of the land of your birth because you immigrated).

[111] *Ep.* 1.8.2.

[112] *Ep.* 1.8.2: See Köhler (1995: 261–263) for discussion of this passage.

Sidonius ends the epistle by asserting the worth of Gaul relative to Ravenna and asking Candidianus to take pity on *Transalpini*, who are not particularly proud of bettering such lowly adversaries as Ravenna (*Ep.* 1.8.3): "si deteriorum collatione clarescant" (if they grow bright in comparison to the worst). The verb *clarescant* makes it all rather personal; this is surely a pun aimed at Candidianus' bright name.[113] There can be no doubt that Sidonius includes himself as one of the *Transalpini* – his use of this toponymic substantive invokes *Ep.* 1.5 where it refers to Sidonius at the very moment that as an outsider he must find his own lodgings in Rome.[114] By strenuously asserting his Gallic credentials, Sidonius' self becomes representative and even emblematic of the changing perceptions in the aristocracies of Gaul and Italy towards one another.[115] The cultural ascendancy of Ravenna, and by extension Italy, is rejected by Sidonius.

Space and its description are important to Sidonius' assertion of his Gallo-Roman self.[116] The description of his villa in *Ep.* 2.2 is a prolonged exercise in self-fashioning, certain aspects of which exhibit distinctly Gallic features, principally the local landscape, fishing, and marble, set inside and next to a Roman villa, modelled on architectural and literary exempla.

Sidonius uses two allusions to Ausonius in *Ep.* 2.2 to draw attention to the Gallic nature of the nearby lake.[117] The first focuses on fishing which was a popular motif in Gallic art and literature (*Ep.* 2.2.12):[118]

> Hinc iam spectabis ut promoveat alnum piscator in pelagus, ut stataria retia suberinis corticibus extendat aut signis per certa intervalla dispositis tractus

---

[113] See pp. 94, 128, 150, 167, 174 for other examples of Sidonius' name puns. Ambrose similarly puns on the meaning of the name Candidianus in *Ep.* 91, which uses three words in quick succession (*splendor, elucet, fulgorem*) that all reference brightness.

[114] Köhler (1995: 264) notes the use of this word in both epistles.

[115] Kaster (1997: 90) links this "return to the local expression of power" to the prominent role of *paideia* in fifth-century southern Gaul. There is little literary tradition of Gallic authors mocking Rome and Italy prior to this period. Ausonius lists Rome as the most famous city of the world at *Ordo urbium nobelium* 1; *Pan Lat.* 12.2 presents a wholly positive image of Rome, which is unsurprising, given it was delivered in Rome. Rutilius' *De reditu suo* is positive in its description of Rome even as it notes the devastation of Gaul in 417 (1.46–154) for which see M. Roberts (2001: 539–540). For an assessment of the attitude of individual Gallic authors of the fourth century towards Rome see Paschoud (1967).

[116] Van Waarden (2011a: 556n15) prefers "self presentation" to "self-fashioning," owing to the latter's origin in New Historicism, but (as Van Waarden acknowledges) its application in Classics is well established, beginning with Riggsby (1995: 123–135).

[117] The description abounds in detail which by and large fits with the identification of the lake as Lac d'Aydat, see Stevens (1933: 185–196), and for a more confident identification Loyen (1970b: 217). Latitude: 45°39'52"N, Longitude: 2°59'9"E.

[118] For fishing as a motif in Late Antique arts and literature see Sivan (1993: 203). Sidonius was certainly familiar with Ausonius' poetry, for which see Geiser (1887: 351–377), and more recently

funium librentur hamati, scilicet ut nocturnis per lacum excursibus rapacissimi salares in consanguineas agantur insidias …

> Here you will now see how the fisherman moves his boat forward out onto the sea, how he spreads his stationary nets with their cork floats and with marks made at fixed intervals the hooked lengths of rope are spread, evidently so that the very greedy trout on their nocturnal excursions through the lake may be drawn into kindred ambushes.[119]

Ausonius' *Mosella* 244–246 describes a similar feat by an angler:[120]

> nodosis decepta plagis examina verrit;
> ast hic, tranquillo qua labitur agmine flumen,
> ducit corticeis fluitantia retia signis;

> he sweeps with knotted nets deceived shoals; And this one, leads out his flowing nets with marked corks, on the tranquil motion as the river glides by.

The method of fishing is very similar: the nets are thrown out, with corks marked along at certain intervals to act as floats. Ausonius notes the deception of fish (*decepta*). Sidonius includes a similar sentiment describing the fisherman's ruse as akin to an ambush at night (*nocturnis excursibus, insidias*). The connection between the two texts is reinforced by their shared use of a specifically Gallic fish, *salares*, a type of trout.[121] Sidonius' use of this specialised term adds authenticity to the fishing scene and gives it a particularly Gallic sentiment.[122]

The second allusion to Ausonius occurs in Sidonius' detailed description of the lake (*Ep.* 2.2.15):

> Is quidem sane circa principia sui solo palustri voraginosus et vestigio inspectoris inadibilis: ita limi bibuli pinguedo coalescit ambientibus sese fontibus algidis, litoribus algosis.

Furbetta (2014–2015b): 107–133). Manitius (1888: 79–80) examines an intense moment of intertextuality between Sidonius' *Carm.* 2.157–63 and Ausonius' *Ludus Septem Sapientum*.

[119] This moment allusively recalls Pliny's *Ep.* 9.7.4 where anglers fishing on a lake are gazed upon from a vantage point.

[120] The method the fisherman employ is recorded in several earlier works, notably Pliny the Elder's *Natural History* (16.6.13) and Ovid's *Tristia* (3.4.1–12), see Yates (1843: 433).

[121] Ausonius *Mosella* 89 and 129; Geisler (1887: 357), Gualandri (1979: 98), and Gruber (2013: 150). Symmachus singled out this fishing scene from Ausonius' *Mosella* for special praise in *Ep.* 1.14, see M. Roberts (1984: 343–344). Adams (2007: 304) notes the peculiarly Gallic connection of this word, formed by these two references, to this epistle of Sidonius and Ausonius' poem. Hoffmann (1996: 663) uses this connection as evidence for the role which vegetation played in clarifying the water.

[122] Sidonius describes the fish in the lake in *Carm.* 18.7-10: "Lucrinum stagnum dives Campania nollet, / aequora si nostri cerneret illa lacus. Illud puniceis ornatur litus echinis: / piscibus in nostris, hospes, utrumque vides" (Rich Campania would not want the Lucrine pond, if it saw

Indeed, around its front it is plugged with holes in its marshy soil and there is no evidence that anyone has visited, such is the sludge of the moist shore which has clumped itself together in the intertwining cold waters, on the shores abundant in seaweed.

Sidonius' use of the recherché adjective *algosus* alludes to Ausonius' description of mussels taken from the south of Gaul (*Ep.* 15.42–43):

> Set primore vado post refugum mare
> algoso legitur litore concolor.

> But after the sea has rescinded, in the first shallows they are picked the same colour as the seaweed-covered shore.

Algosus and *pinguedo* imply the lake's abundance which Sidonius' later remarks upon at *Ep.* 2.2.17.[123] By borrowing from Ausonius specific terminology like *algosus* and *salares* in §12 for his surrounds, Sidonius gives his villa ecphrasis a distinctly Gallic hue, which is projected onto his self as the master of the estate. These allusions, while subtle, are nevertheless encouraged by Ausonius' preeminent position in Gallic literary history and the nature of the scene, as fishing as well as hunting were well-established Gallic motifs in art and literature.

The Roman sentiments of the villa ecphrasis contribute equally to Sidonius' self-fashioning as a Gallo-Roman master of a Gallo-Roman estate.[124] Scholars have long noted the allusive borrowings from Pliny's villa epistles, but other literary allusions in this epistle also contribute to the villa's (and thus Sidonius') Roman sentimentality.[125] Towards the end of the epistle, Sidonius primes the reader to think of Virgil with a brief allusion

---

the surface of our lake. That other shore is decorated with reddish sea urchins: in our fish, dear guest, you will see both). Sidonius presumably means by this final remark that the fish in the lake that borders Avitacum exhibit both features listed in line nine, namely that they are red and like a sea urchin – *echinus* which through its Greek etymology in ἐχῖνος (hedgehog) indicates spikiness. The two most prominent species in modern Lac d'Aydat have prominent red highlights on their fins, and in the case of *perca fluviatilis* prominent dorsal spikes. Similarly the nearby volcanic area provides the lake with nutrients that promote a sustained food source for the fish, fattening them, a point that accords with Sidonius' earlier description of the fertility of the soil in §3 as *terrenus*, and his later description of the surrounding lands' abundance in §19 (*pecorosus, peculiosus*).

[123] Cf. *Ep.* 8.12.1, 7 where Sidonius lists local mussels as a key attraction to induce Trygetius to visit him.

[124] Cf. Myers (2000: 104) who argues that Statius' villa poems in the *Silvae* serve as "architectural symbols of their owner's character and culture." Although, unlike Statius, Sidonius is describing his own villa.

[125] Harries (1994: 10) focuses on the link between *Ep.* 2.2 and Pliny's *Ep.* 2.17 and 5.6. Pavlovskis (1973: 48) argues that *Ep.* 2.2 is largely a reworking of Pliny's villa epistles. Whitton (2013a: 36) notes "other intertextual targets" but does not specify them as his focus is on Pliny.

to the *Georgics* by using the phrase *salicum glaucarum* (grey willows).[126] The next sentence links the space of Sidonius' villa and its use to the Trojans of the *Aeneid* (*Ep.* 2.2.19):

> In medio profundi brevis insula, ubi supra molares naturaliter aggeratos per impactorum puncta remorum navalibus trita gyris meta protuberta, ad quam se iucunda ludentum naufragia collidunt. Nam moris istic fuit senioribus nostris agonem Drepanitanum Troianae superstitionis imitari."

> In the middle of the deepest part [of the water] there is a small island, where above boulders piled up naturally, worn down by the impact of oars from circling ships a turning post sticks out, there jovial shipwrecks collide into one another in play. For it was a custom of our elders to imitate there the contest of Drepanum in the myth of Troy.

Sidonius directly references the boat race in book 5 of Virgil's *Aeneid* (*nam ... imitari*).[127] This allusion connects his estate to a tradition that extends through the elders of Avitacum (*nostri seniores*) to the *Aeneid* and beyond, to Trojan customs.[128] The verb *imitari* describes the elders' imitation of the Trojans, but it also conveys a sense of literary imitation which is particularly apt, given that, in narrating ancient Gallic customs, Sidonius imitates Virgil's description of the Trojans' boat games, the very games which the Gallic boat races imitate.[129] This link is part of a broader myth that the *Arverni* had Trojan origins.[130] The selection of this specific scene invokes the aetiology of Virgil's boat race, which contributes to book 5's establishment of "the continuity of generations and thus of history."[131] Sidonius' placement of the boat race in the scenery around his residence may also echo Virgil's similar use of an autoptic experience near his home to inform this scene in *Aeneid* 5, if as Anderson and Dix note "the boat race in *Aeneid* 5 is ... also an allusion ... to the poet's own experience in his home in the Bay of Naples."[132]

There are, however, important differences between the description in the *Aeneid* and Sidonius' remarks. Whereas Aeneas creates the turning

---

[126] Virgil *Geo.* 2.13, 4.182.

[127] Virgil *Aen.* 5. 151–243.

[128] Braund interprets this passage as potential evidence for the widespread connection of the *Arverni* with the Trojans (1980: 420n6).

[129] Reiff (1959: 107–108).

[130] Roymans (2009: 221), Van Waarden (2010: 348), and Johnston (2017: 201–202). Cf. Sidonius *Carm.* 7.139–140. Sidonius used this connection in *Ep.* 7.7 to link the fall of Clermont to the Visigoths in 475 to the fall of Troy, for which see Mratschek (2013: 256–257) and Johnston (2017: 202–203).

[131] Pavlovskis (1973: 205).

[132] Anderson and Dix (2013: 4).

point, Sidonius notes that it is a naturally occurring phenomenon.[133] He also presents the activity as happening in less agonistic terms through the oxymoronic phrase *iucunda ludentum naufragia collidunt* which juxtaposes the enjoyment that colliding boats bring with the more likely potential for disaster. The comparison with Virgil's boat race continues the presentation of the lake at Avitacum as a sea, which is an ongoing theme throughout the epistle and is part of Sidonius' attempts to position his villa (and villa epistle) against Pliny's villas, both of which enjoy sea vistas.[134] Sidonius' allusion to *Aeneid* 5 emphatically demonstrates *docta otia* as inherent to life at Avitacum and an integral part of the self he projects through the villa ecphrasis, which is Gallic, located next to a lake stocked with local fish, but also Roman, evident in the shared cultural pastime of Rome's mythic founder and Sidonius' compatriots.

A similar degree of local Gallic pride is evident in the description of the marble at Avitacum, which lists in praeteritio some of the most sought after and well-known varieties in the Classical world (*Ep.* 2.2.7):[135]

> Iam si marmora inquiras, non illic quidem Paros Carystos Proconnesos, Phryges Numidae Spartiatae rupium variatarum posuere crustas, neque per scopulos Aethiopicos et abrupta purpurea genuino fucata conchylio sparsum mihi saxa furfurem mentiuntur. Sed etsi nullo peregrinarum cautium rigore ditamur, habent tamen tuguria seu mapalia mea civicum frigidus.

> Now if you inquire about the marble, indeed no Phrygian, Numidian, nor Spartan has deposited pieces of various quarries, there is no Paros, Carystos, or Proconnesos, my rocks do not offer a deceptive scattering of bran, through Ethiopian crags and their precipices coloured with real purple. But even though I am not enriched by the firmness of foreign rocks, still my huts, or cottages, have their own native cold.

The exotic tone of these toponymns is enhanced by the would-be depositors of the marble: Spartans, Numidians, and Phyrgians. *Purpurea* and *conchylio* emphasise the opulence of these foreign goods, which Sidonius belittles as *peregrinarum cautium rigore*, in contrast to his preferred local building material, which maintains a sufficient level of cold in the summer heat

---

[133] Lac d'Aydat has a small island named "ile Saint Sidoine" (island of St Sidonius); see Chaix (1868: 159). This could be the turning point that Sidonius describes.

[134] According to Marlène Lavrieux, a scientific expert on Lac d'Aydat "the lake probably had a smaller surface area in Sidonius' period (than today) as can be inferred by the levels of sediment in the basin which builds up over time" (via email). Sidonius continually represents the lake as a large body of water akin to a sea.

[135] J.B Ward-Perkins (1992: 16), Attanasio, Brilli, and Bruno (2008: 747), Greenhalgh (2009: 492), and Chidiroglou (2011: 51).

(*civicum frigidus*).[136] Sidonius places Gallic material in the same context as eminent imports from Greece, Asia Minor, and North Africa.[137]

Sidonius' villa ecphrasis may be read in two contexts. The first is atemporal – he enjoys the same lifestyle as traditional Roman aristocrats from centuries prior, even the same pastimes as Rome's Trojan ancestors. The second is spatio-temporal: Gaul in the 450s and 460s, as Romans and barbarians battled for control. This context exists outside the imagined villa space, beyond the idyllic pastures, glittering lake, and summer heat. It is largely drawn from the historico-archaelogical record which includes the fortification of villas in response to the threat of barbarians and their destruction. This evidence is substantiated by Sidonius' *Carmen* 22 which describes Pontius' *burgus*, a fortified villa, that is very much a product of the fifth century that cannot affect to be (like Sidonius' villa) from Rome's past. While Sidonius may relax in his large pool, others try to make one out of a hole dug in the ground, and his good friends put up battlements.[138] The atemporality of Sidonius' lifestyle (the fact that his villa could almost have been one of Pliny's) augments his status claim.

Sidonius' pro-Gallic sensibilities maintained their notional permanency even after the fall of Roman Gaul to the Visigoths in 474–475. In books 3–6 repeated veiled references are made to the difficulties of the times.[139] The first words of Sidonius' seventh book of epistles mark the beginning of the very end for the Roman Auvergne (*Ep.* 7.1.1): "Rumor est Gothos in Romanum solum castra movisse" (There is a rumour that the Goths have moved their camp into Roman soil).[140] In *Ep.* 7.5.3 Sidonius reports that of all the cities in *Aquitanica Prima* only the Arverni capital remains. In the next epistle Sidonius calls out Euric for breaking the treaty and (*Ep.* 7.6.4) "[limitem regni] vel tutatur armorum iure vel promovet" (defending or rather expanding the boundary of his kingdom). The tenth and eleventh epistles in the book bemoan Sidonius' inability to meet his addressees in person (*Ep.* 7.11.1): "et ego istic inter semiustas muri fragilis clausus angustias" (shut in among the half burned ruins of a fragile wall).[141] In

---

[136] Sidonius is likely referring to one of the major Gallic marble types, which were quarried from the valley of the Garonne, the Pyrenees, and modern Phillipeville, see Pensabene (2004: 49).

[137] For discussion of the hierarchy of marble see Gauly (2006: 464).

[138] Sidonius' describes Pontius Leontius fortified *burgus* in *Carm.* 22, for Apollinaris and Ferreolus' shoddy baths see pp. 25–27.

[139] See for example *Ep.* 5.12.1, 6.4.1, 6.6.1.

[140] Gibson (2013c: 212) notes the dramatic positioning of this remark at the opening of the book.

[141] Sidonius' syntax recreates the sense of being trapped by enclosing *muri fragilis clausus* within the prepositional phrase *inter semiustas … angustias*. For other examples of this technique see Schwitter (2015: 194–198). In *Ep.* 7.10.1 Sidonius directly blames the political situation for his inability to converse in person with Auspicius.

Ep. 7.11, the last epistle addressed to a bishop in the book, the chronology breaks off; the final moment of the fall of Roman Auvergne is implied; there is no solemn eye witness account of the Visigoths riding into town.[142] In *Ep.* 7.12 wistful nostalgia for the safer periods of Gaul's recent history, when Ferreolus as praetorian prefect of Gaul in 451 came to an accord with the Visigoths under Thorismund, has replaced a perhaps altogether too painful present, still smarting in the late 470s when the book was compiled. Sidonius states (*Ep.* 7.12.) "Gallias tibi administratas tunc, cum maxume incolumes errant" (Gaul then was administered by you, when it was very safe). The temporal markers (*tunc ... cum ... erant*) exacerbate the chronological distance between Gaul's safer days and the epistolary present, which is no longer safe.[143]

While the timeline is not strict – intervening epistles, for example, treat episcopal matters – the arrangement lends itself to a loosely chronological reading which progresses the pseudo-biographical narrative of the collection as a whole: Roman Gaul has fallen; it has passed through the epistolary present and now sits in the recent past. Parts of later letters may still originate, as Sidonius claims, from his earlier days, but in the remainder of book 7, and in books 8 and 9, he never again references Roman Gaul as a present civic entity.[144] This trend corresponds broadly with Sidonius' increased focused on the *Arverni* rather than Gaul as a single entity.

In *Ep.* 4.21 Sidonius sends an invitation to Aper, whose mother was an *Arverna*. The invitation is cast as an imagined address from a single representative of the people, who offers sustained praise of the local surrounds (*Ep.* 4.21.5):

> taceo territorii peculiarem iucunditatem; taceo illud aequor agrorum, in quo sine periculo quaestuosae fluctuant in segetibus undae, quod industrius quisque quo plus frequentat, hoc minus naufragat; viatoribus molle, fructuosum aratoribus, venatoribus voluptuosum; quod montium cingunt dorsa pascuis latera vinetis, terrena villis saxosa castellis, opaca lustris aperta culturis, concava fontibus abrupta fluminibus; quod denique huiusmodi est, ut semel visum advenis multis patriae oblivionem saepe persuadeat.

---

[142] Furbetta (2014–2015a: 143) "Sidoine ne veut pas donner voix à l'histoire de la domination gothique" (Sidonius does not want to give credence to a history of the Gothic conquest).

[143] Castellanos (2013: 219–220).

[144] *Ep.* 9.7.1 refers to the *Arverni* as a geographical locale (*ab Arvernis Belgicum petens*) but no Roman government.

I say nothing of the special charm of the landscape; nothing of that sea of fields, in which lucrative waves bob up and down among the corn without any danger, the more often any hardworking man goes there, the less likely he is to be shipwrecked; it is soft for travellers, abundant for ploughman, gratifying to hunters, the backs of mountains surround it with pastures, their sides with vineyards, earthy parts with villas, rocky parts with forts, shaded parts with groves, open parts with farming, hollows with springs, slopes with rivers, finally, it is the kind of place which, seen once, frequently persuades visitors to forget their homeland.

Sidonius present the Auvergne as an idyllic landscape with each aspect ideally suited to its purpose. The final assertion is ostensibly directed at Aper, but reflects equally on Sidonius, who was from Lyon, and came to live among the Arverni through his wife's family. His comments pick up on specific details of the Auvergne: a region located far from the coast, abundant with forests, and complete with a series of dormant volcanoes, water ways, and earthy soil well suited to viticulture.

Sidonius' pride in Gallo-Roman culture outlasted Roman Gaul. In *Ep.* 8.12 Sidonius focuses on the local seafood, especially regional mussels, as a key attraction to induce Trygetius to visit him (§1):

> Tantumne te Vasatium civitas non caespiti imposita sed pulveri, tantum Syrticus ager ac vagum solum et volatiles ventis altercantibus harenae sibi possident, ut te magnis flagitatum precibus, parvis separatum spatiis, multis exspectatum diebus attrahere Burdigalam non potestates, non amicitiae, non opimata vivariis ostrea queant?

> Does the town of Bazas built not on earth but dust, does the Syrtes-like land and shifting soil and sands flying in changing winds hold you so much that neither the powers-that-be, nor friendships, nor oysters fattened in ponds can bring you to Bordeaux, even though you have been expected for many days and are a short distance away?

Towards the end of the epistle Sidonius returns to the role local seafood plays in the hospitality on offer (*Ep.* 8.12.7):

> veni ut aut pascaris aut pascas; immo, quod gratius, ut utrumque; veni cum mediterraneo instructu ad debellandos subiugandosque istos Medulicae supellectilis epulones. hic Aturricus piscis Garumnicis mugilibus insultet; hic ad copias Lapurdensium lucustarum cedat vilium turba cancrorum.

> come either to feed or to be fed upon; or rather, to do both (which is more pleasing); come with your inland adviser to defeat and subjugate these gourmands with the equipment of the Médoc (i.e oysters). Here the fish of the Adour lords over the mullets of the Garonnel; her horde of cheap crabs is defeated by the forces of Bayonne lobsters.

The food links the location of the hospitality to its consumption.[145] Sidonius jestingly uses battle language to describe the agonistic efforts of the different delicacies (*debellandos, subiugandos, insultet, copias, cedat*). While the substance of the meal is clearly Gallic in origin, the practice of *hospitium*, and the sending of a witty invitation, draws its cultural valency from the traditional custom and behaviour of the Roman aristocracy before the fall of Roman Gaul and the dissolution of the empire in the West into the barbarian successor kingdoms of Europe.[146]

Sidonius' representation of his self as Gallo-Roman may be mapped against the dramatic geopolitical changes of the mid to late fifth century. In this developing notional landscape elites ultimately relied on local recognition for their status claims. So, while elites may draw upon external factors to enhance their status – for Sidonius one may list his prefecture of Rome and his work as a panegyrist for Anthemius – it is Sidonius' clear articulation of local pride which asserts the Gallic credentials of his epistolary self. This self is highly responsive to Italian influences, read through Sidonius' epistles; Rome appears presently as a city in disarray (as opposed to the glory of its youth), Ravenna a rancid cesspit of mosquitos, and Italy a land ravaged by war. Rejection of Italian cultural influences does not entail a curtailing of Roman influences; Sidonius is the city's prefect, enjoys boat races on his lake like the Trojans in Virgil's *Aeneid*, next to his villa like Pliny's, celebrating in a seemingly effortless fashion the traditional markers of the Roman elite: *paideia*, wealth, and political office.[147] Unlike Pliny, or Seneca, or Cicero, Sidonius' epistolary self draws upon a peripheral identity that is shaped against Italian centricity.

The Merging of Sidonius' Episcopal and Literary Selves

Throughout Late Antiquity tension existed between the secular and Christian concept of literary aesthetics. In the late fourth century, Augustine, inspired by Ambrose, defined a new form of Latin aesthetics, one that linked the Christian notion of *humilitas* to a simpler mode of expression, free of the intricate rhetoric embodied in the canon of classical Latin literature he had taught in Milan.[148] This new literary aesthetic

---

[145] For the importance of banquets to Gallo-Roman hospitality see Raga (2014: 65–66).
[146] See for example Catullus 13.
[147] Dewar (2013: 94): "to confer glory on the Avitacum by associating it with the Laurentine villa [Pliny's] was in itself resistance to the tides of change, an assertion and enactment of continuity."
[148] Augustine *De doctrina Christiana* 4.17.34. See also Augustine's remarks in *Conf.* 1.14.23: "Homerus peritus texere tales fabellas et dulcissime vanus est" (Homer was skilled at writing such myths and is very pleasantly pointless).

enabled Augustine to defend the Bible as literature on the grounds that truth itself was beautiful. This transition from one set of aesthetics to another was not without difficulty; Jerome famously vowed to prohibit himself from reading anything but sacred literature, especially not Cicero, yet afterwards still replicated Ciceronian syntax and diction.[149] The difficulty then became how Christian intellects who had received a traditional Roman education based on the very rhetoric of classical authors like Cicero and Virgil could replicate this new, simpler way of writing.[150] According to Markus, both Augustine and Jerome were reacting in part to the conflict that emerged in the mid to late fourth century between Christianity and paganism, itself linked to the "traditional literary culture of educated Romans."[151] Brown argued that this response included an attempt to secularise classical literature and culture.[152]

In Gaul in the early fifth century a multitude of works on Christian themes were expressed in a different, if not altogether simpler, mode of writing.[153] Paulinus of Nola, Prosper of Aquitaine, Paulinus Pellaeus, and Sulpicius Severus all sought to write modestly.[154] Others, like Salvian, used their rhetorical training in a fairly repetitive and monotonous way.[155] In a letter written by an anonymous supporter of Pelagius the author decries (*Ep. ad adolescentum* §3) "Ut Virgilium, Sallustium, Terentium, Tullium et caeteros stultitiae et perditionis auctores non Deum, sed idola legeris praedicantes, tempus vacuum habuisti" (When you read Virgil, Sallust, Terence, Cicero, and other producers of stupidity and ruin, you have not

---

[149] Jerome *Ep.* 22.30, 54.32. Allen (1995: 212). Jerome claims his change was a result of a dream, which Thierry (1963: 37) dated to between 375 and 377. López Fonseca (1998: 340–345) has shown his continued use of secular authors in his writings after that date, Cicero included.

[150] Jerome discourages the reading of secular texts in *Ep.* 128.1. Augustine *De doctrina Christiana* 4.10.24 encourages presbyters to speak so that they are understood. However, Augustine's efforts were, according to Lancel (1999: 93), continually checked by *consuetudo*, by which others like Victorinus and Simplicianus were not impeded.

[151] Markus (1990: 30–31).

[152] Brown (2000: 262–264).

[153] *Humilitas* was an important concern among fifth-century Christian authors, one of whom, perhaps Prosper or Leo, authored the *Epistula ad Demetriadem De Vera Humilitate* which expounded the virtues of humility, for which see Krabbe (1965: 52).

[154] White (1921: 299): "He [Paulinus Pellaeus] is careful to disclaim both literary merit and literary ambition." Van Andel (1976: 140–141) argues that Sulpicius had to embellish his style in the *Chronicle on St Martin* to appeal to "more enlightened members of society" but was able to use his simpler style in the *Vita*. Günther (1997/1998: 33) notes that Sidonius' style was more extravagant than other Gallic authors of his period. Cf. Ennodius' decreased literariness in his *dictio* on Epiphanius' thirtieth anniversary as bishop of Ticinum, written in 496, and his later biography. This change cannot be fully accounted for by the difference between prose and poetic composition.

[155] O'Sullivan (1947: 6); see also Huegelmeyer (1962: 21): "[Prosper] was concerned about writing good verse in the strict Classical tradition, but, above all, he was interested in presenting the truth in clear, forceful, direct language."

chosen the Lord, but the proclaimers of idolatries, then you have wasted your time).[156] In the *Concillia Galliae*, in a list of rules for clergy in Gaul produced circa 475, the sixteenth rule reads: "ut episcopus gentilium libros non legat, haereticorum autem pro necessitate" (that a bishop should not read the books of gentiles and indeed heretics unless out of necessity)[157] This rule indicates the expectations, at least in some circles, as to what a Gallic bishop should and should not be doing circa 475. Nevertheless, *paideia* remained important for bishops. For some, like Synesius of Cyrene, this meant a blatant refusal to accept Christian dogma where it was incompatible with beliefs that were strongly informed by his knowledge of Neoplatonist philosophy.[158]

When Sidonius became the bishop of Clermont circa 470 he needed to negotiate criticism in certain circles of the perceived incompatibility of his classical education and his ecclesiastical profession.[159] His assumption of episcopal office is noted in *Ep.* 3.1, in which Sidonius thanks a relative named Avitus for his donation to the church which he now leads.[160] In a later epistle in book 3, addressed to Riothamus, the king of Aremorica, Sidonius claims that his episcopal rank and social standing affect the range of matters that he can discuss (*Ep.* 3.9.1): "Servatur nostri consuetudo sermonis: … ea semper eveniunt, de quibus loci mei aut ordinis hominem constat inconciliari, si loquatur, peccare, si taceat" (My usual style is in check … events always occur, concerning which it is agreed that a man of my position and rank is in trouble, if he speaks, and sins, if he is silent).[161]

---

[156] For this letter see Markus (1990: 32).

[157] See Desbrosses (2015: 219).

[158] Synesius *Ep.* 105, *Migne Patrologia Graeca XLVI*, 1484A, 1488B: "Φοβοῦμαι δὲ μὴ χαῦνος γενόμενος, καὶ προσιέμενος τὴν τιμήν, ἀμφοῖν διαμάρτω, τοῦ μὲν ὑπεριδὼν, τοῦ δὲ τῆς ἀξίας οὐχ ἐφικόμενος … Δόγματα δὲ οὐχ ἐπηλυγάσομαι, οὐδὲ στασιάσει μοι πρὸς τὴν γλῶτταν ἡ γνώμη" (I fear in becoming frivolous and accepting the honour that I am failing at both [philosophy and the Church] looking askance at one, but not being worthy of the other … I will refuse to teach dogmas, my understanding will not be at variance with my tongue). Bregman (1982: 166–167) notes that the influence of Synesius' Neo-Platonism gives his homilies, delivered as the bishop of Ptolomais, a distinctly pagan appearance.

[159] It is difficult to assess the extent to which Sidonius exaggerated this problem; Rousseau's (1976: 357) scepticism may be warranted given that Sidonius' solution amounts to an emphatic assertion of his *paideia* and Christian credentials. Sidonius avoided resolving this tension earlier. Indeed, as Tomassi (2015: 77–82) has shown, the theology of his panegyrics operates without any explicit reference to Christianity; yet, as Desbrosses (2015: 214) ponders, one wonders why, if the mythological references had no meaning for Sidonius and other literati, did Sidonius largely (abandon) them once he became a bishop, unless he was concerned about their possible reception in certain Christian circles. Mascoli (2016: 23–24) focuses specifically on Sidonius' challenge as a bishop and poet.

[160] *Ep.* 3.1.2. Gibson (2012: 69) notes the parallel with Pliny *Ep.* 3.1, in which he announces his consulship.

[161] Giannotti (2016: 196) infers the implication that Sidonius had written to Riothamus on other occasions.

Quintilian's assertion of suitable usage underpins Sidonius' initial premise (1.6.43–5): "consuetudinem sermonis vocabo consensum eruditorum" (I shall say that the usual style is the consensus of learned men). Sidonius' position and rank (*loci mei aut ordinis*) mark him out as one of Quintilian's educated language users; his claim that he is constrained by his aristocratic and episcopal status acts as a reminder to the reader of his rank, and through the allusion to Quintilian, the *paideia* that such men exhibit.

In *Ep.* 4.10 Sidonius claims that he is reverting to his usual less polished style (§1–2):

> sed dicere solebas, quamquam fatigans, quod meam quasi facundiam vererere, excusatio istaec, etiamsi fuisset vera, transierat, quia post terminatum libellum, qui parum cultior est, reliquas denuo litteras usuali, licet accuratus mihi melior non sit, sermone contexo; non enim tanti est poliri formulas editione carituras.

> even though you used to say, but in a jesting way, that you respected my eloquence, that excuse, if it had ever been true, has now passed, since after my little book was finished, which is somewhat polished, I am composing my remaining letters in my usual style – granted it may not be better for me to be accurate – but there is no point in polishing phrases that will lack publication.[162]

It is unclear what books constituted Sidonius' *libellum*, but by any reckoning, it must have included book 1 of his epistles.[163] His claims that the remainder of his epistles will be composed in *usualis sermo* is linked to his role as a bishop through the noticeable Christian formula of this letter: Helidorus (presumably one of his flock) is referred to as his spiritual son; the value of humility is emphasised early (*siquidem convenit humuliatos humilia sectari*); and Sidonius' ongoing literary endeavour is helped along by Christ's guidance (*praevio Christo*), all of which clearly reminds the reader of his episcopal rank.[164]

The claim that he used *usualis sermo* is disingenuous and perhaps best understood as a blatant case of misdirection rather than a useful indication of stylistic variance. Sidonius' assertion that his current and future endeavours are not polished, as they will not be published, belies the fact that he subsequently circulated them; during that process he could

---

[162] *Ep.* 4.10.1–2: G. Kaufmann (1864: 4) takes Sidonius at his word that he adopted a simpler mode of expression. Amherdt's (2001: 275) scepticism towards Sidonius' claims in this extract is well placed "De telles affirmations ne sont que coquetterie et modestie feinte" (Such statements are merely vanity and feigned modesty).

[163] See pp. 171–174.

[164] *Ep.* 4.10.1–2.

certainly have edited out this literary conceit to avoid a contradiction between his claims and reality. The literary humility cannot be taken at face value, but instead provokes the reader to consider carefully the style that Sidonius employs. Lastly, Sidonius walks back this claim in the same epistle; if Felix writes back to him, perhaps he may be persuaded to return to his old loquacity.[165] There is nothing simple about Sidonius' speech in this epistle, nor can a clear distinction be made between the level of stylistic embellishment in the first two books and the remainder (perhaps with the exclusion of the two books addressed largely to fellow clergy). Instead, the supposed deployment of *usualis sermo* is an emphatic display of *paideia* bound up in the further display of his social standing and episcopal rank. In this epistle Sidonius' self merges its literary and ecclesiastic elements.

The compatibility of these elements is immediately put on display by the next epistle in the collection, in which Sidonius consoles Petreius on the death of his great-uncle Claudianus Mamertus, a Gallic presbyter whom Sidonius knew well. Sidonius eulogises Claudianus (*Ep.* 4.11.1):

> vir siquidem fuit providus prudens, doctus eloquens, acer et hominum aevi loci populi sui ingeniosissimus quique indesinenter salva religione philosopharetur.

> he was indeed far-sighted, wise, learned, eloquent, sharp and the most talented of the men of his age, place, and people, who constantly was the philosopher without injuring his religion.[166]

Eloquence, learning, wisdom, even philosophy need not be juxtaposed to religious office.[167] In the next epistle, *Ep.* 4.12, Sidonius finds himself reading Terence's *Mother-in-law* with his son (§1): "studenti assidebam naturae meminens et professionis oblitus" (I was attending to him as he studied, remembering my nature and having forgotten my profession).[168] The contrast of *meminens* and *oblitus* remind the reader that Sidonius has continued his secular reading.[169] Sidonius' apparent lapse in memory draws attention to his effortless, supposedly natural self which is unable to abandon his *paideia*.

---

[165] *Ep.* 4.10.2.

[166] *Ep.* 4.11.1.

[167] Amherdt (2001: 285).

[168] For the importance of this introduction to the narrative of the epistle see pp. 156–157. Bellès (1998: 52n84) compares Sidonius' claims to Symmachus' studying of Greek with his son in Symmachus *Ep.* 4.20.2.

[169] Gualandri (1979: 10–11) stresses the specific context of this remark to infer that *natura* refers only to Sidonius' role as a father. Sidonius could easily have clarified his meaning if he intended this phrase to be read (only) in this limited way.

The apparent tension between Sidonius' episcopal office and his secular *paideia* and sophisticated style is undermined by ample evidence in books 3, 4, and 5 that they are compatible.[170] In books 6 and 7, which are largely addressed to fellow clergy, this supposed tension manifests itself as the Christian topos of humility combined with authorial humility.[171] Even in those two books Sidonius' classical education is evident. In *Ep.* 6.12 Sidonius compares bishop Patiens of Lyon to Triptolemus. He questions the suitability of this comparison between the holy father and a mythological figure and hence offers a comparison with an example from the Christian, rather than classical, canon (§7): "sed si forte Achaicis Eleusinae superstitionis exemplis tamquam non idoneis religiosus laudatus offenditur, seposita mystici intellectus reverentia venerabilis patriarchae Ioseph historialem diligentiam comparemus" (but if perhaps it offends a religious man to be praised by Greek examples of the Eleusian mystery on the basis that they are inappropriate (putting aside respect for his mystical understanding)[172] we may make a comparison with the historical diligence of the venerable patriarch Joseph). The pretence that Sidonius may have offended the bishop highlights Patiens' own secular knowledge. Ultimately it is up to Patiens to decide whether or not he will be offended by these remarks.[173] In this epistle Sidonius presents himself effortlessly combining the role of bishop with the culture of a secular aristocrat.[174]

Initially Sidonius negotiates the tension between his episcopal and literary selves by asserting that his style changed when he became a bishop.[175] This point is further supported by his remarks that he had stopped writing poetry as it was inappropriate for a bishop to do so.[176] Neither of these

---

[170] Gualandri (1979: 14).

[171] Daly (2000: 19–31). Alciati (2009b: 200) notes "È stato sostenuto che Sidonio non avrebbe avuto nessuna dimestichezza con le questioni teologiche, tuttavia questa dedica e le presunta richiesta monstrano quanto egli sia profondamente implicate nella pubblicazione stessa dell'opera" (It has been argued that Sidonius would have had no familiarity with the theological issues but this dedication [in the *De statu animae*] and the alleged request show how very deeply involved he was in the publication of the work).

[172] Anderson and Warmington (1963: 283) take this phrase as a reference to Joseph's ability to interpret dreams.

[173] Desbrosses (2015: 216) regonises the conceit. If he was genuinely concerned about offending Patiens, he surely would have avoided using the example of Triptolemus.

[174] As MacMullen (1997: 114) has argued, while Augustine preferred a more serious approach to life, Sidonius felt no need to abandon dice, dining and other forms of aristocratic display.

[175] At the end of the collection Sidonius asserts that he would have written martyrdom poetry if he had been given more time to live, for which see p. 82.

[176] Sidonius *Ep.* 4.3.9. Janson (1964: 52) argues that this was just another effort at authorial humility designed to lower the reader's expectation of the rhetorical flourish Sidonius continued to employ in his latter works.

claims are consistently maintained throughout the collection. Rather than taking them at face value or dismissing them out of hand, one may consider how his attempts at self presentation likely responded to societal values and assumptions. As a new bishop, parachuted into the role over career churchmen, Sidonius carefully asserts Christian humility, professing that he has done away with the sophisticated style of his youth.[177] He is thus able to promote a complex self that claims the status and piety of a bishop without dismissing his sophisticated *paideia*, and in so doing offers his entrance into ecclesiastic office as a model to his highly erudite readers, drawn predominantly from the Gallic aristocracy and clergy.

Conclusion

Sidonius' epistles are a dynamic exercise in self-fashioning that promotes his status as a highly educated Gallo-Roman aristocrat and, later, a bishop, as his world underwent profound and lasting changes. As the author of the collection, Sidonius has complete control over how he represents himself, including drawing and implying comparisons for the reader in which he always comes out on top. Thus, while Sidonius' description of make-shift baths in *Ep.* 2.9 may seem to a modern reader quaint, or indicative of decline, or even evidence of technological ingenuity or renewed investment, none of these should be taken as foremost in the minds of Sidonius' literary circle, for whom "rough-and-ready" was not aesthetically appealing. Instead, consideration of the importance of baths to the status of villas and the entertainment of fellow aristocrats points us towards reading the shoddy baths of *Ep.* 2.9 against Sidonius' magnificent domed bathing complex in *Ep.* 2.2. The epistles embrace the publicity of their circulation; offering a view of Sidonius more akin to the carefully arranged image of social media users than private correspondence.

Sidonius' changing representation of self – Henderson's "emphatic egomorphism" – adds different aspects of his status claims together; so Sidonius may keep the high status of secular office and add to that the

---

[177] In *Ep.* 7.9.14 Sidonius includes an address during the episcopal elections in Bourges that has his would-be critics claim that were he to appoint a man with government experience to a role in the clergy they would jump to their feet in protest, saying: "Sidonius ad clericatum quia de saeculari professione translatus est, ideo sibi assumere metropolitanum de religiosa congregatione dissimulat; natalibus turget, dignitatum fastigatur insignibus, contemnit pauperes Christi" (Because Sidonius was brought across to the clergy from a secular career, he is reluctant to take a colleague from the clergy, he swells with pride at his birth, he is exalted by the insignia of his offices, he has contempt for the poor of Christ). Rousseau (1976: 358) cites this decision as an example of how Sidonius was atypical for his episcopal rank. See pp. 150–152.

status of his episcopal rank; he can be a wealthy individual, yet known for his charitable acts to the poor;[178] similarly he may assert a simpler style which nevertheless still displays his extensive *paideia* and ornate Latinity. There need not be consistency in Sidonius' representation of his self, just like there is no need for consistency in any other representation of self.

The temptation to read his changing representation of self against what may be deduced about Sidonius the historical figure from all our sources has been acutely felt by scholarship, yet if we focus on the epistles themselves we can see more clearly how Sidonius tries to manipulate us to view and admire key aspects of his self. In three successive epistles (*Ep.* 4.10–4.12) Sidonius asserts that as a new bishop he has abandoned his more ornate style, leaves open the possibility of a return to that style, praises Claudianus Mamertus for combining his religious office and *paideia*, then discloses, or rather displays, his reading of Terence's *Mother-in-law*.

Sidonius' self is a studied display of tradition and innovation, as a Latin epistolographer cast in the mould of Pliny, but also as an individual whose life and thus self-image spanned the fall of the Roman empire in the West. Despite the challenges this transformative period posed, whenever possible Sidonius tried to project a clear self-representation set against his kaleidoscopic world.

[178] Gregory of Tours 2.22 relates how Sidonius used to give silverware to the poor without his wife knowing. This anecdote cannot be substantiated.

CHAPTER 3

Reading Time: Erzählzeit and Lesezeit

The first two chapters analysed Sidonius' world and how he used his epistles to present a carefully formed self to that world. We have already seen how Sidonius presents a chronologically consistent account in book 7 of the Visigothic acquisition of Roman Gaul, characterises himself relative to others, such as Claudianus Mamertus or Syagrius, uses sophisticated language, and positions his work relative to his epistolary precedents, especially Pliny. The chapters that follow analyse specific aspects of the epistles, showing how Sidonius used time, characterisation, dialogue, and arrangement to develop their narratives. These stories are intricately bound up in his world, full of the profound changes, vivid characters and witty exchanges of his life.

Time is a constant of every narrative; from the very moment an epistle begins to be written the present looms for both the author and reader whose understanding of the author's words is temporally removed from their composition. The epistolary theorist Müller first applied the concept of narrative-time to epistolography (*Erzählzeit*), which he defined as the time it takes for a letter to be read, and distinguished it from narrated time (*erzählte Zeit*), the description and discussion of time in the epistle.[1] Here I use the term *Erzählzeit* to refer to Sidonius' asserted moment of composition. This follows Ricoeur's three tiered framework which includes the actual moment of composition of an epistle, the asserted moment of composition of an epistle, and the discussion of time in the epistle other than the moment of composition (*erzählte Zeit*).[2] The actual moment of composition for Sidonius' epistles can never be definitively known, so here *Erzählzeit* is used to refer to Sidonius' asserted moment of composition.

Erzählzeit is rendered fictitious by the reader; as soon as the epistolary present is read, the epistolary past is understood. So, if a letter writer states "I write to you as the sun sets" the reader understands only that the letter

---

[1] G. Müller (1948: 269–286).
[2] Ricœur (1996: 129–144).

was written at some point in the past when the sun set, not that the letter writer *is* presently writing the letter at sun set. If an epistle is written over a period of time with multiple points referenced by the present, narrative-time's fiction is more transparent.[3] Epistles thus largely sit fixed in a confined present which looks toward the past and future, both distant and near.[4] In its simplest guise, this past is the moment when the epistle was conceived, perhaps in reply to another, and its future is the anticipated moment of the epistle's reading, the so called reading-time *(Lesezeit)*.[5] Time is thus critically important to the writing and reading of epistles. It may undermine or bolster the claims of the author, create suspense, vary narrative sequence, and otherwise enrich the epistolary dynamic.

The majority of Sidonius' epistles avoid defining clearly the epistolary present, frustrating attempts to date each letter accurately. This atemporality is not simply indicative of the turbulence of Sidonius' period; Cicero's letters, written during a comparable period of political disturbance, can be dated with far greater accuracy, in part through their frequent reference to current events or in the case of approximately one third of the collection their inclusion of specific dates.[6] Nevertheless the difficulty of dating many of Sidonius' letters may still be considered representative of the changes that take place during his period as the Visigothic kingdom of Toulouse absorbed the last remnants of Roman Gaul. The theorist Ricœur noted:

> It is clear that a discontinuous structure suits a time of dangers and adventures, that a more continuous linear structure suits a *Bildungsroman* where the themes of growth and metamorphosis predominate, whereas a jagged chronology interrupted by jumps, anticipations and flashbacks, in short, a deliberately multidimensional configuration, is better suited to a view of time that has no possible overview, no overall internal cohesiveness.[7]

The last two books of Sidonius' epistles exhibit the features of a "jagged chronology"; their sequence is deliberately disjointed, flashbacks occur with great regularity, both in letters that Sidonius claims were written earlier, and in those letters with a (more) contemporary *Erzählzeit*. Moments of anticipation become almost exclusively negative as Sidonius struggles to envisage a future for post-Roman Gaul, and even looks forward to his own death.[8]

---

[3] This is what Genette (1980: 222) termed "interpolated narration."

[4] Altman (1982: 122–123).

[5] Ricœur (1996: 129ff).

[6] Gibson (2012: 61). White (2010: 76) proposed that Cicero dated many of his letters when he wrote from abroad so that the eventual recipient could read them in the original order.

[7] Ricœur (1985: 81).

[8] The impact of winter on Sidonius' ink at *Ep.* 9.16.2 may be read figuratively to indicate the physical difficulties he faces writing in his old age see pp. 181–182.

The absence (generally) of datable, fixed epistolary presents in the collection is indicative of Sidonius' focus on the past and future. This past varies, drawing upon a distant nostalgia for a world when Rome was dominant, or at least, not in quite so much difficulty, to a more recent and pessimistic recollection, complete with suffering and strife. The future may equally be optimistic, when Sidonius focuses on specific individuals of the next generation whose character he admires, or pessimistic, as Sidonius envisages the fall of Roman Gaul and lives through it in the last three books of the collection.

Scholarship has interpreted Sidonius' expressions of time as rare opportunities for dating the epistles, even though his chronology is highly obscured, and neither of his epistolary models (Pliny and Symmachus) seemed particularly interested in dating their epistles.[9] Such an interpretation assumes that these moments record precisely (but often not accurately) the exact moment of the epistle's composition.[10] This chapter proposes a different methodology for interpreting Sidonius' *Erzählzeiten*, *erzählte Zeiten*, and his addressee's reported *Lesezeiten* by reading them as narratological tools. Sidonius chose pivotal moments as the setting for the present as a literary strategy designed to enhance the efficacy of the epistolary past and future.[11] They make the narrative-driven epistles more exciting, create anticipation and suspense, and dwell on specific moments framed by a clearly defined past and fenced in by a murky future.

Hanging in the Balance: *Erzählzeiten* as Pivotal Moments[12]

In book 1, three key epistles demonstrate the potential efficacy of selecting a pivotal moment as the *Erzählzeit* of the epistle: *Ep.* 1.5, which describes Sidonius' arrival in Rome; *Ep.* 1.7, which provides an account of the trial of the Gallo-Roman aristocrat Arvandus for treason; and *Ep.* 1.10, which details Sidonius' efforts as the prefect of Rome. These epistles share a similar temporal narratology; their *Erzählzeiten* are precisely defined and

---

[9] For the relative rarity of dates in Latin epistles see Gibson (2012: 61–62); Gibson and Morello (2012: 250) note that the "slipperiness of epistolary time … helps Pliny convey a loose chronology for the work, a vague sense both of quasi-historical record and of forward movement through life." The same may be said for Sidonius, with the exception of the watershed moment of the Visigothic conquest of Clermont, for which see p. 48.

[10] For a recent example see Mathisen (2013).

[11] More pivotal presents occur in the first two books than in the later books, in which Sidonius' perception of reality had worsened. Gibson (2013b: 354) links Sidonius' growing pessimism to a comparable change in Pliny's epistolary collection.

[12] Altman (1982: 117–118, 122–123).

occur at key moments; the epistles look backward to a nostalgic past and forward to an unclear future. Their precise present moments sharpen the excitement for the reader: the consummation of the marriage of the barbarian potentate Ricimer with the Emperor Anthemius' daughter and the alliance between Ricimer and Anthemius hang in the balance; similarly Arvandus has been sentenced to death, but is yet to be executed; Rome is starving, but grain is about to arrive.[13]

The first words of *Ep.* 1.5 foreshadow the *Erzählzeit* of the epistle by mentioning Sidonius' *Lesezeit* of Heronius' epistle, to which he is responding (*Ep.* 1.5.1): "litteras tuas Romae positus accepi" (I received your letter in Rome). This start provides the reader with the ultimate outcome of Sidonius' travelogue. Sidonius indicates that the *Erzählzeit* of the epistle sits between the recent past, embodied in his arrival in the city, and the imminent future which will see Sidonius petition the emperor (*Ep.* 1.5.9–10):

> nunc istaec inter iacendum scriptitans quieti pauxillulum operam impendo. neque adhuc principis aulicorumque tumultuosis foribus obversor. interveni etenim nuptiis patricii Ricimeris, cui filia perennis Augusti in spem publicae securitatis copulabatur.

> now as I write these remarks in a burst in between naps, my focus is on rest for a little while. Nor am I yet acknowledged by the disorderly doors of the emperor and his courtiers. For I arrived while the wedding of the patrician Ricimer was ongoing, to whom the daughter of the eternal Augustus was being coupled in the hope of the safety of the state.

The phrase *scriptitans … impendo* is the first present in the epistle since Sidonius' reporting of his *Lesezeit* of Heronius' epistle. It marks a pivotal moment in the epistle. The frequentative *scribito* taken with the temporal use of *inter* indicates that the *Erzähltezeit* of the epistle is spread out; Sidonius has written the epistle in parts, all of which occur at the precise moment between the marriage of Ricimer and Alypia, and the wedding's consummation. *Neque adhuc* (Nor yet) looks forward to Sidonius' eventual reception at court. The epistolary present is marked backwards in time by the perfect tense verb *interveni*. Sidonius turns this *Erzählzeit* into a vivid description of Rome during the wedding celebration of the emperor's daughter (*Ep.* 1.5.10):

> igitur nunc in ista non modo personarum sed etiam ordinum partiumque laetitia Transalpino tuo latere conducibilius visum, quippe cum hoc ipso

> tempore, quo haec mihi exarabantur, vix per omnia theatra macella, praetoria fora, templa gymnasia Thalassio Fescenninus explicaretur, atque etiam nunc e contrario studia sileant negotia quiescant, iudicia conticescant differantur legationes, vacet ambitus et inter scurrilitates histrionicas totus actionum seriarum status peregrinetur.

> and so now, amid the rejoicing not only of individuals but even classes and parties, it seemed quite advantageous to your *Transalpinus* [Sidonius] to lie low, since at the very moment when these comments were being written by me, the Fescennine cry 'Thalassio' barely began to unfold through all the theatres, markets, official residences, forums, temples, exercise grounds and even now the opposite is true, the schools are silent, business is quiet, courts fall silent, embassies are put off, ambition is absent, and the entire conduct of serious affairs has gone wandering among silly buffoonery.[14]

The second *nunc* (now) in quick succession brings the present back into focus. Sidonius emphatically links this moment to his composition in the phrase *cum hoc ipso tempore, quo haec mihi exarabantur* (at the very moment when these comments were being written by me). The aspect of the imperfect verb *exarabantur* is consistent with Sidonius' claim that the letter was composed over a period of time, and in combination with *hoc ipso tempore* that it is still being written. The moment is pivotal; Rome is in complete disarray awaiting the consummation of the marriage.

The *Erzählzeit* of the epistle sits wedged between the immediate epistolary past and imminent future (1.5.11):

> iam quidem virgo tradita est, iam coronam sponsus, iam palmatam consularis, iam cycladem pronuba, iam togam [senator] honoratus, iam paenulam deponit inglorius, et nondum tamen cuncta thalamorum pompa defremuit, quia necdum ad mariti domum nova nupta migravit.

> now indeed the maiden has been handed over, the husband has placed down his wreath, the man of consular rank his robe, the bridesmaid her decorative gown, the honoured senator his toga, the unremarkable citizen his cloak, and meanwhile the wedding celebration has still not completely ceased raging, since the bride has not yet crossed to the home of her husband.

In a moment the final bedroom act will take place but not quite yet (*nondum, necdum*). The narration which Sidonius has sustained from section two of the epistle awaits the end of the festivity: "qua festivitate decursa cetera tibi laborum meorum molimina reserabuntur, si tamen

---

[14] *Ep.* 1.5.10. Behrwald (2011: 292) rightly focuses attention on Sidonius' description of Rome rather than his brief description of his arrival at the Apostolic church of St. Peter, *contra* Soler (2005: 340–347, 406) who reads the epistle as recording a spiritual pilgrimage. Wolff (2012: 10) also refutes Soler's approach; as do Fournier and Stoehr-Monjou (2014: 11).

vel consummata sollemnitas aliquando terminaverit istam totius civitatis occupatissimam vacationem. vale" (after the festivity has run to a close, the other struggles of my suffering will be revealed to you, if perhaps at some point the finished celebration will bring this very busy holiday of an entire city to an end. Goodbye).

The very specific *Erzählzeit* of *Ep.* 1.5 is an effective narratological tool. Rome is consumed by the wedding festivities. The moment looks forward to an unclear eventuality; the success of the wedding and thus the political union between Ricimer and Anthemius are not yet confirmed. The past is more fixed but no less disconcerting. War and civil strife have plagued Italy, embedded in the epistle by sustained allusions to texts that describe wars and battles from Italy's past, a trend which the reader is encouraged to project forward.[15] Sidonius has chosen this precise moment for its intense political significance. Those who read this epistle after the first book was circulated in the late 460s knew that the marriage was consummated, but also that the hope and promise that Sidonius articulated had proven false.[16] Sidonius uses the present circumstances of the epistle to play on the tension of the moment and the lack of clarity then as to how events would unfold. His numerous asserted moments of composition in between naps hint at the present's fiction, one which he could easily have edited out in subsequent revisions. To do so, however, would have removed the narratological precipice on which the epistle balances, and the political precipice on which Rome totters, reliant on the success of the accord between barbarian potentate and emperor to deal with external threats, principally the Vandal threat from North Africa.

Few moments are more pivotal than when life hangs in the balance. In 468 the Gallo-Roman aristocrat Arvandus was taken to Rome, tried and convicted for treason.[17] He had attempted to negotiate a settlement with the Visigoths independently of the emperor.[18] Sidonius' *Ep.* 1.7 provides a

---

[15] Hanaghan (2017c).
[16] Hanaghan (2017c: 631, 648–649). *Ep.* 1.9. is linked to *Ep.* 1.5, as both are addressed to Heronius. In that epistle Sidonius provides a brief description of Rome after the wedding festivities (*Ep.* 1.9.1): "Post nuptias patricii Ricimeris, id est post imperii utriusque opes eventilatas, tandem reditum est in publicam serietatem, quae rebus actitandis ianuam campumque patefecit" (After the wedding of the patrician Ricimer, that is after the wealth of both empires had been scattered to the wind, at last there has been a return to public seriousness, which has opened the door and a field for conducting business).
[17] See p. 10.
[18] Kulikowski (2013: 87) draws attention to the political embarrassment for the emperor of Arvandus' treasonous attempts to negotiate independently with Euric.

narrative account of these events which historians have subjected to careful analysis. The epistle begins by clearly outlining its *Erzählzeit* (1.7.1):

> Angit me casus Arvandi nec dissimulo, quin angat. namque hic quoque cumulus accedit laudibus imperatoris, quod amare palam licet et capite damnatos. amicus homini fui supra quam morum eius facilitas varietasque patiebantur. testatur hoc propter ipsum nuper mihi invidia conflata, cuius me paulo incautiorem flamma detorruit.

> The fall of Arvandus distresses me, nor do I pretend that it does not distress me. For it amounts to praise of the emperor that it is permissible to love openly even those condemned to death. I have been a friend to that man above and beyond what the ease and variety of his ways allowed. This is evidenced by the ill-will that has recently risen up against me on his account. Its flame has burnt me as I was somewhat incautious.[19]

The distress is current (*angit*).[20] The unspecified *casus Arvandi* quickly becomes apparent; Arvandus has been condemned to death; only the emperor's good will allows men to mourn such doomed individuals (*amare … damnatos*). The epistolary past informs the present: Sidonius has been Arvandus' friend; the perfect tense *fui* outlines this situation and has bearing on the present, including their friendship, which still remains (*amare … damnatos*) despite the circumstances. He has recently suffered a backlash since Arvandus was condemned (*nuper mihi invidia conflata*). Sidonius has been burnt: an analogy for the potentially dangerous repercussions of engaging in imperial politics.[21] The epistle proceeds with its narration, contained in the epistolary past, until at its end, it reaches the present. Arvandus awaits his execution (*Ep.* 1.7.12):

> sed et iudicio vix per hebdomadam duplicem comperendinato capite multatus in insulam coniectus est serpentis Epidauri,[22] ubi usque ad

---

[19] *Ep.* 1.7.1. For the Arvandus affair see Teitler (1992: 309–312) and Harries (1994: 158–166).

[20] The phrase "angit me" is used in two of Pliny's epistles (*Ep.* 5.5.2 and *Ep.* 7.18.1), for which see Harries (1994: 14) and Amherdt (2001: 284). This allusion references Fannia's illness (the focus of Pliny's *Ep.* 5.5) and so foreshadows Sidonius' use of a medical simile later in the epistle, for which see p. 145, and hints that Arvandus may face the same likely outcome as Fannia. This allusion and the medical simile support MacGeorge's (2002: 226) assessment that Arvandus was probably mentally deranged rather than mistaken about what actions constituted treason. For the significance of Fannia's death in Pliny's epistles see Gibson (2015: 205). Köhler (1995: 232) argues that the absence of any epistolary formula in *Ep.* 1.7 suggests the spontaneity of Sidonius' composition of the epistle. The incipit *angit me* is also used by Sidonius in *Ep.* 4.11 regarding the death of Claudianus Mamertus.

[21] See pp. 143–146 for their dialogue.

[22] Sidonius alludes to Tiber island by referring to the temple of Aesculapius (the serpent of Epidaurus) that was once there. In his time there was presumably a jail, for which see Patterson (2013: 6–7). Pietrini (2015: 312) notes that Sidonius does not directly indicate that Anthemius is involved in this process.

inimicorum dolorem devenustatus et a rebus humanis veluti vomitu fortunae nauseantis exsputus, nunc ex vetere senatus consulto Tiberiano triginta dierum vitam post sententiam trahit, uncum et Gemonias et laqueum per horas turbulenti carnificis horrescens.

but then, after the verdict had been suspended for barely a fortnight, he was sentenced to death and thrown onto the island of the serpent of Epidaurus, where he has been stripped of his charm even to the distress of his enemies and spewed out of affairs as if in the vomit of nauseous fortune, now he drags out his life for thirty days following the sentence, in accordance with the ancient decree of the Tiberian senate, fearing hour by hour the hook and the stairs and the noose of an agitated executioner.[23]

The immediate epistolary past, Arvandus' sentence to death and incarceration, breaks into the present: Arvandus is now waiting out the thirty-day period between the sentence in court and the execution (*nunc, trahit*). He is in constant fear (*per horas horrescens*) of the specific execution method that will be employed. Teitler's analysis of the sources shows that Arvandus did in fact escape the death penalty and that Sidonius was unaware of this outcome when the epistle was composed.[24] Such an interpretation is certainly substantiated by the text.

If we consider the *Erzählzeit* of the epistle from a narratological perspective, the pivotal moment on which the epistle balances may inform our understanding of Sidonius' skill as an epistolary author, rather than the "actual moment" when the epistle was written. Sidonius had several reasons for selecting this moment. Firstly, Arvandus is at his most sympathetic. Even his enemies are distressed at his fall (*Ep*.1.7.12): "usque ad inimicorum dolorem devenustatus" ([Arvandus] has been stripped of his charm even to the distress of his enemies). The uncertainty of his fate accentuates his distress (*Ep*. 1.7.13): "illo tamen, seu exspectat extrema quaeque seu sustinet, infelicius nihil est" (but for him, whether he is waiting for the final act or already endures it, nothing is worse). Arvandus is in limbo, awaiting execution, hoping for a pardon. The moment is climactic. If the Arvandus episode is plotted *in toto* as a narrative, his eventual pardon is anti-climactical. Sidonius' epistle preserves the tension of the moment. Lastly, the possibility of Arvandus' pardon remains. The eventual

---

[23] See Behrwald (2011: 294).

[24] Sidonius does not mention Arvandus again in the collection, and so the evidence for his fate is limited to Cassiodorus *Chronica* 1287 s.a. 469 and Paul. Diac. *Hist. Rom.* XV, 2, who both note his exile. Teitler (1992: 311) clearly shows that these later sources are consistent with Sidonius' account if Arvandus' death sentence was commuted to exile. See also MacGeorge (2002: 226).

commutation of his death penalty testifies to the effectiveness of Sidonius and others' advocacy on his behalf.[25]

Sidonius did not revisit Arvandus' fate again in his collection; it would hardly have been politically astute to celebrate his sentence eventually being commuted, especially in a public medium such as widely circulated epistles.[26] One may posit that Sidonius already knew that Arvandus had been pardoned when *Ep.* 1.7 was written, or at least when he inserted the epistle into the first volume of letters. The *pathos* of recording Arvandus' repeated hopes for pardon, if he was in fact executed, may have strained the sensibilities of Sidonius' audience. As a literary construct Arvandus remains in judicial purgatory.

Sidonius favours a pivotal *Erzählzeit* for dramatic effect in some of his shorter epistles too. *Ep.* 1.10 describes Sidonius' efforts to maintain Rome's grain supply, presumably in the face of the heavy disruption caused by the Vandals.[27] The epistle begins with Sidonius recording his *Lesezeit* of a letter by Campanianus, the addressee of *Ep.* 1.10.[28] The present circumstances dominate the last half of the letter (*Ep.* 1.10.2):

> vereor autem, ne famem populi Romani theatralis caveae fragor insonet et infortunio meo publica deputetur esuries. sane hunc ipsum e vestigio ad portum mittere paro, quia conperi naves quinque Brundusio profectas cum speciebus tritici ac mellis ostia Tiberina tetigisse, quarum onera exspectationi plebis, si quid strenue gerit, raptim faciet offerri, commendaturus se mihi, me populo, utrumque tibi.

> but I am afraid that the din of the theatre may sound aloud the hunger of the Roman people and public starvation will be noted down to my bad luck. Indeed, I am preparing to send this very man to the harbour straight away, since I have learnt that five ships set out from Brundisium and have reached the mouth of the Tiber with wheat and honey. If he handles the situation promptly, he will offer its cargo to the expectant people, and commend himself to me, me to the people, and both of us to you.[29]

---

[25] *Ep.* 1.7.13: "nos quidem, prout valemus, absentes praesentesque vota facimus, preces supplicationesque geminamus, ut suspenso ictu iam iamque mucronis exerti pietas Augusta seminecem quamquam publicatis bonis vel exilio muneretur" (We indeed, as much as we are able, those of us who are absent and those present, make representations; we join prayers and requests, that once the death blow has been put to one side (even as the sword tip get now closer and closer) the Emperor's piety may reward this half-dead man nevertheless with confiscation of his property or perhaps exile).

[26] Sidonius similarly avoided mentioning Eparchius Avitus, for which see Mathisen (1979: 165–171) and Rousseau (2000: 253).

[27] Allen and Neil (2013: 79).

[28] For the first half of the letter, which focuses on Sidonius' friendship with Campanianus, see Furbetta (2015b: 349–351).

[29] *Ep.* 1.10.2. See Vitiello's (2002: 491–493) analysis of this epistle's focus on the recommendations involved.

Sidonius' response to the crisis is immediate: he is preparing to send the *praefectus annonae* (prefect of the grain supply) to meet five ships from Brundisium, right at that very moment (*e vestigio paro*). This certainly reads like a literary conceit; given the circumstances Sidonius outlines, a more prudent course may have been to write the epistle after the immediate difficulties had passed. Of course this is what he may have done: namely, set the epistolary present back in time to the dramatic moment when the people were hungry and had begun to blame Sidonius, and yet relief was in sight.[30] The *Erzählzeit* of this epistle shows Sidonius' craft as a story teller at work; constructing the epistolary present to heighten the dramatic effect, rather than the belaboured recording of a pseudo-historian. *Erzählzeiten* that are so specific, that exist in a fleeting moment, may in fact already pass before the addressee's *Lesezeit*. In *Ep.* 1.10, for example, one may envisage the likelihood that the grain was distributed from the boats before Campanianus received the letter.

Sidonius' epistles offer more than a pseudo-historical account of a few decades in Late Antiquity; they aspire to be read and enjoyed. The requirements and expectations of the reader that the narratives contained within should excite is reflected in Sidonius' narratology. Momentuous occasions appeal to narratives. Events which are otherwise mundane can take on new significance and importance, especially when set against the polyvalent future and contextualised by present nostalgia. In epistles 1.5, 7, and 10 the epistolary present occurs in a specific moment: after Sidonius' journey, but before the nuptials are complete; once Arvandus has been sentenced, but prior to his execution; and as the people starve, but the grain to feed them is almost at hand. Changing even slightly the *Erzählzeiten* of these epistles would radically (and detrimentally alter) their narratives; the story of Arvandus' dramatic trial and conviction would peter out in an anti-climactical pardon;[31] Sidonius would write about how the people were hungry for a while but that had all been fixed – without the present threat of violence and revolt looming over the reader; so too perhaps could he have reflected on the ultimately unsuccessful alliance between Anthemius and Ricimer, in an epistle without the intriguing details of the wedding and its celebrations as a metaphor for the state of imperial politics.

Sidonius plays a critical role in each of these epistles. He is the man that saves Rome from hunger, the supportive friend of Arvandus desperately

---

[30] Symmachus describes a comparable circumstance in *Ep.* 3.82, when he sees transport ships sailing to Rome and realises that they will relieve the people's hunger.
[31] For the climax of *Ep.* 1.7 see pp. 143–146.

trying to engender sympathy, or the important envoy, sent to negotiate vital matters with the new emperor. The excitement of the epistles,
developed by his manipulation of time, enhances the focus on Sidonius'
pivotal role in each narrative. His relevancy in a rapidly changing world is
clearly evident; his epistolary self-fashioning may be subtle, but the reader
is once more left in no doubt as to Sidonius' importance.

Erzählzeiten on the Road

Placing the *Erzählzeit* of an epistle during a journey provides the narrative
with temporal and physical settings that interact with one another.[32] In
two epistles, 1.6 and 3.12, Sidonius uses this strategy; in the former the
journey acts as a backdrop and memory-aid for the subject matter, in the
latter the journey becomes a part of the narrative itself.

The *Erzählzeit* of *Ep.* 1.6 is en route to Rome (*Ep.*1.6.1): "Olim quidem
scribere tibi concupiscebam, sed nunc vel maxime impellor, id est cum
mihi ducens in urbem Christo propitiante via carpitur" (Once upon a time
I desired to write to you, but I really am forced to write now, that is, when
by the grace of Christ's atonement the road leading to the city is being trod
by me).[33] As the city looms in the distance and Sidonius contemplates his
own steps he is reminded to write to Eutropius to encourage him to take up
secular office. The *Erzählzeit* provides the literary conceit for beginning the
epistle. Like the *Erzählzeit* of *Ep.* 1.5 it looks both backward and forward.
The epistolary past is referenced in the first words: Sidonius' desire to write
has been held for some time (*olim concupiscebam*), which suggests that
Eutropius has been enjoying his lack of responsibilities over this period.
The future heightens the personal dilemma Eutropius faces (*Ep.* 1.6.4):

> non nequiter te concilii tempore post sedentes censentesque iuvenes
> inglorium rusticum, senem stantem latitabundum, pauperis honorati
> sententia premat, cum eos, quos esset indignum si vestigia nostra
> sequerentur, videris dolens antecessisse?
>
> would it not be awful if, in a session of the assembly, the opinion of a poor
> man of rank were to bear down on you – an inglorious rustic, an old man
> standing, skulking behind young men who are sitting and debating – if you

---

[32] Bakhtin (2002: 17) recognised the importance and frequency of "the road" as a chronotope (combination of space and time) in narratives.

[33] This reference to Christ, one of few in the first two books of epistles (circulated before Sidonius'
episcopacy), may be intended to invoke a parallel with Peter's *quo vadis* moment. Peter's experience
upon arriving in Rome had already become well known in late antiquity, for which see M. Baldwin
(2005: 74–75).

were to realise painfully that those men, not even worthy enough to follow
our footsteps, had surpassed you?

Eutropius still has time to save himself from the indignity of being
surpassed by his inferiors if he acts in the present to assume the responsibilities of office. The epistolary past and future frame this moment
which becomes the pivotal point when Eutropius resolved his dilemma.
The logistics of composing the epistle en route may be explained away;
Sidonius writes the letter when the journey had stopped mid-route; or the
Erzählzeit may be taken as a literary conceit.

In *Ep.* 3.12 Sidonius reports the *Erzählzeit* of a letter sent to a local bishop
to justify his recent actions. He narrates to his second cousin Secundus
an account of his discovery of grave diggers violating his grandfather's
tomb (Secundus' great-grandfather).[34] Sidonius begins with the epistolary
past, in which the majority of the narration takes place (*Ep.* 3.12.1): "Avi
mei, proavi tui tumulum hesterno (pro dolor!) die paene manus profana
temeraverat; sed deus affuit, ne nefas tantum perpetraretur" (The other
day (what grief!) a profane hand had almost desecrated the tomb of my
grandfather, of your great-grandfather; but the Lord was there, so such a
wicked crime was not perpetrated).[35] The action takes place the day before
(*hesterno die*). Sidonius' impromptu reaction is to punish the perpetrators,
after which he realises that he has transgressed the jurisdiction of the local
bishop (3.12.3):

> ceterum nostro quod sacerdoti nil reservavi meae causae suaeque personae
> praescius, in commune consului, ne vel haec iusto clementius vindicaretur
> vel illa iusto severius vindicaret. cui cum tamen totum ordinem rei ut
> satisfaciens ex itinere mandassem, vir sanctus et iustus iracundiae meae
> dedit gloriam, cum nil amplius ego venia postularem, pronuntians more
> maiorum reos tantae temeritatis iure caesos videri.

> I left nothing for the bishop to do, aware of both my own case and his
> character I looked out for the common interest, so that my case would not
> be judged more leniently, and his character would not judge more severely,
> than what was right. But when I wrote to him from my journey about the

---

[34] It is unclear why Apollinaris' tomb had been neglected, although the implication is that Secundus
had failed in his duty. It is possible that Apollinaris' role in Constantine III's uprising may have
made it difficult for his family to celebrate his life with an impressive tomb, especially if he died
during the reign of Honorius (against whom Constantine III had rebelled). Both this epistle and
Ep. 5.9 may be aimed in part at restoring Apollinaris' memory.

[35] Risselada (2013: 302) usefully applies Allan's (2007) narratological framework of abstract, orienta-
tion, climax, aftermath, and coda to this epistle. Nehlsen (1978: 119) uses this epistle as evidence of a
bishop's jurisdiction over graves. Sidonius reserves the phrase *pro dolor* for highly emotive moments,
for which see Van Waarden (2010: 321) and, for this example, Giannotti (2016: 215).

entire matter, as one apologising, he, a holy and righteous man gave glory to my wrath (even though I was asking for nothing more than forgiveness) announcing that those men guilty of such temerity seemed legally punished according to the custom of our ancestors.

Sidonius sends word to the bishop while on his journey (*ex itinere*). The bishop responds (*pronuntians*) offering Sidonius praise beyond the mere forgiveness requested. This presents the reader with two alternatives: either Sidonius has caught the perpetrators, punished them, written to the bishop, received a reply, then written this epistle to Secundus all in the space of a day, or *hesterno die* in the opening of the epistle must be taken more broadly, to denote a period of time that has recently elapsed.[36] The latter is far more likely and readily explicable as a narratological technique. Sidonius has made the epistle succinct and the action more exciting. The letter has an initial complication and resolution: the grave diggers are caught and punished by Sidonius. This is followed by a secondary complication and resolution: the bishop's jurisdiction has been breached and Sidonius has written for forgiveness and received it. The letter could simply have included the first complication; instead multiple characters appear and interact with one another, specifically Sidonius, the grave diggers, the unnamed bishop, Secundus, and (the memory of) their grandfather Apollinaris; making for a more vivid and engaging account.

Time gives the epistle a clear structure. In the case of Sidonius' epistle this takes place over a day, but it could have taken place over a longer period. Pliny in *Ep.* 3.9, for example, uses temporal markers to structure the events of a judicial proceeding which unfolds over a longer period.[37] The mentioning of many days then forms part of the generic excuse for the epistle's length.[38]

Depicting events as happening more quickly and recently can make them more exciting. A useful comparandum to Sidonius' efforts in *Ep.* 3.12 is Pliny's *Ep.* 2.11. In that letter Pliny recounts to Maturus Arrianus the trial of Marius Priscus for misconduct during his governorship of Africa.

---

[36] TLL s.v. II: "sensu latiore: spectat ad tempus nuper praeterlapsum." Three *Lesezeiten* take place within the space of a sentence: the bishop reads Sidonius' letter; Sidonius reads the bishop's response; and Secundus reads this exchange. Sidonius would have been very busy in this theoretical twenty-four period during the day and at night, when he supposedly wrote the epitaph which was inscribed on the gravestone see *Ep.* 3.12.4: "carmen hoc ... nocte proxima feci" (I made this poem last night). For the verse insertion see Wolff (2014b: 210).

[37] Pliny *Ep.* 3.9.18.

[38] Pliny *Ep.* 3.9.37: "Et tamen memento non esse epistulam longam, quae tot dies tot cognitiones tot denique reos causasque complexa sit" (And still remember that this is not a long epistle since it has covered so many days so many developments so many defendants and cases).

The narrative begins (*Ep.* 2.11.1): "Accipe ergo quod per hos dies actum est, personae claritate famosum, severitate exempli salubre, rei magnitudine aeternum" (So listen to what happened over the last few days, made famous by the high rank of the character, scandalous because of the severity of the case, and eternal because of its significance). The temporal indication *per hos dies* refers to recent events that Pliny asserts have just happened.[39] The legal issues of the case are heard and then the witnesses are sent for and arrive in Rome. Pliny notes (2.11.10): "Dilata res est in proximum senatum, cuius ipse conspectus augustissimus fuit. Princeps praesidebat – erat enim consul – ad hoc Ianuarius mensis cum cetera tum praecipue senatorum frequentia celeberrimus" (The case was put off until the nearest senate meeting, the sight of which was very impressive. The emperor was presiding – for he was the consul – January was the month for the hearing when it is very busy in many respects but especially with the number of senators).[40] If Pliny was simply recalling recent events to Maturus Arrianus the detail that it was January is redundant. He could simply have said that the senate was very busy. Instead these remarks are directed at the implied reader who will read Pliny's account of the case. It is unclear how many days are involved, how long it took to get the witnesses to Rome, how long it was until the next meeting of the senate. Pliny's *erzählte Zeiten* provide the story with an internal linear chronology which is made more exciting by being reported as if they had just happened.

The epistolary future of Sidonius' *Ep.* 3.12 is clearly developed (3.12.4):

> sed ne quid in posterum casibus liceat, quos ab exemplo vitare debemus, posco, ut actutum me quoque absente tua cura sed meo sumptu resurgat in molem sparsa congeries, quam levigata pagina tegat. ego venerabili Gaudentio reliqui pretium lapidis operisque mercedem. carmen hoc sane, quod consequetur, nocte proxima feci, non expolitum, credo, quod viae non parum intentus.

> but in order that no accidents may occur in the future, which we should avoid on account of this example, I ask that – immediately even while I am away – the scattered material rise up again into a mound under your care but at my expense, and that a smooth stone cover this mound. I have left behind with the venerable Gaudentius a sum as the fee for the stone and labour. The verse that follows I just composed last night. It is unpolished, I think, because my attention was on my journey.

---

[39] Whitton (2013a: 159).

[40] Pliny's repeated assertions in this epistle as to his own nervousness at speaking in front of such an august body are part of his self-fashioning, as they draw attention to his success in doing so. Whitton (2013a: 170) "this is *amplificatio*, not reportage."

Sidonius chanced upon men who were moving the ground unaware that they had disturbed his grandfather's tomb. The future defilement of the tomb (*in posterum casibus*) is presented as an unlikely scenario if Secundus follows the steps Sidonius outlines. The epistolary past – the narration of the story – and its future – what will happen to Apollinaris' tomb – meets in the present. Sidonius demands that Secundus follows his instructions as he will be unable to carry them out himself owing to his absence (*posco, me absente*).

The *Erzählzeit* hastens this future action; it must happen quickly (*actutum*) lest Apollinaris' tomb remain in disarray, a scattered mass, unmarked by a gravestone. The narrative's present accentuates Sidonius' *pietas*; he has composed the inscription, paid for the stone and the labour involved in inscribing the verse, made arrangements with Gaudentius, and now has written to Secundus asking him to complete the final process at no expense to himself. Sidonius could perhaps have waited until he was back to supervise the work himself, but this will not do – Sidonius' *pietas* demands that the tomb be put right immediately.

A mid-journey *Erzählzeit* places the image of Sidonius writing the letter as constructed in the reader's mind's eye in a defined and described space. This space interacts with Sidonius' narratives temporally; as Rome looms Sidonius is reminded that Eutropius should be with him, or at least, treading the same path to magisterial success; en route the outrage of his grandfather's tomb prompts a flurry of action all of which occurs in a compressed, temporal and physical, epistolary space. In each epistle Sidonius presents a highly effective self-image as either a pious grandson preserving the honour of his family name or as a very successful secular aristocrat inspiring others to serve the state.

Epistolary Time and the Construction of Macro and Micro Chronologies

Ricœur considered time as a common feature of every narrative, which, even if it does not make explicit reference to time, nevertheless unfolds over the time of its telling.[41] Every epistle has therefore a least one *Erzählzeit*. This moment may or may not be asserted or described explicitly. *Erzählzeiten* that record the year of composition may be of great use to the historian in trying to date an epistle's composition, but such information is found

---

[41] Ricœur (1980: 169–173).

in very few extant Latin epistles.[42] Even Cicero's collection which had embedded dates for approximately a third of the corpus rarely includes years in this dating system. Rather than date a letter by its year an author may date a letter by the month or season of its composition, or may structure the narrative of an epistle by using days or even hours to mark the narrative transition from one episode to the next. Such temporal indicators frequently interact with the narrative in important ways: larger temporal units, such as months and seasons (and the sporadic year), may create a "macro chronology" which may influence not only the specific epistle in which they appear, but also other epistles and the collection as a whole.[43] Smaller units such as days and even hours typically have a more limited influence, restricted predominantly to the narrative of the epistle in which they appear.

Seasons play an important structural role in several of Sidonius' epistles. We have already seen, for example, how Sidonius teases Domitius with the delights of his bathing pool during high summer. This epistle cannot work during winter – the pool would have been frozen over. Seasons also exert influence on larger parts of the collection. A clear sense of the progression of time is conveyed to the reader through book 2, from the early summer of *Ep.* 2.2 through to the late autumn of *Ep.* 2.14. This seasonal progression continues into book 3 in the linear *erzählte Zeit* of successive epistles, specifically Constantius' journey to Clermont during winter in *Ep.* 3.2 and Ecdicius' brave fighting with the Visigoths during summer in *Ep.* 3.3.[44] These *erzählte Zeiten* are loosely correlative with the *Erzählzeiten* of these epistles, which must be during or after the respective seasons of each epistle.

Autumn and winter feature in several epistles as months suitable to travel owing to the presence of the Visigoths near Clermont during the summer.[45] In *Ep.* 4.15 Sidonius advises Elaphius to prepare for visitors, as he and others intend to visit him for the opening of a newly completed church (*Ep.* 4.15.3):

> de cetero quamquam et extremus autumnus iam diem breviat et viatorum
> sollicitas aures foliis toto nemore labentibus crepulo fragore circumstrepit

[42] This ultimately begs the question whether dates were only included in epistles to date the events described.

[43] Gibson (2012: 62).

[44] The enemy's inability to bury their dead given the shortness of the night clearly indicates it is summer, but the context also helps as summer was the campaign season, and it seems clear from Sidonius' testimony in *Ep.* 5.6.1 that Clermont was only harried by the Visigoths during summer.

[45] The collection ends during winter, for which see pp. 181–182.

> inque castellum, ad quod invitas, utpote Alpinis rupibus cinctum,
> sub vicinitate brumali difficilius escenditur, nos tamen deo praevio ...
> [veniemus]

> well, even though the end of Autumn is already now shortening the day
> and as the leaves fall in every forest with a crackling crunch it rustles at the
> anxious ears of travellers, and although climbing up to the castle, to which
> you invite me (surrounded as it is by Alpine cliffs), is more difficult in the
> approach of winter, still with God's help ... [I will come]

The dangers of the season recall Constantius' winter journey to visit
Sidonius in Clermont in *Ep.* 3.2. In that epistle the winter conditions
exacerbate Constantius' suffering and piety, as he visits and consoles
the people of Clermont following the destruction caused by the recent
Visigothic raiding.[46] Autumn as a season of travel features again in *Ep.*
5.6 in which Sidonius advises his uncle Apollinaris that he managed a
visit to his brother Thaumastus (one of Sidonius' other uncles) in Vienne
(*Ep.* 5.6.1): "Cum primum aestas decessit autumno et Arvernorum timor
potuit aliquantisper ratione temporis temperari, Viennam veni" (As soon
as summer gave way to Autumn and the Arvernians' fear could subside for
a little while owing to the time of year).

These temporal indications enable the interaction of the text and context. Their effect in the collection goes beyond influencing the specific
narrative of each epistle, to impact intervening epistles that do not specifically reference the season or the year, yet nevertheless get caught up in
the same milieu. They make the reader aware of the passage of time, and
of the influence of historical events on the progression of the epistolary
collection. This effect is aided by Sidonius' occasional oblique reference to
the geopolitical situation, such as the *de temporum statu* of *Ep.* 4.5.

This is a unique effect that is reliant on very specific cyclical circumstances,
namely the Visigothic harrying of Sidonius' see Clermont each summer
from 471 to 474. Seasons do not enable the interaction of text and context to the same extent in other Latin epistolary collections. In Pliny's
collection, for example, the grape harvest parallels his life-time, Spring
and Summer are suited to poetic blooming, and January explains the full
crowd that has gathered to hear one of his cases, but the narrative effect of
these moments is not felt outside of the specific epistles to the same extent
as in Sidonius' collection.[47] Seneca similarly (occasionally) mentions the

---

[46] See pp. 118–119.
[47] For the grape harvest see, for example, Pliny *Ep.* 8.2, 8.15, 9.20, for poetic seasons *Ep.* 1.3.1, 8.21.2,
and for his January court case *Ep.* 6.33.3–4.

month or the season in his collection, but these remarks are rarely invested with any particular importance.[48]

Smaller units of time, such as days and even hours develop micro chronologies in individual epistles. In *Ep.* 3.12, analysed above, the events are relayed as if they took place over the course of a single day, which is broken up into three constitutive parts: the morning of Sidonius' departure; the day of his discovery and punishment of the grave diggers, composition of a letter to the local bishop, reception of a reply; and the night of his poetic composition and the *Erzählzeit* of the epistle proper. Surely too much for a single day's work, but compressing it all into one day makes for a more exciting and engaging account.

For an epistle such as *Ep.* 3.12 that depicts events that take place over a single day, the passage of hours or shorter periods of time (e.g morning, daytime, evening) provide the internal structure of the narrative. In *Ep.* 2.9, for example, Sidonius explains his late arrival to Donidius by detailing a typical day of the entertainment on offer at the estates of Ferreolus and Apollinaris. Regular temporal references would ruin the timelessness of Sidonius' *otium*, which is in fact the basis for his delay. Still, the epistle is not completely atemporal (*Ep.* 2.9.6):

> studiis hisce dum nostrum singuli quique, prout libuerat, occupabantur, ecce et ab archimagiro adventans, qui tempus instare curandi corpora moneret, quem quidem nuntium per spatia clepsydrae horarum incrementa servantem probabat competenter ingressum quinta digrediens.

> while each of us was busying himself with those pursuits, according to his preference, someone came from the head chef to advise us that it was time for refreshment. The fifth hour departing showed that he (who had been keeping an eye on the passage of the hours through periods of the water clock) had come at just the right moment.

Tellingly it is one of the servants, not Sidonius nor his fellow aristocrats, who watch the water clock, so their enjoyment of *otium* may remain undisturbed by consideration of the time. The lunchtime meal structures the day and thus the epistle. Riding helps to keep an afternoon siesta at bay and develops an appetite for the evening meal, before which Sidonius and his friends take a bath (*Ep.* 2.9.9): "hic nobis trahebantur horae non absque sermonibus salsis iocularibusque" (there hours are whiled away by us with no lack of witticisms and joking). Time glides by without anyone

---

[48] Griffin (1976: 400). Gibson (2012: 61) notes Seneca's intention "to foster a time free zone," for discussion of which see Hanaghan (2017d: 203–206).

really noticing, so, Sidonius implies, he can hardly be blamed for the delay
to his journey.[49]

The timelessness of the epistles in book 2 is evident in the difficulty of
dating them accurately, beyond the broad premise that book 2 circulated
before Sidonius' episcopacy ca. 470. This timelessness enhances the book's
thematic unity centred on aristocratic *otium*. This is comparable to the
(largely) timeless quality of Seneca's epistles which facilitates his philosophical contemplation, freeing them somewhat from the political context
of Nero's reign.[50]

While Sidonius only uses hours or short passages of time in his epistles
to structure a day's worth of activities, it is possible for these units of time
to create an even smaller micro chronology. Fronto's exchange of letters
with Marcus Aurelius frequently refers to the hour of the day. These
comments typically provide individual epistles with an internal structure. In *ad M. Caes.* 1.3 Fronto grapples with how he will respond to the
emperor. Early in the epistle he notes the passage of time (2): "Ecce nox
praeteriit, dies hic est alter, qui <iam> prope exactus est, necdum quid aut
quemadmodum tibi rescribam reperio" (Look a night had passed, and this
is the next day, which is now nearly also finished, nor yet do I know what
or how I will respond to you). The passage of time forms the basis of the
end of the epistle (9): "Sed iam hora decimum tangit, et tabellarius tuus
mussat. Finis igitur sit epistulae" (But now the tenth hour is nearly here,
and your clerk is whispering in my ear. Let this be the end of the epistle
then). Ultimately these close micro chronologies collaborate to give the
collection an overall structure, but this structure is unique to the specific
epistolary dynamic of a tutor and emperor writing back and forth to one
another.

The longer the narrative in the epistle the more necessary it is for there
to be a clear internal structure. Sidonius structures some of his longer
narratives by using days as the main chronological unit. In *Ep.* 1.7, which
describes Arvandus' trial, a series of days pass (*pauci medii dies*) between
Sidonius' unsuccessful pre-trial meeting with the defendant and the
hearing in which Arvandus confesses to the charges, unaware of the dire
consequences that await him. In the interval Sidonius leaves, perhaps to
avoid presiding over the case. This departure shifts the narrative function

---

[49] That Sidonius and his friends seem to have spent a lot of time in the baths does not undermine
the agonistic comparison he creates between these baths and his own at Avitacum, for which see
pp. 25–27 and 92.

[50] See Gibson (2012), Rimmel (2015: 130–131), and Hanaghan (2017d: 203–206).

from autoptic to testimonial, as Sidonius can only relay what he heard from others (as he was not there). The passage of days is critical to the telling of the narrative. If Sidonius had tried to compress the events into a single day, as he does in *Ep.* 3.12, his absence from the trial would have been even more conspicuous.

A comparable example may be found in Pliny's description of his uncle's death following the eruption of Vesuvius in *Ep.* 6.16. The progression of events is marked by the passage of days. The first indication of time in the narrative specifies the date and hour when his attention was first drawn to the cloud over Vesuvius.[51] It was the 24th of August at 1pm.[52] A temporal reference follows for the passage of the night that Pliny the elder spent in Pomponianus' house. The next morning the fumes prevented the daylight from forming. Pliny's uncle ventured outside but was overcome by the fumes. Pliny records that his uncle's body was found two days later, on the 26th of August. The strict daily chronology forms a stark contrast between Pliny's perspective of events and his uncle's. To his uncle the events that unfolded during the daytime of the 25th occurred in a bizarre atemporal haze of noxious fumes; to Pliny and the reader, this event fits clearly within the linear progression of time throughout the narrative and its telling. In both Pliny's epistle and that of Sidonius, temporal indicators lend structure to the narrative and vary according to the perspective each author adopts, which is dependent on Pliny's absence from Vesuvius and Sidonius' absence from Arvandus' court.

Lastly, indications that are not strictly temporal may nevertheless construct or imply a macro chronology. These may vary from a change in the author's status, such as Sidonius' acknowledgement that he has become a bishop in *Ep.* 3.1, to temporary ailments that affect the author, such as Fronto's recurrent pain in the neck, which in effect links together a series of otherwise unconnected epistles.[53]

Anticipating and Reporting *Lesezeiten*

Epistles construct a relationship between the author and the reader: both the addressee, who may be conceived of as the public reader, and the

---

[51] Eco (1994: 127ff) provides a dazzling analysis of the temporal aspects of this epistle.

[52] One may posit that the date was included specifically for Pliny's addressee Tacitus, who seemingly requested a detailed account of the events from Pliny to aid him in writing his history of the period; but that would in a way diminish Pliny's own attempt to document and thus preserve a history of the events as they transpired (which since Tacitus' account is not extant has exerted a high degree of influence on historical reconstructions of the event).

[53] Fronto *ad M. Caes.* 5.27, 28, 29, 30, 31. His pain then moves to his gut for *ad M. Caes.* 5.32 and 33.

epistles' wider audience, made up of contemporaries and subsequent generations. This relationship is readily discernible in the I/you of epistolary discourse.[54] As such, the epistolary persona of the author is hyperaware that meaning is made at the moment of reception. This meaning will be contingent to some extent on when this reading takes place – what Müller termed the *Lesezeit*. Ignoring the *Lesezeit* of the addressee may have disastrous consequences; Augustine found this out the hard way by circulating an epistle before Jerome, the addressee, had received a copy to read.[55] This faux pas provoked a series of irksome letters in response.[56] In his epistolary collection Sidonius discusses both his own and the addressees' *Lesezeiten*; Sidonius' typically occurs at the beginning of a letter to position his epistle in response to an earlier epistle from the addressee. Most of those epistles (with the notable exceptions of some letters by Ruricius and one by Claudianus Mamertus) are not extant. It is difficult to determine how authentic Sidonius' comments are; that is, whether or not Sidonius is responding to an actual letter or simply using it as a literary device to introduce and structure his epistle. The addressee's *Lesezeiten* of Sidonius' letter is equally difficult to authenticate; as the author of the epistle Sidonius is in complete control of how the epistle will report the particulars of the addressee such as their rank, location, demeanour, and the anticipated moment when they will read Sidonius' letter. Sidonius' descriptions of the addressee's *Lesezeit* are not trivial; rather they often respond to, and are referenced by, the content of the epistle. The *Lesezeiten* of three epistles (*Ep.* 2.2, 2.12, 4.8) have a clear affect on the narrative contained within; in *Ep.* 2.2 Sidonius tempts Domitius, who is teaching in the city during the summer, with grandiose descriptions of his villa's baths; Sidonius' *Lesezeit*, reported in *Ep.* 2.12, provides the basis for his refusal of Agricola's invitation to go fishing; the *Lesezeit* recorded in *Ep.* 4.8 lends authority to Sidonius' use of the topos of authorial humility by its assertion that he had insufficient time to compose a proper verse for Euodius.

In *Ep.* 2.2 Sidonius describes the summer entertainment on offer at his estate, complete with its impressive array of baths and ice-cold drinks. These comments are directed at his addressee Domitius, who remains in the city without relief from the heat (*Ep.* 2.2.1–2):

> mundus incanduit: glacies Alpina deletur et hiulcis arentium rimarum flexibus terra perscribitur; squalet glarea in vadis, limus in ripis, pulvis in

---

[54] Altman (1982: 118–121).
[55] For a recent summary of the extensive literature on this exchange see Ebbeler (2012: 102–103).
[56] Ebbeler (2012: 102–103).

campis; aqua ipsa quaecumque perpetuo labens tractu cunctante languescit, iam non solum calet unda sed coquitur. Et nunc, dum in carbaso sudat unus, alter in bombyce, tu endromidatus exterius, intrinsecus fasceatus … discipulis non aestu minus quam timore pallentibus exponere oscitabundus oridiris: "Samia mihi mater fuit."

the sky burns, the Alpine ice melts and the earth is being etched by the gaping bends of thirsting cracks, gravel is filthy in the ditches, mud is on the river banks, dust on the plains, even water which flows perpetually has grown slow by its lingering ebb, now not only is the water hot, it is boiling. And now, while one man sweats in linen, another in silk, you wearing a woollen cloak on the outside, wrapped in clothing on the inside … you, yawning, begin to expound to your students, pale no less on account of the heat than from their fear of you: "My mother was from Samos."[57]

This focus on the climate, at the beginning of a letter which describes a villa, is reminiscent of Pliny's *Ep.* 5.6.4.[58] Unlike Pliny's description however, Sidonius focuses only on the heat of summer: the Alps melting, the earth cracking, and the rivers boiling. Sidonius forms a contrast between the *carbasus* and *bombyx* of others,[59] and Domitius, clothed in a woollen cloak (*endromidatus*) and with swathing underneath (*fasceatus*). The chiastic phrase *endromidatus exterius, intrinsecus fasceatus* emphasises that Domitius' attire, like his decision to stay in the city, is ridiculous given the summer heat. Sidonius' remarks allude to Juvenal *Satire* 6.259–260 in which women sweat (*sudant*) wrapped in their *bombyces*, and are characterised, like Domitius, by their incessant complaining.[60] The summer heat is reinforced by *aestu* and *sudat*, but *oscitabundus* also alludes to the sweltering conditions, providing the sense that the summer heat is making Domitius yawn and contributing to his students' pale faces. Sidonius increases his teasing of Domitius by giving him a line from Terence's *Eunuchus* spoken by Thais, the courtesan.[61] Domitius' *Lesezeit* places him at a distinct social disadvantage to Sidonius, who implicitly enjoys the amenities of Avitacum while he continues to swelter throughout the letter.

Discussion of the addressee's *Lesezeit* allows Sidonius to exert control over their response. In *Ep.* 2.12 Sidonius declines an invitation from

---

[57] Squillante (2009: 159) links the heat to the sounds of the villa, yet the more pertinent context is certainly the baths, which Sidonius enjoys and Domitius does not but could were he to visit.

[58] Sidonius' *Ep.* 2.2 has many features in common with this letter of Pliny, see Geisler (1887: 356–358), Harries (1994: 10), and Mondin (2008: 475n96).

[59] Yates (1843: 227).

[60] Colton (1982: 64).

[61] The specific significance of this line is difficult to determine beyond that it was spoken by Thais and Sidonius describes Domitius' dress in terms suitable for a woman's attire. Sidonius and Domitius

Agricola, his brother-in-law, to go fishing, because his daughter, Severiana, has fallen ill.[62] He anticipates that this news will prompt Agricola to visit him immediately (*Ep.* 2.12.1):

> sed dabis veniam, quod invitanti tibi in piscationem comes venire dissimulo; namque me multo decumbentibus nostris validiora maeroris retia tenent, quae sunt amicis quoque et externis indolescenda. unde te quoque puto, si rite germano moveris affectu, quo temporis puncto paginam hanc sumpseris, de reditu potius cogitaturum.

> but you will forgive me for refusing your invitation to accompany you on a fishing trip; seeing that my family is bedridden, nets of grief hold me much more strongly, which cause pain to friends and strangers. And so I think that if you are moved by brotherly affection, at the point in time when you pick up this page, you will think rather of returning.[63]

Sidonius emphasise Agricola's *Lesezeit* with the embellished and exacting phrase *quo temporis puncto paginam hunc sumpseris*. Agricola's reading of the epistle exists in the epistolary future for Sidonius but the present for himself. Sidonius explicitly shapes Agriocola's response. His prediction that Agricola will take up the letter becomes at the moment of reception a post-diction. Agricola's reading lends credibility to Sidonius' claim that he will now think about returning. Sidonius' *Lesezeit* of Agricola's epistle, which presumably contained the invite to go fishing, comes amid Severiana's persistent coughing and fever (*Ep.* 2.12.2–3):

> Severiana, sollicitudo communis, inquietata primum lentae tussis impulsu febribus quoque iam fatigatur, hisque per noctes ingravescentibus; propter quod optat exire in suburbanum; litteras tuas denique cum sumeremus, egredi ad villulam iam parabamus … igitur ardori civitatis atque torpori tam nos quam domum totam … eximimus …

> Severiana, our common concern, disturbed at first by an attack of persistent coughing now is also worn out by fever, and this grew worse at night; because of this she wants to go to our house out of town; when I at last took up your letter, we were already preparing to leave for our little country-house.[64] …

---

may have read this text or shared some other personal experience. Sidonius knew Terence's plays well, see Cain (2013: 380–388) and Amherdt (2001: 311–312).

[62] Sidonius begins by thanking Agricola for gifting him some fish, for which see Williams (2014: 256). This epistle contributes to Sidonius' self-fashioning as a man with familial and community responsibilities, for other examples of which see *Ep.* 5.19 and 6.9.

[63] Bellès (1997: 26) takes this epistle as evidence for the Gallo-Roman elites' enjoyment of fishing trips which along with hunting trips are likely to have been important bonding occasions.

[64] Sidonius is almost certainly referring to *Avitacum*, his estate probably located near Lac d'Aydat. The diminutive force of *villula* is consistent with the language Sidonius' employs in *Ep.* 2.2 to describe

> And so we are taking ourselves and our entire household away from the heat and weariness of the city.[65]

The selection of this moment foregrounds Sidonius' invitation for him to visit them at their country house, where he and his family will surely be by the time Agricola reads the letter. Sidonius' focus on the narrative of Severiana's illness and emotional restraint adds to the sense of urgency. The difference between Sidonius' *Lesezeit* of Agricola's epistle and *Erzählzeit* of his own is momentary; Sidonius was just now preparing to leave (*egredi iam parabamus*) and is leaving that very moment (*eximimus*). His reported *Lesezeit* (narration of the future episode) becomes a part of the *Erzählzeit* of his epistle; the moment when he wrote his letter is defined by its relation to when he read Agricola's, which he claims happened as soon as he picked up his friend's letter.

In *Ep.* 4.8 Sidonius offers an extended discussion of *Lesezeit and Erzählzeit*; he composes a verse inscription for Euodius to put on a bowl to be presented to the Visigothic queen Ragnahilda, the wife of Euric.[66] The considerable pressure Sidonius experienced while reading and replying to Euodius' request lends credibility to his literary humility (4.8.1):

> cum tabellarius mihi litteras tuas reddidit, quae te Tolosam rege mandante mox profecturum certis amicis confitebatur, nos quoque ex oppido longe remotum rus petebamus. me quidem mane primo remoratum vix e tenaci caterva prosecutorum paginae tuae occasio excussit.

> when the letter-carrier gave me your letter which confessed that you were soon to set out with your close friends for Toulouse under the king's command, we also were leaving town for the far distant countryside. Indeed, in the early morning, the chance to read your letter just managed to get me out of being delayed by a persistent crowd of followers.[67]

The focus is on the *occasio paginae*, the moment the letter was delivered to Sidonius, not the letter itself, which he quickly summarises (*qui … confitebatur*). Sidonius' initial *Lesezeit* is checked by his followers who mob around him, which is a clear display of his many friends and supporters.

---

that villa as *tuguria* and *mapalia*, but it is inconsistent with the estate Sidonius describes; the villa boasted nineteen rooms, a bathing complex, and a large swimming pool.

[65] Sidonius invokes Christ's help at the end of the epistle. This stands as an exception to the general absence of Christian terminology in the first two books of epistles which were circulated prior to Sidonius' episcopacy, for which see p. 170.

[66] Euodius may be a descendant of Flavius Euodius who was consul in 386, but such a connection is based solely on the relative obscurity of his name, for which see PLRE II "Euodius."

[67] For the specific circumstances of this epistle see Amherdt (2001: 224–228) and Leatherbury (2017: 36).

At last Sidonius finds a moment to read and respond to Euodius' letter, but only once his journey is already under way (*saltim viator, saltim eques*). Euodius' letter prompts him to halt his journey (4.8.3–4):

> cum tui causa substitissemus ... iam duae secundae facile processerant, iam sol adultus roscidae noctis umorem radio crescente sorbuerat: aestus ac sitis invalescebant eratque in profunda serenitate contra calorem sola quae tegeret nebula de pulvere ... quae cuncta praemissa, domine frater, huc tendunt, ut tibi probem neque animo vacasse me multum neque corpore neque tempore, cum postulatis obtemperavi.

> when we had stopped on your account ... two hours easily had already passed, the blazing sun had absorbed the dampness of the night's dew; heat and thirst grew strong and in the crystal clear sky the only cloud to offer protection against the heat was made of dust ... the point of all this lead-up, my honoured brother, is so that I may show you that I was without much in the way of time, mind or body when I attended to your demands.

Sidonius' initial comments provide the *Erzählzeit* of the verse insertion that follows. The shift in tense from pluperfect (*processerant, sorbuerat*) to imperfect (*invalescebant, erat*) marks the temporal beginning of the verse's composition. The present tense (*tendunt*) is reserved for the *Erzählzeit* of the epistle proper. The point of this lengthy preamble is to develop the circumstances into the literary topos of authorial humility for Sidonius' verses, composed under time pressure and not in an ideal location.[68] Sidonius returns to this point in the epistle, blaming Euodius for his temporal constraints and alleging that the maker of the silver bowl has had more time than the poet, which is perhaps just as well if, as Sidonius complains, the writing material will be more valued at Euric's court than the writing.[69] The *Erzählzeiten* and *Lesezeiten* of this epistle are central features on which the narration and discourse of literary humility rely.

Throughout his collection of epistles Sidonius reports the circumstances which constituted the moment(s) when he read the addressee's epistle to which he is replying. These moments are under his authorial control. They function in *Ep.* 2.12 and 4.8 to frame his response: no he cannot go fishing, his daughter is now sick; if Euodius' epistle had been sent earlier (and he had read it then) he would have had more time to write a better verse inscription. It is not possible for the addressee to challenge Sidonius'

---

[68] Becht-Jördens (2017: 127) contrasts the conditions that Sidonius describes to the *locus amoenus* suited to the composition of poetry.

[69] Becht-Jördens (2017: 133).

authority in making these claims; instead the reader's only option is to accept Sidonius' reported *Lesezeiten* as faits accomplis.

When Sidonius anticipates Domitius' *Lesezeit* of *Ep.* 2.2 the fictional basis of these claims is more apparent; Domitius may have left town already, stopped teaching, or at the very least, chosen to read lines not spoken by the courtesan in Terence's *Eunuchus*. Instead Domitius' persona falls under the sway of Sidonius' authorial control, the abstemious target of the inducements on offer at Avitacum: a cool swim, refreshing drink, and the *docta otia* of villa life.

False Endings and Beginnings: *Erzählzeiten* as Narrative Switch

When the *erzählte Zeit* changes, either by reaching or departing from the present, an opportunity presents for the narrative to alter its direction and tone. This transition in time may be negotiated smoothly or far more abruptly, depending upon whether the change is acute or subtle. In three epistles (8.6, 8.11, and 9.9) Sidonius introduces a narrative switch; in *Ep.* 8.6 and 8.11 this switch is inspired by the arrival of news: in the former a messenger arrives to update Sidonius about the addressee of the epistle; in the latter Sidonius receives news mid epistle of the death of his friend Lampridius. In the last epistle surveyed here, *Ep.* 9.9, the narrative switch is an epistolary conceit – a way of appearing to tack on to an epistle what is really its main point.[70]

Ep. 8.6 is seemingly about to end until the arrival of a messenger breaks the epistle from its present into the epistolary past (*Ep.* 8.6.13):[71]

> exceptis iocis, fac sciam tandem, quid te, quid domum circa. sed ecce dum iam epistulam, quae diu garrit, claudere optarem, subitus a Santonis nuntius; cum quo dum tui obtentu aliquid horarum sermocinanter extrahimus, constanter asseveravit nuper vos classicum in classe cecinisse atque inter officia nunc nautae, modo militis litoribus Oceani curvis inerrare contra Saxonum pandos myoparones, quorum quot remiges videris, totidem te cernere putes archipiratas: ita simul omnes imperant parent, docent discunt latrocinari. unde nunc etiam ut quam plurimum caveas, causa successit maxima monendi.

---

[70] Claudianus Mamertus uses this strategy against Sidonius at *Ep.* 4.2.2: "*illud ... rescripto*," for the circumstances of which see pp. 35–36.
[71] See p. 85 for another example of false closure in an epistle.

jokes aside, make sure that I know what is the latest with you and your household. But look when I was just now about to conclude the letter, which has been prattling along for a while now, suddenly a messenger arrived from Saintes; when I had passed some hours chatting with him about you, he repeatedly affirmed that you had recently sounded the trumpet of war in the fleet and were now occupied with the duties of a sailor, now a soldier, roving the winding shores of the Ocean against the curved warships of the Saxons, and that you think you see the same number of pirate-captains as oars; as they all command and obey, teach and learn to raid as one. And now you should be as careful as possible, for a very good reason for being reminded of this has presented.

The present imperative *fac* commands the addressee Namatius to tell Sidonius about his family. This present is then immediately rescinded; the messenger has arrived, Sidonius spoke to him for some time (*aliquid horarum*) and has learnt that Namatius has taken over command of a boat against the Saxons. The arrival of the letter disrupts Sidonius' supposed attempt to conclude the epistle; it breaks Sidonius' *erzählte Zeit* of the present into the *erzählte Zeit* of the past. This past however only exists relative to the new *Erzählzeit* of the epistle (after the arrival of the messenger and Sidonius' discussion with him). The arrival of the messenger links the first two thirds of the epistle with its end and enables Sidonius to segue into a description of the Saxons and the dangers of fighting them.

This seemingly disorganised arrangement reveals a clear structure when the arrival of the messenger is read as a narratological device. Sidonius ends the epistle by noting that he has included two literary works for Namatius to enjoy: a chronicle by Eusebius and the now lost *Logistoricus* of a work of Varro.[72] Sidonius claims that Namatius will be able to remove the rust not only from his weapons but also from his speech by reading these works in his barracks.[73] The arrival of the messenger thus creates a ring composition by linking the end of the epistle with Sidonius' opening premise (*Ep.* 8.6.1):

> Gaium Caesarem dictatorem, quo ferunt nullum rem militarem ducalius administrasse, studia certatim dictandi lectitandique sibi mutuo vindicavere … in persona unius eiusdemque tempore suo principis viri castrensis oratoriaque scientiae cura certaverit ferme gloria aequipari.
>
> They say no-one has ever managed a military campaign who was more able to command than Gaius Caesar the dictator. The study of composition and

---

[72] Overwien (2009: 103–105) suggests that Sidonius criticises Namatius by drawing a contrast between his Roman and Catholic world, represented by Varro's *Logistorici* and Eusebius' *Chronicle*, and Namatius' Gothic world.

[73] *Ep.* 8.6.18.

reading competed against one another to claim him as their own ... in the character of this one and the same person, the leading man of his time, the study of military science and oratory rivalled one another with equal glory.[74]

Caesar's glory stems from both his knowledge of oratory and warfare (*castrensis oratoriaeque scientiae*).[75] Sidonius proceeds to use the example of Nicetius, a famous Gallo-Roman orator, to provide Namatius with a model of oratorical display, and public service, but hardly military service. The arrival of the messenger, who updates Sidonius on Namatius' military service, renews the relevancy of Caesar's example. Namatius should thus look to Caesar as an example more so than Nicetius and Sidonius. The temporal aspects of the epistle are cleverly manipulated to provide it with a clear internal structure, which despite its length ties together the two main narrative threads: the brilliancy of Nicetius' oratory and the dangers of commanding a vessel against the Saxons. Sidonius uses this structure to stress the importance of *paideia* to Namatius; like Caesar Namatius ought to make sure he keeps up his knowledge of oratory, even while he campaigns.

This use of a false ending to manipulate the *Erzählzeit* of an epistle is also evident in Sidonius' *Ep.* 9.9, written to Faustus, the bishop of Riez. Sidonius extends the letter to introduce a new subject matter.[76] The false ending even includes a formal farewell and a request that Faustus pray for Sidonius (*Ep.* 9.9.2: *vale dicimus. orate pro nobis*). The inclusion of these formalities is clearly a literary conceit which Sidonius could easily have edited out prior to the collection and circulation of the ninth book of his collection. The fiction of this conceit is heightened by the nature of the intrusion; no messenger has come this time, rather Sidonius has simply chanced upon a subject matter. Books written by Faustus passed through the Auvergne, but the carriers denied Sidonius the opportunity to read them. This was not how the literati of late fifth-century Gaul, who valued *paideia* immensely, typically treated each other (*Ep.* 9.9.3):

> sed bene est, bene est, quia chartulam iam iamque complicaturo res forte succurrit, de qua exprobranda si diutius vel laetitia sese mea vel ira cohibuerit, ipse me accepta dignum contumelia iudicabo. venisti, magister,

---

[74] See Overwien (2009: 103–105).

[75] Zecchini (1985: 136): "le brevi citazioni vogliono indicare che il giudizo di Sidonio su Cesare è largamente positivo nonostante la «macchia» non taciuta della guerra civile" (The brief citations tend to indicate that the judgment of Sidonius on Caesar is largely positive notwithstanding the "stain" that is not disregarded concerning the civil war).

[76] See pp. 161 and 176 for this epistle.

in manus meas (nec exulto tantum, verum insulto), venisti, et quidem talis,
qualem abhinc longo iamdiu tempore desideria nostra praestolabantur.

> but it is well, it is well, that a matter happened to occur to me as I was just
> about to fold the letter up, if my happiness or my anger restrains me any
> longer from inspecting it, I will judge myself worthy of the insults I have
> received. You came, my teacher, into my hands (I am not exulting you,
> actually I am insulting you), you came, and in the kind of form which for a
> long while my desire was expecting.

Sidonius was just about to fold up the letter (*chartulam iam iamque
complicaturo*) when his thoughts turned to berating Faustus for not allowing
his book carrier to let him read his more interesting works. Faustus probably
had good reasons for doing so. While he had initially enjoyed considerable
influence over Sidonius, in the early 470s their relationship likely soured
over a dispute between Faustus and Claudianus Mamertus on the nature
of the soul, which began, if Claudianus is to be believed, at Sidonius' insti-
gation, when Sidonius likely did not know that Faustus was the author of
a controversial treatise that had been published anonymously.[77] Sidonius'
peevish tone in *Ep.* 9.9 supports the supposition that their relationship
had deteriorated.[78] He insults Faustus (*insulto verum*) and implies that he
ordered the books to be kept away from Sidonius, despite their proximity
to him (*Ep.* 9.9.3): "tuis libris ... non solum moenia mea, verum etiam
latera radentibus" (as your books were shaving not just my walls, but even
my sides). The narrative switch catches Faustus (and the reader) wholly
unprepared for the string of invectives that follows as Sidonius attacks him
with one rhetorical question after another. Sidonius ends these by inserting
Faustus' persona into the dialogue (*Ep.* 9.9.6): "'ista quorsum?' inquis"
('what's all this about?' You say), which begins in turn the narration of how
he managed to track down and copy the books by pursuing Faustus' book
carrier, Riochatus.[79]

Pliny comparably uses a series of false endings in *Ep.* 3.9 addressed to
Cornelius Minicianus. After narrating judicial proceedings at some length,
Pliny almost forgets to include further details (*Ep.* 3.9.28): "succurrit quod
praeterieram et quidem sero, sed quamquam praepostere reddetur" (what
I had left out occurs to me and I indeed am including it even though

[77] Engelbrecht (1885: 198) argues that Sidonius was angry with Claudianus for criticising Faustus.
Rehling (1898: 44–45) and Alciati (2009b: 201) disagree. For the dispute see Mathisen (1989: 240)
and (1991: 495–496), and Gerth (2013: 171). For Sidonius' involvement see Claudianus *De statu
animae*, preface.
[78] *Ep.* 9.3.1. Wood (1992: 11).
[79] For the specific circumstances of this dialogue see p. 161.

returning to it is out of order). Pliny acknowledges Homer as the source
of his conceit, which he then disavows as intentional.[80] The narrative continues until Pliny stops to remember an additional conclusion.[81] By the
end of the epistle the reader struggles to believe Pliny's attempts at closure
(*Ep.* 3.9.37): "hic erit epistulae finis, re vera finis; litteram non addam,
etiamsi adhuc aliquid praeterisse me sensero. Vale" (this will be the end of
the epistle, really the end; I will not add another word, not even if I feel
that I have still left something out).[82]

A similar plot intrusion to *Ep.* 9.9 is evident in *Ep.* 8.11 addressed to
Lupus which eulogises Lampridius, an orator and friend of Sidonius who
was murdered by his own slaves. This letter has a false beginning, one
which does not mention Lampridius at all, rather than a false ending.[83]
The arrival of the messenger in that epistle may only be assumed; Sidonius
has just learnt of Lampridius' death.[84] The epistle praises Lampridus in
verse and prose but also points out a few shortfalls. At the end Sidonius'
mourning overwhelms his literary persona (*Ep.* 8.11.14):

> longiuscule me progredi amor impulit, cuius angorem silentio exhalare
> non valui. tu interim, si quid istic cognitu dignum, citus indica, saltim ob
> hoc scribens, ut animum meum tristitudine gravem lectio levet. namque
> confuso pectori maeror, et quidem iure, plurimus erat, cum paginis ista
> committerem sola. neque enim satis mihi aliud hoc tempore manu sermone
> consilio scribere loqui volvere libet.

> my love has forced me to go on rather too long, I was not strong enough to
> let go of its anguish in silence. You, meanwhile, if there is anything worth
> knowing, indicate it promptly by writing if only because reading lightens
> my serious mind from its grief. For I am upset, my heart confused, and my
> grief was rightly very great, when I committed these remarks to paper and
> only these, for there is no pleasure for me at the moment to write with my
> own hand, make my own conversation, or mull over any of my thoughts.

---

[80] Pliny *Ep.* 3.9.28.

[81] Pliny *Ep.* 3.9.36.

[82] Kroh (2015: 83) lists this passage as one of several in which Pliny draws attention to the performative
nature of closure; for a detailed study of Pliny's attempts at closure see Whitton (2013c), and for
further discussion of epistle in particular (Hanaghan 2018: 156–159).

[83] This epistle contravenes Sidonius' principle, articulated in one of his programmatic epistles (7.18),
that a letter should discuss a single point; see *Ep.* 7.18.4: "singulae causae singulis ferme epistulis
finiantur" (Individual subject matters are entirely dealt with by each letter).

[84] For Lampridius' character see pp. 121–126. Pliny uses death announcements at the beginning of
certain epistles to introduce a eulogy that usually includes colourful anecdotes and may cover the
circumstances surrounding their death. This happens at the very beginning of those epistles not the
end, see for example *Ep.* 3.1 for the death of Silius Italicus or *Ep.* 7.24.1 for Ummidia Quadratilla.
Wolff (2015a: 193–194) argues convincingly that Pliny's account of the murder of Larcius Macedo in
Ep. 3.14 is Sidonius' model for *Ep.* 8.11.

Sidonius' writing has helped him through the grieving process which becomes his justification for contravening the epistolary norm of brevity.[85] His *Erzählzeit* envisages Lupus' *Lesezeit* of his epistle, and in turn his *Lesezeit* of Lupus' hoped for reply, which he views as the only remedy to free him from his grief. The writing of the letter sits in the past (*cum ... sola*). The *erzählte Zeit* (*hoc tempore*) of the epistle extends its present; the epistolary future is wholly contingent on Lupus reading and replying to Sidonius' letter.[86]

In both *Ep.* 8.11 and 9.9 the narrative switch pivots on the present, but it may equally depend on events that are reported as happening in the past. In *Ep.* 7.14, for example, Sidonius complains to Philagrius that others had recently asserted that they were better friends with him. This happened *proxime* "recently." Sidonius, however, could not keep quiet, and he vehemently put them in their place. They persist with their idiotic argument, which prompts Sidonius into a philosophical defence of his claims that take up the remainder of the letter, one of the longest in the collection.

In each of these epistles the change of the *Erzählzeit* corresponds to a clear change in direction; Sidonius begins to lambast Faustus or mourn Lampridius, or he returns to develop his initial premise, encouraging Namatius to follow Caesar as an example. The insertion of these changes brings the epistolary present into focus, representing it as an interactive moment that corresponds to Sidonius' compositional decisions. The fictional basis of this change is most evident in *Ep.* 9.9 – Sidonius (supposedly) simply thinks it up – but in each of the letters it is a literary conceit with narratological implications.[87]

Sidonius carefully manages and presents his self image; he appears highly interested in Faustus' work, a knowledgeable reader who should not be overlooked, as a sympathetic friend willing to accept Lampridius despite his irksome complexities, or a wise adviser, able to offer Namatius suitably astute advice about navigating the difficulties that confronted him.

Conclusion

An epistle may change direction by interacting with events outside of its notional space. This interaction and the way the events are reported fall

---

[85] For this norm see Constable (1970: 25).

[86] Sidonius' model for this sentiment may well be Pliny's obituary epistle for Junius Avitus (*Ep.* 8.23) at the end of which he claims that grief has overwhelmed his ability to write.

[87] The narratological implications remain even if in *Ep.* 8.6 and 8.11 Sidonius did in fact react to the arrival of news.

completely under the author's control. Sidonius accentuates the impact of these changes by the apparent formal end of the letter, as in *Ep.* 9.9, or by a beginning which quickly yields in significance to the new direction of the narrative, as in *Ep.* 8.11. Reading these changes as purely reflective of actual moments devalues the significance of his authorial control.

Changes in time and direction influence the narratives contained in the epistles by quickening the pace, drawing specific features into focus, or heightening the tension and drama of the plot. Arvandus sits on death row. Domitius endures the summer. Ricimer and the emperor's daughter are yet to couple. Each of these moments holds significance beyond the dating of the moment of composition: Arvandus is at his most pathetic, fully cognizant of the cost of his hubris and about to pay for it with his life. Domitius is at his most ridiculous, inappropriately attired for the summer heat and engaged in unsuitable activities, teaching in the city when he ought to be enjoying the cool waters of Sidonius' baths. Rome is in disarray, a microcosm of what may happen to the empire in the West under the dominion of Ricimer and Anthemius.

Sidonius' audience of contemporaries and posterity is thus encouraged to be sympathetic to Arvandus, to laugh and gloat at Domitius, and to wonder nervously about the fate of the Empire under Anthemius and Ricimer. In narratological terms, because Sidonius manipulates time at the level of the telling, he runs no risk of upsetting contemporaries with a version of events that would jar with their (perhaps more complete) knowledge of Arvandus' story (including the pardoning of his death sentence), as the elements of Sidonius' narrative are filtered through his perspective and fixed to a specific moment in time. The temporality of these epistles is thus integral to their reading, and evidence of Sidonius' careful arrangement of his epistolary narratives.

As time is a constant of every narrative, every epistolary author has the opportunity to manipulate it. Some seize this opportunity more than others; Pliny, for example, masterly uses time and perspective to structure and enhance his account of Vesuvius' explosion. Others barely use time. Seneca's collection, by way of contrast, is almost atemporal.[88] The extent to which authors use time reflects on how bound up their letters are in the events of their world. Thus, Seneca's minimal use of time may be read as part of his philosophical detachment from the Neronian court and an attempt perhaps to rehabilitate his image to posterity. Sidonius' extensive use of time throughout his collection brings his world alive; *causa*

---

[88] See pp. 75–76.

persona tempus provide not only their content, but excitement, contrast, and drama.

Each of Sidonius' epistles is liable to be read as an individual compositional unit, but they also form connections with each other, contained and arranged relative to one another in larger units such as books or the collection as a whole. The manipulation of epistles' temporality may impact not only the specific narrative of a single epistle, but also the narratives of these larger units. Sidonius' lack of a (consistent) chronological arrangement does not prevent a pseudo-biographical narrative being formed by the reading of consecutive epistles in sequence.[89] Certain epistles record watershed moments which in addition to their impact on Sidonius' life also impact the epistles that follow; examples include the fall of Clermont in *Ep.* 7.11 which alters the notional landscape of the remainder of the collection, and Sidonius' acknowledgement of his episcopal rank at the beginning of book 3 which places all subsequent epistles into the period of his episcopacy.[90]

In each case the manipulation of time inevitably draws attention to Sidonius' central importance to the narrative of the epistle. He thus carefully constructs a powerful image as a wise and able friend who uses his extensive learning to help others. The plot of the epistle swirls around his self-fashioning which is never overt enough to detract attention from the central narratives but instead intersects with them at crucial points. Ultimately Sidonius cultivates his persona as a widely read and engaging author.

---

[89] A similar effect is discernible in Pliny's collection, for which see Gibson and Morello (2012: 250): "The slipperiness of epistolary time ... helps Pliny convey a loose chronology for the work, a vague sense both of quasi-historical record and of forward movement through life."

[90] See pp. 52 and 57. This cannot be proven definitively but the collection's maintenance of a largely consistent linear chronology guides the reader towards that assessment. Sidonius never expressly claims that any epistle included after *Ep.* 3.1 was written before his episocopacy.

CHAPTER 4

Reading Epistolary Characters

Sidonius' persona pervades every epistle,[1] interacting with a litany of other characters: bishops, clergy, aristocrats, kings, and emperors. This chapter considers these characters first and foremost as literary constructs, which function within the text as positive and negative *exempla* whose behaviour drives the plot of the epistle forward, creating and subverting an array of narratives set within the last decades of fifth-century Gaul. Sidonius' rich characterisation, like his manipulation of time, is symptomatic of his collection's close engagement with his world and the individuals that he met and interacted with during his life.

Sidonius exerts authorial control over how these characters are described. We have already seen how effective his manipulation of an addressee's character may be: in *Ep.* 2.2 Domitius is stuck in the city during summer, wrapped up in women's clothes, reading the part of the courtesan in Terence's *Eunuchus*.[2] One can hardly envisage that this is how Domitius hoped to be depicted and, for that matter, memorialised in Sidonius' collection. If we deduce from this depiction of Domitius merely that he taught Terence we have surely missed Sidonius' humour, as he writes to Domitius about his enjoyment of his estate's baths and swimming pools.[3] The joke is generated by the disjunction between the addressee and the reader, who is free to laugh at Domitius along with Sidonius.[4] Domitius' depiction thus develops in contrast to Sidonius' and vice versa, as Sidonius fashions his epistolary self as the owner of an impressive estate able to enjoy aristocratic *otium*.[5] This kind of manipulation is not limited to just

---

[1] See pp. 9 and 19.
[2] See pp. 78–79.
[3] Visser (2014: 28, 30) offers a plain reading of Sidonius' depiction of Domitius.
[4] See p. 89.
[5] For this circular epistolary dynamic whereby the author's self is formed in contrast to others whose depictions in turn forms in contrast to the author's see De Pretis (2003: 137).

the addressee; in *Ep.* 2.9 Sidonius' criticism extends to his recent hosts who must live down the ignominy of their shoddy baths.[6]

Unlike Pliny, Sidonius rarely provides background information for the reader unless it is directly necessary for the narrative. Consequently, many of the more minor characters in the collection remain "otherwise unknown."[7] Occasionally Sidonius' remarks about such figures resonate with his wider audience rather than the named addressee. Critics have found these conceits particularly jarring, such as when Sidonius reminds Turnus in *Ep.* 4.24 that his father Turpio was a praetor – Turnus was certainly already aware of that fact, but Sidonius' comments are surely directed at his other readers who otherwise (like us) may not have known who Turnus was and what office his father had obtained.[8]

An individual's depiction may also have fictitious elements. *Ep.* 3.13, for example, offers a detailed invective-laden description of "Gnatho" whose name Sidonius likely borrowed from the parasite in Terence's *Eunuchus*.[9] The literary providence of this name and the unlikelihood of any individual exhibiting all of the negative features Sidonius lists has inhibited reading Gnatho as anything other than a fictional construct, but Sidonius could well have substituted in Gnatho for the original name in the letter, or relied on his son Apollinaris, and readers, to know who Gnatho really was.[10]

---

[6] See pp. 25–27.

[7] See for example *Ep.* 9.6.1: "quid loquar nomen personam? tu recognosces cuncta" (Why should I mention the person by name? You will recognise all the details).

[8] *Ep.* 4.24.1: "Bene nomini, bene negotio tuo congruit Mantuani illud: 'Turne, quod optanti divum promittere nemo auderet, volvenda dies en attulit ultro.' pecuniam pater tuus Turpio, vir tribunicius, mutuam pridem, si recordaris, a Maximo Palatino postulavit impetravitque" (This remark of the Mantuan suits your name well, and your business. "Turnus, what none of the gods dared to promise when you ask, look, the changing of the day has on its own provided"). As Anderson and Warmington (1963: 156n2) noted Sidonius hardly needed to remind Turnus as to his father's rank. Sidonius does not write *vir tribunicius* for Turnus' benefit, but for that of his wider audience, who may not have known who Turpio was. Mathisen (1979: 170) plausibly suggests that Sidonius' lack of clarity as to when Turpio held this office may indicate that it occurred in Avitus' reign. This epistolary necessity is also met by Pliny who mentions facts to an addressee (which the addressee surely knew) for the benefit of his wider readership. Bodel (2015: 8) cites Pliny *Ep.* 3.8.1 as an example of Pliny's use of a "sufficiently distinctive onomastic formula to identify the person for the general reader, even in cases where such specificity would hardly have been necessary for the addressee." For analysis of *Ep* 4.24 see pp. 153–155 and 164–165.

[9] Giannotti (2016: 227). The proverbial use of the name *Gnatho* also occurs in Cicero's *Lael.* 94, but there it is in the plural. See Bertocchi and Maraldi (2006: 91).

[10] According to Anderson and Warmington (1963: 47) "This show-piece likely does not allude to an actually existing person." And Faral (1946 569) says, "cette étrange alliance d'une extrême préciosité et d'un realisme violent font de la pièce une véritable curiosité, qui ne pouvait manquer de retenir l'attention du lecteur" (The strange combination of extreme affectation and graphic violence makes this piece a real curiosity, which could not fail to attract the attention of the reader). Salmon (1961: 520) analyses the influence of Sidonius' Gnatho portrait on the "Wild Man" archetype of medieval literature, noting how smoothly such stories "transition from realism to fantasy." See also

The invective against the Gallo-Roman official Seronatus in *Ep.* 2.1 forms a worthwhile comparandum.[11] Seronatus' description is as hyperbolic and figurative as the treatment of Gnatho; one can hardly envisage Seronatus actually drinking the blood of the local inhabitants, or getting up to the daily mischief which Sidonius lists.[12] The historicity of Sidonius' description of Seronatus, however, has been widely acknowledged (albeit with some allowance for literary embellishment).[13] Scholarship's different treatment of these two characters rests purely on the authenticity of their names, not on the differing degrees of realism in Sidonius' invectives. Seronatus' name (like Gnatho's) fulfils a literary function enabling Sidonius to create a Varro-like etymology (2.1.1)[14]:

> Seronati, inquam: de cuius ut primum etiam nomine loquar, sic mihi videtur quasi praescia futurorum lusisse fortuna, sicuti ex adverso maiores nostri proelia, quibus nihil est foedius, bella dixerunt; quippe etiam pari contrarietate fata, quia non parcerent, Parcas vocitavere.

Ziolkowski (1984: 2–12). Sidonius was not beyond using a literary allusion to refer to a specific person, in *Ep.* 1.11.5 for example Chremes refers to Paeonius, for which see McDonough (1986: 810) and Blänsdorf (1993: 128).

[11] Seronatus was the *vicarius septem provinciarum*, see Mathisen (1979: 169n16); PLRE "Seronatus." His depiction is often compared to Arvandus; see for example Germain (1840: 25), who considered Arvandus a worthy rival to Seronatus. For more recent treatments see Teitler (1992: 316), Heather (1992: 92), and Sarti (2011: 127–128). Furbetta (2014–2015a: 148–149) posits that Sidonius' criticism of Seronatus is based on his dislike of informers.

[12] Goffart's (1980: 246) assessment of *Ep.* 5.13 is equally applicable to *Ep.* 2.1, "The passage is not a factual enumeration of Seronatus' actions, but a highly rhetorical indictment of his character and administration, which should be interpreted accordingly." Still, as Goffart (2006: 133) shows, in conjunction with other evidence the depiction may be used in a limited way.

[13] Rousseau (1976: 364). See also Teitler (1992: 317): "I assume that Sidonius' information [regarding Arvandus and Seronatus], though biased and not at all clear, is basically trustworthy." F.-M. Kaufmann (1995: 127) and Percival (1997: 289) focus on Sidonius' mention of the potholes in Seronatus' way, which Percival asserts "are an incidental, though vivid, detail." Prevot (1999: 69) focuses on Seronatus' sympathy for the Visigoths. The positivist approach to Seronatus' depiction has a long history, stretching back at least as far as De Saavedra Fajardo's 1664 *Corona Gothica*, for which see Villacañas Berlanga's (2008: 181–182) edition. De Saavedra Fajardo used this epistle to substantiate the claim that Theodoric II wrote the first Gothic legal code, citing Sidonius' description of Seronatus' idiotic ways, which includes (*Ep.* 2.1.3): "[Seronatus] leges Theodosianos calcans, Theodoricianasque proponens" ([Seronatus] trampling on the laws of Theodosius and proposing the laws of Theodoric). Harries' (1994: 126n6) assessment is more discerning: "Sidonius' rhetorical complaint in 469 against the evil *vicarius* Seronatus … demonstrates Sidonius' love of assonance, not the existence of a 'Code of Theodoric'."

[14] Sidonius could well be calling Varro out on his more unlikely etymologies, rather than simply applying the rule that names sometimes indicate direct opposites. This etymology is cited by Jerome in *Ep.* 78.35 as coming from Varro, although his source is likely to have been Donatus' *Ars maior* 3.6, for which see Graves (2007: 15). Isidore of Seville 8.11.93 likely follows Jerome in listing this example in a category labelled κατ' ἀντίφρασιν.

> I will say something about Seronatus' name at the very start, it seems to
> me that fortune as if aware of the future played a game, in the manner of
> how our ancestors called wars – the worst of all – *bella* (beautiful) and with
> the same contrarianism called the fates *Parcae* (sparing) because they do
> not spare.

The pun indicates that the literal meaning of "Seronatus" (born-late)
contradicts his underdeveloped personality. It clearly only works if
Seronatus is named.[15] There is likely to have been some risk for Sidonius
in naming and shaming Seronatus in book 2 of the epistles, which was
circulated prior to Sidonius' bishopric at a time when Seronatus may
well have held provincial office.[16] In *Ep.* 5.13 Sidonius references this risk
(5.13.4): "ceteri affligi per suprascriptum damno verentur; mihi latronis et
beneficia suspecta sunt" (others fear to be damaged by the aforementioned
[Seronatus] but to me even the favours of a robber are suspect). His last
mention in the collection occurs in *Ep.* 7.7 where Sidonius mentions frustration at the dithering over Seronatus' execution, which is perhaps the
only silver lining of that letter; a gratuitous and grisly end to the narrative
arc of Seronatus, one which Arvandus was spared.[17]

Sidonius' *paideia* informed the literary and fictitious elements of these
characters. In *Ep.* 5.13, for example, he likens Seronatus to the worst of the
worst, worse than Cacus, the Furies, Verres, or Catiline, the last of which
Sidonius directly links to Seronatus, who, like Sallust's Catiline, drinks
wine mixed with blood.[18] The comments develop Sidonius' assertion in *Ep.*
2.1 that Seronatus is the Catiline of his age (*ipse Catilina saeculi nostri*).[19]
That Seronatus was a historical figure should not limit us in considering the
character Sidonius establishes for Seronatus in his epistles, as the ultimate
villain, a Regulus figure to Sidonius' Pliny, a Roman who abused his office,
engaged in treason, and masqueraded as part of the Gallo-Roman literati.[20]
Conversely, Gnatho's name must not be the only lens through which we
read *Ep.* 3.13, which may tell us far more about Sidonius' own frustrations

---

[15] Gibson (2011: 658): "[Sidonius] was a notorious punster." For a survey of this phenomenon in late
antiquity see Gualandri (2017: 129–131).

[16] For the chronology of the circulation of the epistles see pp. 170–176.

[17] For this comparison see p. 93.

[18] *Ep.* 5.13.3. Gualandri (1979: 122) cites Sallust *Cat.* 22.1 as Sidonius' allusive target, for discussion
of which see also Fascione (2016: 454-4) and Montone (2017: 25). Thome (1993: 57n113) places
Sidonius' beast metaphor in a useful broader literary context.

[19] Schwitter (2015: 83) draws out the ethical implications for Sidonius and his circle of Seronatus' lack
of education.

[20] Kulikowski (2012: 55n11) doubts the historial reliability of Sidonius' rhetoric against Seronatus'
treason.

regarding the corruption of public office holders, education, and morality in Late Antique Gaul than it can about "Gnatho."

This chapter examines Sidonius' portrayal of key figures in the collection: the Visigothic kings Theodoric II and his successor Euric; emperors from Petronius Maximus to Julius Nepos, his friends Lampridius, Ferreolus, and Constantius; and two holy exempla – the widow Eutropia and the archbishop Patiens.[21] Each of these may be read as literary constructs which function within the text and collaborate with one another to create narratives distinct from the specific concerns of his self-fashioning: the changes to the Visigothic kingdom of Toulouse and Roman Gaul, the gradual waning of imperial power, the actions of the Gallo-Roman nobility, and the right and wrongs of the clergy.

Skin-Clad Monarchs: The Rise of the Visigothic Kingdom of Toulouse

Scholarship has held a long interest in Sidonius' description of barbarians in his epistles, especially the Visigothic kings Theodoric II and his brother, murderer, and successor Euric I.[22] In the twentieth century historical debate tried to uncover Sidonius' "real" views on the barbarians, as either the future rulers of medieval Europe or the destroyers of Western civilisation.[23] Uncovering the biases that prompted these works is important, but their methodology still demands re-evaluation and, ultimately, complete refutation.

The modern reader of Sidonius' collection enjoys privileges that the author himself could not have envisaged as he wrote and responded to the immediacy of his present concerns. The portrait of Theodoric, included in the second epistle in the collection, was of some use to Sidonius; it showcased Sidonius' effective engagement with an important political player and diminished the relative difference between Sidonius' Roman Catholicism

---

[21] Ash's (2013) study of Regulus' role in Pliny's collection shows the benefits of reading recurring figures in epistolary collections as literary characters.

[22] Theodoric II has been of particular interest, for the historicity of which see, for example, Chadwick (1955: 310), Loyen (1970a: xli), Reydellet (1981: 71–74), Sivan (1989: 84–90), Harries (1994: 13, 143–144), Heather (1999: 243), Sirks (1996: 154), F-M. Kaufmann (1995: 116), and Castellanos (2013: 284–285). For the literary aspects of Sidonius' description of Theodoric (*Ep* 1.2) see Staubach (1983: 14), Köhler (1995:121), Halsall (2002: 98), and Kitchen (2010: 53–66). Sidonius' description of Sigismer, a barbarian leader, but not Visigothic, has received substantially less attention.

[23] Schuster (1940: 119–126), Bonjour (1981: 109–118), Staubach (1983: 1–16), Sivonen (1997: 430–432), and F-M. Kaufmann (1995). Delaplace (2012: 278) has identified the impact of French historiography in particular on the terms used to describe the Visigothic acquisition of Roman Auvergne.

and Theodoric's Visigothic Arianism.[24] Praise and haughty critiques of the king's habits appear in equal measure: Theodoric is depicted as an adept hunter, but a loot-obsessed hoarder, a regularly frugal diner most of the time, whose gluttonous ways on feast days were notorious.[25] The utility of this epistle was perhaps recycled upon its subsequent arrangement into the first book of epistles, circulated sometime prior to Sidonius' episcopacy, as a reminder to Theodoric's successor Euric that the brother whom he murdered had been a welcome *foederatus* of Roman Gaul.[26]

At some point after the ceding of Clermont to the Visigoths (post 474) when he was wallowing under the terms of his arrest on Euric's orders, Sidonius perhaps had cause to regret his widely circulated portrait of Euric's predecessor, not that anything could really be done to wind that back. Instead Sidonius responded to a new set of circumstances, reluctantly taking it upon himself to include a short panegyrical verse in an epistle, which he promptly sent off to his friend Lampridius, who had managed to manoeuvre his way into the king's good graces.[27] Reading a continuum between that verse and Theodoric's portrait ignores wholeheartedly the specific and immediate nature of Sidonius' concerns.[28] In an earlier epistle (7.6), Sidonius had been forthright in condemning Euric's supposedly militant Arianism, again in response to immediate circumstances, principally the negotiations between the king and a group of four Gallo-Roman bishops appointed to negotiate on the emperor's behalf, one of whom was his addressee Graecus (Sidonius provides this context for the reader at the end of the epistle).[29] Sidonius could ill afford to have a single view of barbarians, as he interacted with them on a political and diplomatic level.[30]

---

[24] Theodoric's portrayal in Avitus' panegyric (*Carm.* 7), delivered 1 January 456 is overwhelmingly positive, understandably given Theodoric played a critical role in Avitus' ascension to the purple, for which see p. 4. Reading the epistle alongside the panegyric may smooth over the complexity of Sidonius' depiction of Theodoric in the epistle. Furbetta (2014–2015a: 137–145), for example, draws extensively on Theodoric's depiction in the panegyric to inform her reading of the epistle, and in so doing focuses on the positive elements to the exclusion of negative features.

[25] *Ep.* 1.2.4–9, Köhler (1995: 151–152).

[26] Sivan (1989: 91–94) and Köhler (1995: 139). Kitchen's (2010: 60) analysis overly extends this argument. Furbetta (2014–2015a: 140) argues for the circulation of the epistle in the late 460s. For Euric's murder of Theodoric II see Heather (1992: 88) and Collins (2008: 113).

[27] See p. 136 for the structural connection between *Ep.* 8.9 and 8.11 both of which pertain to Lampridius. For Sidonius' imprisonment and subsequent release see p. 176 and Hanaghan (forthcoming).

[28] Wood (1992: 12) rightly criticises the validity of that approach.

[29] Van Waarden (2010: 274–276) and Barcellona (2013: 17–18).

[30] Denecker (2015: 418) argues that Sidonius was "strongly biased by the stereotypes he holds of 'barbarians' and members of lower social classes." Castellanos (2013: 202) rightly cautions against making such generalisations "La evidencia que manejamos es lo que estos tipos *quisieron que circulara* en textos que se leían y se copiaban entre la elite aristocrática y clerical" (The evidence we use is what these individuals *wanted to circulate* in texts which were read and copied among the aristocratic

Nevertheless, the juxtaposition of these two letters within the collection opens up the possibility for the reader to create a narrative about Theodoric and Euric. This narrative is not wholly controlled by Sidonius nor completely open-ended. The epistolary theorist Elizabeth Macarthur emphasised that a distinction must be made between "the audible voice of the narrator" heard in each epistle, and the "implied author" – the arranger of the epistles into a collection.[31] Sidonius' control over this narrative is exerted through both these roles. In *Ep.* 8.9, for example, Sidonius stresses to Lampridius the compulsion under which he has written the verses in praise of Euric (*Ep.* 8.9.2–4):

> sed hoc tu munificentia regia satis abutens iam securus post munera facis, quia forsitan satiricum illud de satirico non recordaris: "satur est cum dicit Horatius 'Euhoe'." quid multis? merito me cantare ex otio iubes, quia te iam saltare delectat. quicquid illud est, pareo tamen, idque non modo non coactus verum etiam spontaliter facio … me tamen nequaquam sollicitudo permittit aliud nunc habere in actione, aliud in carmine.

> but you do this taking full advantage of the king's munificence, after receiving some of his gifts you are now free from care, perhaps because you do not recall one satirist's remark about another: "Horace is sated when he says 'Euhoe'." What's the point? You are ordering me to sing for your "deserved" pleasure because it pleases you to dance.[32] However that works, I still obey, I do so not only unforced, but even on my own accord … my anxiety still does not all allow me to conduct myself one way in reality and another way in verse.

Sidonius' claim that he writes the verse on his own accord (*spontaliter*) and not under compulsion (*non coactus*) draws attention to the compelling circumstances of his present circumstances, specifically the anxiety (*sollicitudo*) that dogs him: unable to get repeated audiences with Euric

---

and clerical elite) (emphasis in the original). In addition to being methodologically flawed, such generalisations are fraught with inconsistencies, such as Sidonius' largely positive portrayal of the Visigothic king Theodoric II in *Ep.* 1.2. Furbetta (2014–2015a: 136–148) similarly constructs a continuum between Theodoric's depiction in *Ep.* 1.2 and in *Carm.* 7, but then chooses to separate the description of the Burgundians in *Carm.* 12 from their description in *Ep.* 5.7. Schwitter (2015: 264–265) rightly notes that the complexity and constructed nature of Sidonius' persona prevents the reader from deducing firm views as to his political beliefs or character traits. Wickham (2005: 80) focuses on the central role that changing contexts played in Sidonius developing a variety of positive and negative depiction of barbarians. These various depictions prompt Castellanos (2013: 281) to characterise Sidonius' attitude to the barbarians as ambivalent, but even this moderate claim cannot be deduced with any certainty.

[31] Macarthur (1990: 10), for discussion of which see Hanaghan (forthcoming).

[32] The emphatic position of *merito* has prompted the speech marks around "deserved."

to plead his case directly, instead he must hope that his verses sufficiently impress Lampridius and placate the king.[33] Sidonius' reluctant voice as narrator is all but replaced by the defiant survivalism of his role as "implied author" who unashamedly included the epistle in his eighth book, as the final letter to reference the Visigothic acquisition of Roman Gaul, providing a degree of closure to a narrative in which he tried to prevent the end of Roman Gaul but ultimately failed.[34] The template for the next generation is readily discernible; constructive engagement with the barbarian successor kingdoms has become a political reality; Arvandus now merely seems a few years ahead of his time.[35] The continuum is there to be read: perhaps the grovelling of *Ep.* 8.9 was aimed at making up for the stinging rebuke of Euric in *Ep.* 7.6, in which Sidonius fixates at length on the king's supposedly radical Arianism and Sidonius' direct involvement in resisting Euric's attacks on Clermont.[36] But it is the reader's continuum, the reader's filling in the blanks that knits these disparate epistles into a consistent narrative.

Well before Euric became the Arian monster of *Ep.* 7.6, and the object of Sidonius' momentary sycophancy in *Ep.* 8.9, he is referred to simply as an unnamed king; in *Ep.* 1.7 Arvandus' letter to the Visigoths is described as (*Ep.* 1.7.5) "quam iram regi feroci, placido verecundiam inferrent" (provoking a ferocious king to anger, and a placid one to shame).[37] The king is not named – it must be Euric – but the question remains as to which king

[33] Schwitter (2015: 276) and Gibson (2013c: 215). Sidonius complains at *Ep.* 8.9.5 that the verses would be better if delivered by him in person. In the verse insertion he describes his struggle to gain access to Euric (vv. 17): "[nos] non istic positos semelque visos" ([I am kept] here seen but once); *positus* is clearly a euphemistic take on his incarceration. For his attempted use of Lampridius see Pérez Sánchez (1997: 237).

[34] Schwitter (2015: 280) argues that the main point of the letter is Lampridius' survival strategy (*Überlebensstratagie*) but the focus is equally on Sidonius' belated attempts to weasel his way out the king's bad graces. Wolff (2015a: 196) shows how the epistolary dynamic of *Ep.* 8.9 – Sidonius' grovelling at Lampridius – is reversed by *Ep.* 8.11 in which Sidonius plays the respectable bishop to Lampridius who is clearly depicted as a victim of his slaves and love of astrology, for which see p. 125.

[35] Heather (2005: 340) notes the "military collaboration" of certain Romans with the Visigoths shortly after Arvandus' trial, citing Vincentius' command over Euric's forces in Spain in 473. Individual Romans collaborating with the Visigoths is markedly different from Roman officials doing so on behalf of their command. The term "collaborating" is of limited use since it implies a political betrayal rather than an adaption to a new political reality and constructs a false and overly neat dichotomy between collaboration and resistance. Its use in scholarship, alongside "resistance," may be a remnant of the events of the twentieth century, for another example of which see p. 6n6.

[36] Wood (1992: 12).

[37] Martínez (2014: 117–126) provides a useful synopsis of the geopolitical situation at this precise point. Köhler (1995: 242) argues that *ferox* has positive connotations.

Euric is supposed to be, the ferocious monarch provoked to anger, or the placid one ashamed at his lack of inactivity.[38]

Euric's queen Ragnahilda is named in the collection before he is. In *Ep.* 4.8 Sidonius provides Euodius with a verse to be inscribed on a bowl as a gift for Ragnahilda.[39] Euodius is en route to Toulouse on the order of the king (*rege mandante*).[40] Sidonius narrates Euodius' intention to inscribe the verse on a shell-shaped bowl and then summarises his likely political stratagem[41] (*Ep.* 4.8.5):

> quarum puto destinas vel ventribus pandis singulos versus vel curvis meliore consilio, si id magis deceat, capitibus inscribere; istoque cultu expolitam reginae Ragnahildae disponis offerre, votis nimirum tuis pariter atque actibus patrocinium invictum praeparaturus.

> I suppose that you intend to inscribe individual lines on the undulating bulges of these channels, or better still, if it seems more appropriate, on their curved ridges; you intend to offer Queen Ragnahilda the basin adorned by this refinement, hoping no doubt to secure her irresistible support both for your ambitions and actions.

Euodius hopes to influence the Visigothic court with a good silver bowl.[42] The epistle ends by haughtily acknowledging as much (*Ep.* 4.8.5): "namque in foro tali sive Athenaeo plus charta vestra quam nostra scriptura laudabitur. vale" (for in such forum your writing material will be praised more than my writing). The topos of authorial humility does not wholly exempt the Visigothic court from the implication that shining metals are more valued there than literary culture.[43]

---

[38] *Ep.* 1.7 is dated to 468, see Köhler (1995: 229), two years after Theodoric's death in 466. Sidonius gives Theodoric's murder the same coat of whitewash as Avitus'. Mathisen and Sivan (1999: 28) argue that the epistle indicates the growing power and patronage of the Visigothic court.

[39] For the temporality of this epistle see pp. 81–82, for the verse insertions see Wolff (2014b: 214).

[40] *Ep.* 4.8.1.

[41] Janes (1998: 39) cites Euodius' bowl as an example of the prevalence of "personal gifts ... within high society." Such a reading devalues the political advantage Euodius hopes to gain by way of the gift.

[42] Wolfram (1990: 206, 212, 224) and Hartmann (2009: 19) argue that this epistle indicates that Ragnahilda had some level of education. This is an overly optimistic assessment of Sidonius' assertion that the Visigothic court will be more interested in the bowl than his lines of verse. Wolff (2014b: 214) argues instead that Sidonius' claim highlights the absence of culture among the Visigoths. Williams (2014: 358) takes this claim at face value. Becker-Piriou (2008: 524–525) places Ragnahilda's apparent importance in the broader context of queens developing diplomatic influence during this period.

[43] Gualandri (1979: 24) notes that Sidonius' negative remarks about the Visigothic court inhibit reading this epistle as an indication of his respect for the court. Circulating this epistle post 477 would at least show his fellow Gallo-Romans that the verses do not reflect his attitude towards Ragnahilda and Euric, who had imprisoned him (prior to the epistle's circulation if not composition).

Sidonius' eventual naming of Euric in *Ep.* 7.6 comes only after a lengthy preamble (7.6.2–4):

> tibi defleo, qualiter ecclesiasticas caulas istius aetatis lupus, qui peccatis pereuntium saginatur animarum, clandestino morsu necdum intellecti dentis arrodat. namque hostis antiquus, quo facilius insultet balatibus ovium destitutarum, dormitantum prius incipit cervicibus imminere pastorum. […] Evarix, rex Gothorum, quod limitem regni sui rupto dissolutoque foedere antiquo vel tutatur armorum iure vel promovet.
>
> I lament to you how the wolf of this age, who feasts on the sins of dying souls, snaps at the sheepfolds of the Church with the secret bite of a jaw as yet unnoticed. For the old enemy, so as to jump more easily at the bleating of the abandoned sheep, first of all begins by threatening the necks of the sleeping shepherds … since the old treaty is broken and dissolved Euric the king of the Visigoths is defending or rather extending the boundaries of his kingdom by the force of arms.

The biblical pastoral metaphor suits Sidonius' assertions of the king's virulent Arianism.[44] Sidonius depicts Euric as targeting the Church's leadership and presents himself as uniquely able to perceive the otherwise hidden threat posed by the "old enemy," a term used in Christian texts to refer to the devil.[45] A clear contrast is developed between Sidonius' perspicuity and other bishops' inability to recognise the threat that Euric posed. This contrast is all the stronger given his fellow Gallic bishops' subsequent agreement with Euric to secede his see, which is reported by Sidonius in the very next epistle in the collection.[46] Euric's language has not deceived Sidonius; uncalled for protection is nothing short of invasion. Yet apart from writing of his grievances to Basilius to goad him into action and raise awareness of the changes that are taking place in Roman Gaul there is nothing much that Sidonius can do about it. He carefully marginalises the apparent importance of his geopolitical concerns, making out that Euric's non-Catholic faith is of greater concern (7.6.6):

---

[44] Sidonius' rhetoric, which focuses on Euric's supposedly unbending Arianist persecution of Catholics, tries to conflate the Roman state with the Church, and barbarianism with heresy, see Wood (1992: 12), Santos (1997: 103–104), Barcellona (2013: 17–18), Schwitter (2015: 271), and Hanaghan (forthcoming). For these negotiations see Jiménez Sánchez (2003: 129–130).

[45] Furbetta (2014–2015a: 142), Van Waarden (2010: 291), and Schwitter (2015: 271).

[46] *Ep.* 7.7.2: "facta est servitus nostra pretium securitatis alienae" (Our enslavery has been made the price for others' security). See Mathisen (1993a: 170), Van Waarden (2010: 346), and Castellanos (2013: 177). The presence of *pro dolor* in both epistles, which is noted by Van Waarden (2010: 346), provides an additional link between them. For a critical assessment of Sidonius' evidence for these negotiations see Becker (2014b: 50–52).

sed, quod fatendum est, praefatum regem Gothorum, quamquam sit ob virium merita terribilis, non tam Romanis moenibus quam legibus Christianis insidiaturum pavesco. tantum, ut ferunt, ori, tantum pectori suo catholici mentio nominis acet, ut ambigas ampliusne suae gentis an suae sectae teneat principatum.

but it must be confessed that the aforementioned king of the Visigoths, although he is worth fearing due to his military might, I fear him not so much because he intends to attack our Roman walls but more because he intends to attack our Christian laws. They say that the mention of the name Catholic is so bitter to his mouth, so bitter to his heart, that you would be unsure whether he was the head of his race or the head of his sect.

Sidonius deploys alarmist rhetoric which makes the epistle more exciting and desperate.[47] His reference to Euric as the "aforementioned king of the Goths" (*praefatum regem Gothorum*) distinguishes Euric and the other *rex Gothorum* Theodoric, whose lukewarm Arianism went hand-in-hand with his friendly diplomatic relations with Rome (*Ep.* 1.2.4):[48]

antelucanos sacerdotum suorum coetus minimo comitatu expetit, grandi sedulitate veneratur. quamquam, si sermo secretus, possis animo advertere, quod servet istam pro consuetudine potius quam pro ratione reverentiam.

he seeks out the pre-dawn meetings of his priests with a very small retinue and worships with abundant eagerness. Although if a word may be had privately, you can notice that he keeps this worship up out of habit rather than conviction.

The contrast with Euric is acute; Theodoric worshipped regularly but no real conviction underpins his practice.[49] The brothers' different degrees of Arianism correlate with the status of their relationship to Rome; Theodoric largely behaves as a good *foederatus* should whereas Euric does not.[50]

The praise of Theodoric assists Sidonius' own self-fashioning as an effective diplomat to the Visigothic court.[51] A game of backgammon

---

[47] Castellanos (2013: 176). Tellingly Sidonius preserved his critical tone of Euric in this epistle when it was arranged and circulated after the king released him from prison in the late 470s.

[48] Harries (1994: 128–129), Bellès (1999: 42n62), and Castellanos (2013: 150).

[49] Schwitter (2015: 272) notes the positive aspects of Sidonius' description of the king such as at *Ep.* 7.6.6: "armis potens acer animis alacer annis" (Powerful in arms, sharp of mind, quick for his age). Euric would have been in his mid thirties when Sidonius wrote these remarks. These comments function predominantly to accentuate his disappointment at Euric's bellicose actions and heretical beliefs.

[50] Schwitter (2015: 274).

[51] Harries (1994:143–144) and (1996: 31–44), Köhler (1995: 119), F. M. Kaufmann (1995: 121–123), Loyen (1970a: 4), Stevens (1933: 23), and Reydellet (1981: 71–77).

between Sidonius and the king reads initially as a metaphor for their diplomacy (1.2.7–8):[52]

> quibus horis viro tabula cordi, tesseras colligit rapide, inspicit sollicite, volvit argute, mittit instanter, ioculariter compellat, patienter exspectat. in bonis iactibus tacet, in malis ridet, in neutris irascitur, in utrisque philosophatur.

> In the hours when his heart fixes on the gaming board, he collects the tiles quickly, inspects them carefully, turns them over skilfully, throws them immediately, urges them on jokingly, awaits them patiently. On good throws he is quiet, on bad throws he smiles, on neither is he angry, on both philosophical.

The game ends as the very means by which he succeeds at his diplomatic negotiations with the king (*Ep.* 1.2.8):

> quodque mirere, saepe illa laetitia minimis occasionibus veniens ingentium negotiorum merita fortunat. tunc petitionibus diu ante per patrociniorum naufragia iactatis absolutionis subitae portus aperitur. tunc etiam ego aliquid obsecraturus feliciter vincor, quando mihi ad hoc tabula perit, ut causa salvetur.

> and this may amaze you, often the happiness that comes on these insignificant occasions influences positively the outcome of major negotiations. At such times I am happily beaten if I hope to obtain something, hence my game is lost at that moment so my cause may be saved.

Theodoric is paraded as Sidonius' puppet on important matters, influenced with ease for the paltry sum of a thrown game of backgammon.[53] Sidonius can see the real game that is being played, a view which he shares with the reader.[54]

Sidonius' description of the Visigothic leaders contrasts strongly with the only clearly encomiastic treatment of barbarians in the epistles, which focuses on Sigismer, a prince (*regius iuvenis*), probably a Frank, who was looking to marry into the Burgundian court.[55] In *Ep.* 4.20 Sidonius' offers an autoptic description of the prince as he rides past with his entourage to visit the palace of his beloved's father. The circumstances are not exactly

---

[52] The game is backgammon not simply dice, contra Mathisen and Sivan (1999: 28). Dice on its own would not work well as a metaphor for diplomacy.

[53] Gualandri (1979: 23) notes the absence of any mention in this epistle to the king's learning or interest in literature. This absence may correspond to Sidonius' outsmarting of the king over the game of backgammon.

[54] Sidonius' manipulation of the king should not detract from some of the positive traits he ascribes to Theodoric through the style of his play. Goncalves (2013: 261) lists *virtus, moderatio* and *prudentia*.

[55] Pohl (2006: 125n69). Liebeschuetz (2015: 157–158) compares aspects of Sigismer's appearance to other barbarians described by Sidonius.

clear. Sidonius appears initially to equivocate as to whether the couple are courting or already married, and does not describe who the father was, beyond a vague reference to his *praetorium* which probably refers to a palace.[56] Sigismer is an impressive sight, resplendent in red, white, and yellow clothing that matches his blonde hair, ruddy cheeks, and complexion. His entourage is heavily armed, a terrifying sight even in peace (*Ep.* 4.20.2: *in pace terribilis*). Sidonius sums up the effect on the viewer (*Ep.* 4.20.3): "cuncta prorsus huiusmodi, ut in actione thalamorum non appareret minor Martis pompa quam Veneris" (the whole effect was such that during the wedding the procession appeared to be no less Mars' than Venus').

The epistle may be read against Sidonius' portrayal of the Visigoths. The autoptic perspective that he adopts places Sidonius as the viewer at the Burgundian court, or at least attending a court other than the Visigoths. Sidonius' focus on the barbarians' warlike and threatening appearance even at a time of peace gains further importance from the political context of the late 460s and early 470s, when the Burgundians acted as a counter balance to further Visigothic expansion in Roman Gaul. Visigothic readers of *Ep.* 4.20, or rather, Visigothic advisers, would do well to note the swords, lances, missiles, and shields that the prince's courtiers and allies wear as apparel.[57]

The narrative continuum of Sidonius' depictions of barbarian royalty is constructed by the reader, but Sidonius' manipulation of the broader narrative is still discernible; Euric is clearly unlike Theodoric in many ways. Perhaps Theodoric was a diplomatic lightweight, and perhaps Euric was a virulent Arian; Sidonius' portrayal of these kings cannot be separated from the immediacy of his concerns and the moments in history when it suited Sidonius for Theodoric to appear as a ruler under his thumb, Ragnahilda as the queen through which Euric could be manipulated, and Euric as a sectarian violator of the Catholic faith.[58] Sidonius' persona plays a central role in these depictions, as the Roman diplomat who outwitted Theodoric, the wise bishop who called out Euric for what he was, and the gifted author who writes his way out of trouble. At each point Sidonius carefully manages the epistolary dynamic as well as he can to ensure his positive portrayal; even the grovelling praise of Euric comes across as a case of Sidonius doing what needed to be done.

[56] *Ep.* 4.20.1.
[57] *Ep.* 4.20.3: "eo quo comebantur ornatu muniebantur" (Their dress armed and decorated them).
[58] Wood (1992: 12).

Purpled Emperors: Characters in the Imperial Withdrawal from Roman Gaul

In his early career as a secular aristocrat Sidonius interacted directly with emperors; as a panegyrist for his father-in-law Avitus, Avitus' replacement Majorian, and Anthemius, and as an ambassador and adviser.[59] Their character portrayals emerge in the epistles from his (largely) sporadic references to them: Majorian appears astute and witty, Petronius Maximus an overly ambitious dunce, Anthemius an inept, haughty spendthrift, and Julius Nepos (eventually) as a just and reasonable emperor who follows through on commitments.[60] As Mathisen has adeptly shown, Sidonius' occasional oblique references to Avitus can also be read; given their close personal and political connection, direct mention of his deceased father-in-law may have been too painful or simply too dangerous.[61]

These character portrayals are set within a broader narrative of imperial disengagement from Roman Gaul, evident in the relative abundance of references to specific emperors and their office in the first book, and their gradual reduction culminating in Sidonius' remark in *Ep.* 7.7.4 that the emperor is now absent (*principe absente*).[62] The last contemporary reference to the office of emperor in the collection, at *Ep.* 8.7.2, makes gnomic assertions regarding the nature of its power.[63] There are no references at all to a Roman emperor in book nine, which reflects the political context in the early 480s when the book was likely compiled.[64]

The emperors in Sidonius' epistles can be read as reflections of his fluctuating attitudes towards imperial power and the individuals who wielded it. Sidonius was clearly aware that expressing sensitive opinions could have dire political repercussions, however, thus it is problematic to assume that Sidonius is expressing his "real" opinion about these powerful individuals. These characters reflect on Sidonius' self-fashioning, as a witty dinner companion of Majorian, an educated critic of Petronius Maximus, a (relatively)

---

[59] See pp. 4–6.
[60] The difference in these various portrayals makes it difficult to assert that Sidonius had a single conception of the nature of imperial power, as argued by Barnwell (1992: 15) and Reydellet (1981: 209).
[61] Mathisen (1979: 166): "Where he does refer to him [Avitus] he uses the circumlocution *socer* ... he studiously maintains silence on the emperor himself and makes only euphemistic references to his reign." The exception is *casus vel subsecutorum* in *Ep.* 2.13.3 for which see pp. 112–113.
[62] Gualandri (1979: 40–41).
[63] Contra Anderson and Warmington (1963: 434). Two uses of the word *princeps* in *Ep.* 8.7.2 refer to the office, not a specific individual.
[64] Mathisen (2013: 231).

brave knocker of Anthemius, and a supporter of Julius Nepos, especially when the latter promoted his brother-in-law Ecdicius.

The first emperor to feature in the epistles is Anthemius. In *Ep.* 1.5 Sidonius describes his arrival in Rome as Anthemius' daughter marries Ricimer.[65] Despite being summoned by imperial decree – Sidonius tell us he used the imperial post-horses – access to the emperor is impossible given the circumstances (1.5.10): "neque adhuc principis aulicorumque tumultuosis foribus observer" (nor yet am I observed by the chaotic doors of the emperor and palace attendants).[66] The noun *aulicus* conveys the negativity of court intrigue.[67] Anthemius' chaotic (*tumultuousus*) doors represent his power and authority.[68]

Read in isolation, this remark could perhaps be explained away by the specific circumstances of the moment; chaos has gripped the rest of Rome as the nuptial celebrations are in full swing. Read alongside other references to Anthemius in Sidonius' epistles, this first mention forms part of a larger narrative about the dysfunction of Anthemius' reign. In *Ep.* 1.9 Sidonius laments the pointlessness of the wedding celebration (§1): "post nuptias patricii Ricimeris, id est post imperii utriusque opes eventilitas, tandem reditum est in publicam serietatem, quae rebus actitandis ianuam campumque patefecit" (after the wedding of the patrician Ricimer, that is after the wealth of both empires had been scattered to the wind,[69] at last there has been a return to public seriousness, which has opened the door and widened the field for conducting business). The phrase *post imperii utriusque opes eventilatas* refers to the excessive celebrations that Sidonius described in *Ep.* 1.5.10–11. Its tone is negative; all the expense and fanfare has been pointlessly dissipated.[70]

Anthemius appears briefly in *Ep.* 1.7 as the emperor that Arvandus conspired to undermine by negotiating seperately with the Visigoths. In that epistle Sidonius ostensibly reports Arvandus' labelling of Anthemius as a *Graecus imperator*. The epithet is redundant unless its inclusion is meant to preserve the criticism that underpins Arvandus' remark (which

---

[65] Anthemius is not named but is clearly meant – Sidonius' contemporary audience would have certainly known that his daughter married Ricimer.

[66] *Ep.* 1.5.10. See Harries (1994: 142–145), MacGeorge (2002: 235–236), O'Flynn (1991: 125), and Croke (2014: 106). Mathisen (2009a: 145) lists other cases of intermarriage with barbarians; see also Blockley (1982: 64). See pp. 60–63 for the temporality of this epistle.

[67] Hanaghan (2017c: 646).

[68] Hanaghan (2017c: 646).

[69] Forcellinus and Facciolatus (1831: 197): "eventilitas, h. e. [hoc est] iactatas et dissipitas" (*eventilitas*, that is scattered and dissipated).

[70] Flomen (2009–10: 14) reads into this phrase Sidonius' resentment at Ricimer's focus on Italy.

Sidonius has repeated and so preserved). Similar more overt criticism of Anthemius occurs in Ennodius' *Life of Epiphanius* in which Anthemius is referred to as *Graeculus*, a diminutive which clearly had pejorative force.[71] Ennodius' criticism of Anthemius could be done relatively safely and so more openly, as Anthemius had died more than twenty years earlier.

Anthemius features in *Ep.* 2.1 as the emperor who has bankrupted Rome. This was not a new state of affairs. Avitus, for example, was forced to melt down bronze to pay his Visigothic bodyguards;[72] the Roman economy had never really recovered from the Vandal conquest of North Africa and the Western Roman army had dwindled in numbers for some time – the Vandal sack of 455 met no tangible resistance.[73] These comments play an important role in the developing character portrayal of Anthemius in the collection (*Ep.* 2.1.4): "si nullae a republica vires nulla praesidia si nullae quantum rumor est, Anthemii principis opes statuit te auctore nobilitas seu patriam dimittere seu capillos. Vale" (if there is no strength from the state, if no protection, if, as the rumour has it, the emperor Anthemius has no wealth, then the nobility under your advice has decided either to lose its homeland or its hair. Farewell).[74] Sidonius specifically links Rome's lack of human and pecuniary resources to Anthemius' rule. He cites his source: the rumour mill in Gaul is in overdrive; the state has run out of means. Clearly this is not a positive take on Anthemius' governance.[75]

---

[71] Ennodius *vita Epifani* 54. Castellanos (2013: 154, 227) and Hanaghan (2017c: 635–636). Boshoff (2016: 23) links Sidonius' (and Arvandus') comment (*Graecus imperator*) to Ennodius' (*Graeculus imperator*). Börm (2013: 111) extrapolates that a clear cultural difference existed between Anthemius and the Gallic and Italian aristocracy. The *Historia Augusta* records that some called Hadrian *Graeculus* (*HA* 1.1.5). This use may also have been pejorative.

[72] John of Antioch fr. 202: "Ἀπέπεμπε δὲ καὶ τοὺς Γότθους, οὓς ἐπὶ τῇ σφετέρᾳ ἐπήγετο φυλακῇ, χρημάτων αὐτοῖς ποιησάμενος διανομὴν ἐκ τῶν δημοσίων ἔργων, τοῖς ἐμπόροις χαλκὸν ἀποδόμενος· οὐ γὰρ χρυσίον ἐν τοῖς βασιλικοῖς ταμείοις ἔτυχεν ὄν" (He also sent away the Goths, whom he had brought as his own protection, and made a payment to them from public works through the sale of bronze to merchants; for there was no gold in the imperial treasuries). This translation is adapted from Mariev (2008: 412–413). Roberto (2017: 796) argues that Majorian's fourth novella (*De Aedificiis Publicis*) was written in reaction to Avitus' decision, which was deeply unpopular and resulted in his removal from office.

[73] As Roberto (2017: 779) argues, the Roman army had been in the city in March, but it presumably withdrew before Petronius Maximus was killed and the Vandals arrived, or it remained otherwise inactive during the sack. Pope Leo negotiated with the Vandals before they entered the city, perhaps to secure the rights of sanctuary, for which see Merrills and Miles (2010: 117).

[74] The loss of hair refers to joining the clergy, for discussion of which see Barcellona (2013: 19). Castellanos (2013: 199) dates this epistle's composition to after the defeat of the imperial fleet in June 468. This dating is possible but cannot be shown definitely. The remarks justify and foreshadow Sidonius' decision to become a bishop, which is mentioned for the first time in the collection in *Ep.* 3.1, for which see pp. 52 and 77.

[75] Oppedisano (2017: 1–23) argues that Anthemius' reign gained the support of the Roman senate. Sidonius' characterisation of Anthemius suggests that the emperor enjoyed less support in Gaul.

The reader can hardly feign surprise at Sidonius' remarks; in *Ep.* 1.9 his sober assessment of the fiscal damage of Anthemius' daughter's wedding to Ricimer had foreshadowed this very outcome.[76]

The last reference to Anthemius in the collection occurs in *Ep* 2.3. Sidonius praises Felix, a fellow Gallo-Roman aristocrat, for his recent promotion to the patriciate. He emphatically notes that credit for Felix's rise is due to him alone, not the emperor who has promoted him. While Anthemius is not explicitly named there can be no doubt that he is meant; the position of the epistle in the second book, which was circulated prior to Sidonius' episcopacy, clearly indicates as much. The close proximity of this epistle to *Ep.* 2.1 (which does name Anthemius) further prompts the reader to have Anthemius in mind (*Ep.* 2.3):

> sic quondam Quintum Fabium magistrum equitum dictatorio rigori et Papirianae superbiae favor publicus praetulit; sic et Gnaeum Pompeium super aemulos extulit numquam fastidita popularitas; sic invidiam Tiberianam pressit universitatis amore Germanicus. quocirca nolo sibi de successibus tuis principalia beneficia plurimum blandiantur, quae nihil tibi amplius conferre potuerunt, quam ut si id noluissimus, transiremus inviti.

> and so in the past public support promoted Quintus Fabius the master of the horse above the stern dictator and arrogant Papirius; and so in that way did Gnaeus Pompeius' popularity, which he never spurned, raise him above his rivals; and thus did Germanicus overcome Tiberius' jealously with universal love. So I do not want the emperor's kind deeds to get most of the credit for your success, because they could do nothing more for you than to make us reluctantly let you pass if we had not already wanted to do so.

Sidonius provides three historical exempla of public approval (*favor publicus*) promoting individuals; two of these – Quintus Fabius and Germanicus – develop implied comparisons with Anthemius. Quintus Fabius was a successful master of horse who had won a victory against the Samnites. He had not however been granted permission for the attack and so was subsequently condemned to death by Lucius Papirius who had been appointed dictator. In Livy's account Fabius' father, who had himself been dictator, railed against Papirius' outrageous conduct, castigating him for his arrogance and cruelty.[77] By comparing Felix to Fabius, Sidonius implies a comparison between Anthemius and Papirius, both of whom are not very competent, appear to abuse their power, and act in a haughty and

[76] See p. 63n16.
[77] Livy 8.33.

stern manner.[78] The comparison with Tiberius similarly reflects poorly on
Anthemius; whereas Felix like Germanicus enjoys the love of the people,
Tiberius, and by implication Anthemius, is defined and consumed by his
jealously.[79] Sidonius concludes the comparisons by explicitly asserting that
the emperor deserves no credit for Felix's rise.

Sidonius' critical portrayal of Anthemius, developed in the first two
books of epistles, is all the more significant given that these books were
(both probably) circulated prior to Sidonius' bishopric in late 469 or
early 470, when Anthemius was still very much alive, if heavily occupied
with the affairs of state.[80] Sidonius is clearly careful to avoid direct criticism of Anthemius, preferring to imply rather than assert it directly. The
negativity of his characterisation of Anthemius may indicate the limits of
the emperor's influence in Gaul in the late 460s. Sidonius' portrayal of
Anthemius was feasibly circulated after the disastrous destruction of the
imperial fleet by the Vandals circa June 468.[81] Evidently it suited Sidonius,
once he was safely back in Gaul, to publish epistles which distanced himself from the propaganda of Anthemius' regime.[82]

In the first two books Sidonius includes two more character portrayals
of emperors from the vantage of hindsight: one for Majorian in *Ep.* 1.11 and
the other for Petronius Maximus in *Ep.* 2.13.[83] *Ep.* 1.11 begins with Sidonius'
refusal to send the addressee Montius a satire on the basis that he does
not write them and has never done so.[84] The prelude leads into a narrative
account of an episode when Sidonius was accused of writing a satire (*Ep.*
1.11.2): "temporibus Augusti Maioriani venit in medium charta comitatum,
sed carens indice, versuum plena satiricorum mordacium, sane qui satis

[78] Sidonius' portrayal is in keeping with Livy's, but that is not to say that Sidonius drew directly on
Livy's account, he may well have read a depiction of Papirius that was itself informed by Livy or
the same critical tradition. For Sidonius' knowledge of Livy and allusions to him elsewhere in the
corpus see Mratschek (2013: 259) and Geisler (1887).

[79] Suetonius *vita Tiberi* 52 and Tacitus *Annales* 1.7, 33, 52 et al., for which see Shotter (1968: 194–208).

[80] See pp. 6–7 and 170–173.

[81] Castellanos (2013: 200). For a synopsis of the events see Merrills and Miles (2010: 122–123) and
McEvoy (2014: 251). Heather (2005: 402) estimates that Basiliscus set out in June 468.

[82] Flomen (2009–10: 14–15) argues that Sidonius was more likely to back Anthemius owing to his
efforts to protect the last remnants of Roman Gaul from the Visigoths. This would not have been
apparent to Sidonius in 467 at the time the epistle was written.

[83] In Chafe's (1994: 32–39) framework these epistles are narrated in the displaced mode, where the
narrator is temporally separated from the events described, as opposed to the immediate mode in
which the narrator speaks of recent events. Sidonius largely favours the immediate mode in his
epistles. Allan (2007: 100) usefully illustrates these two modes.

[84] In *Ep.* 4.18 Sidonius threatens his addressee Lucontius with a satirical attack (4.18.6): "versibus
quoque satirographis, si res exegerit, usuri, quos huic carmini lenitate adaequandos falso putabis" (if
the situation demands it, I will even deploy satirical verses, and you will be wrong if you think those
verses will take after this poem with its gentleness).

invectivaliter abusi nominum nuditate carpebant plurimum vitia, plus homines" (In the time of the Emperor Majorian a document circulated in the court lacking an author's name, full of biting satirical remarks which abusively exposed actual names, criticising vices a lot but men more). The temporal setting (*erzählte Zeit*) of the narrative *temporibus Augusti Maioriani ...* ("in the time of the Emperor Majorian ...") identifies for the reader the emperor who features heavily in the last half of the letter.[85] In Arles, rumours and accusations begin to fly, spurred on by Paeonius, that Sidonius was the author of the satire against him. Sidonius describes his arrival in Arles when he was still unaware of these accusations (*Ep.* 1.11.7):

> venio Arelate, nil adhuc (unde enim?) suspicans, quamquam putarer ab inimicis non affuturus, ac principe post diem viso in forum ex more descendo. quod ubi visum est, ilico expavit, ut ait ille "nil fortiter ausa seditio." alii tamen mihi plus quam deceret ad genua provolvi; alii, ne salutarent, fugere post statuas, occulti post columnas; alii tristes vultuosique iunctis mihi lateribus incedere.

> I came to Arles still suspecting nothing (why would I?) although it was thought by my enemies that I would not be there, still on the next day once I had the seen the emperor I went down to the forum as normal. When this was spotted, immediately there was terror, as Lucan says "dissension dared nothing bravely." Some fell down at my knees in an over-the-top manner, others to avoid greeting me fled behind statues, hid behind columns, some sad and stern walked next to me.

To his enemies' surprise Sidonius calmly saunters into town to have a tete-a-tete with Majorian.[86] His appearance prompts a flurry of activity which is conveyed by the run of historical infinitives: *fugere, occuli, mirari*, and *interrogare*.[87] Eventually one of the mob comes up to report the accusations against him. Sidonius sends the interlocutor back with a message that they should reconsider their assumptions and abandon such insolent behaviour. Paeonius the main agitator goes home unsatisfied, carried away by his ghastly sedan bearers.[88]

The narrative progresses to the final scene, a banquet hosted on the next day by Majorian, in which Sidonius cleverly counters the accusations.[89]

---

[85] For this terminology see p. 58. Pliny similarly indicates in one of the narratives in *Ep.* 1.12 that he is describing events that took place during the reign of Domitian (*Ep.* 1.12.6: Domitiani temporibus) to enable the reader to recognise that Domitian is the brigand (*latro*) that Corellius Rufus refers to later in the epistle (*Ep.* 1.12.8).

[86] *Ep.* 1.11.7–8.

[87] Köhler (1999: 413).

[88] *Ep.* 1.11.9, for which see Köhler (1995: 318).

[89] *Ep.* 1.11.10: "postridie iussit Augustus ut epulo suo circensibus ludis interessemus" (On the next day Augustus ordered me to participate in the banquet he hosted at the Circus games).

The position of each invitee is detailed in the epistle, ending with Sidonius' own spot right next to Majorian.[90] Up until this point the emperor has barely featured in the narrative, but it would seem that they are on reasonably friendly terms, made evident in the epistle by Sidonius' prompt access to the emperor upon his arrival, invitation to dinner, and seat of honour next to him; the reader is surely meant to fill in (at least some of) the gaps, specifically by inferring a pre-existing relationship between Majorian and Sidonius.[91]

The narrative turns to the dinner's conversation. Majorian speaks to each guest in turn. Paeonius however is passed over for Athenius, but before the old man can answer, Paeonius interjects.[92] Majorian's response is a study in composure (1.11.12): "subrisit Augustus, ut erat auctoritate servata, cum se communioni dedisset, ioci plenus, per quem cachinnum non minus obtigit Athenio vindictae, quam contigisset iniuriae" (the emperor laughed gently, keeping his authority in tact, when he had given himself over to company, he was full of humour, by that chuckle he enabled Athenius to get his revenge no less than if he had suffered an injury). Majorian laughs, a response that is difficult to read. The verb *subrideo*, which conveys a degree of latency in the action, controls the sense of the noun *cachinnus*, restricting its meaning to a gentle laugh rather than a loud cackle.[93] Importantly Majorian' *auctoritas* remains intact; his response to Paeonius' lack of decorum was presumably shared by his guests. Athenius wittily rebukes Paeonius, prompting Gratian (one of the dinner guests) to remark that the opportunity for a satire had presented itself. Majorian turns to Sidonius (*Ep.* 1.11.13):

> hic imperator ad me cervice conversa: "audio", ait, "comes Sidoni, quod satiram scribas." "et ego", inquam, "hoc audio, domine princeps." tunc ille, sed ridens: "parce vel nobis." "at ego", inquam, "quod ab inlicitis tempero, mihi parco." post quae ille: "et quid faciemus his", inquit, "qui te lacessunt?" et ego: "quisquis est iste, domine imperator, publice accuset: si redarguimur, debita luamus supplicia convicti; ceterum obiecta si non inprobabiliter cassaverimus, oro, ut indultu clementiae tuae praeter iuris iniuriam in accusatorem meum quae volo scribam."

---

[90] For an explanation of the seating arrangement see Köhler (1995: 318–319).

[91] Styka (2008: 64–65) argues that Sidonius was part of a literary circle that Majorian used for his own political purposes, but this is surely an overinterpretation of *Ep.* 1.11. Wickham (2005: 160) similarly proposes that Sidonius held a position at Majorian's court, but there is limited evidence to support this claim.

[92] Lendon (1997: 140) notes that Paeonius' behaviour is an insult to both the emperor and Athenius.

[93] For this specific sense of *sub* prefixes see Zaliznjak and Shmelev (2007: 223). A smile can be interpreted many ways, for an example of which see Uden (2014: 72–75).

then the emperor swivelled his head around to me: "I hear," he said, "Count Sidonius, that you write satire." "And I," I said, "hear that too, Lord Emperor." Then he said jestingly "Just spare me." "But I," I say, "since I steer clear of illegalities, spare myself." After which he said "But what should we do to those who hurt you?" And I say: "Whoever does, Lord Emperor, should accuse me publicly. If I am found guilty, I should pay the correct penalty for someone who is convicted, but if on the other hand I answer the charges in a manner that is not objectionable, I ask with the indulgence of your clemency, short of anything illegal, that I may write what I want against my accuser."

Majorian and Sidonius are presented as having a good rapport; Sidonius parrots Majorian's remark by repeating the verb *audio* which implies the rumour was not true without explicitly acknowledging Majorian's implied question; Sidonius like Majorian had only heard about it from others. Each plays their role with an easy familiarity; Majorian jokingly requests that he not be the subject of any satire, and Sidonius' dutifully agrees to abide by the request, citing his need to obey the law.[94] The witty exchange leads to Majorian seeking advice as to what he should do with Sidonius' accusers. Sidonius offers Majorian a solid legal interpretation in response, which ends with a metaliterary gesture as the epistle is clearly critical of Paeonius (*in accusatorem meum quae scribam*).[95] Majorian immediately acts on Sidonius' advice, glaring at Paeonius to induce his non-verbal acquiescence (*Ep.* 1.11.14): "ad haec ipse Paeonium conspicatus nutu coepit consulere nutantem, placeretne condicio. sed cum ille confusus reticuisset princepsque consuleret erubescenti, ait: 'annuo postulatis, si hoc ipsum e vestigio versibus petas' "[96] (at this he looked at Paeonius and with a nod began to ask him as he faltered whether the condition was acceptable. When Paeonius in his confusion had remained silent and the emperor took heed of his blushing, he said [to me] 'I approve your demands if you make the request right now in verse').

---

[94] Köhler (1995: 326).

[95] Sidonius appears to have had a good, practical understanding of the law. See for example *Ep.* 3.12.3 and 5.19.1. Sidonius' criticism of Paeonius in the epistle does not technically contravene his promise to Paeonius at *Ep.* 1.11.16: "versu nil reponendum" (that nothing would be said in reply in verse), as the epistle is written in prose, not verse.

[96] Sidonius then momentarily stalls Majorian's request by calling for water; by the time the Emperor repeats his condition that the verse composition be spontaneous, Sidonius has readied himself to deliver this two-line ditty (*Ep.* 1.11.14): "scribere me satiram qui culpat, maxime/princeps, hanc rogo decernas aut probet aut timeat" (He who charges that I write satire, most mighty Emperor, I ask you to rule that he should prove it or be afraid).

Paeonius' blushing acts as de facto assent.[97] At the high stakes table of imperial politics Majorian and Sidonius play and win. Paeonius loses – at the end of the dinner he begs Sidonius to forget the whole affair, which the latter, urged on by the others, agrees to do: Sidonius will not lampoon Paeonius (perhaps again) in verse as long as he is never criticised by him in return.[98] Rouseau offers that this dinner party description is "filled with a sense of danger, the danger of being close to men in power."[99] Sidonius must be counted among these powerful men.

Sidonius characterises Majorian as an adept emperor, at ease among a group of political officials, who takes and acts upon advice in a fair and clear-minded manner. The proverbial elephant in the room is his father-in-law. The sources are unclear as to how Avitus died and what level of involvement Majorian had in his downfall, if any; this lack of clarity may well reflect a contemporary lack of certainty.[100] If Majorian was directly involved in Avitus' removal, and was known to have been, offering this portrayal would have further damaged Avitus' memory. Sidonius' panegyric for Majorian at least responded to (and soothed over) the political difficulty of the months after Avitus' reign; placing a positive character sketch in epistles published after Majorian's death in 461 cannot be explained as mere political pragmatism.

Sidonius' purpose in casting Majorian in a positive light takes on new significance when this epistle is placed in the context of book 1 of Sidonius' epistles; the comparison with Anthemius begs to be read. Sidonius was clearly aware of how prevalent such comparisons were; in *Ep.* 2.13 he explicitly rules out comparing one emperor, in this case Petronius Maximus, to others (*Ep.* 2.13.3): "hic si omittamus antecedentium principum casus vel subsecutorum, solus iste peculiaris tuus Maximus maximo nobis documento poterit esse" (if we leave out here the disasters of the emperors who came before and those who followed, that singular man, your Maximus, can on his own provide extensive evidence for this point).[101] The *casus antecedentium* are readily identifiable: Valentinian III, who had murdered Aëtius and was promptly murdered in turn, ending the Theodosian dynasty, and Honorius, who had failed to stop Alaric from

---

[97] Köhler (1995: 326).
[98] According to Mathisen (1979: 168n16) "The accusation was probably justified." Castellanos (2013: 128) detects bitterness in Sidonius' tone, but his telling of events more closely approximates gloating than complaint.
[99] Rousseau (1976: 360n34).
[100] See pp. 4–5.
[101] The name pun is readily discernible: Petronius "the biggest" (*Maximus*) provides the biggest proof (*maximo documento*). Sidonius clearly enjoyed using name puns, for which see Gibson (2011: 655–659) and (2013b: 338), for other examples see pp. 42, 94, 150, 167.

sacking Rome, and had otherwise been largely ineffective.[102] The *casus subsecutorum* surely includes the reigns of Avitus, who ruled for barely more than a year before conflict with Ricimer ended his reign, and perhaps Majorian, whose rule took a turn for the worst when the Vandal navy crushed his armada, rendering Sidonius' bold predictions of a Roman conquest as the rhetorical pith of a panegyric.[103] But in the confines of book 1 of the epistles, Majorian is the better emperor than Anthemius: clever, organised, and fair.

Sidonius portrays Petronius Maximus as a man ambitious for ambition's sake; he passed through the offices of prefect, patrician, and consul, then (*Ep.* 2.13.3): "ceu recurrentibus orbitis inexpletus iteraverat" (unsatisfied he went around again as if the offices were in reoccurring orbits). His eventual rise took an immediate physical toll; all his strength was needed to reach the imperial summit (*ad principis apices abruptum*), but then he suffered from vertigo (*vertiginem*).[104] Petronius is left momentarily tottering at the top, just long enough to consider the nature of imperial power – Sidonius' readers know there is only one way down, and they surely knew that his fall was quick – Petronius was probably stoned to death within two and a half months of seizing the purple.[105]

The character portrayal shifts to a discussion of what Petronius' life was like before his reign (*Ep.* 2.13.4): "profecto invenies hominem beatiorem prius fuisse quam beatissimus nominaretur. [igitur ille,] cuius anterius epulae mores, pecuniae pompae, litterae fasces, patrimonia patrocinia florebant" (you will actually discover that the man was more fortunate before he was called the most fortunate man ... whose banquets, habits, wealth, pomp, letters, magistracies, estates, and clients were flourishing beforehand). All this changed when he became emperor; groaning under the weight of his office he saw that his past life and new role were incompatible (*Ep.* 2.13.4): "perspexit pariter ire non posse negotium principis et

---

[102] Loyen (1970b: 221). Sundwall (1915: 13) follows Sidonius' assessment. Valentinian III and Honorius escape Sidonus' censure in *Ep.* 5.9, but his point there is the shared experiences of his grandfather and Aquilinus, the addressee; belittling the emperors they served under would have been counterproductive, serving merely to undermine the prestige their ancestors won from their palatine service. At *Carm.* 7.359 Sidonius labels Valentinian III *semivir amens* "a mad eunuch" for which see Stroheker (1970: 51). On the influence that ancient criticism has had on scholarship regarding Valentinian III see Humphries (2012: 162).

[103] Mathisen (1979: 169) and Loyen (1970b: 221). Gregory of Tours is ardent in his criticism of Avitus at 2.11, for which see Furbetta (2015c: 5–6). This may represent a departure from his usual reliance on Sidonius as a source, or perhaps his attempts to read into the significance of Sidonius' remarks at *Ep.* 2.13.3.

[104] *Ep.* 2.13.3.

[105] See pp. 4 and 22n23.

otium senatoris" (he saw that he would not be able to undertake equally the business of emperor and the leisure of a senator). At last, Petronius is put out of his misery, his death was (*Ep.* 2.13.4): "novus, celer, acerbus" (strange, quick, harsh).

Petronius stands as a clear exemplum of the dangers of imperial power, functioning in the collection to justify Sidonius' retirement from his secular career.[106] His portrait of Petronius also resonates with the other imperial portraits; the disaster of those who preceded and followed him; Valentinian III, Avitus, Majorian, and Anthemius were all killed in office.[107] Petronius comes across as a good senator, but one wholly unprepared and ill-equipped to be emperor.

In the first two books of Sidonius' collection, written and circulated before he became a bishop, emperors feature heavily; this may be explained by the fact that the letters of book 1 largely detail Sidonius' secular political career and those of book 2 his "retirement" from that path which necessarily includes reflections on the nature of power and politics.[108] The character of an emperor next reappears with a similar frequency in book 5, which describes in several letters the circumstances in the Auvergne in the early 470s when the Visigoths under Euric were attempting to take the city with a series of summer campaigns.[109] In the intervening books (3 and 4) Sidonius offers a single remark on the influence of emperors on events in Gaul amid discussion of the positive qualities of the quaestor Licianus (*Ep.* 3.7.3): "neque ex illo ut ferunt, numero, qui secreta dirigentum principum venditantes ambiunt a barbaris bene agi cum legato potius quam cum legatione" (nor is he from that number, as they say, who go around selling the secrets of the emperors who direct them with the aim of being treated well by the barbarians for their term as a diplomat rather than their diplomatic mission). The waning ability of emperors to control events is readily evident; Sidonius clearly implies that Roman diplomatic efforts are being undermined by the corruption of their officials.[110] The emperor that appointed Licianus as quaestor is not identified.[111]

In *Ep.* 5.6 the character of the emperor reappears, but is not immediately named, instead the epithet *novus* is used to indicate that this emperor is not Anthemius (who was explicitly identified as the current emperor earlier

---

[106] See p. 22.
[107] Avitus perhaps died subsequently; see p. 4n23.
[108] See pp. 5n26 and 22.
[109] Delaplace (2012: 272–278).
[110] Giannotti (2016: 186).
[111] *Ep.* 5.16.

in the collection).[112] In that letter Sidonius cautions his uncle Apollinaris against trying to meddle on behalf of the emperor in the precarious geo-political balance in south-west Gaul, as the emerging Burgundian and Visigothic kingdoms acquired the remaining Roman held territory.[113] The town of Vaison had been lost to the Burgundians.[114] Sidonius dissuades Apollinaris from attempting to bring it back into Roman control – such a move would surely have provoked a swift Burgundian response.

This *novus princeps* features in the next epistle in the collection; the situation is similar, Sidonius reports to the addressee Thaumastus the source of the rumour that his brother was a supporter of the *princeps*. This clearly had become a dangerous position given the prevailing political climate.[115] The shadowy *novus princeps* is finally named in *Ep.* 5.16;[116] Sidonius proudly informs his wife Papianilla that Julius Nepos has appointed his brother-in-law, her brother Ecdicius, to the rank of the patriciate (*Ep.* 5.16.2): "hoc tamen sancte Iulius Nepos, armis pariter summus Augustus ac moribus, quod decessoris Anthemii fidem fratris tui sudoribus obligatam, quo citior, hoc laudabilior absolvit; siquidem iste complevit, quod ille saepissime pollicebatur" (However, Julius Nepos, an emperor equally outstanding in war and in his morals has scrupulously enacted – more quickly and so in a more praiseworthy manner – his predecessor Anthemius' pledge which was compelled by the efforts of your brother; indeed he has brought to fruition what that man was often promising). Nepos is first praised on his own terms; he is equally good in military and moral spheres. It is likely that this letter was written prior to Nepos' flight from Italy to Dalmatia, and so before his *magister militum* Orestes tried to usurp him.[117] In any case, Nepos was still alive when this book circulated. His prompt action in granting Ecdicius his promotion is directly contrasted to Anthemius' dithering; while the latter had often promised it (*saepissime pollicebatur*), Nepos had quickly delivered it (*quo citior*). Sidonius makes sure that Anthemius does not get any acknowledgment; this is consistent with his negative portrayal earlier in the collection.[118]

---

[112] Pliny similarly uses the epithet *optimus* to differentiate Trajan from Nerva and Domitian; see for example *Ep.* 4.22.1.
[113] *Ep.* 5.6.1.
[114] *Ep.* 5.6.2.
[115] *Ep.* 5.7. Furbetta (2014–2015a: 146–148).
[116] Bellès (1998: 103n31), Castellanos (2013: 170), and Giuletti (2014: 108) are surely correct in their identification of Julius Nepos as the *novus princeps* of *Ep.* 5.6.
[117] MacGeorge (2002: 273–286).
[118] See pp. 105–108.

In his first five books of epistles Sidonius' character portrayals of different emperors create a loose narrative that peters out in book 6, which does not mention any emperors, and ends in book 7 with Sidonius' acknowledgement in *Ep.* 7.7 that the emperor is no longer in the picture.[119] Sidonius extensively shapes his material for his literary and rhetorical ends, within bounds that would have been recognisable to his contemporary readers, many of whom would have lived through the reigns of these emperors. Majorian appears as a smooth operator; Petronius Maximus dangerously out of his league; Anthemius paralysed by his indecision; and Julius Nepos as effective, but ultimately too late to make a difference. These portrayals are set in a broader narrative that charts the imperial withdrawal from Roman Gaul, and the collapse of the Empire in the West as a single political entity. Sidonius encourages the reader to read this as a continuum of disasters caused by past and future emperors (*antecedentium principum casus vel subsecutorum*). This narrative is an integral part of Sidonius' self-fashioning as the political survivor, who successfully negotiated the turbulence of wide-sweeping political changes and the dangers of imperial politics; who dined and joked with Majorian, negotiated with Anthemius, avoided Petronius Maximus, while furthering himself and his family.[120]

Plotting Friends: Constantius, Ferreolus, and Lampridius

Individual Gallo-Roman clergy and aristocrats feature as characters in the collection. Constantius, Ferreolus, and Lampridius are a few of the select group who recur, creating smaller narratives within and across individual epistles that are otherwise markedly different from each other. These stories relate to the Visigothic assault on Clermont, the *docta otia* of Gallo-Roman aristocrats, and, in Lampridius' case, his gruesome murder by his own slaves.

Constantius is the addressee of *Ep.* 1.1.[121] He clearly held a prominent position in Sidonius' literary circle (*Ep* 1.1.1): "domine maior … consiliossimus … fautorem non studiorum modo verum etiam studiosorum" (honoured Lord … who is full of wise counsel … a supporter of not only letters but also learned men). The next epistle addressed to Constantius

---

[119] *Ep.* 7.7.1: "principe absente" (now that the emperor is absent), for which see p. 104. Mratschek (2013: 254–255) notes that Licinianus was in Italy, but Sidonius does not explicitly offer that detail.

[120] See the title of Van Waarden's (2010) commentary on the first eleven epistles of book seven "Writing to Survive" and Castellanos (2013: 223). Furbetta (2015b: 353) notes Sidonius' capacity to adapt earlier epistolary models to new political circumstances.

[121] PLRE II "Constantius 10."

offers thanks for his recent visit to Clermont. It contains three distinct narratives that develop out of sequence, each of which is framed by his character. The first describes Constantius' visit to Clermont: he has been to the inhabitants' homes, toured the partly ruined walls, spoken to the people in ways suited to their class, rank, and sex, impressing the young and old alike.[122] This narrative transitions into a series of remarks that Sidonius reports indirectly (3.2.1–2):

> quas tu lacrimas ut parens omnium super aedes incendio prorutas et domicilia semiusta fudisti! quantum doluisti campos sepultos ossibus insepultis! quae tua deinceps exhortatio, quae reparationem suadentis animositas! his adicitur, quod, cum inveneris civitatem non minus civica simultate quam barbarica incursione vacuatam, pacem omnibus suadens caritatem illis, illos patriae reddidisti.

> what tears you poured out, like the father of us all, over the buildings ruined by fire and the half-burnt out homes! How extensively did you grieve at the fields buried by unburied bones! Such was your encouragement, such spirit in urging that there be rebuilding. Added to these achievements is that when you found the city emptied no less by civic strife than by the barbarian assault, urging peace to all men, you gave kindness back to them and them back to their homeland.

Constantius' sympathy for the inhabitants' plight hardens into a plan of action; tears make way for encouragement – the town must rebuild and come together again.[123] The underlying narrative details the city's conflict with the Visigoths: buildings have been levelled and homes burnt; bodies remain unburied; the city is desolate.[124] The people have fled under the pressure of the barbarian assault. Placing the narrative of Clermont's partial destruction inside the narrative of the visit allows Sidonius' to invoke sympathy for the town among his readers, but also echo Constantius' call to rebuild and reinhabit the city. The specific events of the Visigothic assault are not described, only its outcome; the reader is left to imagine and reconstruct the events that have led to the scene. Some sort of battle has taken place outside the walls, which have been fired and collapsed in part. The danger of venturing outside the walls has prevented the burying of bodies.[125]

---

[122] Harries (1994: 226) states "Every summer from 471 to 474 saw the arrival of a substantial Gothic raiding party (at Clermont)."
[123] Giannotti (2016: 126) notes Sidonius' rich language in describing the vivid scene of the city's suffering.
[124] Sarti (2011: 143).
[125] Sidonius details Constantius' struggles against the winter conditions at *Ep.* 3.2.3. The rock-hard icy ground would also have inhibited attempts at burial.

The last narrative in *Ep.* 3.2 details Constantius' journey to Clermont. It sits chronologically between the semi-destruction of the city and his visit. Sidonius lists in quick succession the perils and discomforts Constantius overcame (3.2.3):

> itinerum videlicet longitudinem brevitatem dierum, nivium copiam penuriam pabulorum, latitudines solitudinum angustias mansionum, viarum voragines aut umore imbrium putres aut frigorum siccitate tribulosas, ad hoc aut aggeres saxis asperos aut fluvios gelu lubricos aut colles ascensu salebrosos aut valles lapsuum assiduitate derasas; per quae omnia incommoda, quia non privatum commodum requirebas, amorem publicum rettulisti.

> specifically, the length of the routes, the shortness of the days, the abundance of snow, the scarcity of food, the wide expanses of desolation, the narrow crooks of the guest-houses, the ditches of the road either rotten from the wet rain or roughened by the dry cold, additionally either harsh piles of rocks or rivers slippery with ice or hills uneven to climb, or valleys cut up by constant landslides. Through all these discomforts, since you sought no personal comfort, you won over the love of the people.

Repeated antitheses draw attention to the short days and the abundance of snow, frost, ice and rain which increased the relative personal cost of Constantius' visit in winter.[126] All of this Constantius bore despite his old age and without any special treatment on account of his rank.

Sidonius encourages each individual to have in their mind the image of a venerable Constantius persisting in his journey (3.2.3): "obversatur etenim per dies mentibus singulorum, quod persona aetate gravis infirmitate fragilis, nobilitate sublimis religione venerabilis solius dilectionis obtentu abrupisti tot repagula, tot obiectas veniendi difficultates" (indeed in the mind's eye of each person day after day appears the picture of you weighed down by your age and fragile from your weakness, of noble birth and respected for your piety, you who have broken through so many obstacles, so many difficulties set against your arrival with the only aim one of love). The three narratives in this epistle all rely on Constantius' character as a wise and elderly man for their effect. His visit is a success because he can interact with all the different people, like an able and experienced church leader wisely tailoring his comments to his specific audience. The people appreciate this interaction and, so Sidonius' implies, they appreciate the personal cost that Constantius underwent, as an old man determined to

---

[126] Giannotti (2016: 129–130). Contra Gualandri (1979: 36–37) who argues that Sidonius' embellished language forces the narrated facts into the background.

risk the perils of a winter journey to provide spiritual and emotional res-pite to the town's survivors of the Visigothic assault. Sidonius' description of the town's suffering derives authenticity from Constantius' visit, both he (as the narrator) and Constantius (as the narrated actor) report their autoptic experience of the burnt-out houses, the half-ruined walls, the unburied bodies, and the ensuing desolation.

Throughout the epistle Sidonius appears as a gifted leader of his com-munity, intent on restoring the people's will and prepared to ask a favour of his friend and ecclesiastical superior to ensure that happens. His grati-tude to Contantius reflects equally well on his persona for (presumably) arranging the visit and being so very grateful for the assistance that was forthcoming.

Ferreolus, a Gallo-Roman aristocrat and secular office holder, features in six epistles in Sidonius' collection.[127] In *Ep.* 2.9 Sidonius visits Ferreolus' estate; he has precedence over the other estate master (Apollinaris) owing to his superior rank and age.[128] *Ep.* 7.12 begins with a quasi-apology to Ferreolus to explain why he has not already been honoured by an epistle earlier in the book.[129] The opening describes the imaginary epistle that Sidonius hypothetically would have written to Ferreolus were he to have been included earlier in the collection. This pretence segues into a brief metaliterary reflection as to how the composition of the current epistle began which then dovetails into an extended *praeteritio*. The epistle concludes with some programmatic assertions as to the significance of the epistle's position, addressed to a secular aristocrat but following a series of epistles addressed to clergy. Sidonius explains that clerics must come before mere secular aristocrats – a hierarchy that surely suited the bishop Sidonius at the time of writing but would not have always done so.[130] At no point does Sidonius seem to get to the "real epistle" until its perfunctory sign-off. The epistle clearly plays on its metaliterary fiction, as a shadow of the imagined epistle that was never written. Throughout Sidonius is highly aware of the epistle's literary significance, structure, and positioning.

The closest the epistle comes to depicting anything real is the extended *praeteritio* which fills in the reader on the achievement of Ferreolus' ancestors, providing the background for a succinct *res gestae* of sorts (7.12.3):

---

[127] *Ep.* 1.7, 2.9, 5.5, 7.12, 9.3, 9.15.
[128] *Ep.* 2.9.3.
[129] The first eleven epistles of book seven were addressed to fellow clergy.
[130] See Mathisen (1993a: 93) for these remarks. Rousseau (1976: 362) misreads Sidonius' remarks in *Ep.* 7.12 as an attempt to equate clerical and secular rank.

[publica salutatio] praetermisit Gallias tibi administratas tunc, cum maxume incolumes erant. praetermisit Attilam Rheni hostem, Thorismodum Rhodani hospitem, Aetium Ligeris liberatorem sola te dispositionum salubritate tolerasse, propterque prudentiam tantam providentiamque currum tuum provinciales cum plausuum maximo accentu spontaneis subisse cervicibus, quia sic habenas Galliarum moderarere, ut possessor exhaustus tributario iugo relevaretur. praetermisit regem Gothiae ferocissimum inflexum affatu tuo melleo gravi, arguto inusitato, et ab Arelatensium portis quem Aetius non potuisset proelio te prandio removisse.

[the public greeting] passed over the time when Gaul was administered by you, when it was kept very safe; it passed over the fact that Attila the enemy of the Rhine, Thorismund the guest of the Rhône, Aëtius the liberator of the Loire, were handled by you with only the vigour of your disposition, and on account of your great wisdom and foresight the provincials spontaneously lifted your car onto their shoulders with a great round of applause, since you held the reins of Gaul in such a way that the property owner got relief from being exhausted by the tax burden. It passed over the fact that the most ferocious king of Gothia was influenced by your appeal, sweet but stern, skilful but unhackneyed, and that you removed him from the gates of Arles with a banquet achieving what Aëtius had been unable to do with a battle.

Sidonius takes the reader rapidly through a condensed narrative of the events that took place when Ferreolus was Praetorian Prefect of Gaul. He handles the threat of Attila, the difficulty of Thorismund, and the demands of Aëtius with aplomb, all the while earning popular approval for his efforts to minimise the Gallic tax burden.[131] Sidonius' narrative recollection of this period ends on a neat conceit. Ferreolus succeeded where Aëtius failed by banqueting rather than battling the Visigothic king Thorismund into submission. This tight chronology of events is set against Ferreolus' character. He is clearly highly capable, with an impeccable lineage; his diplomatic triumph over Thorismund and his negotiation of the difficult circumstances prior to Attila's defeat and death appear as the reasonable outcome of his impressive pedigree. Ultimately, however, these achievements are below those of the clergy, to which Sidonius now belongs (*Ep.* 7.12.4): "haec omnia praetermisit, sperans congruentius tuum salve pontificum quam senatorum iam nominibus adiungi; censuitque iustius fieri, si inter perfectos Christi quam si inter praefectos Valentiniani constituerere" (it passed over all these points hoping that your greeting would be joined more fittingly to the names of the priests rather than the senators and

---

[131] See p. 3 for a brief summary of this period.

it judged that it would be more proper if you were placed among the perfect men of Christ than the prefects of Valentinian). The *praeteritio* is clearly a conceit;[132] Sidonius could easily have not mentioned his ranking of secular office against ecclesiastic office. Ferreolus may well have done some remarkable things in his day but their importance is relative to the true calling of Christ.

These comments resonate in the context of book 7 of his epistles, the first eleven of which are addressed to fellow clergy, and with Sidonius' own status and self-fashioning as a bishop who was once a prominent secular office holder. Sidonius makes an implied agonistic comparison between his own achievements and those of Ferreolus. In the secular sphere Ferreolus has excelled, but Sidonius clearly points out that these achievements must be ranked below ecclesiastical success. In that more important sphere Ferreolus has no achievements. This epistle echoes with Sidonius' claims in *Ep.* 7.9 in which he responds to (hypothetical) critics of his past as a secular aristocrat, by presenting a clear endorsement of Sidonius' career change and a stinging criticism of those who only served the Roman state, which had begun well and truly to fall apart in the West by the time this book was circulated post 475. The reader is clearly led to infer that Sidonius made the right decision.

In *Ep.* 8.11 Sidonius describes the murder of his friend Lampridius.[133] He appears as a brilliant orator but a complex and sadly misguided individual. News of his death interrupts the epistle[134] (*Ep.* 8.11.3): "Lampridius orator modo primum mihi occisus agnoscitur, cuius interitus amorem meum summis conficeret angoribus, etiamsi non eum rebus humanis vis impacta rapuisset" (Just now I found out that Lampridius the orator has been killed, the death of that man would have hit my love for him with the greatest pain even if a violent assault has not snatched him away from the affairs of man). The specifics of his death linger behind the anecdotes which Sidonius then offers about his life. A verse eulogy follows, prompting further reflections on their relationship and on Lampridius' character (8.11.4):

> namque crebro levibus ex causis, sed leviter, excitabatur, quod nilominus ego studebam sententiae ceterorum naturam potius persuadere quam vitium; adstruebamque meliora, quatenus in pectore viri iracundia materialiter regnans, quia naevo crudelitatis fuerat infecta, praetextu saltim severitatis emacularetur.

---

[132] The conceit is even clearer in §3 where the verb *praetermisit* occurs in three successive sentences.

[133] Wolff (2015a: 196) dates their friendship to beginning in 450 CE and notes its continuance despite their political differences.

[134] See pp. 87–88.

for he was excited often by insignificant matters but only insignificantly, I nevertheless always tried to convince others that this was his nature rather than a vice. I thought of it in better terms, that the tendency to anger which reigned in his heart, because it had been marked by the stain of cruelty, could at least be excused on the pretext of sternness.

This is not a one-dimensional encomium. Lampridius is a prickly character.[135] Sidonius apologises for his behaviour by encouraging others to accept him for who he was, warts and all. His death results from his bizarre interest in astrology (8.11.9):

illud sane non solum culpabile in viro fuit, sed peremptorium: quod mathematicos quondam de vitae fine consuluit, urbium cives Africanarum, quorum, ut est regio, sic animus ardentior; qui constellatione percontantis inspecta pariter annum mensem diemque dixerunt, quos, ut verbo matheseos utar, climactericos esset habiturus, utpote quibus themate oblato quasi sanguinariae geniturae schema patuisset, quia videlicet amici nascentis anno, quemcumque clementem planeticorum siderum globum in diastemata zodiaca prosper ortus erexerat, hunc in occasu cruentis ignibus inrubescentes seu super diametro Mercurius asyndetus seu super tetragono Saturnus retrogradus seu super centro Mars apocatastaticus exacerbassent.[136]

one aspect of that man was not only worthy of blame but also lethal: he once consulted astrologers about the end of his life, citizens of African cities whose mind – like their region – is rather overheated. Upon inspecting the inquirer's constellation they said in like manner the year, month, and day which would be – I will use the astrological term – climacteric for him. When the image was presented to them it was as if a picture of a bloodied birth had been revealed, since in the year of our friend's birth a favourable rise had directed some sort of calm sphere of planetary bodies into the house of the zodiac, but they growing red by the setting of bloody flames had each been agitated either by Mars asyndetic diametrically above it, or by Saturn retrograde above it perpendicularly, or Mars apocatastatic above it in the middle.

Sidonius' astrological terms (*climactericos, diastemata, zodiaca, tetragono, retrogradus, apocatastaticus*) provide the reader with a glimpse into Lampridius' practice.[137] In Bakhtin's terminology Lampridius inhabits the "exotic alien world" which Sidonius, the hero of the epistle, or at least, the staunch supporter of the Catholic faith, observes as someone fundamentally

---

[135] Wolff (2015a: 195).

[136] Bowersock, Brown, and Grabar provide a clear summary of how astrology was understood to work in late antiquity (1999: 318–319).

[137] By way of contrast, Pliny's description in *Ep.* 2.20 of Regulus' amateur astrological pursuits only uses one specific astrological term *climactericum*.

external to it,[138] indicating to the reader that these terms are not normally part of his vernacular, but rather are those used by the astrologers (*ut verbo matheseos utar*).[139] The Africans convince Lampridius that the sign of a bloodied birth (*sanguinariae geniturae*) was evident in his birth year. One of several potential astrological formations has worsened this sign, making it grow red with bloody flames (*cruentis ignibus inrubescentes*).

Sidonius does not – at this point – explicitly link the connection of the signs to Lampridius' death; but the connection is easily made by the reader: Lampridius asked the astrologers about his death (*de vitae fine*) and they answered with a forecast of a bloodied demise, pre-ordained by the movement and position of astrological bodies. Sidonius gives the astrologers' prediction extensive treatment but frames his account with the assertion that Lampridius' consultation of the astrologers was the fatal act (*peremptorium*). This removes any credit from the astrologers for accurately predicting the nature of his death; Sidonius implies that his efforts to find that out by using such dubious means irrevocably changed it.[140] Further discussion of astrology is put off until he and the addressee Lupus may meet in person.

The death scene receives some detail (8.11.10–11):

> interim ad praesens nil coniecturaliter gestum, nil per ambages, quandoquidem hunc nostrum temerarium futurorum sciscitatorem et diu frustra tergiversantem tempus et qualitas praedictae mortis innexuit. nam domi pressus strangulatusque servorum manibus obstructo anhelitu gutture obstricto, ne dicam Lentuli Iugurthae atque Seiani, certe Numantini Scipionis exitu periit.

> meanwhile on that occasion nothing conjectural happened, nothing obscure, for the time and manner of his predicted death entangled that friend of ours, the rash inquirer of future events, pointlessly oscillating for a long time back and forth. For he was held and strangled at home by the hands of his slaves, his breath cut off, his throat closed off. I will not say that he died like Lentulus, Iugurtha, or Sejanus, but he certainly died like Scipio Numantinus.

[138] Bakhtin (1981: 245). For an application of this terminology see Avlamis (2011: 89–91).

[139] Contra Desbrosses (2015: 214) who interprets this passage as Sidonius showing off his knowledge of astrology. Sidonius however carefully frames his remarks as repeating what the astrologers had relayed to Lampridius, who in turn presumably relayed them to Sidonius. Cf. Wolff (2015b: 195) who notes Sidonius' interest in the subject.

[140] *Ep.* 8.11.9. Sidonius' charge that Lampridius was gullible (*credulus*) is not undermined by the narrative, as proposed by Desbrosses (2015: 225), but rather reinforced, as Sidonius implies that Lampridius empowered the astrologers' prediction by believing it. The account is not paradoxical, contra Wolff (2015a: 195), as Sidonius condemns astrology while recognising its power to harm those who believe in it.

The moment of death is marked by a chiastic flourish (*obstructo anhelitu gutture obstricto*) as Lampridius is choked to death, but whatever sympathy the reader may have held for Lampridius is short lived; Sidonius' condemnatory tone paints him as a rash, dithering fool whose own curiosity caused his ruin. All four of the historical comparanda met a bloodless death just like Lampridius. The nature of his death undermines somewhat the astrologers' prediction by forming a direct contrast to the bloodiness of the astrological signs in §9 (*saunguinariae, cruentis*). Scipio and Iugurtha may be cited additionally for their African connection, and Sejanus and Lentulus may imply that Lampridius had a share in the occasional conspiracy during his life. The complexity of Lampridius' character remains; the first three comparanda (Lentulus, Iugurtha, and Sejanus) are decisively villains in the Roman tradition, whereas Scipio is decisively not.[141] Their combination points to Lampridius' mix of positive and negative character traits.

The narrative turns to a detailed forensic description of the discovery of Lampridius' body, its condition, and the capture and torture of the culprits. Lampridius met his just deserts (8.11.13):

> atque utinam hunc finem, dum inconsulte fidens vana consultat, non meruisset excipere! nam quisque praesumpserit interdicta secreta vetita rimari, vereor huius modi a catholicae fidei regulis exorbitaturum et effici dignum, in statum cuius respondeantur adversa, dum requiruntur inlicita.

> and I wish that he had not deserved to receive this end by consulting meaningless information and trusting it inadvisedly. For whoever undertakes to look into forbidden and banned secrets, I fear that such a man deviates from the rules of the Catholic faith and deserves dark responses concerning their life for enquiring into illicit matters.

Sidonius' tone has transitioned from a mix of sympathy and blame to frustration. His role as narrator is evident in his linking of Lampridius' interest in astrology to his death. That the astrologers happened to get the date right is mitigated by the implication that consulting the astrologers was itself the

---

[141] March (1989: 225ff) details Lentulus' corrupt political practices and involvement with Catiline. Sallust *Cat.* 55.3 records his eventual execution by strangulation. Livy *Per.* 67 simply records that Iugurtha was killed in jail. Plutarch *vita Marii* 12.4 states that he died from starvation. The *Fasti Ostienses* indicates that Sejanus was strangled, for which see Ehrenburg and Jones (1955: 42). This detail is not in Dio Cassius's account at 58.11–45, which does not explicitly indicate that Sejanus was strangled, nor Tacitus' *Annales* (the text has a lacuna). The cause of Scipio's death was unclear. Plutarch *vita Romuli* 27.4 offers several possibilities including strangulation. Like Lampridius' body Scipio's was exposed to onlookers (Plutarch *vita Romuli* 27.5, *vita* Gaii Gracchi 10.4). His *vita Scipionis* is lost.

fatal act. They did not predict what was going to happen to Lampridius but rather doomed him to a specific fate. He would have been far better off if he had not consulted them at all. Sidonius' language strongly condemns astrology for providing pointless answers and orphaning its followers from the Catholic faith.

The epistle contributes to Sidonius' self-fashioning in several ways. Sidonius appears well informed; news reaches him promptly, his retelling of the events represents the contents of the letter as if it will be news to Lupus. Lupus' request for a poem reminds the reader of Sidonius' poetic skill while enabling him to include the literary nicknames Lampridius and Sidonius used for each other, as Orpheus and Phoebus respect-ively.[142] Sidonius describes Lampridius' learning and literary output in some detail; these claims ultimately reflect on Sidonius as a friend with whom Lampridius shared his literary endeavours.[143] Sidonius however is far wiser than his friend; he knows what he can and should do. Consulting astrologers is definitely forbidden; nevertheless its inclusion makes the narrative of the epistle all the more scandalous and exciting.

Reading Lampridius' death in *Ep.* 8.11 with a positivist view offers little certainty – Sidonius' epistles provide our only extant descriptions of the gifted but unusual Gallic orator. Perhaps Lampridius did have a fervent and well-known interest in astrology; Sidonius' knowledge and use of spe-cific terms, and his offer to discuss the astrological aspects at further length with Lupus in due course, suggest that some practice or at least awareness of astrology existed in the Gallic aristocracy and clergy of the mid to late fifth century.[144] One may even suppose that Lupus was interested in that aspect of the story, or that he knew a thing or two about astrology, at least enough to sustain a conversation with Sidonius, and perhaps more, if the moral of Lampridius' death was directed specifically at him.

These "friend" characters drive forward specific narratives which develop alongside and interact with their portrayals: Lampridius' larger than life character corresponds to his sensational death. Ferreolus' brilliant lineage and offices foreground his key role in the events of the early 450s which were critical for Gaul. Constantius' wisdom and holiness provide the hook for three narratives: his journey, and visit, which leads to an eye-witness

---

[142] *Ep.* 8.11.3.
[143] *Ep.* 8.11.6–8.
[144] This is substantiated by Sidonius' direct references to the contemporary teaching and learning of astrologers in §2 of the prose preface to *Carm.* 22, and two mentions of Claudianus Mamertus' interest in astrology in *Ep.* 4.3.5 and 5.2.1, for which see Desbrosses (2015: 222–223), who characterises Sidonius' relationship to astrology as ambiguous.

account of the aftermath of the Visigothic assault. The characters that Sidonius establishes for these three individuals enhance their narratives and the morals these stories offer: personal sacrifice is the mark of a holy man; astrology can get you murdered; ecclesiastical office is more valuable than secular rank. Each depiction contributes to Sidonius' self-fashioning in comparison with Constantius as a strong leader of his community, and in contrast to Ferreolus as a successful member of the clergy and Lampridius whose dabbling with forbidden knowledge brought about his death.

Holy Exempla in Episcopal Narratives

Sidonius' episcopal role is a focalisation point for certain characters in his epistles. Four of these characters stand tall as positive exempla. In *Ep.* 6.2 the widow Eutropia's holiness persists despite the cruel behaviour of the presbyter Agrippinus.[145] In *Ep.* 4.25 and 6.12 the archbishop Patiens does the right thing, using his wisdom and generosity to make a positive impact on the Church and society.[146] In *Ep.* 4.9 and 4.13 Vectius, a *vir illustris*, is presented as an exemplum worth following and then is encouraged to use his status to induce Germanicus to join the clergy. Lastly, in *Ep.* 7.13, Himerius is praised for his diligent following of Lupus as his model and teacher.

Sidonius begins *Ep.* 6.2 with a brief character sketch of Eutropia (6.2.1):

> Venerabilis Eutropia matrona, quod ad nos spectat, singularis exempli, quae parsimonia et humanitate certantibus non minus se ieiuniis quam cibis pauperes pascit et in Christi cultu pervigil sola in se compellit peccata dormire, maeroribus orbitatis necessitate litis adiecta in remedium mali duplicis perfectionem vestrae consolationis expetere festinat

> The venerable matron Eutropia, it looks to me, is an exceptional example, her abstinence and kindness rival one another, she feeds herself with fasting no less than the poor with food and ever vigilant in Christ's service she compels only the sins inside her to sleep, but since the obligation of a legal case has been added to the grief of her loss she is rushing to find your consolation as a remedy for her two ills

Eutropia's epithet *venerabilis* places her on par with the respect offered to bishops.[147] She acts upon her Christian values, helping others, persisting

---

[145] Our knowledge of Eutropia is limited to this one epistle, for which see B. Baldwin (1982: 105). Germain (1840: 10) notes that Eutropia's charitable acts are exceptional.

[146] For the comparison Sidonius draws between Patiens and Triptolemus in *Ep.* 6.12 see p. 55.

[147] See Brown (1992: 77) and Jerg (1970) for the initial use of *venerabilis* in the Church.

despite her bereavement.[148] The extent of this loss is not immediately clear, but she was evidently already suffering before her recent legal trouble arose. Sidonius accounts for his clear sympathy as to her plight (6.2.2):

> igitur praefata venerabilis fratris mei nunc iam presbyteri Agrippini, ne iniuriosum sit dixisse nequitiis, certe fatigatur argutiis; qui abutens inbecillitate matronae non desistit spiritalis animae serenitatem saecularium versutiarum flatibus turbidare; cui filii nec multo post nepotis amissi duae pariter plagae recentes ad diuturni viduvii vulnus adduntur.

> and so the venerable lady (mentioned above) is being worn out by the wily practices – lest it be unfair to have termed them wicked acts – of my brother Agrippinus who only recently became a presbyter. Taking advantage of the matron's vulnerability he does not refrain from blowing worldly cunning against a calm spiritual soul who since she lost her son and a little later her grandson, now has two fresh blows to add to the daily wounds of a widow.

Sidonius' Christian terminology imbues this description with a solemn sanctity. The position of the adjective *venerabilis* adjacent to both *praefata* and *fratis* may be read as applying to Eutropia or Agrippinus, but this very adjective was used earlier to describe her in the opening of the epistle.[149] The reader is thus induced to decide that Eutropia is more deserving of the epithet than Agrippinus. A simpler word order such as *venerabilis praefata* would lose this tension. Figurative language describes Eutropia's suffering (*plagae recentes, vulnus*) implicitly likening her to a martyr. Agrippinus, an inexperienced presbyter, nevertheless pursues her with litigation. Sidonius affects a balanced assessment but clearly induces the reader to side with his advocacy on Eutropia's behalf, *nequitiae* not *argutiae* seem apt; Agrippinus is morally bankrupt to be taking advantage of the most vulnerable in society. Sidonius' frustration is evident in the rhetorical synopsis of Agrippinus' actions as "blowing worldly cunning" against a calm Christian soul.

The contrast of Eutropia's character with that of Agrippinus forms the basis of Sidonius' account of his efforts to mediate the dispute (*Ep.* 6.2.3):

> temptavimus inter utrumque componere, nos maxume, quibus in eos novum ius professio vetustumque faciebant amicitiae, aliqua censentes, suadentes quaepiam, plurima supplicantes; quodque miremini, in omnem concordiae statum promptius a feminea parte descensum est. et quamquam se altius

---

[148] Krause (1991: 551) suggests that Eutropia's wealth enabled her ascetic lifestyle; it probably also funded her legal battle against Agrippinus. Sidonius makes no specific mention of her means.

[149] *Ep.* 6.2.1.

profuturum filiae paterna iactaret praerogativa, nurui tamen magis placuit munificentiae socrualis oblatio.

I tried to mediate between the two, I was especially suited to do so as my profession gave me a new right to do so and my friendships an old one, assessing some points, urging some others, and asking many more; you may be amazed that for every point of the negotiation there was prompter agreement from her side. And although he boasted with the prerogative of a father that he would be a better option for his daughter, the daughter-in-law still preferred her mother-in-law's generous offer.

Sidonius' censure, advice, and requests make little headway; Eutropia's recently widowed daughter-in-law would prefer to stay with her rather than with Agrippinus. There is an implied slight against Agrippinus, whose treatment of his own daughter is clearly worse than Eutropia's, as he seemingly refuses to back down from his stubborn and vexatious litigation.

The dispute is now Pragmatius' problem (6.2.4):

sancta enim Eutropia, si quid vadimonio meo creditis, victoriam computat, si vel post damna non litiget. unde et suspicor vobis unam pronuntiandam domum discordiosam, licet inveniatis utramque discordem.

for the saintly Eutropia, if you give any credence to my assurance, will mark it down as a victory if she avoids litigation after paying some recompense. And so I actually suspect that you will pronounce only one of the households disagreeable even if you find that both are in disagreement.

Sidonius induces Pragmatius to favour Eutropia, whose epithet *sancta* draws attention to her holiness.[150] He provides Pragmatius with a ready-made solution: pay off Agrippinus, but let the grieving widow stay with her kind mother-in-law. In the disagreement Agrippinus' heart is surely in the wrong place; his actions have merely increased the suffering of Eutropia and his daughter.

Sidonius' appraisal of Eutropia's character and his criticism of Agrippinus drive the narrative. The events are related in an initial sequence: Eutropia is a devout Christian, her husband has died, Agrippinus has launched his legal action. The situation is worsened by Eutropia's recent losses, which Sidonius details after his mention of the legal proceeding, yet Agrippinus must have known of Eutropia's grief and launched the action anyway. Sidonius appears as the hard-working bishop trying to do the right thing by his constituents within the bounds laid out by law; his advice to Pragmatius offers a practical solution to the dilemma.[151] The epistle is more

---

[150] Bailey (2016: 39).
[151] Sidonius is likely punning on the etymology of Pragmatius' name from the Greek πρᾶγμα.

dynamic than a mere character sketch; Eutropia's holiness is demonstrated by her actions: feeding the poor, caring for her daughter-in-law, suffering her own personal losses, and putting up with Agrippinus' ill-considered and sanctimonious litigation. Agrippinus forms a clear contrast as he fails to live up to the expectations of his clerical office.

A comparable depiction occurs in *Ep.* 2.8, a letter likely circulated prior to Sidonius' episcopacy, in which he describes the death of Philomathia, a pious daughter and dutiful mother of five.[152] Praise of her character segues into a description of her burial, as her body was conveyed into the tomb by the hands of her relatives and clergy.[153] The moment of her death allows Sidonius to look back on the life that she led and forward to the bereavement of her family, especially her newly widowed husband, childless father, and motherless children. Sidonius includes in the epistle a copy of the epitaph that he wrote for the tombstone that neatly summarises his praise of her character and condolences for her grieving family.[154] In both *Ep.* 2.8 and 6.2 Sidonius merges a letter of praise into a narrative of suffering, by focusing in both cases on the consequences of bereavement.

The bishop Patiens features in four epistles (in three explicitly). These epistles create a narrative of Patiens' effective conduct as a bishop. In *Ep.* 2.10 and 3.12 the references are brief. Sidonius credits the completion of a new church to Patiens (*Ep.* 2.10.2): "quae [ecclesia] studio papae Patientis summum coepti operis accessit, viri sancti strenui, severi misericordis quique per uberem munificentiam in pauperes humanitatemque non minora bonae conscientiae culmina levet" (which [church] the energy of bishop Patiens has brought to the point of completion, a holy and active man, stern and sympathetic, who through his abundant generosity towards the poor and his kindness builds his good conscience equally high).[155] He stands as a model for other clergy, he is holy but still engages in worldly affairs, stern but also sympathetic, and overwhelmingly generous, willing to help others less fortunate.[156] This brief sketch introduces the reader to Patiens' character.

The second reference to him in the collection is not explicit. In *Ep.* 3.12 Patiens is probably the bishop to whom Sidonius refers the incident of the

---

[152] *Ep.* 2.8.1, for discussion of which see Krause (1991: 545).

[153] *Ep.* 2.8.2.

[154] *Ep.* 2.8.3, for which see Wolff (2014b: 208–211).

[155] Bailey (2016: 80) posits that the church in question was probably the Church of St John.

[156] Rousseau (1976: 365) suggests that his praise of Patiens "could have been a vivid warning to himself [Sidonius], just before his consecration, of the adaption required in a man who wished to be a bishop." Patiens shows no sign of adaption or development in the depictions in Sidonius' corpus.

grave diggers defiling his grandfather's tomb.[157] The bishop's reponse in *Ep.* 3.12 is consistent with what the reader may expect of Patiens: he waves away Sidonius' apology and offers him praise for his speedy correction of the outrage.

In *Ep.* 4.25 Sidonius recounts how Patiens conducted the election of a bishop in adverse circumstances. The epistle begins excitedly (*Ep.* 4.25.1):

> Nequeo differre, quin grandis communione te gaudii festinus inpertiam, nimirum nosse cupientem, quid pater noster in Christo pariter et pontifex Patiens Cabillonum profectus more religionis, more constantiae suae fecerit. cum venisset in oppidum suprascriptum provincialium sacerdotum praevio partim, partim comitante collegio, scilicet ut municipio summus aliquis antistes ordinaretur

> I am unable in my haste to put off giving you a share of the wonderful joy, surely you desire to know what Patiens our father in Christ and bishop achieved once he set out for Cabillonum with his characteristic sense of firmness and of duty. When he arrived in the aforementioned town partly preceded and partly accompanied by a group of provincial priests clearly to see to it that someone be ordained as the lead priest of the community

Patiens and his entourage arrive in Cabillonum to conduct the election which was needed as the bishop Paulus had recently died. The townspeople offer the bishop and his advisers a surly welcome; three men had been actively campaigning for the position – *triumviratus conpetitorum* (a triumvirate of rivals).[158] Each of these candidates is unsuited to the role.[159] The first drones on about his aristocratic blood but conveniently ignores his moral deficiency; the second has courted the gourmand voting block – hardly the kind of backers suitable for a bishop; the last had already planned how he intended to divide the church's property among his supporters were he elected.[160] The situation is dire. No candidate represents the interests of the townspeople or the church. Patiens and his episcopal colleague Euphronius put into action a plan to circumvent the triumvirs' electoral ambitions (4.25.3):

> quod ubi viderunt sanctus Patiens et sanctus Euphronius, qui rigorem firmitatemque sententiae sanioris praeter odium gratiamque primi tenebant,

---

Even after Sidonius became a bishop he continued to praise Patiens. The lack of clarity regarding when *Ep.* 2.10 was written and how and how quickly Sidonius became a bishop makes it difficult to reconstruct what Sidonius was thinking when the epistle was written.

[157] See pp. 69–71 and Janes (2000: 8).

[158] *Ep.* 4.25.2.

[159] Becker (2014b: 52–54) draws on this epistle to note the growing politicisation of episcopal elections.

[160] *Ep.* 4.25.2.

consilio cum coepiscopis prius clam communicato quam palam prodito strepituque despecto turbae furentis iunctis repente manibus arreptum nihilque tum minus quam quae agebantur optantem suspicantemque sanctum Iohannem, virum honestate humanitate mansuetudine insignem.

when the holy Patiens and holy Euphronius saw this, these noble men held onto the strength and firmness of their more rational opinion, free of hatred and favour. First their plan was shared with their fellow bishops in secret, then it was put forward openly and, spurning the roar of the raging crowd, with joined hands they suddenly seized their man, who himself had no desire or suspicion at all about what was happening, the holy John, a man outstanding in integrity, kindness, and gentleness.

The two holy men are not influenced by hatred or favour. The climax of the narrative is marked by an alliterative flourish: "consilio cum coepiscopis prius clam communicato quam palam prodito." Out of nowhere, or at least out of near total obscurity, a humble and honest priest is promoted by the bishops. The crowd rages in disgust but too late; the stratagem has worked, acting in concert under the leadership of Patiens and Euphronius the episcopal council have their man.[161] Sidonius concludes the epistle by praising the two bishops for their effective management of the difficult situation.[162] Patiens' importance is far-reaching: he is the preeminent figure in Sidonius' town on account of his episcopal rank as archbishop; this importance in turn extends to the entire province.

Patiens' character is the driving force of the epistle. Much of the action undertaken is implied. The assessment of the candidates' merits (or rather lack thereof) required some investigation, which the bishop as one of the leaders of the episcopal delegation presumably oversaw.[163] The pre-selection of John must have been undertaken somewhat surreptitiously; the towns-people seemingly had no idea what was about to happen.[164] Patiens is

---

[161] For an assessment of Euphronius' role in this and another episcopal election see Castellanos (2013: 237–238).

[162] *Ep.* 4.25.5.

[163] This process may be understood as an "implied dialogue" for which see p. 165.

[164] Hanson (1970: 3–4). Comparison with the election in Bourges may shed light on the nature of the process. In *Ep.* 7.8 Sidonius sounds out Euphronius' views on his candidate Simplicius (the son of Eulogius). This happens in the collection before Sidonius endorsed Simplicius in *Ep.* 7.9, a chronology that surely reflects that Sidonius sought Euphronius' advice before he publicly endorsed Simplicius. *Ep.* 7.8.2 indicates as much "quia Simplicium, spectabilem virum, episcopum sibi flagitat populus Biturix ordinari, quid super tanto debeam negotio facere, decernas" (since the people of Bourges demand that Simplicius, a man of rank, be ordained as their bishop, decide what I should do about this significant business). Diefenbach (2013: 91–92) argues that it reflects well on Sidonius that Simplicius' lack of clerical experience does not disqualify him from clerical office, since Sidonius similarly lacked such experience prior to his appointment as a bishop.

clearly a formidable adversary: cunning, a good judge of character, brave, and a gifted leader.

In *Ep.* 6.12 Sidonius narrates the action that Patiens took to relieve large parts of Gaul from crippling starvation. In that letter the focus is placed squarely on Patiens' charity and generosity to others; these aspects round out his impeccable character as a key leader in the Gallic Church. The epistle begins with a gnomic assertion that a life led for others is truly worth living. This assertion transitions into a synopsis of the many acts that Patiens has done for others: spreading charity to those near and far, including improving and renovating churches. This is a reference to Patiens' first mention in the collection as the bishop who oversaw the renovation of the church in Lyon.[165] Patiens has also battled against heretics and converted barbarians to the orthodox faith.[166] Sidonius allows that others have helped carry out these deeds, but for one act Patiens alone deserves the credit (*Ep.* 6.12.5):

> post Gothicam depopulationem, post segetes incendio absumptas peculiari sumptu inopiae communi per desolatas Gallias gratuita frumenta misisti, cum tabescentibus fame populis nimium contulisses, si commercio fuisset species ista, non muneri. vidimus angustas tuis frugibus vias; vidimus per Araris et Rhodani ripas non unum, quod unus impleveras, horreum.

> after the Visigothic devastation, after the crops were consumed by fire, at your own expense you sent free supplies of grain through the desolate lands of Gaul for the public need, even though you would have done too much for the people, wasting away from hunger, if that supply had been a sale, rather than a gift. I have seen the roads crammed with your grain; I have seen by the banks of the Saône and the Rhône more than one barn which you alone have filled.

Gaul has been left devastated by the Visigothic incursions.[167] Patiens relieves the hunger of the people by releasing grain from his supply, giving it freely rather than selling it at a (surely inflated) price.[168] Sidonius praises Patiens by drawing examples from both Christian and Classical literature, likening him to both Triptolemus (who had two ships where Patiens has used two rivers) and to Joseph (who carefully stored grain to survive a

---

[165] See p. 129.

[166] *Ep.* 6.12.4.

[167] Allen and Neil (2013: 79) allow that the destruction of grain could be the result of a natural disaster, but the phrase *post Gothicam depopulationem* strongly implies that the Visigothic incursion was the cause.

[168] Harries (1994: 227) is right to note that in normal circumstances Patiens would have sold the grain. Sidonius' point is that Patiens did not exploit the people's suffering by selling the grain at an inflated price but instead gave it away for free. See also Harries (1992a: 91).

seven year famine).[169] His popularity is attested from one end of Gaul to the other.

Patiens thus epitomises the best that the Church offers in times of acute crisis. The epistle ends with Sidonius noting that the peoples' starvation at least afforded them the opportunity to appreciate his enormous generosity.[170] His character drives the specific narrative of the grain distribution forward. This story resonates with the broader narrative of the Visigothic plundering and destruction of Gaul, and within the epistle of Patiens' other good acts. The link to Patiens' renovation of the church in Lyon places this epistle in a continuum with *Ep.* 2.10. Its display of Patiens as a church leader of all of Gaul fosters a similar link to *Ep.* 4.25; Patiens is everyone's bishop.

Vectius is mentioned in two epistles: in *Ep.* 4.9 Sidonius sings his praises to Industrius, and he is the addressee of *Ep.* 4.13. In the first epistle Sidonius offers a detailed assessment of his behaviour, virtues, and physical appearance: he treats his household well, is a generous but sober host, is skilled at hunting, dresses and carries himself well, and speaks in a dignified manner. Sidonius signals out his Christian learning and practice for special praise; Vectius religiously reads the Psalms and is almost a monk (*Ep.* 4.9.3): "monachum complet non sub palliolo sed sub paludamento" (he fulfils the role of a monk at least in custom if not costume).[171] The point of Sidonius' praise is to present Vectius as an exemplum for others to follow (*Ep.* 4.9.5):

> qua industria viri ac temperantia inspecta ad reliquorum quoque censui pertinere informationem, si vel summotenus vita ceteris talis publicaretur, ad quam sequendam praeter habitum … omnes nostrae professionis homines utilissime incitarentur, quia … plus ego admiror sacerdotalem virum quam sacerdotem.

> once I looked into this man's moderation and diligence I decided that it would be relevant to other's instruction, if such a life was shown to others far and wide, and it might be very useful in encouraging all men of my profession to follow it, except with regards to their clerical dress … since I admire a priestly man more than a man who happens to be in the priesthood.

Ep. 4.13 begins with a character sketch of Germanicus. Unlike Vectius, he is only described in physical terms: his gait, strength, stamina, and

---

[169] See p. 55.
[170] *Ep.* 6.12.9.
[171] The literal contrast is between a monk's habit and the dress of a military man, for the specifics of Sidonius' word play see Bellès (1998: 46n62). Vectius' portrait is briefly discussed by Wolff (2017: 81).

vitality have allowed him, despite his age, to avoid serving the Church in the same capacity as his son and father.[172] Sidonius urges Vectius to entice Germanicus into the clergy, lest he become an embarrassment for his family. The epistles are clearly linked, not only by their close proximity in the same book, but also as the only epistles in the collection to mention Vectius. However, they offer different models of correct behaviour.[173] In *Ep.* 4.9 Vectius' lack of clerical status makes his exemplum all the more powerful to Sidonius, who explicity favours him over those who are clerics in name only.[174] In *Ep.* 4.13 Germanicus' failure to join the Church is the basis for Sidonius' criticism. It may be sufficient, and even admirable, for Vectius to behave as he does without clerical rank, but Germanicus falls into a separate category, because both his father and son were clerics. Sidonius' focus on Germanicus' physical appearance comes at the expense of praising his other qualities. This is thrown into sharp relief by the implied comparison with Vectius which makes Germanicus appear vain and self-centered.

Sidonius' praise of Himerius in *Ep.* 7.13 follows loosely the same structure as his praise of Vectius in *Ep.* 4.9: both read religious literature, exercise careful moderation, are great companions, and are skilful and learned speakers.[175] Himerius, however, was a member of the clergy; his exact position is not clear – Sidonius refers to him with the general term *antistes* – but he seems to exert a degree of influence over others which is in keeping with someone with important responsibilities.[176] Himerius' character and behaviour remind Sidonius of Lupus, who recieves reflected praise, as the holy bishop who taught Himerius and whose exemplum Himerius has in turn followed. This praise is also cast onto Himerius' worldly father, Sulpicius, to whom the epistle is addressed (*Ep.* 7.13.5):

> totum te nobis ille iam reddidit; totam tuam temperantiam religionem, libertatem verecundiam et illam delicatae mentis pudicissimam teneritudinem iucunda similitudine exscripsit. quapropter quantum volueris deinceps frui secreto, indulgere secessui, licebit indulgeas; quandoquidem nos in fratre meo Himerio avum nomine, patrem facie, utrumque prudentia iam tenemus.

> he now completely resembles you, in my opinion; he has copied out, with pleasing similarity, your restraint, religious duty, freedom, modesty and that

[172] *Ep.* 4.13.2.
[173] Raga (2014: 78).
[174] Rousseau (1976: 358).
[175] *Ep.* 7.13.1–4.
[176] *Ep.* 7.13.1.

most beautiful tenderness of a delightful mind. Consequently enjoy your seclusion as much as you want, indulge in your retirement, it is your right to indulge, since we have in my brother Himerius, his grandfather in name, his father in appearance, and in wisdom the both of you.

Sidonius' encouragement to Sulpicius to enjoy his lifestyle is based on the piety and success of his son Himerius, whose devotion and sacrifice excuses Sulpicius from the obligation to involve himself in the community.[177]

Eutropia and Patiens are the main characters in emotionally charged narratives. Their holiness, Christian values, generosity, charity, and wisdom hold them in good stead: in Eutropia's case through the deaths of her husband, son, and grandson, and in Patiens' case the renovation of a church, the adjudication of Sidonius' ad hoc punishment of the grave diggers, and on a larger scale, the conduct of a challenging episcopal election and the relief of starvation through Gaul. The narrative of each epistle interacts with the development of their characters. Eutropia's sanctity forms a clear contrast to Agrippinus' aggressive and litigious behaviour. The various epistles that detail Patiens' actions and character collude to make a broader narrative that details his effective execution of the office of archbishop of Gaul. There was probably some benefit and certainly no harm to Sidonius in interweaving through his epistles the career highlights of his ecclesiastic superior.[178] Patiens and Vectius stand as a model for what clergy ought to be like.[179] This model gains relevancy from the negative exempla of clergy and would-be clergy which feature: people like the triumvirs who campaign immorally for their election to the vacant bishopric or Agrippinus who has only just become a presbyter and is already proving himself unworthy of his lowly church rank or Germanicus who is overly obsessed with his own appearance at the expense of fulfilling his Christian duty.

These depictions reflect positively on Sidonius. In Eutropia's case he appears as a committed bishop focused on protecting the vulnerable in his community against those who are unsympathetic to their plight.[180] His advocacy is practical and selfless; Sidonius has little to gain from a favourable outcome other than peace of mind that the widow has managed to get some relief from her worldly suffering. Patiens' numerous positive appearances make an equally important contribution to Sidonius' image as a grateful and supportive member of the church, able to work effectively

---

[177] Raga (2014: 77–78).
[178] Mratschek (2016: 311) shows that the social standing of addressees does not necessarily correlate with their prominence in Sidonius' collection, but it surely does in Patiens' case.
[179] See Chapter 5.
[180] Harries (1994: 211–212).

alongside his superiors to assuage the people's suffering or ensure that the right sort of people assume positions of responsibility. Sidonius' praise of Vectius and Himerius shows the characteristics that he values, and in Vectius' case his commitment to judging men according to their intrinsic worth rather than rank, even if they are fellow clergy.

Conclusion

Altman theorised that the fragmentary nature of epistles may be likened to dots which appear to form lines, creating the semblance of continuities at the moment of reception.[181] This model may usefully be applied to Sidonius' characters, the individuals whom he describes and who interact with his persona in the epistles. Sidonius' control over these characters, what Macarthur termed "the audible voice of the narrator" is significant; his control over what continuities are to be read requires consideration of Sidonius' role as the "implied author" – the arranger of the epistles. This distinction may help to follow the characters whose narratives are spread throughout multiple epistles.

Lampridius' death in *Ep.* 8.11 comes as a shock to Sidonius' narratorial voice; the recasting of the epistle's *Erzählzeit* dramatically marks the impact of the news on Sidonius' persona.[182] The shock to the reader is considerably less, marking a neat conclusion to a narrative arc focused on the gifted but troubled orator that only has to stretch from *Ep.* 8.9, when he is first mentioned in the collection as its addressee. Sidonius' role as implied author is clearly discernible to the reader; the letter to Lampridius precedes the letter about his death and so maintains a comforting chronological order.

Sidonius' role as implied author becomes more difficult to read when the broader narratives of the collection are considered: the emergence of the barbarian successor kingdoms, the demise of Roman power in Gaul, and the actions of the clergy and aristocracy. Macarthur argued that the immediacy of the letter-writer's concerns obstructs their longer perspective:

> In the epistolary form, present moments are recounted without knowledge of the future ... Rather than recounting a series of past events that can be seen, retrospectively, to lead to a particular outcome epistolary characters describe present events with no knowledge of the larger story in which these events may ultimately play a role.[183]

[181] Altman (1982: 167–169).
[182] See pp. 87–88.
[183] Macarthur (1990: 8).

Joining the dots between two epistles separated by only one intervening epistle is less problematic perhaps than connecting epistles from numerous books, written at different moments in history, and which responded to the immediacy of those moments. Narratives thus exist within Sidonius' collection that cannot easily be understood as the result of his work as the implied author. This does not prevent our reading of these narratives; the epistles, for example, chart the rise of the barbarian kingdoms in Gaul, but this narrative demands interpretation of the extent of Sidonius' authorial control over it. Its highly fragmentary nature and its subject matter render it improbable that Sidonius and his circle of Gallo-Roman literati were determined to keep for posterity the story of how the west was lost.

Sidonius' persona is a continuum that runs through each epistle in the collection.[184] It is the immoveable lens through which we unavoidably read all of the characters in the collection. At times this self-reflection is readily discernible, but it becomes harder to see when others are ostensibly his focus. In *Ep.* 7.9 Sidonius reflects on the career of another Gallo-Roman, Simplicius, the son of Eulogius (*Ep.* 7.9.19–20):

> si humanitas requirenda est, civi clerico peregrino, minimo maximoque, etiam supra sufficientiam offertur, et suum saepius panem ille potius, qui non erat redditurus, agnovit. si necessitas arripiendae legationis incubuit, non ille semel pro hac civitate stetit vel ante pellitos reges vel ante principes purpuratos. [...] postremo iste est ille, carissimi, cui in tenebris ergastularibus constituto multipliciter obserata barbarici carceris divinitus claustra patuerunt.

> if his kindness is queried, he is available to the citizen, cleric, stranger, to the most insignificant person and to the most important, above and beyond what is needed, and quite often the man who was not going to repay took his alms. If the need to undertake an embassy became urgent, not just once he stood up for his city before skin-clad kings or before purpled princes ... Finally this is the man, my dear friends, for whom when he was locked up in a dark jail cell, the abundantly bolted doors of a barbarian prison divinely opened.

Simplicius is praised for his generosity and service, especially his representation to "skin-clad kings" and "purpled emperors."[185] He no doubt did both; Sidonius otherwise would have looked quite ridiculous praising him. Unlike Simplicius, however, Sidonius' public readers have a broader

---

[184] This includes *Ep.* 4.2, which was written by Claudianus Mamertus and addressed to Sidonius.
[185] Harries (1992a: 94) lists this as an example of growing importance of diplomatic experience for bishops.

context in which to place this epistle: its book, the collection as a whole, and Sidonius' other achievements. The epistolary doublespeak is perceptible; Sidonius' self is a readable stand-in for Simplicius – epistles are inherently about the author even when they appear not to be.[186]

The narratives and characters of individual epistles may be read on their own terms without specific connection to others. The portrait of Eutropia and account of her legal struggle against Agrippinus is self-reliant; it may be contextualised by its position in book 6, or linked to Sidonius' portraits of other women in the collection, but it is not reliant on these connections for its own narrative. Sidonius' self is still there to be seen: the thoughtful bishop trying to protect the grieving widow from a callous churchman.

Sidonius' character-driven narratives blend different modes of story telling. In *Ep.* 3.2 the didactic mode details Constantius' tour of war-torn Clermont as he wanders through the town, speaks to the people, witnesses the damage and atrocities, and then encourages them to return and rebuild. This transitions into the introspective mode; Sidonius reflects on the greatness of his character, his generosity and charity, and notes that the townspeople are thinking along similar lines, focusing on the extensive personal cost to Constantius of undertaking the journey. The epistle concludes in the summative mode: the perils of Constantius' journey are listed in asyndeton. These three modes effectively interweave the different narrative strands of the epistle which are bound together by Constantius' character.

Sidonius' authorial control must affect our reading of how he portrays others in the collection. Such portrayals exhibit factual and fictional elements; the truth will only ruin a good story, and Sidonius' epistles have plenty of these.

---

[186] Sidonius' praise of Gaudentius in *Ep.* 1.4 reflects on his own career advancement, for which see pp. 20–21. Becker's (2014b: 52–54) analysis of this epistle is limited, as she does not consider Sidonius' background as an envoy, for which see p. 3. Brennan (1985: 318) highlights the importance of Sidonius' praise of his candidate's wife in contrast to his refusal to back candidates who had been married twice or who had a monastic background and therefore limited worldy experience. Like Simplicius, Sidonius was also freed from barbarian imprisonment, for which see Hanaghan (forthcoming) and p. 7.

CHAPTER 5

Narrating Dialogue

The author's voice may be heard in every word of an epistle as the epistolary "I" dominates its discourse. All voices in an epistle are controlled by the author; dissent is thus a fiction, allowed only within the bounds that the author sets. Altman recognised the potential for deceit that underpins all purported remarks in an epistle:

> instead of faithfully registering and reproducing dialogues … [epistles] offer concise analyses … dialogue is condensed into its salient elements and filtered through the [author's] intelligence.[1]

Filtering is an apt term for the apparent reproduction of past or present dialogues; but epistles are not constrained merely to assert what was and is being said, but may also convey what will or should be said. In this aspect the author's control over the addressee's likely words is comparable to the manipulation of *Lesezeit*, anticipated dialogue becoming in effect a vocalised form of anticipated thought. As Miles has shown, Augustine deployed this epistolary strategy to put down dissenting views in the North African church by studiously recording his debates, circulating them, and even imagining his opponents' responses, squeezing them out of any opportunity for further dissent.[2]

Genette theorised that all narrative discourse was reported (diegetic); that the authorial control over dialogue was such that even speech that appeared to imitate (mimetic) actual speech would always fall short.[3] In Latin indirect speech is not mimetic,[4] as two major syntactical changes

---

[1] Altman (1982: 113).

[2] Miles (2008: 139–147).

[3] Genette (1980: 228–231).

[4] Kroon's (2002: 192–195) analysis of dialogue in Pliny's *Ep.* 7.27 drew upon Chafe, Bakker, and Rosén in listing indirect speech as mimetic. She argued that indirect speech all but replicated direct speech forms. Chafe (1994: 214), however, was far more restrained in his consideration of indirect speech, noting its various distal features (which ultimately make it diegetic to at least some degree). Bakker (1997: 37–38) used mimetic in a very precise way for Greek and especially Thucydides, noting that

take place when speech is reported, namely the accusative subject and infinitive verb. To these may also be added more subtle changes that can occur to pronouns and to verbs in subordinate clauses. All of these mark the diegetic nature of indirect speech in Latin.

Genette's consideration of the diegetic nature of indirect speech is thus more applicable to Latin. He proposed considering dialogue as sitting on a spectrum, on one end of which was direct transcription, which lacked external evidence that speech was occurring such as an introductory verb, and on the other end was indirect speech that was wholly consumed by the narrative process.[5] The narrative may also simply imply that speech has occurred by reporting its outcome without the markers of indirect speech (extradiegetic).

These levels of narrative discourse interact with the different functions of the narrator to tell the story (narrative), interrupt it (directing), address the reader directly (communicative), profess autopsy (testimonial), or to assert a gnomic truth (ideological).[6] Lastly (for our purposes) dialogue in any form or for any function may vary the speed of the epistle; direct discourse occurs at the same pace of the narrative, while indirect discourse may either quicken the pace by summarising or slow it by elaborating.[7]

Sidonius uses direct, indirect, and implied dialogue throughout his epistles to vary the narrative speed, shift the discourse's function, construct climaxes and epistolary characters (as outlined in Chapter 4). His use of dialogue corresponds broadly with the reduction in aristocratic movement in Late Antique Gaul, as it allowed correspondents, who could not physically meet one another, to keep up the pretence of an ongoing conversation.[8] This chapter examines the various narratological implications of Sidonius' direct, indirect, and implied dialogues. It argues that these textual moments may be understood as fictional constructs rather than the accurate reproduction of real speech.[9]

"the mimetic mode of Thucydidean narrative is related to a specific use of the imperfect that has to be distinguished from the better-known use of the imperfect in the diegetic mode." Risselada (2013: 298) applies Allan's (2007: 93ff) analysis to Latin epistles, but does not discuss indirect and direct dialogue. Rosén (1980: 34–35) analyses a comparable use of the imperfect tense form in Pliny, but this still does not support Kroon's claim that indirect discourse is mimetic, as Latin cannot use the imperfect tense in indirect discourse.

[5] Genette (1980: 165–167, 265): "The narrative of events, however, whatever its mode, is always narrative, that is, a transcription of the (supposed) non-verbal into the verbal. Its mimesis will never be anything more than an illusion of mimesis."

[6] Genette (1980: 254–257).

[7] Genette (1980: 85–92, 166).

[8] See p. 13.

[9] Gualandri (1979: 14) argues that the address in *Ep.* 7.9 cannot be taken as an indication of how Sidonius spoke to his flock since the audience of that address included a higher proportion of educated individuals especially fellow clergy.

Switching Focalisation

Epistolary diction's apparent mimicry of speech conceals changes in focalisation more than other genres. The reader may hear all the words of an epistle in their own imagined version of the author's voice, even when the direct speech of others is represented. Thus a shift in focalisation from indirect to direct speech may be less discernible in epistles as the authorial "I" is so dominant.

In several epistles Sidonius clearly marks the narratorial direction the epistle will take, often in response to a request, real or otherwise, from the addressee. Such beginnings establish the "narrative" function of the narrator, which Sidonius may later switch to a communicative function to bring impetus to the narrative, or to the testimonial function to assert his authority, or even on the rare occasion to the ideological function to grapple with some gnomic truth. Dialogues play a key role in the shift in narrative function of four very different epistles: *Ep.* 1.2, which describes the Visigothic king Theodoric II; *Ep.* 1.7, which outlines Arvandus' trial; *Ep.* 5.17, which describes a celebration at a church in Lyon; and *Ep.* 7.9, which includes Sidonius' announcement of the new bishop of Bourges.

Sidonius indicates in the opening of *Ep.* 1.2 that the letter will describe the Visigothic king Theodoric from head to toe and in action as he goes about his daily routine.[10] The second person is reserved to mark the narrative's transition from describing Theodoric's physique (*Ep* 1.2.4): "si actionem diurnam, quae est forinsecus exposita, perquiras" (if you enquire as to his daily routine, which is on public display). The relative clause clarifies that what follows is not the result of Sidonius' unique autoptic experience, anyone who has had business at the Visigothic court could offer a similar description, yet Sidonius does in fact go on to reveal details that only a privileged few could know, ranging from Theodoric's morning prayers, to dining habits and even his attitude to backgammon, the last of which relies on a dramatic shift in narrative function.[11]

Second person verbs (*possis, cupias, eligas, eligis, elegeris*) provide the detailed account of Theodoric's routine with impetus.[12] The gaze of the reader is separate from Sidonius' autoptic view, instead the second person *videas* imagines what Agricola and Sidonius' wider audience would see were they to attend the court.[13] Sidonius' persona is nowhere to be seen in

[10] *Ep.* 1.2.1.
[11] See pp. 142–143.
[12] *Ep.* 1.2.4–5.
[13] *Ep.* 1.2.6.

the image he presents of the court, not even as he resumes the narrative, using the impersonal *redeatur* "returning" rather than a first person verb.[14]

The narrative builds towards the climactic backgammon scene.[15] The king is quite a good player. Observance of his technique engenders a shift in the function of the discourse from telling the story (narrative) to a communicative function, as Sidonius offers a psychoanalytical assessment of the king's personality (1.2.8): "dicam quod sentio: timet timeri" (I will say what I think: he fears to be feared).[16] The absence of any indirect speech marker, either in the phrase *quod sentio*, or for the verb *timet*, lends this remark a mimetic hue. Sidonius could have stressed his reporting of this view by using an indirect statement after *dicam*. The narrator is back in the picture, but not yet sat at the table (*Ep.* 1.2.8):

> quodque mirere, saepe illa laetitia minimis occasionibus veniens ingentium negotiorum merita fortunat. tunc petitionibus diu ante per patrociniorum naufragia iactatis absolutionis subitae portus aperitur. tunc etiam ego aliquid obsecraturus feliciter vincor, quando mihi ad hoc tabula perit, ut causa salvetur.

> and this may amaze you, often the happiness that comes on these insignificant occasions influences positively the outcome of major negotiations. At such times I am happily beaten if I hope to obtain something, and so my game is lost in the moment so my cause may be saved.

The reader's amazement at Sidonius' diplomatic chicanery is enhanced by the dramatic insertion of his persona into the scene. The description of Theodoric playing backgammon now retrospectively has Sidonius' persona sitting opposite the king. The narratorial function is testimonial, nearly anyone who attended the court presumably could provide a general outline of the king's routine, but not everyone has played backgammon with the king. Sidonius' persona promptly leaves the epistolary space, reappearing again at the end of the epistle to assert his commitment to accord with the generic rules and reflect on the completed epistle.[17]

In *Ep.* 1.2 the only person to speak is Sidonius. Even then his speech is contained within the epistolary form, with the exception perhaps of his testimonial outburst, which may be better punctuated so as to bring out its affected mimesis of spoken discourse "dicam, quod sentio, 'timet timeri'."[18] The changes from first, second, and third person alter the focalisation of

---

[14] *Ep.* 1.2.7.

[15] See p. 102 for the impact of this scene on Sidonius' characterisation of Theodoric.

[16] For the literary precedents to this remark see Köhler (1995: 156).

[17] *Ep.* 1.2.10: "ego non historiam sed epistulam efficere curavi" (I have undertaken not to produce a history but an epistle). See p. 115.

[18] *Ep.* 1.2.8.

the narrative as the reader witnesses Theodoric's physique and routine through Sidonius' eyes or as a fly on the wall when Sidonius' persona is injected into the epistle.

Direct speech is instrumental to *Ep*. 1.7, which describes Arvandus' conviction for treason.[19] The main evidence against Arvandus was a letter that had been intercepted addressed to the Visigothic king (Euric), and his secretary's testimony that he had authored the incriminating letter. If his version of Arvandus' trial is a reasonable reflection of what took place, his dear friend inadvertently confessed to treason. Sidonius deemphasises this confession (which given its acceptance by the judges would be arguably the natural climax to any such forensic narrative) by not using direct speech to convey Arvandus' outburst.

Prior to the confession Sidonius outlines Arvandus' propensity for such outbursts by developing a clear contrast between his diligent behind-the-scenes work on Arvandus' behalf and his friend's own self-destructive behaviour. Sidonius and Auxanius (a bishop) come to learn of the moves that are being made against Arvandus (*Ep*. 1.7.6):

> Hanc epistulam laesae maiestatis crimine ardere iurisconsulti interpreta-bantur. me et Auxanium, praestantissimum virum, tractatus iste non latuit, qui Arvandi amicitias quoquo genere incursas inter ipsius adversa vitare perfidum barbarum ignavum computabamus.

> The legal advisers were explaining that this letter was red hot treason. This discussion did not escape me and Auxanius, an exceptional man; we were of the view that it would be disloyal, barbarous, cowardly to avoid Arvandus' friendship, regardless of its form, during that man's difficulties.[20]

They determined that Arvandus could not be abandoned; the misappro-priation of "disloyal, barbarous, cowardly" forms a neat contrast, whereas Sidonius and Auxanius behave in a loyal, cultured, and brave manner, Arvandus' subsequent behaviour deserves the very hypothetical criticisms suitable for Sidonius and Auxanius were they to abandon their friend in his moment of crisis.[21] Together they inform Arvandus of the plot that is being hatched against him (*Ep*. 1.7.6):

> deferimus igitur nil tale metuenti totam perniciam[22] machinam, quam summo artificio acres et flammei viri occulere in tempus iudicii meditabantur,

---

[19] For the circumstances see p. 6; for the temporality of *Ep*. 1.7 see pp. 63–66.

[20] Sidonius' use of a tricolon in asyndeton accentuates the rhetorical flourish of his remarks.

[21] Squillante (2014: 283) catalogues Sidonius' uses of the adjective *barbarus* and shows that it always carries a negative connotation.

[22] For the emendation *perniciam* see Köhler (1999: 232).

scilicet ut adversarium incautum et consiliis sodalium repudiatis sibi soli
temere fidentem professione responsi praecipitis involverent.

we therefore detail to the man who feared nothing of the sort the dangerous scheme, which the keen and fiery men were planning to hide until
the defining moment in court, evidently in order to entwine their reckless
opponent in a hasty public reply, who after repudiating the advice of his
close friends was boldly putting trust in himself alone.

Sidonius barely narrates his report to Arvandus, summarising with the
phrase *perniciam machinam* what the reader has gleaned from the beginning of the epistle. Instead, the narrative function shifts to the testimonial,
as Sidonius conveys aspects of the situation to the reader without indicating that these aspects were conveyed to Arvandus, principally that his
adversaries were fierce and flaming mad, that they were plotting to keep
this information from Arvandus until the moment of the trial, and that
they had accurately gauged his impulsive character. All of this is conveyed
to the reader in direct discourse but not to Arvandus, whose conversation
with the bishops is contained within the indirect speech. Arvandus appears
quick to cut off his wiser friends. They still manage, however, to urge a
plan of action on their incarcerated friend (1.7.6):

dicimus ergo, quid nobis, quid amicis secretioribus tutum putaretur.
suademus nil quasi leve fatendum, si quid ab inimicis etiam pro levissimo
flagitaretur; ipsam illam dissimulationem tribulosissimam fore, quo facilius
exitiosam suscitarent illi persuasionem securitatis.

and so we said, what was thought by us, his closest friends, to be the safe
option. We urged him to confess nothing even if it seems trivial, even if it is
asked by his enemies as if it were very insignificant, [we advised] that their
deception would be very tricky, so as to incite more easily in him a fatal
sense of security.

Arvandus is ignorant of the danger he is in and the potential advantage
that may be derived by confounding his opponents' secret tactics. Denial,
or at least the avoidance of a confession, might buy Arvandus enough time
to allow his own furtive coalition (*amicis secretioribus*) to influence the
course of events.

Arvandus' inability to appreciate the cloak and dagger efforts of his
friends and enemies manifests itself in a dramatic outburst that foreshadows
his later confession (*Ep.* 1.7.7):

quibus agnitis proripit sese atque in convicia subita prorumpens: "abite,
degeneres", inquit, "et praefectoriis patribus indigni, cum hac superforanea
trepidatione; mihi, quia nihil intellegitis, hanc negotii partem sinite

curandam; satis Arvando conscientia sua sufficit; vix illud dignabor admittere, ut advocati mihi in actionibus repetundarum patrocinentur."

once he picked up on the gist of our comments he burst forward breaking out into sudden abuse: "Go away, you degenerates," he said "and men unworthy of your prefect forebears, taking your unnecessary worry with you, let me take care of this part of the business, since you don't understand any of it; for Arvandus his conscience is enough, I will hardly condescend to allow advocates to represent me in proceedings of extortion."

The two *pro* compounds (*proripit, prorumpens*) indicate the alacrity of Arvandus' response; he is in a hurry but has nowhere to go because he is still in jail.[23] He bursts forth into direct speech, spitting at Auxanius and Sidonius the worst possible insult for men of their rank, that their behaviour is beneath their standing, *degeneres* literally ignoble, and unworthy of their prefect forebears.[24] The alliterative plosives (*proripit, prorumpens, praefectoribus patribus*) leaves the reader momentarily witness and proxy target of Arvandus' diatribe. Arvandus' pompous stupidity is evident in the third person reference to himself by name and assertion that he scarcely deems it proper to have representation in the case.[25] He alone will be the arbiter of what is right (*dignabor*) not Auxanius and Sidonius (*indigni*). Sidonius' testimonial function as narrator becomes momentarily ideological (*Ep.* 1.7.7): "discedimus tristes et non magis iniuria quam maerore confusi; quis enim medicorum iure moveatur, quotiens desperatum furor arripiat?" (we departed sadly and confused no more by the insult than by grief; for what doctor would rightfully be excited, whenever madness takes a desperate man?). Arvandus' speech has betrayed his madness. It will soon betray his guilt.

The proceedings of the trial are narrated in a detached and dejected tone (*Ep.* 1.7.10):

epistula post provinciale mandatum, cuius supra mentio facta, profertur; atque, cum sensim recitaretur, Arvandus necdum interrogatus se dictasse proclamat. respondere legati, quamquam valde nequiter, constaret, quod ipse dictasset. at ubi se furens ille quantumque caderet ignarus bis terque repetita confessione transfodit, acclamatur ab accusatoribus, conclamatur

---

[23] Sidonius uses a series of historical infinitives in between these two scenes to describe Arvandus' strutting around town, which exacerbates his shock at how the courtroom proceedings unfold, for which see Köhler (1999: 412).

[24] Sidonius reminds the reader twice of Arvandus' plebeian rank, at *Ep.* 1.7.3 and 11, as noted by Wickham (2005: 155n5). These comments foreshadow and respond to Arvandus' attempted criticism of Sidonius and Auxanius as men unworthy of their rank.

[25] *Ep.* 1.7.7.

a iudicibus reum laesae maiestatis confitentem teneri. ad hoc et milibus
formularum iuris id sancientum iugulabatur.

after the provincial commission, the letter, mentioned above, was brought
forward; and as it was gradually read aloud, without even being asked
Arvandus shouted out that he had dictated it. The delegates responded, but
in a very mean way, that it was agreed that he had dictated it. But when in
a rage, ignorant of the extent of what was about to go down, he did himself
in by repeating his confession two or three times, it was shouted forth by
the accusers and shouted in agreement by the judges that he be determined
to be confessing to the charge of high treason (lèse-majesté). On top of this
by a thousand legal precedents which sanction it he was sentenced to death.

Arvandus does not even wait to be interrogated (*necdum interrogatus*) before
proclaiming that he is the author of the epistle in question. Another *pro*
compound *proclamat* invokes his earlier propensity for outbursts. The par-
ticiple *furens* reasserts Sidonius' gnomic claim that his counsel of Arvandus
was like a doctor trying to treat a madman (*furor*), which the allusion at the
very beginning of the epistle to Pliny's *Ep.* 7.9 has signposted by invoking
a comparison between Fannia's illness and Arvandus' situation.[26] This time
there is no direct speech, instead his shouting (*proclamat*) is drowned out
by two passive *clamo* compounds in asyndeton, first by the accusers in the
alliterative phrase *acclamatur ab accusatoribus*, and then by the judges who
unanimously and immediate convict (*conclamatur a iudicibus*). The shift
from the active to passive voice accentuates Arvandus' loss of control.

The words of Arvandus' hot-tempered outburst against Sidonius and
Auxanius (*praefectoriis patribus indigni*) resound in Sidonius' tempered
reporting of his demotion from patrician rank (*Ep.* 1.7.11): "confestim
privilegiis geminae praefecturae, quam per quinquennium repetitis
fascibus rexerat, exauguratus et, plebeiae familiae non ut additus sed ut
redditus, publico carceri adiudicatus est" (immediately he was disinvested
of the privileges of the double prefecture, which he had held for successive
five year periods, and he was assigned to the state prison, not entering but
rather returning to a plebeian family). Sidonius' use of direct speech in this
epistle indicates the climax according to his focalisation point; after his
dramatic and climactic outburst against Sidonius and Auxanius, Arvandus'
confession becomes a mere fait accompli.

Direct speech typically features in an epistle at the narrative's defining
moment. In Pliny's *Ep.* 1.12, for example, direct speech features twice,
on both occasions the speaker is Corellius Rufus, whose death Pliny is

---

[26] See p. 64n20.

describing. On the first occasion he tells Pliny that there is no point in prolonging his life given the pain of his illness. The second moment is in response to the doctor offering him food "Κέκρικα" "I have made up my mind."[27] Code-switching to Greek makes this remark stand out all the more.[28] Both instances of direct speech lend these pivotal moments an added sense of vivacity. The dynamic of the direct speech in Sidonius' *Ep.* 1.7 is markedly different; unlike Pliny's epistle the natural climax of the story is not enhanced, instead direct speech emphasises an earlier, less significant moment that then foreshadows the narrative's eventual end.

In the epistle Sidonius preserves his testimonial function for what he may personally testify to – he was surely not to know that his epistle would be our only contemporary account of the trial. Preserving the testimonial function for his autoptic experiences maintains his authority as an eyewitness to some but not all the events. Sidonius' authority is kept at a distance from the legally dubious claim that Arvandus was unaware that seizing the purple by force was only one of several acts that constituted treason. Rather than constructing a dramatic dialogue of the confession in direct speech, as if he were there, Sidonius reports what he was subsequently told had transpired.[29] Arvandus' limited understanding of Roman law is at least in keeping with his reckless and boastful character.[30]

This epistle reflects on the nature of epistolary communication. The authorship of Arvandus' *own* epistle may have been in doubt if he had not confessed. This is the only likely reason why Sidonius and Auxanius advised him to confess nothing even if it seemed trivial (*nil quasi leve fatendum*).[31] Epistolary speech is not as easily linked to the speaker as vocal speech even when it appears mimetic, like Arvandus' incriminating letter, written by his own secretary and presumably dictated by him, it can only be, as Genette concluded, degrees of diegetic.

[27] Whitton (2013b: 9n56) notes Pliny's borrowing of Κέκρικα from Cic. *Att.* 13.31.3.
[28] Cicero uses codeswitching in a comparable fashion in *Att.* 13.42, which begins with a dialogue reported in direct speech, for the analysis of which see Swain (2002: 151–152). Mullen (2015: 217–227) links Fronto's use of codeswitching to his use of Cicero as a model. For Pliny's use of codeswitching see Rochette (2010: 289) and (2013: 472–475, 478).
[29] *Ep.* 1.7.9: "sic post comperi nam inter ista discesseram" (I found out about it afterward, for in the meanwhile I had left). Harries (1994: 160) notes that the emotional strain may have been too much for Sidonius. Sivan (1989: 93) implies that Sidonius wanted to distance himself politically from Arvandus. Köhler (1995: 247) suggests that Sidonius may not have held his position only at the beginning of the trial.
[30] *Ep.* 1.7.2.
[31] *Ep.* 1.7.6.

A shift in focalisation is key to the dramatic rhapsodic challenge narrated in *Ep.* 5.17.[32] Sidonius indicates to the addressee Eriphius that he will send him the verses he requested only after he has detailed the context of their composition with a lengthy preface. The account begins in the narrative function.[33] A great mass of both sexes had gathered at the tomb of St Justus for an annual celebration. Sidonius reminds Eriphius that illness prevented his attendance, comments that are surely directed more at his wider audience than at his actual addressee, who surely knew that he was not there and why.[34] After the vigils Sidonius and some others play a ball game.[35] At the end of the game, Sidonius breaks from his narrative function into the testimonial function to relate in direct speech his conversation with Philomathius, an older man who had been quite the ball player in his youth but was the first to withdraw from the game. Sidonius graciously (or so he tells us) joined Philomathius to prevent the older man's humiliation.[36] The conceit is readily apparent when one considers that Sidonius not only shared Philomathius' retirement from fatigue with Eriphius but subsequently circulated the epistle (and those remarks) in his collection. Philomathius is the first to speak (*Ep.* 5.17.9):

> Quo [linteo] dum per otium genas siccat: "vellem", inquit, "ad pannum similis officii aliquod tetrastichon mihi scribi iuberes." "fiat", inquam. "sed quod meum", dixit, "et nomen metro teneret." respondi possibilia factu quae poposcisset. et[37] ipse: "dicta ergo." tunc ego arridens: "ilico scias Musas moveri, si choro ipsarum non absque arbitris vacem."

> As he leisurely dries his cheeks with the cloth, "I would like," he says, "you please to arrange for a four-verse ditty to be written for the cloth in keeping with its service to me." "Let it be so," I say. "But," he said, "it should also have my name in the meter." I answered that what he demanded was possible to do. And he [said] "go on then," then I smiling at him [answered]: "Surely you would know that the Muses may be upset, if I am not far away from critics when I devote myself to their harmonious song."

---

[32] The poetics of this epistle, as noted by Fo (1991: 65), connect well with Sidonius' display of belletrism.

[33] For this terminology see p. 141.

[34] Cf. Sidonius' reminder to Turnus of his father's rank for which see p. 92n8.

[35] Schwitter (2015: 72–77) has convincingly argued that Sidonius' syntax imitates the movement and position of players.

[36] Schwitter (2015: 198) somewhat overstates the case in labelling Sidonius' depiction of Philomathius as a satirical description, but he is surely right to draw attention to its negative elements. Wickham (2005: 158n12) picks up on Sidonius' pride in his ability to play ball at his age.

[37] Luetjohann's text (1887: 91) includes *ait* before the *et* but this is not well attested in the manuscript tradition, is semantically and syntactically unnecessary, and slows the narrative speed of the exchange.

Philomathius' tone is initially polite.[38] The imperfect (*vellem, iuberes*) rather than present subjunctive verbs remove any immediacy from his request. Sidonius' brief response "fiat" is also in direct speech. Philomathius' stipulation that his name be included in the composition receives an acknowledgment from Sidonius in indirect speech that this is possible, implying that he can and will do so. Sidonius' use of indirect speech concedes the impetus in the dialogue to the older man. His imperative *dicta* and Sidonius' narratorial decision to spare his remark from an introductory verb (unlike the other exchanges in the dialogue so far: *inquit*, *inquam*, *dixit*, and *respondi*) quicken the pace. Sidonius tries to get one over Philomathius with his witty response by laughing at him. Philomathius' rejoinder ends the dialogue (*Ep.* 5.17.9):

> respondit ille violenter et perurbane, ut est natura vir flammeus quidamque facundiae fons inexhaustus: "vide, domine Solli, ne magis Apollo forte moveatur, quod suas alumnas solus ad secreta sollicitas." iam potes nosse, quem plausum sententia tam repentina, tam lepida commoverit.

> but he replied passionately and very charmingly, as by nature he is fiery and a sort of inexhaustible fountain of wit, "Ensure, Lord Sollius, that Apollo is not perhaps upset, because you are seducing his pupils at secret meetings just with you." You can already tell the applause that such a sudden and charming sentiment provoked.

His droll reply is bookended by two descriptions, one that speaks to his wit and acumen, the other that notes the applause that followed, indicating that a crowd has quickly gathered or was already there, the entire exchange lasts for less than a minute, assuming Sidonius' indirect speech records an answer that approximates the brevity of his first response.

Sidonius has complete narratorial control over how he reports and ostensibly records his exchange with Philomathius. He has allowed himself to be beaten in the battle of wits (at least in the epistle). The crowd's applause stems from two aesthetic principles, first that Philomathius response was immediate (*repentina*), comebacks thought of subsequently count for nothing, and second that it was witty, the *fons facundiae* did not disappoint with the purpled sibilance at the end of his remarks (*suas alumnas solus ad secreta sollicitas*). These two principles are offered to the reader to induce their application onto Sidonius' verse composition. The insertion of his four-line ditty into the epistle is not followed by the crowd's reaction, applause or otherwise, instead Sidonius adopts the narrative function once

---

[38] This is especially so if *mihi* is understood as an ethic dative.

more to relate that at that very moment (*vix suprascripta peraravera, hora monente*) it was announced that the bishop was leaving the *receptorium* and so the group dispersed.[39]

Sidonius' shift from the narrative function to testimonial and back again makes the exchange with Philomathius more vivid. His defeat in their witty exchange is followed by the requested verse, which was the professed point of the epistle. Rather than simply provide the addressee with a copy of the verse, Sidonius carefully details an account that reflects well on himself, as a fit ball player, sympathetic friend, witty companion (albeit not the wittiest), and gifted extempore poet.[40]

The longest example of direct speech in the collection is contained in *Ep.* 7.9, which includes a version of an address Sidonius gave in Bourges during an episcopal election.[41] This epistle is in many ways a special case because it uses a formal epistolary sign-off before the address: "memor nostri esse dignare, domine papa"; but unlike other epistles where Sidonius creates a false ending, there is no second sign-off. The epistle ends with Sidonius still in the testimonial function of the oration. If the address is counted as part of the epistle, rather than an addendum, *Ep.* 7.9 is clearly the longest in the collection. Sidonius is not at all concerned with the epistle's length. This lack of concern may simply indicate that Sidonius did not consider the address to be part of the epistle proper, and therefore saw no reason to excuse its length. The point of inserting the address in the epistle was (at least in part) to preserve it for posterity, an aim which the selection of the addressee may hint at – the epistle is addressed to Perpetuus, the namesake of perpetuity.[42]

Sidonius begins by expressing his *humilitas*. The new bishop then outlines the difficulties he must negotiate as the selection of one type of candidate is likely to cause offence to others (*Ep.* 7.9.9):

> aures ilico meas incondito tumultu circumstrepitas ignobilium pumilionum murmur everberat conquerentum: 'hic qui nominator', inquiunt, 'non

---

[39] This is a convenient if not wholly fictitious *erzählte Zeit* that prevents the reader from knowing how the crowd responded to Sidonius' poem.

[40] Gregory of Tours 2.22 and Gennadius of Marseilles 92 both mention Sidonius' ability to speak extemporaneously, for which see Wolff (2014a: 249–250). One of their sources for this was surely Sidonius, who describes several such occasions throughout his epistles.

[41] Hanson (1970: 3–4) and Norton (2007: 78–80).

[42] Visser (2014: 30) suggests that Sidonius may have addressed *Ep.* 2.2 to Domitius to invoke an intertextual connection to Pliny's *Ep.* 2.17 and 5.6, both of which were addressed to Domitius Apollinaris. Sidonius extensively alludes to both of these epistles throughout *Ep* 2.2 for which see Gualandri (1979: 96), Mratschek (2008: 374), Harries (1994: 10), Pavlovskis (1973: 48), and Whitton (2013a: 36); for discussion of *Ep.* 2.2 see pp. 42–47. Gibson (2011: 655–659) convincingly argues that Sidonius plays a similar interetextual game with Pliny's collection in the addressee for *Ep.* 1.1 and 9.16, for which see p. 177.

episcopi, sed potius abbatis complet officium et intercedere magis pro animabus apud caelestem quam pro corporibus apud terrenum iudicem potest.' sed quis non exacerbescat, cum videat sordidari virtutum sinceritatem criminatione vitiorum?

immediately the murmuring of unworthy squirts rattles around, beating my ears engulfed by their chaotic uproar. They say "This man who would be nominated does not fulfil his role as a bishop but rather a monk and is more able to intercede on behalf of our souls in front of a heavenly judge than for our bodies in front of an earthly judge." But who would not grow exasperated, when he sees the integrity of virtues muddied by the allegation of vices?

Direct speech is contained within the direct speech of the address that is itself in epistolary form. No-one will be able to dispute the selection of a monk and avoid being characterised as an *ignobilis pumillio* "unworthy squirt."[43] Becker notes that Sidonius' use of a hypothetical objector distances his persona from the claims that are made.[44] The strategy is all the more potent as Sidonius may well be reworking the very language of certain lobbyists in the audience, some of whom, he infers, tried to bribe him.[45]

The direct speech establishes the tone of the remarks that follow, which use indirect discourse to record how Sidonius imagines his critics may respond: a humble man is thought downtrodden, an upright man arrogant, a poorly educated man a joke, a well-educated man conceited, and so the list continues.[46] Even a cleric will be judged wanting for his lack of experience, which appears an especially sore point for Sidonius who had himself only recently assumed episcopal rank.[47] Some (perhaps in the audience) come in for especially savage condemnation (*Ep.* 7.9.12): "nituntur regere ecclesiam, quos iam regi necesse erit per senectam" (some strive to guide the Church who because of their old age will soon need to be guided themselves).

To slow the pace of his remarks and so dwell on an *ad hominem* attack Sidonius reverts to more imagined direct speech (7.9.14):

si militarem dixero forte personam, protinus in haec verba consurgitur: 'Sidonius ad clericatum quia de saeculari professione translatus est, ideo sibi assumere metropolitanum de religiosa congregatione dissimulat; natalibus turget, dignitatum fastigatur insignibus, contemnit pauperes Christi.'

---

[43] Cf. Miles (2008: 139–147).
[44] Becker (2014b: 53).
[45] *Ep.* 7.9.15.
[46] *Ep.* 7.9.10.
[47] *Ep.* 7.9.5–6.

if I perhaps even mention a military man, immediately these comments arise "Sidonius since he was brought across to clergy from a secular career, he is repressing his feelings about taking a metropolitan candidate from a religious assembly; he swells with pride at his birth, he is exalted by his secular rank, he has contempt for the poor of Christ."

Sidonius does not respond to this criticism, at least, not directly, instead his speech turns away from Church politics to scripture, quoting from *Acts* 8.18–24 and then *Luke* 1.5–17 to substantiate beginning the biography of his nominee Simplicius (the son of Eulogius) with a description of his famous forebears (*Ep.* 7.9.23): "parentes ipsius aut cathedris aut tribunalibus praesederunt" (his forebears presided either over sees or courts).[48] They impress Sidonius as they would have also impressed the writer of the gospel who also began his eulogy of John with discussion of that man's ancestors.[49] The response to the imagined *ad hominem* is readily discernible: Sidonius is clearly an able bishop who uses scripture authoritatively as required. From that point the speech continues in Sidonius' voice, save for a brief hypothetical interlocutor who asks Sidonius for his sources regarding Simplicius.[50]

In the four epistles analysed Sidonius uses direct speech in different but important ways. In *Ep.* 1.2 the break from the narratorial mode to the communicative creates an epistolary soliloquy in which Sidonius can "speak" to the addressee outside of the narration to offer his own analysis of the significance of the story. The absence of his persona in the narrative function enables a switch to the testimonial, which sees Sidonius identify himself as the king's backgammon opponent, and in effect retrospectively inserts his persona into the earlier (narratorial) backgammon scene. Similar switches in function are evident in *Ep.* 1.7 where the break from the narratorial mode to the testimonial creates the dramatic precursor to Arvandus' public confession, as he harangues both Sidonius and Auxanius for offering him advice. A further shift to the ideological mode introduces an analogy in which Sidonius is the doctor treating Arvandus the madman. This moment foreshadows Arvandus' own mad ranting in court where no-one, not even Sidonius (who is conspicuously absent) can save him from himself. In *Ep.* 5.17 and 7.9 Sidonius switches narrative modes to exert control over his readers' reaction, encouraging them to project the aesthetics

---

[48] Geisler (1887: 370) and Anderson and Warmington (1963: 348–349). Sidonius names the *Gospel of Luke* at *Ep* 7.9.17.

[49] *Gospel of Luke* 1.5–7.

[50] *Ep.* 7.9.23.

that the crowd appreciate in Philomathius' wit onto Sidonius' verse, or to respond sympathetically to his efforts in what appear to be exceptionally trying circumstances. In each epistle Sidonius shifts focalisation points for narrative effect, to deride a king, cut Arvandus loose, alter the reception of a poem, or promote himself and his episcopal nominee.

Narrative Speed

Sidonius varies the narrative speed of his epistles, dwelling on certain moments, and summarising or even omitting others. The shift between indirect and direct dialogue is a key way that the speed of an epistle may be manipulated. Direct speech is read at (roughly) the same pace as the spoken word, and so its mimesis extends from reporting exactly what was said to include also how long it took to say it. The speed of indirect speech cannot be so clearly calculated; it may be quicker than the speech it reports, summarising with a few words what may have taken many, or it may be slower as it focuses on particulars, providing additional information regarding content, mode of delivery, or tone.

In *Ep.* 4.24 Sidonius relates to Turnus how he interceded on behalf of Turnus' father Turpio with his creditor Maximus.[51] Indirect dialogue begins the scene the day before the interview. Sidonius is struck by the change he sees in Maximus' appearance and behaviour, and so asks the bystanders what religious order he is in, only to be told that he does not follow one in particular.[52] Sidonius' intercession on Turpio's behalf is in indirect speech (*Ep.* 4.24.5):

> Turpionis nostri rogata profero, allego necessitates, extrema deploro, quae duriora maerentibus amicis hinc viderentur, quod faenore ligatus corpore solveretur: meminisset ergo professionis novae, sodalitatis antiquae, exactorumque circumlatrantum barbaram instantiam indultis tantisper indutiis moderaretur; et, si decessisset aeger, tribueret heredibus annui luctus tempus immune; si, quod optarem, pristinam Turpio salutem recuperasset, indulgeret exhausto per otium facultatem convalescendi.

> I brought forward the requests of our friend Turpio, I asserted his needs, deplored his final circumstances, which [I said] seemed to his grieving friends all the worse because he was being removed from his body while still tied down by debt. I urged him therefore to remember his new profession, our old friendship, and so lessen the barbaric insistence of the

---

[51] Bellès (1997: 70) summarises the epistle. See also Rousseau (1976: 359–360).
[52] *Ep.* 4.24.3–4.

debt-collectors barking all around by [allowing] the indulgence of a period
of respite in the meantime, and should the sick man pass away, to offer the
heir a suspension of the debt for the period of a year of mourning, if, as
I desire, Turpio recovered to pristine health, to grant the worn out man the
opportunity to get better in peace and quiet.

The initial part of Sidonius' pleading is quickly summarised by three
short phrases made up of two interlocking chiasmi (*rogata profero, allego
necessitates, extrema deploro*).[53] The relative and causal clauses that follow
detail why the situation is so abject, Turpio is dying and unless the debt
is cleared, he will pass it on to his heirs. The subjunctive mood of the
verbs *viderentur* and *solveretur* indicates that these comments are part of
Sidonius' plea and stems from his perspective. He uses four verbs in the
subjunctive to report the commands that he gave to Maximus: *meminisset,
moderaretur, tribueret*, and *indulgeret*. If these verbs were in the present
tense, or in the case of the defective verb *memini* in the perfect tense, and
if the protases were also in the present or future tense, these remarks would
be as mimetic as possible of real speech, and so would be punctuated by
direct speech marks. On the other hand, if Sidonius wanted to stress the
reporting of these remarks he could have used indirect statements and
constructions of obligation. Instead the use of finite verbs in the imperfect
(and pluperfect) subjunctive makes these remarks appear a close paraphrase
of what Sidonius said that falls just short of direct quotation. Reporting
this exchange makes his pleas sound more measured and controlled; his
persuasive argument is condensed, "filtered" through his intelligence into
its most effective form.

The contrast with Maximus' reply is acute (4.24.6):

> adhuc rogabam, cum repente vir caritatis flere granditer coepit non moram
> debiti sed periculum debitoris; frenatoque singultu: "absit a me," inquit, "ut
> haec reposcam clericus ab aegro, quae vix petissem miles a sospite. sed et
> liberos eius ita diligo, ut etiam, si quid adversum cesserit amico, nil sim ab
> his amplius postulaturus quam mei officii ratio permittit."

> I was still pleading, when suddenly the kind man began to cry abundantly
> not at the delay of the debt but at the danger to the debtor; he reined in
> his sobbing and said "Let it be beyond me as a cleric to demand from a
> sick man what I would hardly have sought as a government official from a
> healthy man. But I love his children so much that even if something bad
> happened to my friend, I would still demand nothing more from them than
> the sum of my part."

---

[53] Amherdt (2001: 497) notes the intense rhetoric of Sidonius' language.

Maximus bursts into tears, shamed by Sidonius' reproach into giving up the interest on the loan. His use of the present jussive subjunctive is much more vivid than Sidonius' more indirect use of the imperfect. The use of the first person in the remarks (*me, reposcam, petissem, diligo, sim, mei*) adds to the realism of his remarks.

He urges Sidonius to include in his letter to Turpio a letter from him (4.24.6):

> quapropter scribe sollicitis quoque plus credant litteris tuis, meas iunge, quisquis ille fuerit languoris eventus, quem tamen fratri prosperum optamus, quod et annuum solutioni spatium prorogabo et superpositam medietatem, quae per usurae nomen accrevit, indulgeam, sola simpli restitutione contentus.'

> accordingly write to the concerned parties and to lend further credibility to your letter, add on one from me that whatever the outcome of his illness, which I still would like to be positive for my brother, that I will extend the term of payment to a year and I will wave the extra half which has accrued by way of interest, I will be happy with simply the restitution of the principal.

Presumably there was no need for Sidonius to draft and attach the additional letter, his direct quotation of Maximus acts in lieu of the additional epistle. Sidonius' reply to Maximus is again consumed within indirect discourse, including his claim that Maximus had bought himself a place in heaven by his generosity.[54]

In *Ep.* 4.24 Maximus' reply in direct speech is more vivid than Sidonius' previous and subsequent comments. Direct speech is naturally more dramatic, the very words spoken, or at least, the very words that seem to have been spoken, lend vivacity to the dialogue. The pace of the epistle slows during Maximus' reply, each word supposedly spoken corresponds directly to the time taken to read that word. Sidonius' remarks that prelude Maximus' speech abbreviate his haranguing, summarising quickly his tone (*allego, deploro*). The indirect speech that reflects Sidonius' actual words slows the pace, but still remains short of the mimesis that direct speech affects. It is possible to recover Sidonius' actual words, but this is a step the reader must take alone. Conversely Sidonius' indirect speech after Maximus' direct reply elaborates his response, dwelling on his episcopal benediction, rather than ending his acceptance with a simpler expression of thanks.

---

[54] *Ep.* 4.24.7.

By using a mix of direct, indirect, and semi-indirect speech Sidonius manipulates the pace of the narrative, summarising or elaborating it for narratological effect, to make Maximus' reply more dramatic, and to summarise the less dramatic aspects of his own speech, without losing the more impressive rhetoric that Maximus has bought a seat in heaven, and the possibilities facing the dying Turpio. Sidonius appears as a gifted speaker, able to move Maximus to tears, and grateful (on Turnus' behalf) for the forthcoming generosity, which Turnus would do well to accept graciously.

Direct and indirect speech are important to *Ep.* 4.12, which is addressed to Simplicius and Apollinaris. Sidonius begins that letter by comparing the stirring of minds to a shipwrecking sea, both of which may be disturbed by an adverse change in circumstances, either unwelcome news or a dangerous storm.[55] This beginning suggests that the narrative will be interrupted.

Sidonius and a young relative were reading Terence together, when a messenger, a slave of the household (*puer familiaris*) arrived (4.12.2): "cui nos: 'quid ita?' et ille: 'lectorem', inquit, 'Constantem nomine pro foribus vidi a dominis Simplicio et Apollinare redeuntem; dedit quidem litteras quas acceperat sed perdidit quas recepit'" (To whom I said "What is it?" And then "a reader" he said "Constans by name, I saw him in front of the gates returning from lords Simplicius and Apollinaris; he gave them the letter which he had taken but lost what he got in return"). Constans is either too timid to confront Sidonius himself or is beaten to it. Instead the boy becomes the bearer of bad news. His remarks are emphatic. The reader Constans is the problem. The slave represents his actions as occurring on his own initiative. He has perhaps overheard Constans explaining the predicament to the household's slaves upon his arrival. This is not a trivial matter. Epistolary exchange was important to the Gallo-Roman aristocracy, losing an epistle reflected poorly on the intended recipient, who would obviously be unable to reply to the contents of the letter and so fulfil the reciprocity that such exchange demanded.[56]

Sidonius' furious response is contained within indirect speech. His sunny outlook gives way to a storm of sadness, picking up on the meteorological analogy with which the letter began. He raged for many days (*per plurimos dies*), refusing to grant an audience to the "hermam stolidissimum" (moronic blockhead) – a reference both to a stone head

---

[55] *Ep* 4.12.1.
[56] Stanley's (2011: 140, 149–150) theorisation of epistolary exchange shows the prominence of expectations of reciprocity, for which see pp. 8–9.

carving (in the use of Herma) and to Constans' failed role as a messenger.[57] Sidonius' supposed anger, if real, would stand out as a rare exception to his otherwise impeccable self-fashioning.[58] Two other functions loom as more likely: it enhances the apology that Sidonius offers to Simplicius and Apollinaris; and resonates with the metaliterary force of Sidonius' reading of Terence's *Mother-in-law*, with which the letter begins, as the epistle plays out like a stock scene from Roman comedy, complete with the angry master and incompetent slave.

Eventually Sidonius grants Constans an audience, asking him if there is a least a verbal message that was intended to accompany the lost letter (*Ep.* 4.12.4): "respondit ipse, quamquam esset trepidus et sternax et prae reatu balbutiret ore, caecutiret intuitu, totum quo instrui, quo delectari valerem, paginis quae intercidissent fuisse mandatum" (he responded, although nervous and apologetic and blabbering in his speech like a defendant, his sight blinded, that all which I would be able to be instructed by, pleased by, had been ordered to be put on to the pages which had disappeared). Constans stammers and stutters, taking twenty words to convey his response, in which only the last five words say much at all. Sidonius' reporting of Constans' reply conveys the trembling tone of the grovelling messenger. The epistle ends with a change in function from testimonial to communicative, providing Sidonius' reply with a renewed sense of urgency: Simplicus and Apollinaris should rewrite the letter and promptly send it back to Sidonius.[59]

In *Ep.* 4.23, addressed to Proculus, Sidonius manipulates the speed of the narrative by varying the degree of detail used in indirect speech. He relates a conversation that he had with Proculus' son, who had run away after disobeying his father.[60] The son's dialogue is quickened by the indirect speech and condensed into its salient points (*Ep.* 4.23.1): "qui te relicto deliquisse se maeret, obrutus paenitendi pudore transfugi" (he grieves that after abandoning you he has wronged you, and is devastated by the shame of his sorrowful escape). Neither of these claims expressly indicate a speech act, but the implication is still made that Sidonius' comments represent a synopsis of what Proculus' son had said to him. Sidonius then explicitly indicates that Proculus' son filled him in on what had happened, using a

---

[57] TLL *s.v.* 1. This interpretation reads *Herma* as a pun on *Hermes* which is validated by the context of a message delivery, for which see Bellès (1998: 54n88).

[58] Nathan (2000: 178) takes Sidonius' description of his anger as an accurate account of his response to the circumstances.

[59] *Ep.* 4.12.4.

[60] For this letter see Amherdt (2001: 472–482).

meagre three words to indicate what was said (*Ep.* 4.23.1): "audito culpae tenore" (once I had listened to an account of the offence). Sidonius' reply, which is also conveyed in indirect speech, is far slower (*Ep.* 4.23.1):

> corripui latitabundum verbis amaris vultu minaci et mea quidem voce sed vice tua dignum abdicatione cruce culleo clamans ceterisque suppliciis parricidalibus. ad haec ille confusus inrubuit, nil impudenti excusatione deprecatus errorem, sed ad cuncta convictum cum redarguerem, verecundiae iunxit comites lacrimas ita profluas ubertimque manantes, ut secuturae correctioni fidem fecerint.

> as he skulked I jumped upon him with bitter words, a threatening face and my own voice (but actually playing your part) as I shouted that he was worthy of disinheritance, the cross, the sack and all the other punishments for parricides. He blushed at these remarks, confused, but did not compound his mistake with a shameful excuse, but when I convicted him on all points, he added tears to his sense of shame, crying and weeping copiously in such a way that his tears confirmed that he would follow through on making amends.

Sidonius' reporting of his speech includes vivid details. The alliterative rhetorical sting in the phrase "dignum abdicatione cruce culleo clamans ceterisque suppliciis parricidalibus" sounds more like the words Sidonius used than the sombre reporting of what was said.[61] Proculus' son's reactions speak for him, as he blushes and cries at Sidonius' vehement prosecutorial attack. The narrative switches from the testimonial function to the communicative as Sidonius asks Proculus to forgive his son, and envisages how that scene will unfold, as the ashamed son is greeted by his forgiving father.

Sidonius manipulates speech in *Ep.* 4.12 and 24 to quicken or slow the pace of the narrative. Thus Constans' dialogue is slowed as he appears to stammer particularly badly while apologising for the ineptitutde that led him to lose the letter for Sidonius. Similarly the effect of Sidonius' pleading is made more dramatic by Maximus' reply in direct speech, in which the narrative slows to focus on each word that Maximus says, which is important given that these constitute the exact outcome that Sidonius has won for Turnus, and ultimately functions as a pseudo-epistle from Maximus himself. Sidonius manages to make indirect speech more vivid than it might otherwise be by reporting remarks using finite verbs that more closely mimic direct speech. In *Ep.* 4.23

---

[61] Arjava (1998: 154) takes this remark as evidence that Sidonius considered abandonment in the same class as parricide; but as Bellès (1998: 77n162) and Cook (2012: 241) argue, the phrase is highly rhetorical. Sidonius may well be exaggerating what punishments are suitable to enhance Proculus' son's sense of shame.

changes in narrative speed take place within the indirect speech, as Sidonius embellishes his criticism of Proculus' son and condenses what is said in return.

Imagined Speech

Epistolary authors may invent an interlocutor to turn their narratives at least partly into dialogues. Seneca's addressee Lucilius, for example, may very well be fictitious.[62] Even if he is not, Seneca's frequent epistolary conversations with him involved some level of creative licence. Epistolary monologues may also be imagined, their time, space and even their participants altered from the reality of the author's experience. Sidonius uses imagined speech in his epistles in two distinct ways, to spur on the narrative by inserting the persona of the addressee, which asks a single question and then fades back to join the implied reader outside of the narrative, or to separate his persona as narrator from the persona of the speaker. This second technique is evident in *Ep.* 7.9, in the *ad hominem* attack that Sidonius makes against himself, by using the imagined voice of a detractor rather than his authorial voice to do so. That example, analysed above, is its own special case, as the imagined dialogue of the hypothetical detractor occurs within Sidonius' public address.

In certain epistles Sidonius uses the epistolary convention of an imagined interlocutor or co-opts another persona's voice to carry the narrative forward. Such a beginning may be found in many epistolary authors and is rightly considered to be a generic trope.[63] Sidonius' extensive use of this convention has a varied and important narrative effect in many of his epistles, enabling changes in the narrative speed and almost seamless shifts from one narrative function to another.

Many of the epistles begin by asserting that they are responding to a request from the addressee. This request may be for specific information, such as the portrait of Theodoric, or for the inclusion of a verse, or even simply for a letter.[64] Some of these requests are put into direct speech. *Ep.* 2.1, for example, begins with Sidonius asserting that the Arverni must tolerate two problems at once, prompting the involvement of the addressee's persona (*Ep.* 2.1.1): " 'quaenam' inquis" ("Which are those?" you say). The epistle thus assumes a communicative rather than narrative function; Sidonius relates the flaws of Seronatus as if he is speaking to

---

[62] See Wilson (1987: 119n3).
[63] Constable (1970: 14–20).
[64] *Ep.* 1.2.1. Requests for verses are prominent towards the end of the collection see for example 8.9; 9.12, 13, 14, 15, 16.

us, but he clearly is not. His words' attempted mimesis of speech is evident in the verbs he uses, which reference the oral composition of the letter: *inquam* and *loquar*, rather than *scribo*. The resulting epistle is free from the confines of the narrative mode and so resists the pressure to cite specific occasions of when Seronatus made a joke in Church or otherwise acted inappropriately.[65]

A worthwhile comparandum may be found in the second epistle to mention Seronatus (*Ep.* 5.13). In that letter there is no imagined interlocutor, nor any verbs of speaking, instead Sidonius narrates specific events: Seronatus is hurrying to Toulouse, his stooge Evanthius is clearing the road to Clausetia so the great whale of a man will complete his journey.[66] The shift to the communicative function at the end of the epistle maintains the non-verbalised form of the communication (*Ep.* 5.13.4): "In summa, de Seronato vis accipere quid sentiam? Ceteri affligi per suprascriptum damno verentur mihi latronis et beneficia suspecta sunt" (In sum, do you want to learn what I think about Seronatus? Others fear to suffer damage from that man, but even the kind acts of a robber are suspect to me). The verb *accipere* may mean "to listen," but not as explicitly as a verb like *audire*; Sidonius' reference to Seronatus as the man *written* about above (*suprascriptum*) maintains the written (rather than affected spoken) discourse of the epistle.[67]

Ep. 4.6, addressed to Sidonius' uncle Apollinaris, begins by referring to a message that the former had sent (*Ep.* 4.6.1):

> Per Faustinum antistitem non minus mihi veteris contubernii sodalitate quam novae professionis communione devinctum verbo quaepiam cavenda mandaveram: dicto paruisse vos gaudeo. siquidem prudentibus cordacitus insitum est vitare fortuita, sicut itidem absurdum, si coeptis audacibus adversetur eventus, consurgere in querimonias et inconsultarum dispositionum culpabiles exitus ad infamanda casuum incerta convertere.

> Through the priest Faustinus, to whom I am bound no less by the bond of an old friendship than by the fellowship of my new profession, I passed onto you earlier a word of warning. I am pleased that you have obeyed my remark. Just as it is a well-established principle for wise men to avoid haphazard occurrences, it is equally ridiculous, if bold undertakings turn out badly, to launch into complaints and turn the blameworthy consequences of arrangements that were not thought through into an attack on the vagaries of chance.

---

[65] *Ep.* 2.1.3.
[66] *Ep.* 5.13.1.
[67] TLL *s.v.* 4: "sensibus, praesertim auditu."

Faustinus did not deliver an epistle but a verbal message (*verbum*) which Apollinaris listened to him speak (*dicto*) and has subsequently followed. Sidonius shifts from the narrative function to the ideological. His remarks clearly need exposition, which he begins by inserting Apollinaris as the interlocutor.[68]

Sidonius is clearly asking himself a question and then answering it, but the effect is quite different to a deliberative question posed in the first person, as in *Ep.* 9.3, addressed to Faustus the bishop of Riez (*Ep.* 9.3.7): "sed ista quorsum stolidus allego?" (but to what end do I sense-lessly make these accusations?). In the first person Sidonius can be self-deprecating, and equally respectful of his addressee, whose persona remains un-manipulated.[69] In Faustus' case Sidonius had perhaps good reason to treat him carefully, given the fallout from the attack against him in the *De statu animae*, written by Sidonius' friend Claudianus Mamertus.[70] The second letter to Faustus in book 9 is far chattier in tone (*Ep.* 9.9.1):

> Longum tacere, vir sacratissime, nos in commune dequestus es; cognosco vestrae partis hinc studium, nostrae reatum non recognosco. namque iampridem iussus garrire non silui litteris istis antecurrentibus, quibus tamen recensendis, cum Reios advenerant, qui tunc Aptae fuistis, aptissime defuistis.

> My most pious Lord, you have bitterly complained that I have been silent for a long time; I acknowledge the intention on your side, I do not acknow-ledge guilt on my side. Actually I have been asked to chat for a while now, but I was not silent in the letter preceding this one, which when it had reached Riez, you then were in Apt, and very aptly were not there to read it.[71]

He even says goodbye (*ave dicto mox vale dicimus*) in the false ending, rather than use the standard epistolary sign-off to a bishop (*memor nostri esse dignare, domine papa*) with which the epistle eventually ends. When he inserts an interlocutor, it is now Faustus' persona rather than his own, in the second person: *ista quorsum? inquis* and then in the phrase *nunc quaeris*. The difference in the two letters to Faustus may be partially explained in socio-historical terms; if the intervening exchange of letters had improved

---

[68] Sidonius uses the same epistolary formula in this epistle as in *Ep.* 3.8: "'quorsum istaec.' ais. fateor" ("'What is the point?' You say. I confess").

[69] For an extended analysis of this epistle see Schwitter (2015: 267–270).

[70] For details pertaining to the circumstances of this controversy in southern Gaul see Mathisen (1989: 235–244) and Brittain (2001: 240–243).

[71] This is another name pun which plays on the (potential) literal meaning of the toponym Apta. Sidonius usually puns on the meaning of individuals' names rather than places, for examples of which see pp. 42, 94, 128n151, 150, 167, 174.

their relationship Sidonius may have felt able to adopt the more relaxed epistolary convention of inserting the addressee's persona into the epistle, rather than chatting to his own persona as in *Ep.* 9.3.

Sidonius use of these imagined interlocutors is an epistolary convention. In each epistle the addressee's persona has at most a few words to say. They are imaginary to the extent that their involvement in a spoken exchange is fictitious, but epistolary interlocutors may also have more to say. The epistolary convention can be extended to a more complex question and answer. In the hypothetical dialogue in Pliny's *Ep.* 1.9, for example, he reflects on what he actually does when he is in the city, which leads him to consider how mundane these activites are in hindsight (1.9.2–3):

> Nam si quem interroges "Hodie quid egisti?," respondeat: "Officio togae virilis interfui, sponsalia aut nuptias frequentavi, ille me ad signandum testamentum, ille in advocationem, ille in consilium rogavit." Haec quo die feceris, necessaria, eadem, si cotidie fecisse te reputes, inania videntur, multo magis cum secesseris. Tunc enim subit recordatio: "Quot dies quam frigidis rebus absumpsi!"

> For if you ask someone "What did you do today?" He may respond: "I attended a ceremony for a toga *virilis*, I went to an engagement party or wedding, that man asked me to witness his court case, that one to witness a will, that other one for advice. On the day that you did these things they seemed necessary but if you think back to what you did yesterday, the same things seem pointless, especially after you have left town. For then the thought looms "How many days did I spend on such trivial matters!"

Pliny uses the hypothetical locutor to list a series of activities, perhaps so that no specific person may take offense. This is the kind of activity that he gets up to, helping out three different friends in different ways.[72] The reflection is summed up by Pliny's direct speech. This cleverly combines the testimonial and ideological narrative function. The reader is induced into thinking that this is actually what Pliny thought at a particular point in time after a visit to Rome, and to reflect that his idea is correct by applying it to their own experience. His ubiquitous self-fashioning is still there; Pliny comes across as a generous and selfless supporter of his friends' activities.

Sidonius uses a similarly more developed epistolary interlocutor in *Ep.* 9.11, in which he apologises to Lupus for not sending him a collection of

---

[72] Leach (2003: 155–158) notes the programmatic force of these activities which feature in subsequent epistles.

his epistles, but instead sending them on to others through Lupus. By way of defence he conjures a hypothetical other (9.11.5):

> dixisset alius: 'neminem tibi praetuli, nullas ad ullum peculiares litteras dedi: quem praelatum suspicabare, unius epistulae forma contentus abscessit, atque ea quidem nihil super praesenti negotio deferente: tu, qui te quereris omissum, tribus loquacissimis paginis fatigatus potius in nausiam concitaris, dum frequenter insulsae lectionis verbis inanibus immoraris.'

> someone else would have said 'I have preferred no-one over you, I have not sent special letters to anyone, the man whom you suspect was preferred to you, happily went away with the formality of one letter, and even that brought up nothing relevant to the current business, you, who complain that you have been passed over, have been worn out by three very talkative letters or rather forced into feeling unwell since you immerse yourself frequently in the pointless remarks of an awkward text.

The prosopopoeia marks a change in Sidonius' tone from the grovelling obsequity of the epistle's opening to a more direct refutation of Lupus' claims. Equally it allows Sidonius to exaggerate his usual self-deprecation. The spirited defence of Sidonius' treatment of Lupus turns to the arrangement of the epistles (*Ep.* 9.11.5): "reverentiae tuae meritorumque ratio servata est, quod sicut tu antistitum ceterorum cathedris, prior est tuus in libro titulus" (a reckoning of your status and achievements is preserved because just as you are the first of the other seated bishops, your title is first in the book).[73] Lupus' positioning in the collection matches his prominence.[74] The prosopopoeiac interlocutor thanks Lupus for his accurate transcriptions of Sidonius' epistles. Sidonius reverts to his own voice to end the monologue (9.11.7): "haec et his plura fors aliquis" (this and much more the other man might say). Sidonius' persona continues in its indirect politesse, begging further pardon by refusing to concede that Lupus has more affection for Sidonius than he does for Lupus.

The blurring of real and epistolary speech is evident in how Sidonius describes the epistle to Lupus (9.11.9): "ecce habes litteras tam garrulas ferme quam requirebas: quamquam sunt omnes, si quae uspiam tamen sunt, loquacissimae. Namque in audentiam sermocinandi quem non ipse compellas" (there you are, a letter almost as chatty as the one you were needing, although all the others, if any are still out there, are all very

---

[73] Sidonius is referring to book 6 of the epistles, which is exclusively addressed to clergy, and begins with an epistle addressed to Lupus.

[74] *Ep.* 9.11.5: "tuo praeter tibi deputatas frequenter illustrantur alienae" (excepting the letters to you, others' epistles are also decorated by your name). He is mentioned in *Ep.* 4.17.3, 7.13.1, 8.15.1, and is the addressee of 6.1, 6.4, 6.9; 8.11, and 9.11.

talkative. Is there anyone that you could not compel into a frank conversation?). It is full of chatter in a literal sense, the interlocutor speaks for
roughly one fifth of the time and right in the centre of the epistle. The
words *garrulas, loquacissime, sermocinandi* refer to the content of the epistle
as if it were speech.[75] The letter ends, however, by reflecting on its written
form (*Ep.* 9.11.10): "copiosus hilarere, si meae culpae defensio potius tibi
scripta feratur quam satisfaction" (you may laugh a lot, if the letter written
to you turns out to be more a defence of my guilt than recompense for it).
Lupus can listen to Sidonius *speak* once, subsequently he will have to read
what is *written* (*scripta*); the act of rereading will go some way towards dis-
pelling the discourse's mimesis of spoken dialogue.

Sidonius also uses imagined speech to distance his persona from
remarks that could be considered overly confrontational or direct if they
were presented simply as Sidonius' own. In *Ep.* 4.21, for example, Sidonius
encouraged Aper to imagine what the Arverni would say to him to get him
to visit (*Ep.* 4.21.3): "[Arvernos] quos palam et coram dicere puta: 'quid
in te mali tantum, ingrate, commisimus, ut per tot annos quondam
humum altricem nunc velut hosticum solum fugias?'" (Imagine that these
Arverni are openly speaking to you face-to-face "What great wrong have
we committed against you, you ingrate, so that you have avoided now for
so many years the very earth that raised you, as if it was enemy soil?").
Sidonius is able to adopt a more critical tone without seeming to cause
offense by imagining that the entire population is addressing Aper, at the
same time his comments carry the (imaginary) weight of the communal
opinion. After haranguing Aper and praising the Auvergne at some length,
Sidonius breaks from the imaginary interlocutors to confess the epistolary
ruse (*Ep.* 4.21.6): "haec unus tibi omnium civium, certe bonorum, voto
petitu vice garrio" (I alone say these words to you, but I do so with the
will, intent, and role of all the citizens, at least all the good ones). Imagined
speech may equally be found alongside epistolary discourse that affects to
be real speech. Sidonius concludes *Ep.* 4.24, analysed above for its changes
in narrative speed, by warning Turnus not to reject the renegotiated terms
of his father's loan from Maximus (*Ep.* 4.24.8):

> non est cur dicere incipias: "habeo consortes necdum celebrata divisio est;
> avarius me constat esse tractatum quam coheredes; frater ac soror sub annis
> adhuc tutelaribus agunt; sorori necdum maritus, fratri necdum curator,
> curatori necdum satisdator inventus est."

---

[75] Marinova (2014: 100) lists *alloquim, afflatus, colloquium, sermo, salve* (subst.), *salutatio* as synonyms
for *epistula* metonymically derived from the idea that the letter represents "one half of a dialogue."

this is not grounds to start to say "I have co-heirs nor yet has the division of the estate been made; it is agreed that I have been exploited more than them; my brother and sister are still young enough to need a guardian; there is not yet a husband for my sister, nor a tutor for my brother, nor yet has a guarantor been found for the tutor."

Sidonius increases the reader's sympathy for Turnus by adopting direct speech for how he may respond, making the appeal all the more personal.[76] The tricolon emphatically ends the imagined reply by summarising Turnus' situation.[77] The reader may hope that Turnus was able to pull himself and his family out of trouble, perhaps if he had failed Sidonius may have spared him the ignominy of having his private difficulties advertised for all to read.

Imagined dialogue lets an epistolary author mimic a conversation with others, including the addressee. Unlike reported speech, imagined dialogue is not limited to what was said; it thus has far greater narrative flexibility, possibilities may be excluded, such as Sidonius' caution to Turnus not to advocate for better terms, or included, such as when Lupus is saved by a proxy imagined target from bearing the direct brunt of Sidonius' rhetoric. These imagined dialogues are clearly fictional and so free Sidonius to develop rich alternatives to the pretence of an epistle's reality.

Implied Speech

Implied speech exists beyond the diegesis of the narrative; it is a connection between speech and events that the reader may or may not entertain. Consequently, Sidonius' authorial control over the implication of his narrative is less immediately apparent. Questioning how information was conveyed to the various actors in the narrative may nevertheless bring extradiegetic speech to the fore. Implied dialogue can fulfil a unique narrative effect by lending Sidonius' authority to whatever claims are made.

In some instances implied speech is a mere word or two away from indirect speech. In *Ep.* 7.4, for example, Sidonius gently castigates Fonteius, the bishop of Vaison,[78] for his generous bestowing of gifts on Vindicius,

---

[76] Amherdt (2001: 502).

[77] The rhetorical force of the letter is maintained by the chiasmus at its end (after Turnus' imaginary words), for which see Amherdt (2001: 503). *Ep.* 4.24.8: "si moram patitur, quicquid propter misericordiam concesserat pie, iuste reposcit propter iniuriam" (if he suffers a delay, whatever he has piously conceded owing to his sympathy, he may rightly demand it back owing to your unlawful conduct).

[78] In *Ep.* 5.6 Sidonius refers to the Burgundian acquisition of Vaison, for which see p. 115.

who recently visited him (*Ep.* 7.4.1): "testis horum est Vindicius noster, qui segnius domum pro munificentiae vestrae fasce remeavit, quoquo loco est, constanter affirmans, cum sitis opinione magni, gradu maximi, non tamen esse vos amplius dignitate quam dignatione laudandos" (my dear Vindicius is the source of this information; he meandered home more slowly because of the burden of your generosity, wherever he is, he always affirms, even though you are greatly esteemed and of the highest station, that you nevertheless should still be praised no more for your honour than for your rank). Sidonius clearly implies that Vindicius has said these words to him, but his language falls just short of explicitly indicating as much.[79] The indefinite adjective *quoquo* and the adverb *constanter* together leave open the possibility that word has reached Sidonius about Vindicius' remarks. Vindicius may alternatively have written to Sidonius, informing him of Fonteius' generosity.

The implied speech need not be brief. In *Ep.* 6.8, addressed to Graecus, the bishop of Marseilles and a recurrent character in the collection, Sidonius endorses the character of Amantius by relating the man's exemplary integrity as a buyer's agent.[80] He indicates to Graecus the source of his remarks (*Ep.* 6.8.2.): "inter dictandum mihi ista suggesta sunt, ne ob hoc dubito audita fidenter asserere, quia non parum mihi intumos agunt quibus est ipse satis intumus" (These comments were suggested to me as I wrote, but I do not hesitate on that account to assert confidently what I have heard, since they with whom he is quite intimate, behave no less intimately with me). Sidonius clearly implies that he has written what he was told by intermediaries who know him and Amantius well.

In a follow up letter (*Ep.* 7.2) to Graecus, Sidonius narrates at some length how the same Amantius, now described as a *callidus viator*, tricked him into providing a letter of recommendation (presumably the previous letter) that advanced him further in Marseilles than it ought.[81] Sidonius apologises twice for the length of the narrative, which details how the young man managed to marry the daughter of a wealthy family on false pretences.[82] Sidonius clearly has been told this story by somebody, perhaps

---

[79] Van Waarden (2010: 224).

[80] Mathisen (2003b: 46).

[81] *Ep.* 7.2.1: "ignorantiae siquidem meae callidus viator imposuit. nam dum solum mercatoris praetendit officium, litteras meas ad formatae vicem, scilicet ut lector, elicuit" (a cunning traveller took advantage of my ignorance. For even though he was only a merchant, he managed to get a canonical letter of introduction from me, on the basis that he was a Reader). Colton (1985: 281) notes this as a borrowing from Martial 3.57.1: *Callidus imposuit nuper mihi copo Ravennae* but the borrowing of *callidus viator* from Horace *Sat.* 1.5.90 should also be noted.

[82] Van Waarden (2010: 127–135) and Krause (1991: 552n89).

the man's mother-in-law who broke off her legal efforts against Amantius when the couple started presenting her with grandchildren, or perhaps she or someone else wrote to Sidonius to tell him the story.[83]

Implying rather than reporting speech may provide the contents of the story with Sidonius' authority as author. In *Ep.* 6.4 he narrates how a woman was kidnapped in a raid by brigands and subsequently sold as a slave. Her family have related their story to Sidonius who in turn relates it to Lupus.[84] His exchange with them was presumably in person; they had travelled to the Auvergne and so could well have sought his assistance directly as the local bishop, or subsequently when it became known to them that the woman had been sold to Sidonius' business adviser and had subsequently died. A mix of actual evidence, rumour, and implied speech combine to create the narrative. A certain Prudens signed off on the deal as *adstipulator* – Sidonius adds that this was his actual name (*hoc viro nomen*) to deter the reader from reading a name-pun and draw attention to how inappropriate his name is. Prudens, as it happens, had been anything but prudent in the business deal that went badly wrong. Sidonius asks Lupus to intercede directly by meeting the parties in person. The efficacy of direct speech is clearly needed to resolve the dispute.

The implied "speech" may be an epistle rather than an actual speech act. In *Ep.* 5.19, for example, Sidonius narrates the scandalous story of two household members absconding without first marrying, one from his house and another from Pudens'.[85] It is unclear whether Pudens made his request to Sidonius face-to-face or in writing, but the latter is surely more likely (*Ep.* 5.19.1): "sed concientiae tuae purgatione praelata petere dignaris culpae calentis impunitatem" (but after revealing that you were free from being complicit you deemed to ask that there be no punishment for this blatant offense).

The precise source of implied speech may be undefined in other ways. As the barbarian conquest of Roman Gaul unfolded the rumour mill went into overdrive. Rumour is Sidonius' source when he states at the beginning of *Ep.* 7.1 that the Visigoths have finally occupied Roman soil. When rumours have a particular source they lose their indefinite status, and may be considered as a precise form of implied speech. In *Ep.* 6.10, which

---

[83] Jones (2009: 100–103) credits Amantius with using the "rhetoric of inclusion" to find a way into the aristocracy. Mathisen (2003b: 46–49, 143).

[84] *Ep.* 6.4.3. For the structure of this epistle see Furbetta (2015b: 353).

[85] Grey (2008: 302) analyses this epistle in depth. Pudens' name may be another name pun given the impropriety involved.

foreshadows the Visigothic invasion, Sidonius relates the struggles of the
deacon who is carrying the letter to Censorius, the bishop of Auxerre (*Ep.*
6.10.1):[86]

> hic cum familia sua depraedationis Gothicae turbinem vitans in territorium
> vestrum delatus est ipso, ut sic dixerim, pondere fugae; ubi in re ecclesiae,
> cui sanctitas tua praesidet, parvam sementem semiconfecto caespiti advena
> ieiunus iniecit, cuius ex solido colligendae fieri sibi copiam exorat.

> this man, avoiding the whirlwind of Gothic ransacking, was carried off along
> with his family into your territory by the very burden of his flight, so to speak;
> where on the property of the church, over which your sanctity presides, the
> hungry arrival planted a small amount of seed on some half-ploughed soil,
> he desperately asks that he be allowed to harvest the entire amount.

The events that have affected the letter bearer are related by Sidonius in
the narrative mode, switching to the communicative to request (*exorat*)
that he accede to the bearer's request to yield the crop from the church's
land without paying the required dues (6.10.2): "quem si domesticis fidei
deputata humanitate foveatis, id est, ut debitum glaebae canonem non
petatur, tantum lucelli praestitum sibi computat (peregrini hominis ut
census, sic animus angustus), ac si in patrio solo rusticaretur" (if you were
to favour him with the kindness due a family member of the faith, by not
collecting the tribute from the rented-land, then he (whose strength of
mind, like his property, is that of a foreigner) will think that small amount
of profit surpasses what he would get if he could farm his native soil).
The implication clearly is that Sidonius has asked the bearer what specifically he would like from Censorius. This request implies a dialogue
between Sidonius and the letter bearer. The resulting request is filtered by
what Sidonius thinks is reasonable, and is arranged in the way most likely
to meet a positive response, asking for the right to yield the crop before
asking for the remission of the dues.

   Implied discourse fulfils a narrative role that cannot be fulfilled by
indirect or direct discourse. It may lend authority to the narrative that
stems neither from the autopsy that direct speech may convey, nor the specific sources (a letter, or precise individual) that typically precede indirect
discourse. Instead the authority of the narrator is all consuming. Cracks
may still appear; in such epistolary moments implied speech loses its
extradiegetic concealment and becomes a part of the diegetic narrative,
able to be read and interpreted like other forms of speech.

---

[86] For other examples of Romans with less wealth fleeing see Mathisen and Sivan (1999: 36).

Conclusion

Epistolary discourse imitates spoken discourse. This near mimesis enabled epistles to bridge the communicative gap between author and addressee. Within the affected spoken discourse of the epistle, different layers of speech may exist, direct, indirect, implied, or imagined. Sidonius uses each of these for varying narratological effect, to quicken or slow the narrative, switch function, and indicate or conceal his sources. These effects are important. They bring exchanges to life, flesh out rich characters, create narrative tension, and build and release climaxes. Dialogue provides Sidonius with ample scope for manipulation as he displays his strategic thinking while losing to Theodoric in backgammon, desperately counsels Arvandus, and tries to appease or cajole his peers in the Gallo-Roman aristocracy and clergy. They help Sidonius shape his persona, as a witty and clever speaker, able to respond dynamically to the challenges of his age, from promoting the right candidate to an ex tempore poetic composition.

Altman argues that "interior dialogue" was inherently fictitious:

> Interior dialogue is haunted be an air of falseness. When the partner's words are imagined, the letter writer is addressing a manipulated pseudo-presence; when they are quoted the dialogue borders on artifice. Interior dialogue is an attempt to approximate a conversation of the here and now, which both grows out and is doomed by the epistolary situation.[87]

Sidonius' imagined dialogues are fictitious; the addressee can no more interrupt his authorial voice than bridge the physical gap between author and addressee. As the author of the epistles Sidonius is in full control. Altman's artifice is present to some extent in every dialogue that Sidonius includes in the epistles, including even his own. We have no way of knowing how Sidonius spoke, or whether all the epistles were actually sent. Instead we have a body of rich narratives that exploit the opportunities that epistolography offers to vary dialogues, imagining them, reporting them, recording them, or at least, affecting to do so. These efforts ultimately enable a more complex interaction between dialogue and plot.

[87] Altman (1982: 140).

CHAPTER 6

Arrangement

Sidonius' epistles were circulated during his lifetime and arranged in nine books.[1] Three main factors influenced their arrangement: the release of books and groups of books over time; his attempts to follow Pliny's collection; and his efforts to bring closure and assert some narratological control as the implied author of the collection. These factors acted in concert with one another. So, while books 1 and 2 may be dated to before Sidonius' episcopacy, the arrangement of each book and division of epistles is thematic: book 1 treats Sidonius' career as a secular office holder and book 2 his enjoyment of aristocratic *otium*. The division approximates Pliny's but also reveals Sidonius' efforts to create specific narratives, stretched over each book and the collection as a whole. The narrative arc of these early books is particularly evident when their last letter is read against their remainder; in book 1, for example, *Ep.* 1.11 neatly concludes Sidonius' office-holding years by offering reflections on his career from the vantage point of one who has "retired" from secular politics. Similarly, the final epistle (2.14) in book 2 completes a thematic ring structure by presenting a mirror image of the circumstances in *Ep.* 2.2, which begins by chastising the addressee Domitius for staying in the city when he could otherwise be enjoying the *otium* of Sidonius' estate. *Ep.* 2.14 presents the converse: Sidonius is stuck in the city and the allure of the countryside and the year's surprisingly bumper vintage tempt him to leave for the country, even though it is mid-winter, the seasonal opposite to the high summer of *Ep.* 2.2.[2] This textual connection is reinforced by the book's thematic treatment of aristocratic *otium* which is embedded by sustained allusions

---

[1] See Harries (1994: 7). It is possible that book 9 may have circulated posthumously, especially if Sidonius' died ca. 479 rather than 485, for discussion of which see p. 7n43.

[2] Cf. Pliny's juxtaposition of the seasons in *Ep.* 9.36 and 9.40, for which see Gibson (2015: 189). See also Gibson and Morello's (2012: 188) analysis of Pliny *Ep.* 7.2, where daily routines merge into the routines adopted according to the season.

to Martial's epigrams.[3] In the final epistle in the book Sidonius alludes to one of Martial's epigrams (2.14.2): "[si] destinas illic ... ninguidos menses in otio fulginoso sive tunicata quiete transmitter" (if you intend to pass the snowy months there in gloomy *otium* or tunic-clad peace). The phrase *tunicate quiete* singles out Martial's lament to Faustinus (10.51.5–6):[4]

> Quos, Faustine, dies, qualem tibi Roma Ravennam
> abstulit! o soles, o tunicate quies!
>
> What days Faustinus, does Rome deprive you of, what Ravenna lifestyle,
> O' suns, o' tunic-clad peace!

The arrangement of book 2 thematically follows Pliny, intertextually engages with Martial, appears chronologically before Sidonius' episcopacy, and presents Sidonius enjoying idyllic *otium* and the hospitality of his friends.

This chapter assesses the internal evidence for the process Sidonius followed in collating and circulating individual books and the collection as a whole. This evidence is read alongside Sidonius' attempts to engage with the structural arrangement of Pliny's letter collection. It analyses Sidonius' role as the implied author of the epistles and shows how the arrangement of the epistles contributes to specific narratives formed between epistles, including the pseudo-biographical narrative of the collection. Lastly, it examines the closural dynamics of individual epistles and the collection, as the last epistles envisage Sidonius' death.

Editing and Circulation

Sidonius edited, arranged, and circulated his epistles and so exerted direct authorial control over each epistolary book. Indications of this process may be found throughout the collection. In the opening epistle Sidonius characterises Constantius' request as asking for whatever letters (*Ep.* 1.1.1) "paulo politiores [fluxerint] ... retractatis exemplaribus enucleatisque" (have poured out a little more polished ... once the examples have been edited and simplified). In that letter Sidonius also asks Constantius to play a role in readying the epistles for circulation by requesting that he purge (*defaecandas*) and file them (*limandas*) into shape. The extent to which

---

[3] For the thematic unity of content in the first two books see Gibson (2012: 62), Harries (1994: 9–17), and Whitby (1995: 42).

[4] Geisler (1887: 360) lists this as one of his verbal connections between Sidonius and Martial, as does Wolff (2014c: 297).

this language reflected the reality of Sidonius' editing process is difficult to gauge; *politus* and *limo* are typical for programmatic prefaces, as is the general humility of his tone.[5]

A similar difficulty emerges for Sidonius' programmatic remarks in *Ep.* 7.18.1:

> nam petitum misimus opus raptim electis exemplaribus quae ob hoc in manus pauca venerunt, quia mihi nil de libelli huiusce conscriptione meditanti hactenus incustodita nequeunt inveniri. sane ista pauca, quae quidem et levia sunt, celeriter absolvi. Quamquam incitatus semel animus necdum scripturire desineret, servans hoc sedulo genus temperamenti, ut epistularum [*] produceretur textus, si numerus breviatur.

> for I sent the work demanded as soon as examples were chosen. Accordingly, only a few came to hand. Because I gave no thought to the composition of this my little book, those letters which were not kept safe were unable to be found. In fact these few, which really are trifles, I have quickly finished off. Although once my mind got into it, it could not stop writing, but I diligently kept to the principle, that the text of the letters should be extended, if their number is cut short.

Sidonius dwells on the speed of his composition and arrangement (*raptim*, *celeriter*) but these remarks are again reasonably typical for programmatics, and they accord closely with Sidonius' final programmatic remarks in *Ep.* 9.16: "raptim coactimque translator festinus exscripsi" (I copied them out like a hurried transcriber, quickly and briefly).[6] This affected disregard for his epistolary project sits awkwardly with the clear principles of arrangement that may be found throughout the collection. His last claim is equally enigmatic. The manuscripts of Sidonius vary on whether a "*non*" ought to be placed at the point of the asterix.[7] If *non* is placed at the asterix, the *ut* clause must be a result clause without a demonstrative in the main clause. This grammatical construction is not unattested, but it is unusual, and it may explain the possible removal of *non* from the other manuscript traditions. If the *non* is absent, Sidonius' comments contradict his well attested respect for epistolary brevity and his professed awareness that longer letters may provoke boredom in his readers.[8] This is the exact point

---

[5] Cf. Catullus 1.2: "arida modo pumice expolitum" ([this little book] recently polished out with dry pumice). For these terms see Batstone (1998: 133) and Pricoco (1965: 94). Hernández Lobato (2012: 411–412) argues that Catullus 1 is Sidonius' model for *Carm.* 9. 9–13, and Sidonius may well be drawing upon it here as well.
[6] See p. 181.
[7] Luetjohann (1887: 125).
[8] Köhler (1995: 14). See for example *Ep.* 6.11.2: "nam prudentiae satis obviat epistulari formulae debitam concinnitatem plurifario sermone porrigere" (for it belies good sense to extend with

that Sidonius goes on to make (*Ep.* 7.18.2): "pariter et censui librum, quem lector delicatissimus desiderares, et satis habilem nec parum excusabilem fore, si, quoniam te sensuum structurarumque levitas poterat offendere, membranarum certe fascibus minus onerarere" (equally I also thought the book which you, my most precious reader wanted would be manageable and reasonable, because the lightness of its sentiments and organisation caused offence, if you were at least not burdened by bundles of pages). At the end of the letter Sidonius draws attention to the speed with which the reader may finish his letters; extending them would slow the reader down.[9]

The evidence for Sidonius' process of composition and arrangement is his own remarks, yet these may well be distorted by the tropes and allusions that he uses. It is not possible to read the letters in their original, pristine, and unedited form. Attempts to do so by reading, for example, *Ep.* 1.5 and 1.9 as two halves of the same "original" letter remain highly speculative.[10] Since Sidonius wrote and then collated each epistle, each epistle has two moments of composition: its initial drafting in response to certain circumstances, and then its subsequent revision and inclusion in the collection.[11]

The opening epistle introduces a single volume (*unum volumen*), which probably refers just to book 1, and looks forward to the circulation of more epistles if the initial offering meets with success. It is possible that *volumen* indicates more than simply the epistles in book 1, perhaps a collection comprised of books 1 and 2, which pertain to events in his life that pre-date his ordainment as a bishop, or to books 1–7, especially as the last epistle in book 7 (*Ep.* 7.18) responds intratextually to the programmatic concerns of

---

abundant language the careful arrangement needed for the epistolary form). For the importance of brevity in Late Antique letters see Abram (1998: 23–35).

[9] *Ep.* 7.18.4: "nec faciet materia ut immensa fastidium, quia cum singulae causae singulis ferme epistulis finiantur, cito cognitis in quae oculum intenderis ante legere cessabis quam lecturire desistas" (the subject matter will not produce boredom like an immense topic, since individual points are entirely dealt with by each letter. What your eyes falls upon will be quickly understood, you will cease reading before you bring a stop to it).

[10] Köhler (1995: 265) and Anders (2010: 186) (following Köhler) argue that *Ep.* 1.5 and 1.9 are two halves of the same letter which was split to confine with generic constraints of length. The two are clearly paired; *Ep.* 1.5 treats the journey and arrival to Rome while *Ep.* 1.9 describes Sidonius' conduct of politics in Rome. They are, however, separate letters; indeed the final two sections of *Ep.* 1.5 function clearly as a conclusion, and conversely the beginning of *Ep.* 1.9 is an introduction rather than a continuation of a piece. They may have originally constituted a single letter, but such a suggestion can only be conjecture. A similar epistolary dynamic between two epistles is evident in Pliny's *Ep.* 6.16 and 6.20.

[11] The exception to this general rule may be letters that were already arranged in the collection when they were sent. These likely included the programmatic letters that refer to their own position such as *Ep.* 1.1, 7.18 and 9.16, and also *Ep.* 7.12, which relies on its position for its narrative force, for which see p. 119.

the opening epistle (*Ep.* 1.1) and both letters are addressed to Constantius, a fact that Sidonius draws attention to with a prominent quotation from Virgil (*Ep.* 7.18.1): "'A te principium tibi desinet'" ("begun by you, it will end with you").[12]

Ep. 8.1 alleges that Petronius, the addressee, has asked Sidonius for more epistles; Sidonius notes his previous circulation (*superior vulgatus*), presumably of books 1–7, but nevertheless agrees to comply to Petronius' demands. The additional letters are termed *addenda voluminis*, the metaphoric sea-journey of the opening epistle continues;[13] Sidonius is at pains to write well (*Ep.* 8.1.3): "sicut adhibendam in conscriptione diligentiam, ita tenendam in editione constantiam" (just like how care must be taken when composing, so too loyalty is needed when publishing). The noun *constantia* puns on Constantius' name and role in revising books 1–7. The final letter of book 8 is again addressed to Constantius, and honours him for his role in assisting Sidonius to produce his epistles. Sidonius emphatically denies that he has enough material to make any further addition, nevertheless a ninth book followed in professed imitation of Pliny, which Sidonius characterises as a late addition (*sera coniunctio*) to the eight already in circulation (*octo superiorum voluminibus*).[14]

Few of Sidonius' early epistles can be dated accurately, but even if we can date their composition – *Ep.* 1.10 was written when Sidonius was the urban prefect of Rome in 467(at least this is what Sidonius claims) – it is still not possible to date their precise circulation. Sidonius likely arranged and distributed books 1 and 2 prior to becoming a bishop in 469/470, if only because boasting about his villa (*Ep.* 2.2) and secular political achievements (*Ep.* 1.2–1.11) may not have been considered suitable behaviour for a new member of the clergy.[15] The collection of books 1–7 took

---

[12] Virg. *Ecl.* 8.11.

[13] Hanaghan (2017a: 255–260).

[14] *Ep.* 9.11.5 refers to previous circulation and arrangement of book 6 by reminding Lupus that he was the addressee of *Ep.* 6.1.

[15] See Harries (1994: 7) and Mathisen (2013: 226, 231). Mommsen (1887: li) suggested dating of book 2 to after the death of Anthemius. This may be discounted given that Sidonius clearly made subtle and latent criticism of Anthemius during the emperor's lifetime, including in his panegyric for Anthemius, for which see Boshoff (2016: 15), who detects "a current of unease and ambivalence surrounding the new, foreign emperor." See Harries (forthcoming), Hanaghan (2017c), and pp. 105–108. Schwitter (2015: 24) posits that the second book was not part of the pre-episcopal circulation, and instead favours the circulation of books 2 to 7 as a single volume post 477. This division devalues the important programmatic role of *Ep.* 1.1 and 7.18 for a collection made up of the first seven books. While it is possible that book 2 was circulated once Sidonius was a bishop, it remains doubtful given that Sidonius probably would have been conflicted over the circulation of a book that celebrated his aristocratic otium.

place in the late 470s after the fall of Clermont.[16] This may be inferred, as book 7 describes the fall of Clermont and clearly represents the first seven books as constituting a single unified collection.[17] There is no specific evidence to suggest that books 3, 4, 5, 6, or 7 circulated independently of that collection. The opening and closing epistles of book 8 and 9 indicate that Sidonius considered these books to be additions; but compelling structural allusions to Pliny's collection (discussed below) suggests that both addenda were planned, and not, as Sidonius makes out, simply an afterthought.[18]

In *Ep.* 1.1 Sidonius indicates that he is sending the *volumen* to Constantius so that he may revise them; this could be lip-service to Constantius – the language is typical of prefaces and programmatic concerns – or it may be a genuine request for assistance. Sidonius may have also used a bookseller (*bybliopola*) to help him distribute his epistles; elsewhere he states that such a man may include the poetic epitaph that he has just composed for the noblewoman Philomathia (*Ep.* 2.8.2) "ceteris epigrammatum meorum voluminibus" (along with the other volumes/pages of my epigrams). Sidonius plausibly sent his epistles to this bookseller (or some other) for reproduction and binding, but this claim cannot be made definitively. In *Ep.* 5.15 he sheds some light on how copies of works may be made (*Ep.* 5.15.1):

> bybliopolam nostrum [insinuo] … librum igitur hic ipse deportat heptateuchi, scriptum velocitate summa, summo nitore, quamquam et a nobis relectum et retractatum. defert volumen et prophetarum, licet me absente decursum, sua tamen cura manuque de supervacuis sententiis eruderatum, nec semper illo contra legente, qui promiserat operam suam; credo, quia infirmitas fuerit impedimento, quominus pollicita compleret.

> I introduce my bookseller to you … and so he brings with him an edition of the heptateuch, which he has written at great speed, and with great energy, although it was read over and revised by me. He also has with him a book of the prophets, written out while I was away, but he has proofed it carefully with his own hand of any superfluous material, the other man who always proofreads had promised to do it, but was prevented from carrying out the revisions because illness intervened, I believe.

---

[16] Harries (1994: 7–9) and Mathisen (2013: 231). It is feasible, however, given the negative depiction of Anthemius in books 1 and 2, that Sidonius circulated the epistles after the defeat of the imperial navy by the Vandals circa June 468, for which see p. 108.

[17] Köhler (1999: 99–100); see also Mrastchek (2016: 310), who considers the first eight books as the main collection.

[18] *Ep.* 8.1.1 and 8.16.1, 5, for which see Harries (1994: 8–9), and *Ep.* 9.1.1 and 9.16.1. For Sidonius' structural use of Pliny see Gibson (2011: 655–659), (2012: 69), (2013b), and (2013c: 198–200, 206–219).

The bookseller is a skilled copyist, and there is clearly a system in place to ensure errors are corrected. The same process may have been used for Sidonius' epistles, but his comments fall short of confirming as much. In *Ep.* 2.9.4 Sidonius likens his friends' libraries to *armaria exstructa byblipolarum* (the piled-up crates of the booksellers), which might suggest that he has had some first-hand experience with the production and distribution of his work.

Works were also distributed and copied less formally. In *Ep.* 4.16 Sidonius assures Ruricius that copying works does not constitute theft. Later in the collection Sidonius relates how he managed to track down Faustus of Riez's bookseller on his travels, and make copies of Faustus' work there and then.[19] Similarly, in *Ep.* 9.7 Sidonius informs Remigius that an acquaintance had returned from Rheims with copies of his recent work (a book of prayers), which he was able to see because he managed to bribe or otherwise cajole Remigius' bookseller into granting him permission. One expectation of receiving a work in certain circumstances was that the recipient should make their own copy and then send the original on to someone else. At the beginning of *Ep.* 9.11 Sidonius paraphrases the letter from Lupus to which he is responding (*Ep.* 9.11.1): "propter libellum, quem non ad vos magis quam per vos missum putastis, epistulam vestram non ad me magis quam in me scriptam recepi" (because of that book, which you think was not sent to you but rather through you, I have received a letter not written to me but rather against me). The *libellum* in question likely pertains to an epistolary book or collection of books that made their way to Lupus by way of a third party, perhaps with instructions to pass the work on to someone else once he had finished making his copy. Sidonius envisages such a journey for his poetry in *Carm.* 24, as it travels from house to house, meeting and being read by each of his friends in turn. The book will travel at speed (*Carm.* 24.51): "quamvis rapido ferare cursu" (however quickly you rush on your way). This remark is broadly suggestive of Sidonius' expectation that each friend will not read through the original at their own leisurely pace, but rather make a copy, and then send on the original to the next friend that Sidonius lists.

In Pliny's Footsteps

Sidonius may well have circulated his epistles in the steps that he outlines, but this is difficult to know as his arrangement closely follows Pliny's,

---

[19] *Ep.* 9.9.

whose nine books of epistles (not counting book 10) had exactly one hundred more than Sidonius' and included the last two books as addenda. Sidonius' opening epistle directly paraphrases Pliny's[20] and definitively states his intention to use him as a model (*Ep.* 1.1.1): "Gai Plinii disciplinam maturitatemque vestigiis praesumptiosis insecuturus" (to follow the *disciplina* and maturity of Gaius Pliny with presumptuous footsteps).[21] As Gibson has argued, the literal meaning of the names of Sidonius' first and last addressees, Constantius and Firminus, create a journey from "standing strong" to "steadfast" that mirrors Pliny's literal use of Clarus and Fuscus' names in his collection to create a journey from light to darkness (and from "C" to "F").[22] This intertextual engagement does not necessarily undermine Sidonius' claims as to how the collection formed; indeed it is possible that Sidonius followed through on his decision to imitate Pliny by actually releasing his epistles in the same steps that Pliny claims to have used, including ending the collection prematurely in book 7, and then adding books 8 and 9 as addenda.[23]

Other connections link Sidonius' epistles to Pliny's: his villa epistle, which combines elements from Pliny's two villa epistles, the thematic grouping of the first two books, and even specific numerically focused allusions. Sidonius' *Ep.* 4.3, for example, praises Claudianus Mamertus' Greek by drawing upon Pliny's praise of Arrius Antoninus which is also the third epistle in his fourth book (Sidon. *Ep.* 4.3.8):

> [hymnus] dulcis elatus, et quoslibet lyricos dithryambos amoenitate poetica … quid multis? arbitro me in utroque genere dicendi nec Athenae sic Atticae nec Musae sic musicae iudicabuntur

> [the hymn] is sweetly uplifting, and those lyrics and dithyrambs with poetic charm … what else? From my perspective in both kinds of speaking neither Athenians will be judged so Attic, nor the Muses so musical …

Pliny's language is very similar (*Ep.* 4.3.4–5):

> Quantum ibi humanitatis, venustatis, quam dulcia illa … Callimachum me vel Heroden, vel si quid his melius, tenere credebam … Hominemne

---

[20] Köhler (1995: 99): "[Sidonius übernimmt] die einleitende Floskel des Plinius […] zwar an gleicher Stelle und in ähnlicher Konstruktion, aber so, daß jedes einzelne Wort durch ein Synonym ersetzt wird" (Sidonius adopts Pliny's introductory phrase … at the same point and in a similar construction, but so that every individual word is replaced by a synonym).

[21] Sidonius also mentions Symmachus and Cicero by name, for discussion of which see pp. 14–15.

[22] Gibson (2011: 655–659), (2013b 338–339), and (2013c: 198–202) shows the extensive structural engagement of Sidonius' collection with Pliny's.

[23] See pp. 173–175.

Romanum tam Graece loqui? Non medius fidius ipsas Athenas tam Atticas
dixerim. Quid multa?

Such great elegance, charm, such sweetness … I thought I was holding a
copy of Callimachus or Herodas, or even something better than them …
Is it, that a Roman speaks so in Greek? I would not even say that Athens is
so Attic. What else?

The verbal echoes are extensive. Arrianus' poetry has charm (*venustatis*)
and sweetness (*dulcia*), Claudianus' is also sweet (*dulcis*) and has charm
(*amoenitate*).[24] When Pliny appears unsure how to continue he exclaims
quid multa, Sidonius *quid multis*. Both Arrianus' and Claudianus'
command of Attic is so strong that it would show up an Athenian (*Athenas
tam Atticas, Athenae sic Atticae*). Pliny's praise of Arrianus stands as a literary model that Sidonius can rework and redeploy to his own context,
appropriating the praise of a Greek epigrammatist for a Gallic presbyter.
The precise positioning of the two epistles as the third instalment of the
respective fourth books enhances their intertextual connection.[25]

Sidonius' intense engagement with Pliny's letters has a clear effect on
the arrangement of the collection, both for individual epistles and whole
books.

Comedic and Tragic Ends

Every epistle has an end, as does each epistolary book and collection.[26]
This section analyses how Sidonius exploits the closural opportunities of
the genre for individual epistles and the collection as a whole. According
to Altman epistles ultimately have two possible endings: a final definitive
sign off, the "tragic closure" or a momentary pause in an ongoing dialogue,
the "comedic closure."[27] This dynamic may not be evident in every epistle,
but it is evident in every epistolary collection, which either has a definitive end of some sort or does not. Seneca's collection for example has no
noticeable end, whereas the collections of both Pliny and Sidonius have
multiple ends, the last of which is clearly marked as definitive. Altman

[24] Sidonius lauds Claudianus for combining his poetic charm with historical veracity, for which see
Amherdt (2001: 33).
[25] Gibson (2012: 69) similarly reads a connection between Sidonius' assertion of his episcopacy
and Pliny's announcement of his consulship, both of which occur in *Ep.* 3.1 of their respective
collections.
[26] Fragmentary epistles may not, but if the incompletion was unintentional, they would have had a
beginning and ending at some point.
[27] Altman (1982: 148–150).

defined tragic closure as when an epistolary author is compelled to stop writing, often owing to their death. A comedic end occurs when an epistolary author chooses to stop writing owing to circumstances or their whimsy. An author may also choose to stop writing, and then die, which may alter the reception of their final work as their "last work," rendering it with a degree of seriousness which it lacked at the moment of composition. Open-ended epistles that imply a further exchange are by definition comedic, the epistolary author has chosen rather than been forced to end the epistle. Whether an ending is open or closed, comedic or tragic, is ultimately determined by the reader rather than something that is innate to the text.[28]

The most easily identifiable comedic end is when an epistolary author and addressee close the physical distance between themselves which prevents the epistle from bridging their spatial gap. This kind of comedic finale is readily apparent in *Ep.* 4.19, which as the shortest epistle in the collection may be quoted in full (*Ep.* 4.19.1): "Et moras nostras et silentium accusas. utrumque purgabile est; namque et venimus et scribimus. vale" (You accuse me both of delay and silence. Both of these can be dismissed; for I am both on my way and writing. Goodbye).[29] Sidonius and Florentius were apart. This is soon to be remedied. The arrival of Sidonius' epistle and person will fix Florentius' two complaints: that he has not written and has been delayed in visiting. The comedy is formed by the absurdity of the epistolary dynamic: one can envisage Sidonius arriving immediately after his letter carrier or perhaps even delivering the letter himself.

Other comedic closures in Sidonius' collection are not as extreme. In *Ep.* 4.1 Sidonius indicates to Probus his commitment to maintain their friendship through their exchange of epistles, which is necessitated by their physical distance from one another.[30] A chiastic flourish induces Probus to maintain their epistolary communication (4.1.5): "etsi sede absumus, adsimus affectu" (although we are distant from each other's homes, let us be close in affection). The epistle leaves open the likely further exchange of letters between Probus and Sidonius. The fact that Probus does not receive another letter in Sidonius' collection invites a revisionist re-reading of the end of the epistle (4.1.5): "cuius [amicitiae] intemeratae partes, quantum spectat ad vos, a nobis in aevum, si quod est vitae reliquum,

---

[28] Fowler (1997: 4–5).

[29] Amherdt (2001: 420–421).

[30] Squillante (2014: 279) notes that their affinity is formed not only by their familial connection but also their shared educational experience.

perennabuntur" (in as much as it pertains to you, my share of our friendship will be kept endlessly pure by me for the course of my life, however much of it remains). Either Sidonius or Probus died before he could send another epistle to Probus, or at least, include one in his collection.[31] Re-reading *Ep.* 4.1 gives an otherwise positive epistle a new, far gloomier feel. A tragic reading of comedic ends is one consequence of the end of the collection, which creates an opportunity to read the notional open-ended nature of certain epistles against the closed tragic reality of the end of the collection.

In the last book Sidonius subtly foreshadows his own death. In the second epistle in book 9 Sidonius refers to himself as a (*Ep.* 9.2.3) "novus clericus peccator antiquus" (a new cleric but an old sinner). The contrast is clearly between new and old but really only works if Sidonius is an old man. Two letters later Sidonius reminds his fellow bishop Graecus (*Ep.* 9.4.2) "quod ad promissa convivia patriarcharum vel ad necta caelstium poculorum per amaritudinum terrenarum calices perveniretur" (that the journey to the promised banquets of the patriarchs and the nectar of heaven's cups passes through drinks of earthly bitterness).[32] The epistle ends by noting how insignificant such earthly cups are compared to what Christ drank on the cross (*Ep.* 9.4.3): "qui invitat ad caelum" (who calls us to heaven). Heaven barely features in the earlier epistles,[33] yet appears again four epistles later (9.8.2):

> orate, ut optabili religiosoque decessu vitae praesentis angoribus atque onere perfuncti, cum iudicii dies sanctus offulserit cum resurrectione, agminibus vestris famulaturi … iungamur; quia secundum promissa caelestia, quae spoponderunt filios dei de nationibus congregandos, si nos reos venia soletur, dum vos beatos gloria manet, etsi per actionum differentiam, non tamen per locorum distantiam dividemur.

> pray, that after a pleasant and devout death and we have brought an end to our current struggles and burden, when the holy day of judgment shines with the resurrection, that I may be joined to your group in service … since according to heaven's promises, which have assured us that the sons of the Lord will come together from all nations, if forgiveness may comfort me in sin, while glory awaits you saints, and if we are not divided by the difference of our actions, then we will not be divided by the distance between our locations.

---

[31] For an example of this methodology applied to some of Pliny's epistles see Gibson (2015: 220).

[32] Cf. Ambrose *Ep.* 15 where he uses the image of drinking bitterness (*hausi … amaritudinem*) to describe his reaction to the news that Acholius is dead.

[33] *Ep.* 6.12.1, 6.12.6, 7.9.7.

In heaven the suffering that they will endure on earth will end, including the mental anguish of their physical separation, so there will be no need for epistles in heaven. In both epistles the tragic end of the parting of author and addressee on earth looks forward to the comedic closure of their reunion in heaven. A similar use of heaven features at the end of Jerome's *Ep.* 60 which was written to Heliodorus to console him on the death of his nephew Nepotian (*Ep.* 60.19): "haec [caritas] semper vivit in pectore; ob hanc Nepotianus noster absens praesens est et per tanta terrarum spatia divisos utraque conplectitur manu" (this [love] always lives in our heart; accordingly our absent Nepotianus is present and holds by the hand each of us although we are separated by distant lands). Jerome reworks Nepotian's tragic end on earth into an omnipresent reunion with both the author and addressee, but ultimately the conceit that underpins this claim is laid bare, neither of them can actually hold or talk to Nepotian.[34]

Death lurks behind Sidonius' focus on the afterlife, which dramatically increases in the ninth book of epistles. A mere six epistles later Sidonius emphatically acknowledges that he is bedridden with illness.[35] By the last epistle in the collection his efforts to write have become affected by the wintry conditions (9.16.2):

> raptim coactimque translator festinus exscripsi, tempore hiberno nil retardatus, quin actutum iussa complerem, licet antiquarium moraretur insiccabilis gelu pagina et calamo durior gutta, quam iudicasses imprimentibus digitis non fluere sed frangi. sic quoque tamen compotem officii prius agere curavi, quam duodecimum nostrum, quem Numae mensem vos nuncupatis, Favonius flatu teporo, pluviisque natalibus maritaret.

> quickly and concisely I hurriedly transcribed, copying it out, I was not at all slowed down by the wintry time of year in completing promptly what was asked, although the page, unable to be dried because of its iciness, slowed down the copyist and ink was harder than the pen, even so I hastened to carry out the completion of my duty, before in the twelfth month, which you term the month of Numa, the West wind with its warm air and native rains comes to fertilise.

These comments highlight Sidonius' mortality. Winter time is symbolic of death; it is nearly the end of the year which stands metaphorically for

---

[34] Jerome *Ep.* 60.19, for which see Scourfield (1993: 227–228), who cites John Chrysostom *vid. Iun.* 3 as a comparable example. Similar claims emerge in Christian theology such as in Ambrose's treatise on the death of his brother Satyrus which concludes by looking forward to his reunion with Satyrus in heaven (*De Excessu Fratris sui Satyri* 2.135).

[35] *Ep.* 9.14.1.

his lifetime.[36] The cold has not slowed him down, but even still his secretary must contend with ink freezing and the nib breaking. Sidonius is in a hurry to finish in time. The inserted verse directly references the approach of his death (9.16.3 vv40–48):

Nec recordari queo, quanta quondam scripserim primo iuvenis calore, unde pars maior utinam taceri possit et abdi!	Nor am I able to recall, how many things I once wrote in the first energy of youth, hence I wish that most of it would be able to be silenced and buried!
Nam senectutis propiore meta, quicquid extremis sociamur annis, plus pudet, si quid leve lusit aetas, nunc reminisci.	For as the end of old age becomes nearer, regardless of what I do in my final years, the more it shames me to remember now, what levity youth played

Old age is getting closer. Sidonius contrasts his youthful folly (*iuvenis calore, leve lusit aetas*) with his more recent endeavours (*quicquid extremis sociamur annis*). The praeteritio (*nec recordari queo*) gives way to the act of remembering (*reminisci*) which causes shame (*pudet*), despite attempts to forget (*taceri, abdi*). The end of the collection becomes "tragic" in its aftermath. Sidonius' (implied) death prevents him from adding to the collection.[37] The early writings of Sidonius' youth may refer specifically to his poetry, which becomes the focus of his regret. The verse ends with Sidonius' assertion that if he had more time on earth he would write martyrdom poetry.[38] He cites the example, drawn from Prudentius, of when Saturninus was gored to death by a bull as the kind of topic such poetry would cover.[39]

The epistle ends with a reversion to prose (*Ep.* 9.16.4):

> Redeamus in fine ad oratorium stilum materiam praesentem proposito semel ordine terminaturi, ne, si epilogis musicis opus prosarium clauserimus, secundum regulas Flacci, ubi amphora coepit institui, urceus potius exisse videatur.

> Let us at the end return to the rhetorical style to conclude the present material once and for all with the proposed rule, so that following the rules

---

[36] Gibson (2013c: 219) notes the parallel with Pliny's collection which also ends during winter and (2013b: 354) argues that Sidonius' end is more optimistic as it looks forward to the imminent advent of spring.

[37] What D.H. Roberts (1997: 262) termed a historical ending, where historical events that occurred after the end of the text provide closure to the narrative.

[38] *Ep.* 9.16.3 vv. 60–84.

[39] Prudentius, *Hymn in Honour of the Eighteen Holy Matyrs of Saragossa*, 4.160–164. See Herrera (1981: 160–161) and Mratschek (2016: 316–320).

of Flaccus it does not seem that a pitcher was produced (if I ended my prose work with a rhythmical epilogue) when an amphora started to form.

This passage alludes to Horace's *Ars Poetica* (21–23):[40]

> Amphora coepit institui,
> currente rota cur urceus exit?
> sit quod vis, simplex dum taxat et unum.

> An amphora began to be built. Why as the wheel runs is a pitcher produced? Finally, let it be what you want, but let it be a single entity.

The allusion is clearly established by Sidonius' reference to Horace as *Flaccus*, the direct quotation of *Amphora coepit institui*, the use of *urceus*, and the Sapphic metre, which lends the entire verse a Horatian colour.[41] Horace's concern is that if a work exhibits diverse features it will lack sufficient coherency.[42] Sidonius displays the same concern: by introducing short poems in his final letters he may jeopardise the coherency of his epistolary corpus as a whole.[43] This concern resonates more broadly with the unity of a collection of epistles that cover an eclectic mix of events, individuals, and moments.[44]

Sidonius died shortly after, or perhaps even before, the last book of epistles was circulated.[45] If he died afterwards a contemporary reader could have read the ninth book without knowing that Sidonius was dead. If he died beforehand then the context of his death would have provided his contemporary reader with an external closure to the collection. The precise dating of Sidonius' death relative to the circulation of book 9 only impacts our understanding of how his contemporaries read the closural dynamics of the ninth book in the late 470s and early 480s, not our reading of the ninth book, nor how every reader read Sidonius' collection after his death.

Ricœur's argument is worth repeating "a jagged chronology interrupted by jumps, anticipations and flashbacks, in short, a deliberately multidimensional configuration, is better suited to a view of time that has no

---

[40] Bellès (1999: 220n233).
[41] For the significance of the Sapphic metre see Morgan (2010: 181ff).
[42] Brink (1971: 102–103).
[43] As Brink (1971: 103) argues, Sidonius' concern is specifically on the unity of a collection composed in verse and poetry. See also Condorelli (2015: 493).
[44] *Ep.* I.I.I "… prout eas causa persona tempus elicuit" "… as each event, character, moment has produced them [the epistles]."
[45] Mathisen (2013: 223) dates Sidonius' death to approximately 485 and dates the circulation of book 9 to 481, but an alternate reading to Sidonius' epitaph may date his death to 479, for which see Furbetta (2014) and (2015a). This could either force the circulation of book nine to be brought forward or may open the possibility that Sidonius finished the book, and then requested it be circulated after his death.

possible overview, no overall internal cohesiveness."[46] The clear thematic divisions unravel. His claims that books 8 and 9 are addenda may excuse this lack of continuity, but it does little to offer the reader any sense of closure.[47] Ultimately a closural force is felt through Sidonius' encouragement to read the epistles as a pseudo-biographical narrative in which his own death provides a definitive and clearly marked end. The "old sinner" has died; winter has finally won.

---

[46] Ricœur (1985: 81).
[47] Matthews' (1975: 346) claims that Sidonius tries to project continuity despite great changes taking place. This is a fair assessment of the opening of the collection but not the end at which point the "great changes" have clearly affected the narrative.

Epilogue

This book has examined Sidonius' persona, manipulation of time, characterisation, use of dialogue, and arrangement. These elements are somewhat dependant on each other. Dialogue, for example, may affect characterisation: Arvandus' haughty condemnation of others confirms Sidonius' depiction of his arrogance. Equally, temporality may affect arrangement, especially with epistles that cover the same topic or involve the same individuals. The epistle addressed to Lampridius could have been positioned after the epistle that details his murder, but such an arrangement would have jarred the general progression of time that persists throughout the collection's "jagged chronology." In every aspect Sidonius' persona looms, as the careful author, close friend, confidant, wise bishop or passionate Gallo-Roman. This epilogue offers a holistic assessment of one epistle in the collection (2.13) which features elements in each category which may be read in concert with one another. It ends with a brief reflection on the place of Sidonius' epistles in Latin literature.

Ep. 2.13 "On the Dangers of Imperial Politics"

Ep. 2.13 is addressed to Serranus, about whom nothing is known other than what may be deduced from this epistle.[1] He was a supporter of Petronius Maximus and likely knew Sidonius in some capacity.[2] It begins with the circumstances that prompted Sidonius to write (*Ep.* 2.13.1):

> Epistulam tuam nobis Marcellinus togatus exhibuit, homo peritus virque amicorum. quae primoribus verbis salutatione libata reliquo sui tractu, qui quidem grandis est, patroni tui Petronii Maximi imperatoris laudes habebat; quem tamen tu pertinacius aut amabilius quam rectius veriusque

---

[1] See PLRE II "Serranus" and Henning (1999: 74).

[2] Sidonius' reference to him as *dominus frater* at the end of the letter is dripping with irony given the tone of the letter and so is not reliable as evidence for a close friendship.

felicissimum appellas, propter hoc quippe, cur per amplissimos fascium titulos fuerit evectus usque ad imperium. sed sententiae tali numquam ego assentior, ut fortunatos putem qui reipublicae praecipitibus ac lubricis culminibus insistunt.

The advocate Marcellinus showed me your letter; he is a talented individual who has many friends. With its first words it offers a gentle greeting, and then for the rest of its length, which is quite significant, it praises your patron, the emperor Petronius Maximus, whom you still label "the most fortunate" with more persistence and affection than accuracy or truth, the basis for this is that he progressed through a great number of offices and made it as far as all the way to emperor. But I will never agree with that sort of an opinion, which puts forward that the fortunate are those who stand on the lofty and slippery heights of government service.

Marcellinus is praised, both for his talent, presumably as an advocate, and his circle of friends that surely included Sidonius. The opening creates an *Erzählzeit* for Sidonius' reply which has come shortly after he read Serranus' letter. The verb *exhibuit* indicates that Serranus' letter was not addressed to Sidonius, but that Marcellinus took it upon himself to divulge its contents anyway. Sidonius' praise of Marcellinus contrasts with the total absence of any praise for Serranus. This absence of praise is highlighted by criticism of Serranus' letter, not only for its content and motivation, but also its length, which contravenes the generic expectation that letters should be brief.[3] Serranus is painted as Petronius Maximus' man and prone to the same vanity for power as his patron. Sidonius' opinion carries the weight of his own public service and resonates with his personal experience in the inauspicious court of his father-in-law Avitus, and so his argument naturally assumes the qualities that he denies Serranus, namely that it is correct and true.

Sidonius shifts from the testimonial function, as he describes how he happened to read Serranus' letter, to the communicative, when he asserts his own opinion regarding the nature of power, and then to the ideological as he details the stress that confronts rulers (*Ep.* 2.13.2): "nam sicut hominibus reges, ita regibus dominandi desideria dominantur" (for just as kings rule over men, love of ruling rules kings).[4] A similarly balanced

---

[3] Ebbeler (2009: 277) recognises the pejorative force of Jerome's implication that Augustine had ignored epistolary brevity by his reference to one of Augustine's letters as a *liber* rather than a *libellus*. Sidonius' language effects the same slight.

[4] For this terminology see Chapter 5. Squillante (2007–08: 254) argues that Sidonius alludes to the opening of Augustine's *De civitate dei* which also plays on the verb *dominari*. Rousseau (2000: 256) links this sentiment to Sidonius' advice to Ecdicius in *Ep.* 3.3.9 to avoid high politics owing to the dangers involved.

and pithy remark neatly summarises his conundrum (*Ep.* 2.13.3): "nec sustinebat dominus esse, qui non sustinuerat esse sub domino" (he was unable to be master who could not be under a master).

The epistle obliquely references the disastrous emperors who came before and after Petronius.[5] Petronius' early (successful) life forms a contrast to his ambitious later life that ended with his own bizarre death.[6] After which Sidonius reverts to the testimonial function, inserting dialogue for Petronius in direct speech which a third party (Fulgentius) claimed to have overheard and has presumably relayed to Sidonius. As Petronius' reign seemingly started to unravel, he was heard expressing envy for Damocles who was only king for the day.[7]

Sidonius shifts to the narrative mode, segueing into a detailed account of who Damocles was, complete with inserted direct dialogue between Damocles and his prince Dionysius. The feast begins, the sword dangles, and Damocles quickly has cause to regret his brash statements. Sidonius concludes the epistle in a combination of the communicative and ideological mode (*Ep.* 2.13.8): "quapropter ad statum huiusmodi, domine frater, nescio an constet tendere beatos, patet certe miseros pervenire" (accordingly, my lord brother, I do not know whether it may be agreed that those who reach such a position are "blessed" but it is clear that they are wretched).

The epistle has three interwoven narratives. The first details the circumstances by which Sidonius managed to read Serranus' letter, the second focuses on Petronius Maximus as an example of ambition causing disaster, and the last features the famous Damocles. These three narratives interact with one another. Sidonius' use of Damocles as an example is suggestive of the disdain that he has for Serranus, who writes long letters, supports Petronius Maximus, and does not know the story of Damocles well enough to understand the significance of Sidonius' blatant reference. The *Erzählzeit* gives Sidonius' response impetus, as if he could not stand by while Serranus' views went unchallenged.

These narratives take on new proportions when Sidonius' role as the implied author of the epistle, the author who decided to select this epistle, include it in the second book of the collection, and circulate it. The second book is thematically unified around aristocratic *otium*, and in a way this epistle is too, in that Sidonius argues strongly against ambitious *negotium*.[8]

---

[5] See pp. 112–113.
[6] See p. 114.
[7] See pp. 22–23.
[8] Montone (2017: 36).

This argument is accentuated by the good life that individuals like Petronius Maximus could have enjoyed if only their lust for power had not corrupted them. He could have dined with friends, visited others, played ball, read literature, bathed in a villa; but instead he died, bludgeoned to death by a mob. The epistle reflects directly onto Sidonius' persona and acts as further justification for his decision to retire from secular politics, in effect smoothing the transition into book 3 and rationalising Sidonius' decision to become a bishop. *Ep.* 2.13 is a good example of how Sidonius developed complex and multi-layered narratives contained within the epistolary form.

Placing Sidonius' epistles in a broader literary context can prove difficult. Despite the abundance of epistles from Late Antiquity, few exhibit the manipulation of the narrative for literary effect to the same extent. In this regard there is a stark difference between Sidonius' epistles and the efforts of his (near) contemporaries in Late Antique Gaul, such as Ruricius of Limoges and Avitus of Vienne. Some of Synesius of Cyrene's epistles perhaps come closest for their literary flair and ambition. At times shades of other epistolary authors loom; Jerome's characterisation is a worthy comparandum to Sidonius', similarly Augustine's extensive use of dialogue, but no-one Late Antique author consistently approximates Sidonius' unique narrative technique and language.

Sidonius' letters are closest to Pliny's. This is entirely intentional: Sidonius is upfront about this ambition from the beginning of the collection and was clearly committed to making the connection meaningful and clear. This intense engagement raises the question as to whether Sidonius succeeds in placing his work in Pliny's shadow. Ultimately the relevancy of Pliny's example must be weighed against its irrelevancy; Rome falls, the Visigoths take Clermont, as the events in the background seep into Sidonius' epistles. The pessimism of the final books turns the whole into a performance that is never to be repeated. Sidonius is not just the next Pliny, he is the last Pliny.

Timeline 378–485

Sidonius	(Western) Roman Empire	Barbarians
	378 Valens dies at the battle of Adrianople. Theodosius becomes the emperor in the East.	378 Goths defeat Valens' army in the battle of Adrianople, destroying large parts of it, including many veterans. The Roman army never recovers.
	391 Theodosius I dies, the last ruler of a unified Roman Empire. His sons inherit: Arcadius in the East and Honorius in the West.	
		400 Rhine frontier 'collapses' – large groups of barbarian peoples move inside the borders of the Western Roman Empire.
407 Sidonius' grandfather is involved in Constantius III's failed ursurpation in Gaul and Spain.		
		410 Alaric sacks Rome, then dies.
		418 Theodoric I becomes king of the Visigoths.
	423 Honorius dies.	
	425 (ca) Valentinian III becomes emperor.	
		429 Vandals cross into North Africa.

(continued)

430 (ca) Sidonius is born.

435 Vandals establish a
kingdom in North Africa.

450 (ca) Sidonius marries
Pappianilla, Avitus' daughter.

451 battle of the Catalaunian
plains: Theodoric I dies and
Thorismund becomes king of
the Visigoths.

453 Thorismund is murdered
by his brother Theodoric II
for the Visigothic throne.
Attila dies.

454 Aëtius (magister
militum) is assassinated.

455 (Mar) Valentinian III
is assassinated. Petronius
Maximus becomes emperor.

455 (May) Petronius
Maximus dies.

455 (Jun) Avitus is   455 (Jun) Vandals sack Rome.
proclaimed emperor
in Gaul.

456 (Jan) Sidonius delivers
a panegyric for Avitus.

456 (Sep)-457? Avitus dies.

457 Majorian becomes
emperor.

459 Sidonius delivers a
panegyric for Majorian.

461 Majorian dies. Libius
Severus replaces him.

465 Libius Severus dies.

466 Euric murders his
brother Theodoric II for the
Visigothic throne.

467 Sidonius travels to   467 Anthemius becomes
Rome   emperor. His daughter
                               Alypia marries the barbarian
                               potentate Ricimer.

468 Sidonius delivers a
panegyric for Anthemius.
Sidonius serves as prefect of
Rome. Arvandus' trial for
treason takes place.

469–470 Sidonius returns
to Gaul, circulates his
poetry and some of his
epistles (books 1 and 2),
and is appointed the
bishop of Clermont.

471 Euric begins to harry
Clermont.

472 Anthemius and
Ricimer die. The next
emperor, Olybrius also dies.
Glycerius' reign begins.

474 Julius Nepos forces
Glycerius' abdication and
begins his reign.

474–475 Euric's attacks on
Clermont stop. Clermont
is seceded to the Visigothic
kingdom of Toulouse.

475 Sidonius is
imprisoned by Euric.

475 Romulus Augustus is
installed as emperor.

476 Romulus Augustus
dies.

? Sidonius is released
and circulates books 1–7
of the epistles.

? Sidonius circulates book
8 and then book 9 of the
epistles

480 Julius Nepos dies.

? 485 (ca) Sidonius dies.

Catalogue of Contents and Addressees

	Addressee	Subject
Book 1		
1.1	Constantius	A programmatic introductory letter, modelled on Pliny *Ep.* 1.1, that offers a *volumen* of letters in need of revision and proofing.
1.2	Agricola	A physical description of Theodoric II, Visigothic king (453–466), and account of a typical day at his court.
1.3	Philomathius	A mock apology for Sidonius' political ambitions and an account of Gaudentius' rise to the rank of vicarius.
1.4	Gaudentius	Congratulations to Gaudentius for his political success.
1.5	Heronius	A travelogue of Sidonius' journey to Rome from Gaul, and a description of Rome during the wedding celebrations of the barbarian potentate Ricimer and the emperor Anthemius' daughter, Alyppia.
1.6	Eutropius	An encouragement to Eutropius to take up public service.
1.7	Vincentius	An account of Sidonius' ultimately unsuccessful attempt to help Arvandus, the praetorian prefect of Gaul (464–469), avoid conviction for *Lèse majesté*.
1.8	Candidianus	A jocular comparison of Ravenna and Rome.
1.9	Heronius	A follow-up to 1.5 which describes the aftermath of the wedding and Sidonius' attempts to ingratiate himself with the Roman political class.
1.10	Campanianus	An account of Sidonius' difficulties, as the urban prefect of Rome, to manage the city's grain supply.
1.11	Montius	A *recusatio* for a satire and an account of when Sidonius was accused of authoring a satire but managed to convince the emperor Majorian over dinner that no charges should be laid.
Book 2		
2.1	Ecdicius	Invective against Seronatus.
2.2	Domitius	Description of Sidonius' villa, Avitacum.

2.3	Felix	Congratulations to Felix for his promotion to the patriciate.
2.4	Sagittarius	A letter of recommendation, requesting Sagittarius befriend Proiectus.
2.6	Pegasius	An endorsement of Menstruanus, a mutual friend.
2.7	Explicius	Advice to Explicius to be fair and prompt in judging the merits of a case.
2.8	Desideratus	Eulogy and epitaph for the noblewoman Philomathia.
2.9	Donidius	An apology for being late owing to the the hospitality that Ferreolus and Apollinaris have shown Sidonius as a guest at their estates.
2.10	Hesperius	Praise of Hesperius as a learned man, followed by a description of a church recently built in Lyon and the epigram (included) which Sidonius composed to be inscribed on the church.
2.11	Rusticus	A formal courtesy letter that notes the physical separation between author and addressee.
2.12	Agricola	A refusal to join Agricola on a fishing trip as Sidonius' daughter is unwell.
2.13	Serranus	Reflections on the dangers of imperial power with specific reference to Petronius Maximus' disastrous reign.
2.14	Maurisius	Promise to visit Marusius on his estate.

Book 3

3.1	Avitus	Praise of their close friendship and thanks for Avitus' charitable donation to Sidonius' church.
3.2	Constantius	Description of Constantius' visit to war-torn Clermont and thanks for the comfort and spiritual leadership that he provided to the suffering townspeople.
3.3	Ecdicius	Praise of Ecdicius for his efforts defending the Arverni from the Visigoths.
3.4	Felix	Introduction of one of Sidonius' letter carriers, Gozolas, and description of the geopolitical situation of Clermont, wedged between the Visigoths and Burgundians.
3.5	Hypatius	A request that Hypatius agree to let Sidonius' friend acquire a parcel of land.
3.6	Eutropius	Congratulations to Eutropius on his career advancement.
3.7	Felix	A letter admonishing Felix for not replying to Sidonius which then describes the character of Licinianus who had been sent to resolve the tension between the Arverni and the Visigoths.
3.8	Eucherius	A letter of thanks to Eucherius for his achievements.
3.9	Riothamus	A letter of recommendation asking Riothamus to intercede on behalf of Sidonius' letter carrier in a dispute that he has with some Bretons regarding their acquisition of his slaves.

(*continued*)

3.10	Tetradius	A letter of introduction for Theodorus, an upright and diligent friend of Sidonius'.
3.11	Simplicius	A letter of praise for Simplicius and apologies for Sidonius' delay in writing to him.
3.12	Secundus	A narrative of Sidonius' actions in punishing grave-robbers from desecrating his grandfather's tomb (Secundus' great-grandfather) and instructions for Secundus to oversee its timely repair, including a new epitaph that Sidonius has composed.
3.13	Apollinaris	An invective against 'Gnatho'.
3.14	Placidus	Thanks to Placidius for his generous encouragement of Sidonius' literary pursuits.

Book 4

4.1	Probus	Praise of Probus and reflections on their shared childhood.
4.2	*From Claudianus Mamertus to Sidonius	A letter chiding Sidonius for not acknowledging the publication of Claudianus' treatise on the nature of the soul (*De statu animae*) which was dedicated to Sidonius.
4.3	Claudianus Mamertus	A letter in reply to 4.2 which (ostensibly) praises Claudianus using hyperbole.
4.4	Simplicius and Apollinaris	A letter of introduction for the letter-carrier Faustinus.
4.5	Felix	A follow-up letter to Felix again asking him to reply.
4.6	Apollinaris	Another letter, sent through Faustinus, which warns Apollinaris not be complacent given the dangerous circumstances.
4.7	Simplicius	A letter criticising the letter-carrier for being a rustic fool.
4.8	Euodius	A letter describing the circumstances of its composition in reply to Euodius and his request for a poem (included) that he can inscribe on a silver dish to present to Ragnahilda, the Visigothic queen.
4.9	Industrius	Praise of Vectius.
4.10	Felix	Another letter requesting word from Felix.
4.11	Petreius	A eulogy for Claudianus Mamertus and a copy of his epitaph which Sidonius composed in verse.
4.12	Simplicius and Apollinaris	A description of the circumstances that led to the letter carrier losing the message that they had written for Sidonius and a request for them to resend it.
4.13	Vectius	Praise of Germanicus.
4.14	Polemius	Praise of Polemius for his conduct as the praetorian prefect of Gaul and comparison between secular and clerical office.
4.15	Elaphius	Congratulations to Elaphius for completing his baptistery.
4.16	Ruricius	A letter thanking him for his stylish letter and noting that making a copy of a work does not constitute a 'theft.'

(*continued*)

Book 7

7.1	Mamertus	An account of Visigothic raiding and thanks to Mamertus for instigating a new schedule of prayers (rogations).
7.2	Graecus	Apologies for inadvertently misrepresenting who Amantius was, which segues into a second, more reliable letter of recommendation for Amantius.
7.3	Megethius	A letter accompanying a copy of Sidonius' sermons (which are not extant).
7.4	Fonteius	An account of Vindicius' return from Fonteius, laden with gifts, and a summary of his praise of Fonteius.
7.5	Agroecius	An account of Sidonius' role in a clerical election in Bourges.
7.6	Basilius	A plea for Basilius to lobby the Gallo-Roman negotiators to rethink their agreement with Euric, the Visigothic king, to cede Clermont.
7.7	Graecus	A letter of complaint regarding the Visigothic acquisition of Clermont and the suffering that the Arverni went through during the barbarian attacks, followed by criticism of the negotiators and the treaty that they signed with Euric.
7.8	Euphronius	A request for advice given that the people of Bourges want to elect Simplicius as their bishop.
7.9	Perpetuus	An account of Sidonius' role in the election of the bishop of Bourges and a copy of the address that he gave to the assembly.
7.10	Graecus	Apologies to Graecus that Sidonius is unable to visit because of the dire circumstances confronting Clermont.
7.11	Auspicius	Apologies for Sidonius' lack of time for his friendship with Auspicius, followed by a recommendation for Petrus.
7.12	Ferreolus	Praise of Ferreolus and his achievements.
7.13	Sulpicius	Praise of Sulpicius' son, Himerius.
7.14	Philagrius	An account of a meeting, in which others claimed that they were closer friends with Philagrius than Sidonius, followed by a defence of their friendship, and philosophical reflections on the nature and limitations of the human condition.
7.15	Salonius	A complaint that Sidonius never sees Salonius and his brother because they are always farming.
7.16	Chariobaudus	A report that indicates Chariobaudus' freedmen have successfully completed their allotted task.
7.17	Volusianus	Sidonius agrees to Volusianus' request to write a funerary poem for Abraham, a recently deceased abbot, includes the poem in the letter, and describes Abraham's successor Auxanius.
7.18	Constantius	A programmatic letter that book-ends a volume that included books 1–7.

(continued)

Book 8

8.1	Petronius	Programmatic letter, acquiescing to Petronius' request for more letters.
8.2	Johannes	Praise of Johannes for his learning.
8.3	Leo	An introduction of some works that Sidonius has copied for Leo, followed by complaints regarding his imprisonment by Euric.
8.4	Consentius	Description of Consentius' estate and poetry, which Sidonius claims not to write as he is a bishop devoted to serious matters.
8.5	Fortunalis	Praise of Fortunalis.
8.6	Namatius	Praise of the Gallo-Roman orator Flavius Nicetius, and an account of when Sidonius witnessed him speak, followed by inquiries regarding Namatius' hunting and naval service against the Saxons.
8.7	Audax	Criticism of the old elite and praise of Audax for continuing to improve his family's standing.
8.8	Syagrius	An invitation for Syagrius to visit Sidonius.
8.9	Lampridius	A response to Lampridius' request for verses (enclosed).
8.10	Ruricius	Praise of Ruricius for his learning.
8.11	Lupus	A courtesy letter that segues into an account of the murder of Lampridius by his own slaves, a poem that Sidonius composed to mark the occasion of his death, and reflections on his unique character traits and behaviour.
8.12	Trygetius	An invitation for Trygetius to visit Sidonius.
8.13	Nunechius	Praise of Nunechius' character and a recommendation for Promotus, the letter-carrier.
8.14	Principius	Praise of Principius.
8.15	Prosperus	Praise of Annianus and Sidonius' apologies for being unable to finish a history of Attila's campaign.
8.16	Constantius	A programmatic end to book 8 (the first addendum).

Book 9

9.1	Firminus	A programmatic letter introducing the second addendum (book 9).
9.2	Euphronius	A refusal to write a theological or exegetical work.
9.3	Faustus	A letter that reiterates Sidonius' friendship with Faustus and praises him for his knowledge, learning and oratory.
9.4	Graecus	Praise of Graecus.
9.5	Julianus	A letter hoping for further correspondence between Sidonius and Julianus now that peace has been agreed.

9.6	Ambrosius	An account of how a young man ended his romance with a slave-girl and has married a woman of suitable social standing.
9.7	Remigius	An account of how a traveller managed to copy one of Remigius' works from his bookseller, followed by praise of that work.
9.8	Principius	A letter hoping that Principius and Sidonius will meet in heaven.
9.9	Faustus	A request for a letter, followed by complaint that Faustus had not willingly shared his recent work with Sidonius and an account of how Sidonius managed to get access to it anyway, and an extended praise of that work and its philosophical erudition.
9.10	Aprunculus	A letter of recommendation.
9.11	Lupus	A defence against Lupus' criticisms of Sidonius, including that Sidonius has preferenced others over Lupus by sharing his work with them first.
9.12	Oresius	Praise of Oresius and a refusal to comply with his request for poetry, which Sidonius refuses to write, but is prepared to send if he can find poetry that he has already written.
9.13	Tonantius	A request for a poem which Sidonius sends (included in the letter), and a second poem and an account of the circumstances of its composition.
9.14	Burgundius	A request for poetry which Sidonius sends (included in the letter). Commiserations, as they are both unwell and Burgundius is unable to travel to Rome; examples of different kinds of palindromic verses, a request for Burgundius to send Sidonius his recent work, followed by praise of Burgundius.
9.15	Gelasius	A request for poetry which Sidonius sends (included in the letter). Apologies for not including a letter to Gelasius earlier in the collection and inclusion of some request poetry.
9.16	Firminus	A programmatic letter that ends the collection, including the ninth book, and includes a verse insertion of eighty-four lines.

Bibliography

Abram S.L. (1994) *Latin Letters and their Commonplaces in Late Antiquity and the Early Middle Ages*, Dissertation (Indiana University).

(1998) "Brevity in Early Medieval Letters," *Florilegium* 15, pp. 23–35.

Adams, J.N. (2007) *The Regional Diversification of Latin, 200 BC–AD 600* (Cambridge, Cambridge University Press).

Alciati, R. (2009a) "Eucher, Salvien et Vincent: les Gallicani doctores de Lérin," in *Lérins, une île sainte; de l'Antiquité au Moyen Âge; Collection d'études médiévales*, Y. Codou and M. Lauwers (eds) (Turnhout, Brepols), pp. 105–119.

(2009b) *Monaci, Vescovi e Scuola nella Gallia Tardoantica* (Rome, Edizione di Storia e Letteratura).

Allan, R. J. (2007) "Sense and Sentence Complexity. Sentence Structure, Sentence Connection, and Tense-Aspect as Indicators of Narrative Mode in Thucydides' Histories," in *The Language of Literature. Linguistic Approaches to Classical Texts*, R.J. Allan and M. Buijs (eds) (Leiden, Brill), pp. 93–121.

Allen, M. (1995) "The Martyrdom of St. Jerome," *Journal of Early Christian Studies* 3, pp. 211–213.

Allen, P. (2015a) "Christian Correspondences: The Secrets of Letter-Writers and Letter-Bearers," in *The Art of Veiled Speech. Self-Censorship from Aristophanes to Hobbes*, H. Baltussen and P.J. Davis (eds) (Philadelphia, University of Pennsylvania Press), pp. 209–232.

(2015b) "Rationales for Episcopal Letter-Collections in Late Antiquity," in *Collecting Early Christian Letters from the Apostle Paul to Late Antiquity*, B. Neil and P. Allen (eds) (Cambridge, Cambridge University Press), pp. 18–34.

Allen, P. and B. Neil (2013) *Crisis Management in Late Antiquity (410–590 CE). A Survey of the Evidence from Episcopal Letters* (Leiden, Brill).

Altman, J. G. (1982) *Epistolarity: Approaches to a Form* (Ohio, Ohio State University Press).

Amherdt, D. (2001) *Sidoine Apollinaire, Le quatrième livre de la correspondance* (Berlin, Peter Lang).

(2004) "*Rusticus politicus*. Esprit de caste? L'agriculture et la politique chez Sidoine Apollinaire. Réalité et lieux communs," *Hermes* 132, pp. 373–387.

(2013) "Sidonius in Francophone Countries," in *New Approaches to Sidonius Apollinaris*, J.A. Van Waarden and G. Kelly (eds) (Leuven, Peeters), pp. 23–36.

Anders, F. (2010) *Flavius Ricimer, Macht und Ohnmacht des Weströmischen Heermeisters in der Zweiten Hälfte des 5. Jahrhunderts* (Frankfurt am Main, Peter Lang).

Anderson, C.A. and T.K. Dix (2013) "Vergil at the Races: The Contest of Ships in Book 5 of the *Aeneid*," *Vergilius* 59, pp. 3–21.

Anderson, W.B. (1936) *Sidonius: Poems and Letters I* (London, Loeb Classical Library).

Anderson, W.B and E.H. Warmington (1963) *Sidonius: Poems and Letters II* (London, Loeb Classical Library).

Arjava, A. (1998) "Paternal Power in Late Antiquity," *Journal of Roman Studies* 88, pp. 147–165.

Arnold, E.F. (2014) "Fluid Identities: Poetry and the Navigation of Mixed Ethnicities in Late Antique Gaul," *European Journal of Literature, Culture and Environment* 5, pp. 88–106.

Ash, R. (2003) "'Aliud Est Enim Epistulam, Aliud Historiam ... Scribere' (*Epistles* 6.16.22)," *Arethusa* 36, pp. 211–225.

(2013) "Drip-Feed Invective: Pliny, Self-Fashioning, and the Regulus Letters," in *The Author's Voice in Classical and Late Antiquity*, A. Marmodoro and J. Hill (eds) (Oxford, Oxford University Press), pp. 207–232.

Attanasio D., M. Brilli, and M. Bruno (2008) "The Properties and Identification of Marble from Proconnesos (Marmara Island, Turkey): A New Database Including Isotopic, EPR and Petrographic Data," *Archaeometry* 50, pp. 747–774.

Auerbach, E. (1958) *Literary Language and Its Public, in Late Latin Antiquity and in the Middle Ages*, trans. Ralph Manheim, Bollingen Series LXXIV (New York, Bollingen Foundation).

Avlamis, P. (2011) "Isis and the People in the *Life of Aesop*," in *Revelation, Literature, and Community in Late Anitquity*, P. Townsend and M. Vidas (eds) (Tübingen, Mohr Siebeck), pp. 65–102.

Babic, M. (2015) "Pôžitky vidieckej vily v neskororímskej Galii. Sidonius Apollinaris, *Ep.* 2.2," *Kultúrne dejiny* 6, pp. 87–99.

Bailey, L. (2016) *The Religious Worlds of the Laity in Late Antique Gaul* (London, Bloomsbury Academic).

Bakhtin, M.M. (1981) *The Dialogic Imagination: Four Essays* (Austin, University of Texas Press).

(2002) "Forms of Time and of the Chronotype in the Novel: Notes Towards a Historical Poetics," in *Narrative Dynamics, Essays on Time, Plot, Closure, and Frames*, B. Richardson (ed.) (Columbus, Ohio State University Press), pp. 15–24.

Bakker, E. J. (1997) "Verbal Aspect and Mimetic Description in Thucydides," in *Grammar as Interpretation, Greek Literature in its Linguistic Contexts*, E.G. Bakker (ed.) (Leiden, Brill), pp. 7–54.

Baldwin, B. (1982) "Some Addenda to the Prosopography of the Later Roman Empire," *Historia: Zeitschrift für Alte Geschichte* 31, pp. 97–111.

Baldwin, M.C. (2005) *Whose Acts of Peter?* (Tübingen, Mohr Siebeck).

Balmelle, C. (2001) *Les Demeures Aristocratiques D'Aquitaine, Société et culture de l'Antiquité tardive dans le Sud-Ouest de la Gaule* (Bordeaux, Université Michel de Montaigne).

Banchich, T.M. (trans.) (2009) *Aurelius Victor, Epitome de Caesaribus* (Buffalo, Canisius College).

Banniard, M. (1992) "La Rouille et la Lime: Sidoine Apollinaire et la Langue Classique en Gaule au Ve Siècle," in *De Tertullien aux Mozarabes*, L. Holtz et al. (eds) (Paris, Institut d'Études Augustiniennes), pp. 413–427.

Barcellona, R. (2013) "La "conversione" della cultura: una trasformazione tardoantica," *Chaos e Kosmos* 14, pp. 1–23.

Barnes, T.D. (1983) "Review: Late Roman Prosopography: Between Theodosius and Justinian," *Phoenix* 37, pp. 248–270.

Barnwell, P.S. (1992) *Emperors, Prefects and Kings, The Roman West, 395–565* (Chapel Hill, University of North Carolina Press).

Batstone, W.W. (1998) "Dry Pumice and the Programmatic Language of Catullus I," *Classical Philology* 93, pp. 125–135.

Beard, M. (2002) "Ciceronian Correspondences: Making a Book Out of Letters," in *Classics in Progress*, T.P. Wiseman (ed.) (Oxford, Oxford University Press), pp. 103–144.

Becht-Jördens, G. (2017) "Ein Waschbecken mit Versinschrift des Sidonius als Danaergeschenk für die Gotenkönigin Ragnahild. Zur Bedeutung von Materialität, Handwerks- und Dichtkunst im Diskurs der Ohnmächtigen (Sidon. epist. IV 8)," *Antike und Abendland* 63, pp. 125–153.

Becker, A. (2014a) " 'Ethnicité, identité ethnique. Quelques remarques pour l'Antiquité tardive," *Gerión* 32, pp. 289–305.

(2014b) "Les évêques et la diplomatie romano-barbare en Gaule au Ve siècle," in *L'empreinte chrétienne en Gaule du IVe au IXe siècle*, M. Gaillard (ed.) (Turnhout, Brepols), pp. 45–59.

Becker-Piriou, A. (2008) "De Galla Placidia à Amalasonthe, des femmes dans la diplomatie romano-barbare en Occident?," *Revue Historique* 647, pp. 507–543.

Behrwald, R. (2011) "Das Bild der Stadt Rom im 5. Jh. Das Beispiel des Sidonius Apollinaris," in *Rom und Mailand in der Spätantike. Repräsentationen städtischer Räume in Literatur, Architektur und Kunst*, T. Fuhrer (ed.) (Berlin, De Gruyter), pp. 283–302.

Bellès, J. (1997) *Sidoni Apol·linar Lletres 1–3* (Barcelona, Fundació Bernat Metge).

(1998) *Sidoni Apol·linar Lletres 4–6* (Barcelona, Fundació Bernat Metge).

(1999) *Sidoni Apol·linar Lletres 7–9* (Barcelona, Fundació Bernat Metge).

Bertocchi, A. and M. Maraldi (2006) "*Menaechmus quidam*. Indefinites and Proper Nouns in Classical and Late Latin," in *Latin vulgaire, latin tardif VII: actes du VIIème Colloque international sur le latin vulgaire et tardif, Séville, 2–6 septembre 2003*, C. Arias Abellán (ed.) (Sevilla, Universidad de Sevilla Secretariado de Publicaciones), pp. 89–108.

Beutler, R. (1937) "Der lateinische Neuplatonismus und Neupythagoreismus und Claudianus Mamertus in Sprache und Philosophie by Franz Bömer," *Gnomon* 13, pp. 552–558.

Blänsdorf, J. (1993) "Apollinaris Sidonius und die Verwandlung der römischen Satire in der Spätantike," *Philologus* 137, pp. 122–131.

Blockley, R.C. (1982) "Roman-Barbarian Marriages in the Late Empire," *Florilegium* 4, pp. 63–79.

Bodel, J. (2015) "The Publication of Pliny's letters," in *Pliny the Book-Maker, Betting on Posterity in the Epistles*, I. Marchesi (ed.) (Oxford, Oxford University Press), pp. 13–108.

Bömer, F. (1936) *Der lateinische Neuplatonismus und Neupythagoreismus und Claudianus Mamertus in Sprache und Philosophie* (Leipzig, Otto Harrassowitz).

Bonjour, M. (1981) "Sidonius Apollinaris inter Romanos et barbaros," in *Acta Treverica*, R. Schnur and N. Sallman (eds) (Leichlingen, Brune), pp. 109–118.

(1982) "Personnification, allegorie et prosopopée dans les Panégyriques de Sidoine Apollinaire," *Vichiana*, 11, pp. 5–17.

Borius, R. (1965) *Vie de Saint German d'Auxerre* (Paris, Les Éditions du Cerf).

Börm, H. (2013) *Westerom, von Honorius bis Justinian* (Stuttgart, W. Kohlhammer).

Boshoff, L. (2016) "Looking Eastwards: The *Regina Orientis* in Sidonius Apollinaris' *Carmen 2*," in *From Constantinople to the Frontier: the City and the Cities*, N.S.M. Matheou, T. Kampianaki, and L.M. Bondioli (eds) (Leiden, Brill), pp. 11–24.

Bowersock, G.W., P. Brown, and O. Grabar (1999) *Late Antiquity, A Guide to the Postclassical World*, repr. 2000 (Cambridge, MA, Harvard University Press).

Braund, D.C. (1980) "The Aedui, Troy, and the Apocolyntosis," *The Classical Quarterly* 30, pp. 420–425.

Bregman, J. (1982) *Synesius of Cyrene, Philosopher-Bishop* (Berkeley, University of California Press).

Brennan, B. (1985) "'Episcopae': Bishop's Wives Viewed in Sixth-Century Gaul," *Church History* 54, pp. 311–323.

Brink, C.O. (1971) *Horace on Poetry: The "Ars Poetica" II* (Cambridge, Cambridge University Press).

Brittain, C. (2001) "No Place for a Platonist Soul in Fifth-Century Gaul? The Case of Mamertus Claudianus," in *Society and Culture in Late Antique Gaul, Revisiting the Source*, R.W. Mathisen and D. Schanzer (eds) (Aldershot, Ashgate), pp. 239–262.

Brocca, N. (2003–04) "Memoria poetica e attualità politica nel panegirico per Avito di Sidonio Apollinare," *Incontri triestini di filologia classica* 3, pp. 279–295.

Brown, P. (1971) *The World of Late Antiquity: 150–750 AD* (London, Thames and Hudson).

(1992) *Power and Persuasion in Late Antiquity: Towards a Christian Empire* (Madison, University of Wisconsin Press).

(2000) *Augustine of Hippo: A Biography* (London, Faber).

Burgess, R.W. (1987) "The Third Regnal Year of Eparchius Avitus: A Reply," *Classical Philology* 4, pp. 335–345.

Burton, P. (2009) "The Discourse of Later Latin," in *A Companion to Late Antiquity*, P. Rousseau (ed.) (Chichester, Wiley-Blackwell), pp. 327–341.

Cabouret, B. (2012) "D'Apicius à la table des rois «barbares»," *Dialogues d'histoire ancienne Supplément 7*, pp. 159–172.

Cain, A. (2013) "Terence in Late Antiquity," in *A Companion to Terence*, A. Augoustakis and A. Traill (eds) (Oxford, Wiley-Blackwell), pp. 380–398.

Cameron, Alan. (1965) "The Fate of Pliny's Letters in the Late Empire," *Classical Quarterly* 15, pp. 289–298.

Cameron, Averil. (1993) *The Later Roman Empire, AD 284–430* (London, William Collins).

Castellanos, S. (2013) *En el final de Roma (ca. 455–480)* (Madrid, Marcial Pons).

Chadwick, N.K. (1955) *Poetry and Letters in Early Christian Gaul* (London, Bowes and Bowes).

Chafe, W. (1994) *Discourse, Consciousness, and Time* (Chicago, University of Chicago Press).

Chaix, L.A. (1868) *Saint Sidoine Apollinaire et son siècle* (Clermont-Ferrand, Ferdinand-Thiabud).

Chalon M. et al. (1985) "Memorabile factum: Une célébration de l'évergétisme des rois Vandales dans l'Anthologie Latine," *Antiquités africaines* 21, pp. 207–262.

Champomier, J. (1938) *Esquisse pour un portrait de Sidoine Apollinaire* (Paris, Debresse).

Checon de Freitas, E. (2008) "Entre a *Galliae* a *Francia*," *Brathair* 8, pp. 50–78.

Chidiroglou, M. (2011) "Karystian Marble Trade in the Roman Mediterranean Region. An Overview of Old and New Data," *Bollettino di Archeologia online* 1, pp. 48–56.

Chronopoulos, T. (2010) "Brief Lives of Sidonius, Symmachus, and Fulgentius Written in Early Twelfth-Century England?" *Journal of Medieval Latin* 20, pp. 232–291.

Cloppet, C. (1989) "À propos d'un voyage de Sidoine Apollinaire entre Lyon et Clermont-Ferrand," *Latomus* 48, pp. 857–868.

Collins, R. (2008) *Visigothic Spain 409–711* (Oxford, Blackwell).

Colton, R.E. (1982) "Echoes of Juvenal in Sidonius Apollinaris," *Res Publica Litterarum* 2, pp. 59–74.

(1985) "Some Echoes of Martial in the Letters of Sidonius Apollinaris," *L'Antiquité Classique* 54, pp. 277–284.

Condorelli, S. (2012) "Dal parassita della commedia all'impudicus di Sidonio Apollinare (Epist. 3, 13, 1–4)," *Paideia* 67, pp. 409–427.

(2015) "L'inizio della fine: l'epistola IX 1 di Sidonio Apollinare tra *amicitia* ed istanze estetico-letterarie," *Bollettino di Studi Latini* 45, pp. 489–511.

Connant, J. (2012) *Staying Roman, Conquest and Identity in Africa and the Mediterranean, 439–700* (Cambridge, Cambridge University Press).

Conring, B. (2001) *Hieronymus als Briefschreiber, Ein Beitrag zur spätantiken Epistolographie* (Tübingen, Mohr Siebeck).

Consolino, F.E. (1974) "Codice retorico e manierismo stilistico nella poetica di Sidonio Apollinare," *Annali della Scuola Normale Superiore di Pisa. Classe di Lettere e Filosofia* 4, pp. 423–460.

(2011) "*Recusationes* a confronto: Sidonio Apollinare *Epist.* IX 13,2 e Venanzio Fortunato *carm.* IX 7," in *Il calamo della memoria. Riuso di testi e mestiere letterario nella tarda antichità IV*, L. Cristante and S. Ravalico (eds) (Trieste, Edizioni Università di Trieste), pp. 101–125.

Constable, G. (1970) *Letters and Letter-collections*, Typologie des sources du moyen age occidental 17 (Turnhout, Brepols).

Conybeare, C. (2000) *Paulinus Noster: Self and Symbols in the Letters of Paulinus of Nola* (Oxford, Oxford University Press).

(2012) "*The Letters of Symachus: Book 1* by Michelle Renee Salzman, and Michael Roberts (review)," *Journal of Late Antiquity* 5, pp. 412–414.

Cook, J. G. (2012) "Crucifixion in the West: From Constantine to Recceswinth," *Zeitschrift für Antikes Christentum / Journal of Ancient Christianity* 16.2, pp. 226–246.

Courcelle, P. (1948) *Histoire littéraire des grandes invasions germaniques*, repr. 1964 (Paris, Hachette).

Creese, M. (2006) *Letters to the Emperor: Epistolarity and Power Relations from Cicero to Symmachus*, Dissertation (University of St. Andrews).

Croke, B. (2014) "Dynasty and Aristocracy in the Fifth Century," in *The Cambridge Companion to Attila*, M. Maas (ed.) (Cambridge, Cambridge University Press), pp. 98–124.

Curtius, E. R. (1953) *Europäische Literatur und lateinisches Mittelalter*, trans. Willard R. Trask (New York, Harper and Row).

Daly, W.M. (1987) "*Christianitas* Eclipses *Romanitas* in the Life of Sidonius Apollinaris," in *Religion, Culture and Society in the Early Middle Ages*, T.F.X. Noble and J.J. Contreni (eds) (Kalamazoo, Medieval Institute Publications), pp. 7–26.

(2000) "An Adverse Consensus Questioned: Does Sidonius's *Eucharisticon* (*Carmen* XVI) Show that he was Scripturally Naïve?," *Traditio* 55, pp. 19–71.

Dalton, O.M. (1915) *The Letters of Sidonius I* (Oxford, Clarendon Press).

Damon, C. (2010) "*Quid tibi ego videor in epistulis*, Cicero's *verecundia*," in *Valuing Others in Classical Antiquity*, R.M. Rosen and I. Sluiter (eds) (Leiden, Brill), pp. 375–390.

Dark, K. (2005) "The Archaeological Implications of Fourth- and Fifth-Century Descriptions of Villas in the Northwest Provinces of the Roman Empire," *Historia: Zeitschrift für Alte Geschichte* 54, pp. 331–342.

De La Broise, R.M. (1890) *Mamerti Claudiani vita eiusque doctrina de anima hominis*, Dissertation (Paris).

De Pretis, A. (2003) ""Insincerity," "Facts," and "Epistolarity": Approaches to Pliny's Epistles," *Arethusa* 36, pp. 127–146.

De Saavedra Fajardo, D. (2008) *Coronoa Gótica* [1664], J.L Villacañas Berlanga (ed.) (Murcia, Ediciones Tres Fronteras).

Deißmann, A. (1908) *Licht vom Osten. Das Neue Testament und die neuentdeckten Texte der hellenistisch-römischen Welt* (Tübingen, Mohr Siebeck).

Delaplace, C. (2012) "The So-Called "Conquest of the Auvergne" (469–475) in the History of the Visigothic Kingdom. Relations between the Roman Elites of Southern Gaul, The Central Imperial Power in Rome and the Military Authority of the Federates on the Periphery," in *Shifting Cultural Frontiers in Late Antiquity*, D. Brakke, E. Watts, and D. Mauskopf Deliyannis (eds) (Farnham, Ashgate), pp. 271–281.

(2015) *La fin de l'Empire romain d'Occident. Rome et les Wisigoths de 382 à 531* (Rennes, Presses Universitaires de Rennes).

Denecker, T. (2015) "Language Attitudes and Social Connotations in Jerome and Sidonius Apollinaris," *Vigiliae Christianae* 69, pp. 393–421.

(2017) *Ideas on Language in Early Latin Christianity: From Tertullian to Isidore of Seville* (Leiden, Brill).

Desbrosses, L. (2015) "L'Ancien Monde chez Sidoine: prégnance et signification du modèle païen," in *Une antiquité tardive noire ou heureuse? Colloque international de Besançon, 12 et 13 novembre 2014*, S. Ratti (ed.) (Besançon, Presses Universitaires de Franche-Comté), pp. 209–226.

Dewar, M. (2013) *Leisured Resistance. Villas, Literature and Politics in the Roman World* (London, Bloomsbury).

Diefenbach, S. (2013) ""Bischofsherrschaft." Zur Transformation der politischen Kultur im spätantiken und frühmittelalterlichen Gallien," in *Gallien in Spätantike und Frühmittelalter. Kulturgeschichte einer Region*, G.M. Müller and S. Diefenbach (eds) (Berlin, De Gruyter), pp. 91–152.

Dill, Samuel. (1904) *Roman Society from Nero to Marcus Aurelius* (London, Macmillan).

(1910) *Roman Society in the Last Century of the Western Empire* (London, Macmillan).

(1926) *Roman Society in Gaul in the Merovingian Age* (London, Macmillan).

Drinkwater, J.F. (1978) "The Rise and Fall of the Gallic Iulii: Aspects of the Development of the Aristocracy of the Three Gauls under the Early Empire," *Latomus* 37.4, pp. 817–850.

(1983) *Roman Gaul, The Three Provinces 58 BC–AD 260* (Oxford, Routledge).

(1987) *The Gallic Empire. Separatism and Continuity in the North-Western Provinces of the Roman Empire A.D. 260–274* (Stuttgart, Historia Einzelschriften Heft 52).

(1989) "Gallic Attitudes to the Roman Empire in the Fourth Century A.D.: Continuity or Change?," in *Labor Omnibus Unus. Gerold Walser zum 70. Geburtstag*, H.E. Herzig and R. Frei-Stolba (eds) (Stuttgart, Historia Einzelschriften Heft 60), pp. 136–153.

(1998) "The Usurpers Constantine III (407–411) and Jovinus (411–413)," *Britannia* 29, pp. 269–298.

(2001) "Women and Horses and Power and War," in *Urban Centers and Rural Contexts in Late Antiquity*, T.S. Burns and J.W. Eadie (eds) (East Lansing, Michigan State University Press), pp. 135–146.

(2013) "Un-Becoming Roman. The End of Provincial Civilisation in Gaul," in *Gallien in Spätantike und Frühmittelalter. Kulturgeschichte einer Region*, G.M Müller and S. Diefenbach (eds) (Berlin, De Gruyter), pp. 59–78.

Drinkwater, J.F. and H. Elton (eds) (1992) *Fifth Century Gaul: A Crisis of Identity?* (Cambridge, Cambridge University Press).

Duckett, E.S. (1930) *Latin Writers of the Fifth Century* (New York, H. Holt and Co).

Dunbabin, K.M.D. (1989) "*Baiarum Grata Voluptas*: Pleasures and Dangers of the Baths," *Papers of the British School at Rome* 57, pp. 6–46.

Ebbeler, J. (2001) *Pedants in the Apparel Of Heroes? Cultures of Latin Letter-Writing from Cicero to Ennodius*, Dissertation (University of Pennsylvania).

(2009) "Tradition, Innovation and Epistolary Mores," in *A Companion to Late Antiquity*, P. Rousseau (ed.) (Chichester, Wiley Blackwell), pp. 270–284.

(2012) *Disciplining Christians, Correction and Community in Augustine's Letters* (Oxford, Oxford University Press).

Eco, U. (1994) *The Limits of Interpretation*, first published 1990 (Bloomington, Indiana University Press).

Ehrenberg, V. and A.H.M. Jones (1955) *Documents Illustrating the Reigns of Augustus and Tiberius* (Oxford, Oxford University Press).

Eigler, U. (1997) "Horaz und Sidonius Apollinaris. Zwei Reisen und Rom (mit Tafel 1)," *Jahrbuch für Antike und Christentum* 40, pp. 168–177.

Elg, A.G. (1937) *In Faustum Reiensem Studia, Commentatio academica* (Uppsala, Almqvist and Wiksell).

Engelbrecht, A. (1885) "Untersuchungen über die Sprache des Claudianus Mamertus," *Sitzungberichte der Wiener Akademie* 110, pp. 423–537.

(1889) "Studien über die Schriften des Bischofes von Reii Faustus," *Jahres-Bericht des Gymnasiums der k. k. Theresianischen Akademie*, pp. 1–104.

(1890) "Beiträge zur Kritik und Erklärung der Briefe des Apollinaris Sidonius, Faustus und Ruricius," *Zeitschrift für die österreichischen Gymnasien* 6, pp. 481–497.

Fagan, G.G. (1999) *Bathing in Public in the Ancient World* (Ann Arbor, University of Michigan Press).

Fanning, S. (1992) "Emperors and Empires in Fifth-Century Gaul," in *Fifth-century Gaul: A Crisis of Identity?*, J. Drinkwater and H. Elton (eds) (Cambridge, Cambridge University Press), pp. 288–297.

Faral, E. (1946) "Sidoine Apollinaire et la technique litteraire du Moyen Age," *Studi e testi* 122, pp. 567–580.

Fascione, S. (2016) "Seronato, Catilina e la *moritura libertas* della Gallia," *Koinonia* 40, pp. 453–462.

Fauriel, M. (1836) *Histoire de la Gaule Méridionale sous la Domination des Conquérants Germains*, Tome Premier (Paris, Paulin).

Fitzgerald, W. (2007) *Martial: The World of the Epigram* (Chicago, University of Chicago Press).

Flomen, M. (2009–10) "The Original Godfather: Ricimer and the Fall of Rome," *Hirundo* 8, pp. 9–17.

Fo, A. (1991) "Percorsi e sogni geografici tardolatini," *Aion* 13, pp. 51–71.

Fögen, T. (1999) "Bezüge zwischen antiker und moderner Sprachnormentheorie," *Listy filologické* 121, pp. 199–219.

Forcellinus, A. and J. Facciolatus (1831) *Totius Latinitatis Lexicon II* (Schneebergae, C. Schumanni).

Forman, R.J. (1995) *Augustine and the Making of a Christian Literature, Classical Tradition and Augustinian Aesthetics* (Lewiston, E. Mellen Press).

Fortin E. (1959) *Christianisme et culture philosophique au cinquième siècle, La Querelle de L'âme Humaine en Occident* (Paris, Études Augustiniennes).

Fournier, M. and A. Stoehr-Monjou. (2013) "Représentation idéologique de l'espace dans la lettre 1, 5 de Sidoine Apollinaire: cartographie géo-littéraire d'un voyage de Lyon à Rome," (version 1) *Conference L'espace dans l'Antiquité. Utilisation, function et representation, organised by P. Voisin and M. de Béchillon*, Paris, pp. 1–20.

(2014) "Cartographie géo-littéraire et géohistorique de la mobilité aristocratique au Ve siècle d'après la correspondence de Sidoine Apollinaire: du voyage officiel au voyage épistolaires," *Belgeo* 2014(2), pp. 1–19.

Fowden, G. (2004) *Art and the Umayyad Elite in Late Antique Syria, Quṣayr ʿAmra* (Berkeley, University of California Press).

Fowler, D.P. (1989) "First Thoughts on Closure: Problems and Prospects," *Materiali e discussion per l'analisi dei testi classici* 22, pp. 75–122.

(1997) "Second Thoughts on Closure," in *Classical Closure, Reading the End in Greek and Latin Literature*, D.H. Roberts, F.M. Dunn, and D. Fowler (eds) (Princeton, Princeton University Press), pp. 3–22.

Frye, D. (2003) "Aristocratic Response to Late Roman Urban Change: the Examples of Ausonius and Sidonius in Gaul," *The Classical World* 96, pp. 185–196.

Furbetta, L. (2014) "Un nuovo manoscritto di Sidonio Apollinare: una prima ricognizione," *Res publica litterarum* 37, pp. 135–157.

(2014–2015a) "Empereurs, rois et délateurs. Esquisse d'étude sur la représentation du pouvoir et de ses dégénérescences dans l'oeuvre de Sidoine Apollinaire," *RET* 4, pp. 123–154.

(2014–2015b) "Tracce di Ausonio nelle lettere di Sidonio Apollinare (appunti di lettura)," *Incontri di filologia classica* 16, pp. 107–133.

(2015a) "L'epitaffio di Sidonio Apollinare in un nuovo testimone manoscritto," *Euphrosyne* 43, pp. 243–254.

(2015b) "La lettre de recommandation en Gaule (Ve-VIIe siècles) entre tradition littéraire et innovation," in *Gouverner par les lettres, de l'Antiquité à l'époque contemporaine*, A. Bérenger and O. Dard (eds) (Metz, Université de Lorraine), pp. 347–368.

(2015c) "Sidonio Apollinare nei Libri Historiarum di Gregorio di Tours: qualche riflessione," *Mélanges de l'École française de Rome – Moyen Âge* 127–2, pp. 1–13.

Fürst, A. 1999. *Augustins Briefwechsel mit Hieronymus* (Münster, Aschendorff).

Gamberini, F. (1983) *Stylistic Theory and Practice in the Younger Pliny* (Hildesheim, Olms-Weidmann).

Ganz, D. (1995) "Theology and the Organization of Thought," in *The New Cambridge Medieval History II*, R. McKitterick (ed.) (Cambridge, Cambridge University Press), pp. 758–785.

Gauly, B.M. (2006) "Das Glück des Pollius Felix. Römische Macht und privater Luxus in Statius' Villengedicht *silv.* 2, 2," *Hermes* 134, pp. 455–470.

Geary, P.J. (2009) "What Happened to Latin?," *Speculum* 84, pp. 859–873.

Geisler, E. (1885) *De Apollinaris Sidonii Studiis*, Dissertation (Bratislava).

    (1887) "Loci Similes Auctorum: Sidonio Anteriorum," in *Gai Sollii Apollinaris Sidonii epistulae et carmina*, C. Luetjohann (ed.) (Berlin, Monumenta Germaniae Historia), pp. 351–416.

Gemeinhardt, P. (2011) "Wozu Bildungsgeschichte in der Theologie? Gesprächsimpulse aus kirchengeschichtlicher Perspektive," *Zeitschrift für Religionspädagogik* 10, pp. 190–207.

Genette, G. (1980) *Narrative Discourse: An Essay in Method*, Jane E. Lewin (tran.) (Ithaca, Cornell University Press).

Germain, A.C. (1840) *Essai Littéraire et Historique sur Apollinaris Sidonius* (Montpellier, Boehm).

Gerth, M. (2013) *Bildungsvorstellungen im 5. Jahrhundert n. Chr., Marcrobius, Martianus Capella und Sidonius Apollinaris* (Berlin, Walter de Gruyter).

Giannotti, F. (2016) *Sperare Meliora, il terzo libro delle Epistulae di Sidonio Apollinare, introduzione, traduzione e commento* (Pisa, Edizione ETS).

Gibson, R.K. (2003) "Pliny and the Art of (in) Offensive Self-Praise," *Arethusa* 36, pp. 235–254.

    (2011) "<CLARUS> Confirmed? Pliny, Epistles I.1. and Sidonius Apollinaris," *Classical Quarterly* 61, pp. 655–659.

    (2012) "On the Nature of Ancient Letter Collections," *Journal of Roman Studies* 102, pp. 56–78.

    (2013a) "Letters into Autobiography: The Generic Mobility of the Ancient Letter Collection," in *Generic Interfaces in Latin Literature*, T.D. Papanghelis et al. (eds) (Berlin, de Gruyter), pp. 387–416.

    (2013b) "Pliny and the Letters of Sidonius: From Constantius and Clarus to Firminus and Fuscus." *Arethusa* 46, pp. 333–355.

    (2013c) "Reading Sidonius by the Book," in *New Approaches to Sidonius Apollinaris*, J.A. Van Waarden and G. Kelly (eds) (Leuven, Peeters), pp. 195–220.

    (2015) "Not Dark Yet: Reading to the End of Pliny's Nine-Book Collection," in *Pliny the Book-Maker, Betting on Posterity in the Epistles*, I. Marchesi (ed.) (Oxford, Oxford University Press), pp. 185–221.

Gibson, R.K. and R. Morello. (2012) *Reading the Letters of Pliny the Younger* (Cambridge, Cambridge University Press).

Gillett, A. (1995) "The Birth of Ricimer," *Historia: Zeitschrift für Alte Geschichte* 44, pp. 380–384.

    (1999) "The Accession of Euric," *Francia* 26.1, pp. 1–40.

    (2003) *Envoys and Political Communication in the Late Antique West, 411–533* (Cambridge, Cambridge University Press).

    (2012) "Communication in Late Antiquity: Use and Reuse," *Oxford Handbook of Late Antiquity* S.F. Johnson (ed.) (Oxford, Oxford University Press), pp. 815–848.

Gilson, E. (1995) *History of Christian Philosophy in the Middle Ages* (New York, Random House).

Giuletti, I. (2014) *Sidonio Apollinare, Diffensore della Romanitas, Epistulae 5, 1–13: Saggio di Commento*, Dissertation (Università degli Studi di Macerata).

Goffart, W.A. (1980) *Barbarians and Romans, A.D. 418–584: The Techniques of Accommodation* (Princeton, Princeton University Press).

(2006) *Barbarian Tides: The Migration Age and the Later Roman Empire* (Philadelphia, University of Pennsylvania Press).

Goncalves, V. (2013) "*Aleae aut Tesserae?* Les Significations d'une Opposition Ludique dans la Rome D'Ammien Marcellin," *AnTard* 21, pp. 257–264.

Graves, M. (2007) *Jerome's Hebrew Philology: A Study Based on his Commentary on Jeremiah* (Leiden, Brill).

Greenhalgh, M. (2009) *Marble Past, Monumental Present, Building with Antiquities in the Mediaeval Mediterranean* (Leiden, Brill).

Grey, C. (2008) "Two Young Lovers: An Abduction Marriage and its Consequences in Fifth-Century Gaul," *Classical Quarterly* 58.1, pp. 286–302.

Griffin, M.T. (1976) *Seneca, A Philosopher in Politics* (Oxford, Clarendon).

(1982) "The Lyons Tablet and Tacitean Hindsight," *Classical Quarterly* 32, pp. 404–418.

Grotowski, P. (2010) *Arms and Armour of the Warrior Saints: Tradition and Innovation in Byzantine* (London, Brill).

Gruber, J. (2013) *D. Magnus Ausonius, Mosella: Kritische Ausgabe, Übersetzung, Kommentar* (Berlin, Walter de Gruyter).

Gualandri, I. (1979) *Furtiva Lectio* (Milan, Cisalpino-Goliardica).

(2017) "Words Pregnant with Meaning: The Power of Single Words in Late Latin Literature," in *The Poetics of Late Latin Literature*, J. Elsner and J. Hernández Lobato (eds) (Oxford, Oxford University Press), pp. 125–148.

Günther, R. (1997/1998) "Ansätze eines Bedeutungswandels sozialer und politischer Termini bei latinischen Schriftstellern des 5. Jahrhunderts unter besonderer Berücksichtigung des Sidonius Apollinaris," *Kodai* 8/9, pp. 31–52.

Halsall, G. (2002) "Funny Foreigners: Laughing with the Barbarians in Late Antiquity," in *Humour, History and Politics in Late Antiquity and the Early Middle Ages*, G. Halsall (ed.) (Cambridge, Cambridge University Press), pp. 89–113.

Hanaghan, M.P. (2017a) "All in a Word or Two; Micro Allusions in Sidonius' Programmatic Epistles," *International Journal of the Classical Tradition* 24.3, pp. 249–261.

(2017b) "Avitus' Characterisation in Sidonius' *Carmen 7*," *Mnemosyne* 70.2, pp. 262–280.

(2017c) "Latent Criticism of Anthemius and Ricimer in Sidonius' *Epistula* 1.5," *Classical Quarterly* 67.2, pp. 631–649.

(2017d) "Note de lecture: The Temporality of Seneca's *Epistles*," *Latomus* 76.1, pp. 203–206.

(2018) "Pliny's Epistolary Directions," *Arethusa* 51.2, pp. 137–162.

(forthcoming) "Sidonius Apollinaris and the Making of an Exile Persona," in *Mobility and Exile at the End of Antiquity*, D. Rohmann, J. Ulrich, and M. Vallejo Girves (eds) (Frankfurt, Peter Lang).

Hanson, R.P.C. (1970) "Church in Fifth-Century Gaul: Evidence from Sidonius Apollinaris," *The Journal of Ecclesiastical History* 21, pp. 1–10.

Harries, J.D. (1992a) "Christianity and the City in Late Roman Gaul," in *The City in Late Antiquity*, J. Rich (ed.) (London, Routledge), pp. 77–98.

(1992b) "Sidonius Apollinaris, Rome and the Barbarians: A Climate of Treason?," in *Fifth-Century Gaul: A Crisis of Identity?*, J. Drinkwater and H. Elton (eds) (Cambridge, Cambridge University Press), pp. 298–308.

(1994) *Sidonius Apollinaris and the Fall of Rome, AD 407–485* (Oxford, Clarendon Press).

(1996) "Sidonius Apollinaris and the Frontiers of *Romanitas*," in *Shifting Frontiers in Late Antiquity*, R.W. Mathisen and H.S. Sivan (eds) (Aldershot, Variorum), pp. 31–44.

(forthcoming) "East versus West: Sidonius, Anthemius and the Empire of Dawn," in *Festschrift for Ian Wood*, N. Kıvılcım Yavuz, R. Broome, and T. Barnwell (eds).

Hartmann, M. (2009) *Die Königin im frühen Mittelalter* (Stuttgart, Verlag W. Kohlhammer).

Haverling, G. (1988) *Studies on Symmachus' Language and Style* (Gothenburg, Acta Universitatis Gothoburgensis).

Heather, P. (1992) "The Emergence of the Visigothic Kingdom," in *Fifth-Century Gaul: A Crisis of Identity?*, J. Drinkwater and H. Elton (eds) (Cambridge, Cambridge University Press), pp. 84–94.

(1999) "The Barbarian in Late Antiquity: Image, Reality and Transformation," in *Constructing Identities in Late Antiquity*, R. Miles (ed.) (London, Routledge), pp. 234–258.

(2005) *The Fall of the Roman Empire: A New History* (London, Macmillan).

(2009) "Why Did the Barbarians Cross the Rhine?," *Journal of Late Antiquity* 2, pp. 3–29.

Hebert, B. (1988) "Philosophenbildnisse bei Sidonius Apollinaris; Eine Ekphrasis zwischen Kunstbeschreibung und Philosophiekritik," *Klio* 70, pp. 519–538.

Heinzelmann, M. (1976) "L'aristocratie et les évêchés entre Loire et Rhin, jusqu'à la fin du VIIe siècle," *Revue d'histoire de l'Eglise de France* 62, pp. 75–90.

Henderson, J. (2002) *Pliny's Statue, The Letters, Self Portraiture and Classical Art* (Exeter, University of Exeter Press).

Henke, R. (2008) "Eskapismus, poetische Aphasie und satirische Offensive: Das Selbstverständnis des spätantiken Dichters Sidonius Apollinaris," in A.H. Arweiler and M. Möller (eds) *Vom Selbst-Verständnis in Antike und Neuzeit. Notions of the self in Antiquity and beyond*, Transformationen der Antike 8 (Berlin, De Gruyter), pp. 155–173.

Henning, D. (1999) *Periclitans res publica. Kaisertum und Eliten in der Krise des weströmischen Reiches 454/5–493 n. Chr* (Stuttgart, Franz Steiner Verlag).

Herbert De La Portbarré-Viard, G. (2011) "Venance Fortunat et la representation litteraire du décor des villa après Sidoine Apollinaire," in *Decór et Architecture en Gaule*, C. Balmelle, H. Eristov, and F. Monier (eds) (Bordeaux, Aquitania), pp. 391–401.

Hernández Lobato, J.M. (2012) *Vel Apolline muto: estética y poética de la Antigüedad tardía* (Bern, Peter Lang).

(2014) *El Humanismo que no fue. Sidonio Apollinar en el Renaciemento* (Bologna, Pàtron).

Herrera, I. R. (1981) *Poeta Christianus, Essencia y misión del poeta cristianoen Ia obra de Prudencio* (Salamanca, Universidad Pontificia de Salamanca).

Herschkowitz, D. (1995) "Pliny the Poet," *Greece and Rome* 42, pp. 168–181.

Hodkinson, O. and P.A. Rosenmeyer. (2013) "Introduction," in *Epistolary Narratives in Ancient Greek Literature*, O. Hodkinson, P.A. Rosenmeyer, and E. Bracke (eds) (Leiden, Brill), pp. 1–36.

Hoffer, S. (1999) *The Anxieties of Pliny the Younger* (Atlanta, American Philological Association).

Hoffmann, R.C. (1996) "Economic Development and Aquatic Ecosystems in Medieval Europe," *The American Historical Review* 101, pp. 631–669.

Hooper, F. and M. Schwartz (1991) *Roman Letters, History from a Personal Point of View* (Detroit, Wayne State University Press).

Horvath, Á.T. (2000) "The Education of Sidonus in the Light of his Citations," *Acta Classica Universitatis Scientiarum Debreceniensis* 34, pp. 151–162.

Howland, J.W. (1991) *The Letter Form and the French Enlightenment: The Epistolary Paradox* (Paris, Peter Lang).

Huegelmeyer, C.T. (1962) *Carmen De Ingratis S. Prosperi Aquitani, A translation with an Introduction and a Commentary*, Dissertation (Catholic University of America, Washington, DC).

Humphries, M. (2012) "Valentinian III and the City of Rome (425–455): Patronage, Politics, Power," in *Two Romes: Rome and Constantinople in Late Antiquity*, L. Grigs and G. Kelly (eds) (Oxford, Oxford University Press), pp. 161–182.

Hutchings, L. (2009) "Travel and Hospitality in the Time of Sidonius Apollinaris," *Journal of the Australian Early Medieval Association* 5, pp. 65–74.

Janes, D. (1998) *God and Gold in late Antiquity* (Cambridge, Cambridge University Press).

(2000) "Treasure, Death and Display from Rome to the Middle Ages," in *Treasure in the Medieval West*, E.M. Tyler (ed.) (York, York Medieval Press), pp 1–10.

Janson, T. (1964) *Latin Prose Prefaces, Studies in Literary Conventions* (Stockholm, Almquist and Wiksell).

Jerg, E. (1970) *Vir venerabilis: Untersuchungen zur Titulatur der Bischöfe in den ausserkirchlichen Texten der Spätantike als Beitrag zur Deutung ihrer öffentlichen Stellung* (Vienna, Herder).

Jiménez Sánchez, J.A. (2003) "Julio Nepote y la agonía del Imperio Romano de Occidente," *Faventia* 25, pp. 115–137.

Johnson, W.A. (2010) *Readers and Reading Culture in the High Roman Empire: A Study of Elite Communities* (New York, Oxford University Press).

Johnston, A.C. (2017) *The Sons of Remus: Identity in Roman Gaul and Spain* (Cambridge, MA, Harvard University Press).

Jones, A. E. (2009) *Social Mobility in Late Antique Gaul, Strategies and Opportunities for the Non-Elite* (Cambridge, Cambridge University Press).

Judge, E.-A. (2010) *Jerusalem and Athens, Cultural Transformation in Late Antiquity* (Tübingen, Mohr Siebeck).

Kaster, R. (1997) *Guardians of Language: The Grammarian and Society in Late Antiquity* (Berkeley, University of California Press).

Kaufmann, F.-M. (1995) *Studien zu Sidonius Apollinaris* (Frankfurt am Main, Peter Lang).

Kaufmann, G. (1864) *Die Werke des Cajus Sollius Apollinaris Sidonius als eine Quelle für die Geschichte seiner Zeit* (Göttingen, Universitäts-Buchdruckerei).

Kelly, G. (2008) *Ammianus Marcellinus, the Allusive Historian* (Cambridge, Cambridge University Press)

Kelly, H.A. (1993) *Ideas and Forms of Tragedy from Aristotle to the Middle Ages* (Cambridge, Cambridge University Press).

King, P.D. (1972) *Law and Society in the Visigothic Kingdom* (Cambridge, Cambridge University Press).

Kitchen, T.E. (2010) "Sidonius Apollinaris," in *Ego Trouble. Authors and Their Identities in The Early Middle Ages*, R. Corradini et al. (eds) (Vienna, Austrian Academy of Sciences), pp.53–66.

Koch, A. (1895) *Der heilige Faustus, Bischof von Riez* (Stuttgart, Jos. Roth'sche Verlagshandlung).

Köhler, H. (1995) *C. Sollius Apollinaris Sidonius Briefe Buch 1* (Heidelberg, Universitätsverlag C. Winter).

(1998) "Der Geist ist offenbar im Buch wie das Antlitz im Spiegel: Zu Sidonius epist. I 2, III 13, VII 14," in *Mousopolos Stephanos: Festschrift für Herwig Görgemanns*, M. Baumbach et al. (eds) (Heidelberg, Universitätsverlag Winter), pp. 333–345.

(1999) "Der historische Infinitiv in den Briefen des Sidonius," in *Latin vulgaire – latin tardif, Actes du Ve Colloque international sur le latin vulgaire et tardif*, R. Kettemann and H. Petersmann (eds.) (Heidelberg, 5–8 septembre 1997) (Heidelberg, Universitätsverlag Winter), pp. 409–418.

(2013) "Sidonius in German-Speaking Countries," in *New Approaches to Sidonius Apollinaris*, J.A. van Waarden and G. Kelly (eds) (Leuven, Peeters), pp. 37–46.

(2014) *C. Sollius Apollinaris Sidonius, Die Briefe* (Stuttgart, Hiersemann).

Krabbe, M.K.C. (1965) *Epistula ad Demetriadem de Vera Humilitate, A Critical Text and Translation with Introduction and Commentary*, Dissertation (The Catholic University of America, Washington, DC).

Krause, J.-U. (1991) "Familien- und Haushaltsstrukturen im spätantiken Gallien," *Klio* 73.2, pp. 537–562.

Kroh, K. (2015) "Der laute und der leise Plinius. Vom Umgang mit exemplarischen Ordnungen in epist. 3, 1 und 3, 5," in *Was bedeutet Ordnung – was ordnet Bedeutung?*, C.D. Haß and E.M. Noller (eds) (Berlin, De Gruyter), pp. 71–96.

Kroon, C.H.M. (2002) "How to Write a Ghost story? A Linguistic View on Narrative Modes in Pliny *Ep.* 7.27," in *Donum Grammaticum: Studies in*

Latin and Celtic Linguistics in Honour of Hannah Rosén, L. Sawicki and D. Shalev (eds) (Leuven, Peeters), pp. 189–200.

Kröner, H.O (1989) "Q. Symmachi rotunditas, C Plinii disciplina maturitasque," *Actas del VII Congreso Español de Estudios Clásicos* 2, pp. 639–652.

Kulikowski, M. (2000) "Barbarians in Gaul, Usurpers in Britain," *Britannia* 31, pp. 325–345.

(2008) "*Carmen* VII of Sidonius and a Hitherto Unknown Gothic Civil War," *Journal of Late Antiquity* 1, pp. 335–352.

(2012) "The Western Kingdoms," in *The Oxford Handbook of Late Antiquity*, S.F. Johnson (ed.) (Oxford, Oxford University Press), pp. 31–59.

(2013) "Sundered Aristocracies, New Kingdoms, and the End of the Western Empire," in *Gallien in Spätantike und Frühmittelalter. Kulturgeschichte einer Region*, G.M Müller and S. Diefenbach (eds) (Berlin, De Gruyter), pp. 79–90.

Küppers, J. (2005) "Autobiographisches in den Briefen des Apollinaris Sidonius," in *Antike Autobiographien*, M. Reichel (ed.) (Cologne, Weimer u. Wein), pp. 251–277.

Laes, C. (2013) "Polyglots in Roman Antiquity. Writing Socio-Cultural History Based on Anecdotes," *Literatūra* 55, pp. 7–26.

Lancel, S. (1999) *St. Augustine*, English translation (London, SCM Press).

Leach, E. W. (2003) "*Otium* as *Luxuria*: Economy of Status in the Younger Pliny's Letters," *Arethusa* 36.2, pp. 147–165.

Leatherbury, S. (2017) "Writing (and Reading) Silver with Sidonius: The Material Contexts of Late Antique Texts," *Word and Image* 33.1, pp. 35–56.

Lendon, J.E. (1997) *Empire of Honour, the Art of Government in the Roman World* (Oxford, Clarendon Press).

Leppin, H. (2013) "Überlegungen zum Umgang mit Anhängern von Bürgerkriegsgegnern in der Spätantike," in *Vergeben und Vergessen? Amnestie in der Antike*, K. Harter-Uibopuu and F. Mitthof (eds) (Vienna, Holzhausen), pp. 337–358.

Levick, B.M. (1978) "Antiquarian or Revolutionary? Claudius Caesar's Conception of His Principate," *AJPh* 99, pp. 79–105.

Lewis, C.M. (2000) "Gallic Identity and the Gallic *Civitas* from Caesar to Gregory of Tours," in *Ethnicity and Culture in Late Antiquity*, S. Mitchell and G. Greatrex (eds) (London, Duckworth), pp. 69–81.

Liebeschuetz, J.H.W.G. (2004) "The Collected Letters of Ambrose of Milan: Correspondence with Contemporaries and with the Future," in *Travel, Communication and Geography in Late Antiquity*, L. Ellis and F.L. Kidner (eds) (Aldershot, Ashgate Publishing), pp. 95–107.

(2015) *East and West in Late Antiquity* (Leiden, Brill).

Lievestro, C.T. (1956) "Tertulian and the Sensus Argument," *Journal of the History of Ideas* 17, pp. 264–268.

Liverani, P. (2013) "Saint Peter's and the city of Rome between Late Antiquity and the Early Middle Ages," in *Old Saint Peter's, Rome*, R. McKitterick et al. (eds) (Cambridge, Cambridge University Press), pp. 21–34.

López Fonseca, A. (1998) "San Jerónimo, lector de los cómicos latinos: cristianos y paganos," *Cuadernos de filología clásica: Estudios latinos* 15, pp. 333–352.

López Kindler, A. (2003) "Sidonius Apollinaris: Mitläufer im spätrömischen Gärungsprozess oder Zeuge des Glaubens?," in *Urbs aeterna: actas y colaboraciones del Coloquip Internacional Roma entre la Literature y la Historia: homenaje a la profesora Carmen Castillo*, M. Pilar et al. (eds) (Pamplona, Ediciones Universidad de Navarra), pp. 835–849.

Loretto, F. (1977) *L. Annaeus Seneca: Epistulae morales ad Lucilium. Liber I* (Stuttgart, Reclam).

Loyen, A. (1942) *Recherches Historiques sur les Panégyriques de Sidoine Apollinaire* (Paris, E. Champion).

(1970a) *Sidoine Apollinaire, Tome II Lettres* (Paris, Société d'Édition Les Belles Lettres).

(1970b) *Sidoine Apollinaire, Tome III Lettres* (Paris, Société d'Édition Les Belles Lettres).

Lucht, B. (2011) *Gastfreundschaft und Landleben bei Sidonius Apollinaris am Beispiel von epist. 2,9 an Donidius* (Berlin, Polyptoton II).

Luetjohann, C. (1887) *Gai Sollii Apollinaris Sidonii Epistulae et Carmina* (Berlin, Monumenta Germaniae Historica).

Macarthur, E. (1990) *Extravagant Narratives, Closure and Dynamics in the Epistolary Form* (Princeton, Princeton University Press).

MacGeorge, P. (2002) *Late Roman Warlords* (Oxford, Oxford University Press).

MacMullen, R. (1997) *Christianity and Paganism in the Fourth to Eighth Centuries* (New Haven, Yale University Press).

Maguire, H. (1999) "The Good Life," in *Late Antiquity, A Guide to the Postclassical World*, repr. 2000, G.W. Bowersock, P. Brown, and O. Grabar (eds) (Cambridge, MA, Harvard University Press), pp. 238–257.

Manitius, M. (1888) "Zu Ausonius und Apollinaris Sidonius," *Jahrbücher für classische Philologie* 137, pp. 79–80.

Manuwald, G. (2003) "Eine 'Schule' für Novum Comum (epist. 4, 13). Aspekte der liberalitas des Plinius," in *Plinius der Jüngere und seine Zeit*, L. Castagna and E. Lefèvre (eds) (Munich, K.G. Saur Verlag), pp. 203–217.

March, D.A. (1989) "Cicero and the 'Gang of Five'," *The Classical World* 82, pp. 225–234.

Marchesi, I. (2008a) *The Art of Pliny's Letters: A Poetics of Allusion in Private Correspondence* (Cambridge, Cambridge University Press).

(2008b) "Review: William Fitzgerald, *Martial: The World of the Epigram*," *Bryn Mawr Classical Review* 2008.01.23.

(2015) "Introduction," in *Pliny the Book-Maker, Betting on Posterity in the Epistles*, I. Marchesi (ed.) (Oxford, Oxford University Press) pp. 1–12.

Mariev, S. (2008) *Ioannis Antiocheni Fragmenta Quae Supersunt Omnia* (Berlin, De Gruyter).

Marinova, E. (2014) "Duties and Epistolarity: Semantic Transformations of officium in Latin Epistolography, 4th–5th c.," *Lucida Intervalla* 43, pp. 99–117.

Markus, R.A. (1990) *The End of Ancient Christianity* (Cambridge, Cambridge University Press).

Martínez, M.P. (2014) "El final del Imperio romano de Occidente en Tarraco. La inscripción de los emperadores León I y Anthemio (467–472 d.C.)," *Pyrenae* 45, pp. 117–138.

Mascoli, P. (2001) "Gli Apollinari e l'eredità di una cultura," *Invigilata Lucernis* 23, pp. 131–145.

(2002) "Un nobile galloromano: Apollinare il Vecchio," *Annali della Facoltà di lettere e filosofia dell'Università di Bari* 45, pp. 183–197.

(2010) *Gli Apollinari. Per la storia di una famiglia tardoantica* (Bari, Quaderni di « Invigilata Lucernis » 39).

(2016) *Amici di penna: dall'epistolario di Sidonio Apollinare*, Biblioteca tardoantica 10 (Bari, Edipuglia).

Mathisen, R.W. (1979) "Sidonius on the Reign of Avitus: A Study in Political Prudence," *Transaction of the American Philological Association* 109, pp. 165–171.

(1981) "Epistolography, Literary Circles and Family Ties in Late Roman Gaul," *Transactions of the American Philological Association* 111, pp. 95–109.

(1984) "Emigrants, Exiles and Survivors: Aristocratic Options in Visigothic Aquitania," *Phoenix* 38, pp. 159–170.

(1985) "The Third Regnal Year of Eparchius Avitus," *Classical Philology* 80, pp. 326–335.

(1988) "The Theme of Literary Decline in Late Roman Gaul," *Classical Philology* 83, pp. 45–52.

(1989) *Ecclesiastical Factionalism and Religious Controversy in Fifth-Century Gaul* (Washington, DC, Catholic University of America Press).

(1991) "Review: *De Gratia: Faustus of Riez's Treatise on Grace and Its Place in the History of Theology,* by Thomas A. Smith," *The Catholic Historical Review* 77, pp. 495–496.

(1993a) *Roman Aristocrats in Barbarian Gaul: Strategies for Survival in an Age of Transition* (Austin, University of Texas Press).

(1993b) "For Specialists Only: The Reception of Augustine and his Teachings in Fifth-Century Gaul," in *Collectanea Augustiniana, Augustine: Presbyter Factus Sum*, J.T. Lienhard, E.C. Müller and R.J. Teske (eds) (New York, Peter Lang), pp. 29–41.

(1996) "Review: *Sidonius Apollinaris and the Fall of Rome AD 407–485*, by Jill Harries," *International Journal of the Classical Tradition* 3, pp. 246–250.

(1997) "Les Barbares intellectuels dans l'Antiquité tardive," *Dialogues d'histoire ancienne* 23, pp. 139–145.

(2001) "The Letters of Ruricius of Limoges and the Passage from Roman to Frankish Gaul," in *Society and Culture in Late Antique Gaul: Revisiting the Sources*, R.W Mathisen and D. Shanzer (eds) (Aldershot, Ashgate), pp. 101–115.

(2003a) *People, Personal Expression, and Social Relations in Late Antiquity*, Volume I (Ann Arbor, University of Michigan Press).

(2003b) *People, personal expression, and social relations in Late Antiquity*, Volume II (Ann Arbor, University of Michigan Press).

(2005) "Bishops, Barbarians and the "Dark Ages": The Fate of Late Roman Educational Institutions in Late Antique Gaul," in *Medieval Education*, R.B. Begley and J.W. Koterski (eds) (New York, Fordham University Press), pp. 3–19.

(2009a) "Provinciales, Gentiles, and Marriages between Romans and Barbarians in the Late Roman Empire," *Journal of Roman Studies* 99, pp. 140–155.

(2009b) "The Use and Misuse of Jerome in Fifth Century Gaul," in *Jerome of Stridon: His Life, Writings and Legacy*, A. Cain and J. Lössl (eds) (Farnham, Ashgate), pp. 191–208.

(2013) "Dating the Letters of Sidonius," in *New Approaches to Sidonius Apollinaris*, J. A. van Waarden and G. Kelly (eds) (Leuven, Peters), pp. 221–248.

(2014) "La creation et l'utilisation de «dossiers» dans les lettres de Sidoine Apollinaire," in *Présence de Sidoine Apollinaire*, R. Poignault and A. Stoehr-Monjou (eds) (Clermont-Ferrand, Centre de Recherches A. Piganiol – Présence de l'Antiquité), pp. 205–214.

Mathisen, R.W. and H. Sivan (eds) (1996) *Shifting Frontiers in Late Antiquity* (Aldershot, Variorum).

(1999) "Forging a New Identity: The Kingdom of Toulouse and the Frontiers of Visigothic Aquitania (418–507)," in *The Visigoths: Studies in Culture and Society*, A. Ferreiro (ed.) (Leiden, Brill), pp. 1–62.

Matthews, J. (1971) "Gallic Supporters of Theodosius," *Latomus* 30, pp. 1073–1099.

(1975) *Western Aristocracies and the Imperial Court, A.D. 364–425* (Oxford, Oxford University Press).

(2000) "Roman Law and Barbarian Identity in the Late Roman West," in *Ethnicity and Culture in Late Antiquity*, S. Mitchell and G. Greatrex (eds) (London, Duckworth and the Classical Press of Wales), pp. 31–44.

Max, G E. (1979) "Political Intrigue During the Reigns of the Western Roman Emperors Avitus and Majorian," *Historia: Zeitschrift für Alte Geschichte* 28, pp. 225–237.

McCutcheon, R.W. (2016) "A Revisionist History of Cicero's Letters," *Mouseion: Journal of the Classical Association of Canada* 13.1, pp. 35–63.

McDonough, C.J. (1986) "Hugh Primas 18: A Poetic Glosula on Amiens, Reims, and Peter Abelard," *Speculum* 61, pp. 806–835.

McEvoy, M. (2014) "Between the Old Rome and the New: Imperial Co-Operation *ca.* 400–500 CE," in *Byzantium, its Neighbours and its Cultures*, D. Dzino and K. Parry (eds) (Brisbane, Australian Association for Byzantine Studies), pp. 245–268.

McKay, A.G. (1975) *Houses, Villas and Palaces in the Roman World* (Baltimore, Johns Hopkins University Press).

McLynn, N.B. (1993) "Review: *Fifth-Century Gaul: A Crisis of Identity?* by John F. Drinkwater and Hugh Elton," *Classical Review, New Series* 43, pp. 352–354.

Merrills, A. and R. Miles (2010) *The Vandals* (Malden, Wiley-Blackwell).

Miles, R. (2005) "The Anthologia Latina and the Creation of Secular Space in Vandal Carthage," *Antiquité Tardive* 13, pp. 305–320.

(2008) " 'Let's (Not) Talk About It': Augustine and the Control of Epistolary Dialogue," in *The End of Dialogue in Antiquity*, S. Goldhill (ed.) (Cambridge, Cambridge University Press), pp. 139–147.

Militello, C. (2005) "I *Symmetika Zêtêmata* di Porfirio, fonte del *De statu animae* di Claudiano Mamerto," *Auctores Nostri* 2, pp. 141–159.

Mitchell, S. (2014) *A History of the Later Roman Empire, AD 284–641: The Transformation of the Ancient World* (Chichester, Wiley Blackwell).

Mohrmann, C. (1955) *Latin Vulgaire, latin des Chrétiens, latin medieval* (Paris, Klincksieck).

Mommsen, T. (1887) "Praefatio in Sidonium," in *Gai Solii Apollinaris Sidonii Epistulae et Carmina*, C. Luetjohann (ed.) (Berlin, Weidmann), pp. xliv–liii.

Mondin, L. (2008) "La misura epigrammatica nella tarda latinità," in *Epigramma longum. Da Marziale alla tarda antichità. From Martial to Late Antiquity*, Atti del Convegno internazionale, Cassino, *29–31 maggio 2006*, A.M. Morelli (ed.) (Cassino, Università degli Studi di Cassino), pp. 397–494.

Montone, F. (2017) "Vita e svaghi di un aristocratico del V secolo. Il secondo libro dell'epistolario di Sidonio Apollinare," *Salternum* 21, pp. 23–45.

Moorhead, J. (2007) "Clovis' Motives for Becoming a Catholic Christian," *Journal of Religious History* 13, pp. 329–339.

Morgan, L. (2010) *Musa Pedestris: Metre and Meaning in Roman Verse* (Oxford, Oxford University Press).

Morello, R. (2015) "Pliny's Book 8: Two Viewpoints and the Pedestrian Reader," in *Pliny the Book-Maker: Betting on Posterity in the Epistles*, I. Marchesi (ed.) (Oxford, Oxford University Press), pp. 149–182.

Moss, J.R (1973) "The Effects of the Policies of Aetius on the History of Western Europe," *Historia* 22, pp. 711–731.

Mratschek, S. (2008) "Identitätsstiftung aus der Vergangenheit: Zum Diskurs über die trajanische Bildungskultur im Kreis des Sidonius Apollinaris," in *Die christlich-philosophischen Diskurse der Spätantike: Texte, Personen, Institutionen, Akten der Tagung vom 22.-25. Februar 2006 am Zentrum der Antike und Moderne der Albert-Ludwigs-Universität Freiburg*, T. Fuhrer (ed.) (Stuttgart, Philosophie der Antike Band 28), pp. 363–380.

(2013) "Creating Identity from the Past: The Construction of History in the Letters of Sidonius," in *New Approaches to Sidonius Apollinaris*, J.A. Van Waarden and G. Kelly (eds) (Leuven, Peters), pp. 249–272.

(2016) "The Letter Collection of S.A.," in *Late Antique Letter Collections*, C. di Sogno, B. Storin, E. Watts (eds) (Berkeley, California Press 2016), pp. 309–336.

Muhlberger, S. (1990) *The Fifth-Century Chroniclers, Prosper, Hydatius, and the Gallic Chronicler of 452* (Leeds, Francis Cairns).

Mullen, A. (2015) " 'In Both our Languages': Greek-Latin Code-Switching in Roman Literature," *Language and Literature* 24, pp. 213–232.

Müller, C. (2013) *Kurialen und Bischof, Bürger und Gemeinde – Untersuchungen zu Kontinuität von Ämtern, Funktionen und Formen der 'Kommunikation' in der gallischen Stadt des 4.-6. Jahrhunderts*, Dissertation (Freiburg).

Müller, G. (1948) "Erzählzeit und erzählte Zeit," *Festschrift für P. Kluckhorn*, repr. in Müller, G. (1968) *Morphologische Poetik*, E. Müller (ed.) (Tübingen, M. Niemeyer), pp. 269–286.

Murray, O. (1965) "The 'Quinquennium Neronis' and the Stoics," *Historia: Zeitschrift für Alte Geschichte* 14, pp. 41–61.

Myers, K.S. (2000) "*Miranda Fides*, Poet and Patrons in Paradoxographical Landscapes in Statius' Silvae," *Materiali e discussioni per l'analisi dei testi classici* 44, pp. 103–138.

(2005) "Docta Otia: Garden Ownership and Configurations of Leisure in Statius and Pliny," *Arethusa* 38, pp. 103–129.

Nathan, G. (2000) *The Family in Late Antiquity: The Rise of Christianity and the Emergence of Tradition* (London, Routledge).

Nauta, R.R. (2006) "The *Recusatio* in Flavian Poetry," in *Flavian Poetry*, R.R. Nauta, H.-J. Van Dam and J.J.L. Smolenaars (eds) (Leiden, Brill), pp. 21–40.

Neger, M. (2015) "Pliny's Martial and Martial's Pliny: the Intertextual Dialogue between the Letters and the Epigrams," in *Autour de Pline Le Jeune. En hommage à Nicole Méthy*, O. Devillers (ed.) (Bordeaux, Ausonius Éditions), pp. 131–144.

Nehlsen, H. (1978) "Der Grabfrevel in den germanischen Rechtsaufzeichnungen," in *Zum Grabfrevel in vor- und frühgeschichtlicher Zeit*, H. Jankuhn, H. Nehlsen, H. Roth (eds) (Göttingen, Vandenhoeck und Ruprecht), pp. 107–168.

Newlands, C. (1991) "Silvae 3.1 and Statius' Poetic Temple," *Classical Quarterly* 41, pp. 438–452.

(2013) "Architectural Ecphrasis in Roman Poetry," in *Generic Interfaces in Latin Literature*, T.D. Papanghelis et al. (eds) (Berlin, de Gruyter), pp. 55–78.

Nickisch, R.M.G. (1991) *Brief* (Stuttgart, J.B. Metzler).

Noreña, C. (2007) "The Social Economy of Pliny's Correspondence with Trajan," *American Journal of Philology* 128, pp. 239–277.

Norton, P. (2007) *Episcopal Elections 250–600: Hierachy and Popular Will in Late Antiquity* (Oxford, Oxford University Press).

Obermaier, A. (1999) *The History and Anatomy of Auctorial Self Criticism in the European Middle Ages* (Amsterdam, Rodopi).

O'Daly, G. (1987) *Augustine's Philosophy of Mind* (Berkeley, University of California Press).

O'Flynn, J.M. (1983) *Generalissimos of the Western Roman Empire* (Edmonton, University of Alberta Press).

(1991) "A Greek on the Roman Throne: The Fate of Anthemius," *Historia: Zeitschrift für Alte Geschichte* 40, pp. 122–128.

O'Sullivan, J.F. (1947) *The Writings of Salvian, the Presbyter* (Washington, the Catholic University of America Press).

Ogilvy, J.D.A. (1963) "*Mimi, Scurrae, Histriones*: Entertainers of the Early Middle Ages," *Speculum* 38, pp. 603–619.

Oost, S.I. (1964) "Aëtius and Majorian," *Classical Philology* 59, pp. 23–29.

(1970) "D. N. Libivs Severvs P. F. AVG," *Classical Philology* 65, pp. 228–240.

Oppedisano, F. (2017) "L'insediamento di Antemio (467 d.C.)," *Aevum* 91.1, 1–23.

Overwien, O. (2009) "Kampf um Gallien. Die Briefe des Sidonius Apollinaris zwischen Literatur und Politik," *Hermes* 137, pp. 93–117.

Pagán, V. (2010) "The Power of the Epistolary Preface from Statius to Pliny," *Classical Quarterly* 60, pp. 194–201.

Paschoud, F. (1967) *Roma Aeterna* (Geneva, Institute Suisse).

Patterson, D.J. (2013) "Adversus Paganos: Disaster, Dragons, and Episcopal Authority in Gregory of Tours," *Comitatus: A Journal of Medieval and Renaissance Studies* 44, pp. 1–28.

Pavlovskis, Z. (1962) *The Influence of Statius upon Latin Literature before the Tenth Century*, Dissertation (Cornell University).

(1973) *Man in an Artificial Landscape, the Marvels of Civilisation in Imperial Roman Literature* (Leiden, Brill).

Pensabene, P. (2004) "Amministrazione dei marmi e sistema distributive nel mondo Romano," in *Marmi Antichi*, G. Borghini (ed.) (Roma, De Luca Editori d'Arte), pp. 43–54.

Percival, J. (1997) "Desperately Seeking Sidonius: the Realities of Life in Fifth-century Gaul," *Latomus* 56, pp. 279–292.

Pérez Sánchez, D. (1997) "Realidad social, asentamiento bárbaro y prejuicios ideológicos en la Galia del siglo V a través de la obra de Sidonio Apolinar," *Gerión* 15, pp. 223–241.

Perkins, K.L.P (2007) *The Education of Princess Mary Tudor*, Dissertation (Louisiana State University).

Peter, H. (1901) *Der Brief in der römischen Literatur, litterargeschichtliche Untersuchungen und Zusammenfassungen* (Hildesheim, Olms).

Pietrini, S. (2015) "Il processo di Arvando. Il racconto di Sidonio Apollinare," in *Ravenna Capitale, Guidizi, Giudici e norme processuali in Occidente nei secoli IV-VIII*, G. Bassanelli (ed.) (Santarcangelo di Romagna, Maggioli Editore), pp. 301–322.

Pohl, W. (2006) "Telling the Difference: Signs of Ethnic Identity," in *From Roman Provinces to Medieval Kingdoms*, T.F.X. Noble (ed.) (London, Routledge), pp. 99–138.

Poignault, R. and A. Stoehr-Monjou (eds) (2014) *Présence de Sidoine Apollinaire* (Clermont-Ferrand, Centre de Recherches A. Piganiol – Présence de l'Antiquité).

Postel, V. (2011) "Libertas und Litterae: Leitbegriffe der Selbstdarstellung geistlicher und weltlicher Eliten im frühmittelalterlichen Gallien und Italien," in *Théorie et pratiques des élites au Haut Moyen Âge*, F. Bougard (ed.) (Turnhout, Brepols) pp. 169–186.

Potter, D.S. (1999) *Literary Texts and the Roman Historian* (London, Routledge).

Prévot, F. (1993) "Deux fragments de l'épitaphe de Sidoine Apollinaire découverts à Clermont-Ferrand," *Revue de l'Antiquité Tardive* 1, pp. 223–229.

(1999) "Sidoine Apollinaire et l'Auvergne," in *L'Auvergne de Sidoine Apollinaire à Grégoire de Tours: Histoire et archéologie. 13e Journées internationales d'archéologie mérovingienne, Clermont-Ferrand, 3–6 oct. 1991*, B. Fizellier-Sauget (ed.) (Clermont-Ferrand, Presses Université Blaise-Pascal), pp. 63–80.

Pricoco, S. (1965) "Studi su Sidonio Apollinare," *Nuovo Didaskaleion* 11, pp. 70–150.

Prosopography of the Later Roman Empire (1971–1992) vol. 1, ed. A. H. M. Jones et al. (Cambridge, Cambridge University Press, 1971); vols 2 and 3, ed. J. R. Martindale (Cambridge, Cambridge University Press, 1980–1992) (abbreviated PLRE).

Raffaelli, R. (2007) "Die Metrische Präsentation des Terenztexts in der Antike: der Codex Bembinus," in *Terentius Poeta*, P. Kruschwitz, W.-W. Ehless, and F. Felgentreu (eds) (Munich, Verlag C.H. Beck), pp. 73–91.

Raga, E. (2014) "L'influence chrétienne sur le modèle alimentaire classique: la question de l'alternance entre banquets, nutrition et jeûne," in *L'empreinte chrétienne en Gaule, du IVe au IXe siècle*, M. Gaillard (ed.) (Turnhout, Brepols), pp. 61–87.

Rehling, B. (1898) *De Fausti Reiensis, Epistula Tertia*, Dissertation (Oldenburg).

Reich, H. (1903) *Der Mimus, ein litterar-entwickelungsgeschichtlicher Versuch* (Berlin, Weidmannsche Buchhandlung).

Reiff, A. (1959) *Interpretatio, imitatio, aemulatio, Begriff und Vorstellung literarischer Abhängigkeit bei den Römern*, Dissertation (Cologne).

Reydellet, M. (1981) *La Royauté dans la Littérature Latine De Sidoine Apollinaire à Isidore de Séville* (Rome, École française de Rome).

Ricœur, P. (1980) "Narrative Time," *Critical Inquiry* 7, pp. 169–190.

(1985) *Time and Narrative*, Volume 2, trans. K. McLaughlin and D. Pellauer (Chicago, University of Chicago Press).

(1996) "The Time of Narrating (Erzählzeit) and Narrated time (Erzählte Zeit)," in *Narratology: An Introduction*, S. Onega and J.A. García Landa (eds) (London, Longman), pp. 129–144.

Riggsby, A.M. (1995) "Pliny on Cicero and Oratory: Self-fashioning in the Public Eye," *The American Journal of Philology* 116, pp. 123–135.

Rimell, V. (2015) "Seneca and Neronian Rome: In the Mirror of Time," in *The Cambridge Companion to Seneca*, S. Bartsch and A. Schiesaro (eds) (Cambridge, Cambridge University Press), pp. 122–134.

Risselada, R. (2013) "Applying Text Linguistics to the Letters of Sidonius Apollinaris," in *New Approaches to Sidonius Apollinaris*, J.A. Van Waarden and G. Kelly (eds) (Leuven, Peeters), pp. 273–304.

Robert, R. (2011) "La description du Burgus de Pontius Leontius entre réalité et objet de memoire littéraire (Sidoine Apollinaire, Carm. 22)," in *Decór et Architecture en Gaule*, C. Balmelle, H. Eristov and F. Monier (eds) (Bordeaux, Aquitania), pp. 377–390.

Roberto, U. (2017) "Dépouiller Rome? Genséric, Avitus et les statues en 455," *Revue historique* 684, pp. 775–801.

Roberts. D.H. (1997) "Ending and Aftermath in Ancient and Modern Narrative," in *Classical Closure: Reading the End in Greek and Latin Literature*, D. Roberts, F. Dunn and D. Fowler (eds) (Princeton, Princeton University Press), pp. 251–274.

Roberts, M. (1984) "The *Mosella* of Ausonius: An Interpretation," *Transactions of the American Philological Association* 114, pp. 343–353.

(1989) *The Jeweled Style: Poetry and Poetics in Late Antiquity* (Ithaca, Cornell University Press).

(1995) "Martin Meets Maximus: The Meaning of a Late Roman Banquet," *Revue des Études Augustiniennes* 41, pp. 91–111.

(2001) "Rome Personified, Rome Epitomized: Representations of Rome in the Poetry of the Early Fifth Century," *American Journal of Philology* 122, pp. 533–541.

Rochette, B. (2010) "Greek and Latin Bilingualism," in *A Companion to the Greek Language*, E.J. Bakker (ed.) (Malden, MA, Wiley-Blackwell), pp. 281–294.

(2013) "Traces du bilinguisme dans la correspondance de Pline le Jeune," in *Polyphonia Romana. Hommages à Frédérique Biville 2*, A. Garcea, D. Vallat and M-K Lhommé (eds) (Hildesheim, Olms), pp. 469–481.

Rosén, H. (1980) "*Exposition und Mitteilung* – the Imperfect as a Thematic Tense-Form in the Letters of Pliny," in *On Moods and Tenses of the Latin Verb: Two Essays*, H. Rosén and H.B. Rosén (eds) (Munich, William Fink Verlag), pp. 27–48.

Ross, A. (2016) *Ammianus' Julian, Narrative and Genre in the Res Gestae* (Oxford, Oxford University Press).

Rousseau, P. (1976) "In Search of Sidonius the Bishop," in *Historia: Zeitschrift für Alte Geschichte* 25, pp. 356–377.

(2000) "Sidonius and Majorian: The Censure in *Carmen* V," *Historia: Zeitschrift für Alte Geschichte* 49, pp. 251–257.

Rowan, C. and D. Swan (2015) "Victory, Torcs and Iconology in Rome and Britain," *Journal of the Numismatic Association of Australia* 26, pp. 71–90.

Roymans, N. (2009) "Hercules and the Construction of a Batavian Identity in the Context of the Roman Empire," in *Ethnic Conflicts in Antiquity: The Role of Power and Tradition*, T. Derks and N. Roymans (eds) (Amsterdam, Amsterdam University Press), pp. 219–238.

Russell, J.C. (1994) *The Germanization of Early Medieval Christianity: A Sociohistorical Approach to Religious Transformation* (Oxford, Oxford University Press).

Salmon, P. (1961) "The Wild Man in "Iwein" and Medieval Descriptive Technique," *The Modern Language Review* 56, pp. 520–528.

Salzman, M.R. (2004) "Travel and Communication in The Letters of Symmachus," in *Travel, Communication and Geography in Late Antiquity*, L. Ellis and F.L. Kidner (eds) (Aldershot, Ashgate Publishing), pp. 81–94.

Salzman, M.R. and M. Roberts. (2011) *The Letters of Symmachus: Book 1* (Atlanta, Society of Biblical Literature).

Santos, D. (1997) "Sidonio Apolinar y la descomposición del poder imperial en la Galia," *Anales de historia antigua y medieval* 30, pp. 93–106.

(2011) "La Importancia Política de Ejército Renano durante el Siglo IV," *Studia Historia. Historia Antigua*, 29, pp. 277–291.

Sarti, L. (2011) *Perceiving War and the Military in Early Christian Gaul (ca. 400–700 A.D)* (Leiden, Brill).

Schaff, P. and H. Wace (1892) *A Select Library of Nicene and Post-Nicene Fathers of the Christian Church*, Volume 3: *Theodoret, Jerome, Gennadius, Rufinus* (Michigan, W M. B. Eerdmans).

Schirok, E. (2005) "*Ecce altera quaestio, quomodo hominibus sit utendum*: Seneca über den Umgang mit Menschen," in *Seneca: Philosophus et Magister. Festschrift für Eckard Lefevre zum 70. Geburtstag*, T. Baier and G. Manuwald (eds) (Berlin, Rombach Verlag), pp. 225–254

Schröder, B.J. (2007) *Bildung und Briefe im 6. Jahrhundert. Studien zum Mailänder Diakon Magnus Felix Ennodius* (Berlin, De Gruyter).

Schuster, M. (1940) "Die Hunnenbeschreibungen bei Ammianus, Sidonius und Iordanis," *Wiener Studien* 58, pp. 119–130.

Schwitter, R. (2015) *Umbrosa Lux, Obscuritas in der lateinischen Epistolographie der Spätantike* (Stuttgart, Franz Steiner Verlag).

Scourfield, D. (1993) *Consoling Heliodorus: A Commentary on Jerome, Letter 60* (Oxford, Clarendon Press).

Shanzer, D. and I. Wood (2002) *Avitus of Vienne, Letters and Selected Prose* (Liverpool, Liverpool University Press).

Sharrock, A. (2000) "Intratextuality: Parts and (W)holes in Theory," in *Intratextuality: Greek and Roman Textual Relations*, A. Sharrock and H. Morales (eds) (Oxford, Oxford University Press), pp. 1–39.

Shotter, D.C.A. (1968) "Tacitus, Tiberius and Germanicus," *Historia: Zeitschrift für Alte Geschichte* 17, pp. 194–214.

Simonetti, M. (1976) "Le Fonti del De Spiritu Sancto di Fausto di Riez," *Siculorum Gymnasium* 29, pp. 413–425.

Sirks, A.J.B. (1996) "Shifting Frontiers in the Law: Romans, Provincials, and Barbarians," in *Shifting Frontiers in Late Antiquity*, R. W. Mathisen and H. S. Sivan (eds) (Aldershot, Variorum), pp. 146–157.

(2013) "The *episcopalis audentia* in Late Antiquity," *Les justices alternatives et leurs avatars, Droit et Cultures, Revue Internationale interdisplinaire* 65, pp. 79–88.

Sivan, H.S. (1989) "Sidonius Apollinaris, Theodoric II, and Gothic-Roman Politics from Avitus to Anthemius," *Hermes* 117, pp. 85–94.

(1993) *Ausonius of Bordeaux* (London, Routledge).

Sivonen, P. (1997) "The Good and the Bad, the Civilised and the Barbaric: Images of the East in the Identities of Ausonius, Sidonius, and Sulpicius," *Studies in Latin Literature and Roman History* 8, pp. 417–440.

(2006) *Being a Roman Magistrate: Office-holding and Roman Identity in Late Antique Gaul* (Helsinki, Suomalaisen Kirjallisuuden Seura).

Sogno, C. (2014) "The Ghost of Cicero's Letters: Epistolography and Historiography in Senatorial Letter Writing," *Journal of Late Antiquity* 7, pp. 201–222.

Soler, J. (2005) *Écrituees du Voyage, Héritages et inventions sans la littérature latine tardive* (Paris, Institut d'Études Augustiniennes).

Squatriti, P. (1992) "Marshes and Mentalities in Early Medieval Ravenna," *Viator* 23, pp. 1–16.

Squillante, M. (2007–08) "La felicità e il potere: l'exemplum di Damocle nella rielaborazione tardoantica," *Incontri triestini di filologia classica* 7, pp. 249–260.

(2008) "Scrittori della tarda latinità: identità culturale e difesa della persona," in *Ebraismo e Letteratura*, S. Manferlotti and M. Squillante (eds) (Naples, Liguori), pp. 35–56.

(2009) "La bibliotheca di Sidonio Apollinare," *Voces* 20, pp. 139–159.

(2014) "… tanta curiositate discusserat atque intellexerat, ut … paratum haberet competens sine aliqua dilatione responsum: l'uomo di cultura tra V e VI sec.," in *Il miglior fabbro. Studi offerti a Giovanni Polara*, A. De Vivo and R. Perrelli (eds) (Amsterdam, Hakkert), pp. 273–286.

Stanley, L. (2011) "The Epistolary Gift, the Editorial Third-Party, Counter-Epistolaria: Rethinking the Epistolarium," *Life Writing* 8, pp. 135–152.

Staubach, N. (1983) "Germanisches Königtum und lateinische Literatur," *Frühmittelalterliche Studien* 17, pp. 1–54.

Stein, E. (1959) *Histoire du Bas-Empire*, I-II (Paris, Desclée de Brouwer).

Stevens, C.E. (1933) *Sidonius Apollinaris and his Age* (Oxford, Oxford University Press).

Stickler, T. (2002) *Aëtius: Gestaltungsspielräume eines Heermeisters im ausgehenden Weströmischen Reich* (Munich, C.H Beck).

Stirling, L.M. (2005) *The Learned Collector: Mythological Statuettes and Classical Taste in Late Antique Gaul* (Ann Arbor, University of Michigan Press).

Stroheker, K.F. (1965) *Germanentum und Spätantike* (Zürich, Artemis Verlag).

(1970) *Der senatorische Adel im spätantiken Gallien* (Darmstadt, Wissenschaftliche Buchgesellschaft).

Strunk, T.E. (2013) "Domitian's Lightning Bolts and Close Shaves in Pliny," *The Classical Journal* 109, pp. 88–113.

Styka, J. (2008) "Życie literackie w Arles (Arelate) na podstawie twórczości Sydoniusza Apollinarisa," *Symbolae Philologorum Posnaniensium Graecae et Latinae* 18, pp. 49–69.

(2011) "Cursus honorum im Spätantiken Gallien im Lichte der Briefe Sidonius Apollinaris," *Classica Cracoviensia* 14, pp. 303–318.

Sundwall, J. (1915) *Weströmische Studien* (Berlin, Mayer and Müller).

Swain, S. (2002) "Bilingualism in Cicero? The Evidence of Code-Switching," in *Bilingualism in Ancient Society: Language Contact and the Written Word*, J.N. Adams, M. Janse and S. Swain (eds) (Oxford, Oxford University Press), pp. 128–167.

Szidat, J. (2010) *Usurpator tanti nominis, Kaiser und Usurpator in der Spätantike (337–476 n. Chr.)* (Stuttgart, Franz Steiner Verlag).

Tarrant, R.J. (1997) "Aspects of Virgil's Reception in Antiquity," in *The Cambridge Companion to Virgil*, C. Martindale (ed.) (Cambridge, Cambridge University Press), pp. 56–72.

Teitler, H.C. (1992) "Un-Roman Activities in Late Antique Gaul: The Cases of Arvandus and Seronatus," in *Fifth Century Gaul: A Crisis of Identitity?*, J. Drinkwater and H. Elton (eds) (Cambridge, Cambridge University Press), pp. 309–318.

Teske, R.J. (2001) "Augustine's Theory of Soul," in *Cambridge Companion to Augustine*, N. Kretzmann and E. Stump (eds) (Oxford, Oxford University Press), pp. 116–123.

Thébert, Y. (2003) *Romain D'Afrique du Nord et Leur Contexte Méditerranéen* (Rome, École Française de Rome).

Thierry, J.J. (1963) "The Date of the Dream of Jerome," *Vigilae Christianae* 17, pp. 28–40.

Thome, G. (1993) *Vorstellungen vom Bösen in der lateinischen Literatur. Begriffe, Motive, Gestalten* (Stuttgart, Franz Steiner Verlag).

Thraede, K. (1970) *Grundzüge griechisch-römischer Brieftopik* (Munich, Verlag C.H. Beck).

Tibiletti, C. (1979) "Libero arbitrio e grazia in Fausto di Riez," *Augustinianum* 19, pp. 259–285.

Tomassi, C.O. (2015) "Teo-teleologia in Sidonio Apollinare: tra modulo encomiastico e provvidenzialità dell'impero," in *Poesia e teologia nella produzione Latina dei secoli IV–V*, F. Gasti and M. Cutino (eds) (Pavia, Pavia University Press), pp. 73–105.

Traub, H.W. (1955) "Pliny's Treatment of History in Epistolary Form," *Transactions of the American Philological Association* 86, pp. 213–232.

Twyman, B.L. (1970) "Aetius and the Aristocracy," *Historia: Zeitschrift für Alte Geschichte* 19, pp. 480–503.

Uden, J. (2012) "Love Elegies of Late Antiquity," in *A Companion to Roman Love Elegy*, B.K. Gold (ed.) (Oxford, Blackwell), pp. 459–475.

—— (2014) "The Smile of Aeneas," *American Journal of Philology* 144, pp. 71–96.

Uytterhoeven, I. (2007) "Housing in Late Antiquity: Thematic Perspectves," in *Housing in Late Antiquity, from Palaces to Shops*, L. Lavan et al. (eds) (Leiden, Brill), pp. 25–66.

Van Andel, G.K. (1976) *The Christian Concept of History in the Chronicle of Sulpicius Severus* (Amsterdam, Adolf M. Hakkert).

Van Dam, R. (1985) *Leadership and Community in Late Antique Gaul* (Berkeley, University of California Press).

—— (1992) "The Pirenne Thesis and Fifth-Century Gaul," in *Fifth-Century Gaul: A Crisis of Identity* (Cambridge, Cambridge University Press) pp. 321–34.

—— (1998) *Leadership and Community in Late Antique Gaul* (Berkeley, University of California Press).

Van Waarden, J.A. (2010) *Writing to Survive: A Commentary on Sidonius Apollinaris Letters Book 7 Volume 1: The Episcopal Letters 1–11* (Leuven, Peeters).

(2011a) "Episcopal Self-Presentation: Sidonius Apollinaris and the Episcopal Election in Bourges AD 470," in *Episcopal Elections in Late Antiquity*, J. Leemans et al. (eds) (Berlin, Walter De Gruyter), pp. 555–561.

(2011b) "Sidonio Apollinare, poeta e vescovo," *Vetera Christianorum* 48, pp. 99–113.

(2013a) "Sidonius in the 21st Century," in *New Approaches to Sidonius Apollinaris*, J.A. van Waarden and G. Kelly (eds) (Leuven, Peeters), pp. 3–22.

(2013b) "Review: Jesús Hernández Lobato, J.M. *Vel Apolline muto: estética y poética de la Antigüedad tardía,*" *Bryn Mawr Classical Review* 2013.02.20.

Van Waarden, J.A. and G. Kelly (eds) (2013) *New Approaches to Sidonius Apollinaris* (Leuven, Peters).

Van Wageningen, J. (1905) "De Damoclis gladio," *Mnemosyne New Series* 33, pp. 317–329.

Vessey, D. (1972) "Aspects of Statius' *Epithalamion,*" *Mnemosyne* 25, pp. 172–187.

Visser, J. (2014) "Sidonius Apollinaris *Ep.* II.2. The Man and his Villa," *Journal of Late Antique Religion and Culture* 8, pp. 26–45.

Vitiello, M. (2002) "Fine di una *magna potestae*. La prefettura dell' Annona nei secoli quinto e sesto," *Klio* 84, pp. 491–523.

Ward-Perkins, B. (2005) *The Fall of Rome and the End of Civilization* (Oxford, Oxford University Press).

Ward-Perkins, J.B. (1992) *Marble in Antiquity: Collected Papers of J.B. Ward-Perkins* (London, British School at Rome).

Ware, C. (2012) *Claudian and the Roman Epic Tradition* (Cambridge, Cambridge University Press).

Watson, F. (1912) *Vives and the Renascence Education of Women* (New York, Green and Co, and London, Arnold).

Watson, Lindsay. (2003) *A Commentary on Horace's Epodes* (Oxford, Oxford University Press).

Watson, Lynette. (1998) "Representing the Past, Redefining the Future: Sidonius Apollinaris' Panegyrics of Avitus and Anthemius," in *The Propaganda of Power: The Role of Panegyric in Late Antiquity*, M. Whitby (ed.) (Boston, Brill), pp. 177–198.

Webb, R. (2008) *Demons and Dancers: Performance in Late Antiquity* (Cambridge MA, Harvard University Press).

Weigel, G. (1938) *Faustus of Riez, An Historical Introduction* (Philadelphia, The Dolphin Press).

Wessel, S. (2008) *Leo the Great and the Spiritual Rebuilding of Rome* (Leiden, Brill).

Whitby, M. (1995) "Review: Good Friends in Late Antiquity, Symmaque ou le rituel épistolaire de l'amitié littéraire. Recherches sur le premier livre de la correspondance by P. Bruggisser," *The Classical Review* 45, pp. 42–44.

White, H.G.E. (1921) *Ausonius*, II (London, William Heinemann and G.P. Putnam's sons).

White, P. (2010) *Cicero in Letters: Epistolary Relations of the Late Republic* (Oxford, Oxford University Press).

Whittaker, D. (1993) "Landlords and Warlords in the Later Roman Empire," in *War and Society in the Roman World*, J. Rich and G. Shipley (eds) (London, Routledge), pp. 277–302.

Whitton, C. (2013a) *Pliny the Younger, Epistles Book II* (Cambridge, Cambridge University Press).

(2013b) "Quintilian in Brief: Modes of Intertextuality in Pliny's *Epistles*," *Working Papers on Nervan, Trajanic and Hadrianic Literature* 1.6, pp. 1–19.

(2013c) "Trapdoors: The Falsity of Closure in Pliny's Epistles," in *The Door Ajar: False Closure in Greek and Roman Literature and Art*, F. Grewing, B. Acosta-Hughes, and A. Kirchenko (eds) (Heidelberg, Universitätsverlag Winter), pp. 43–61.

(2015) "Grand Designs: Unrolling Epistles 2," in *Pliny the Book-Maker: Betting on Posterity in the Epistles*, I. Marchesi (ed.) (Oxford, Oxford University Press), pp. 109–143.

Wickham, C. (2005) *Framing the Early Middle Ages: Europe and the Mediterranean, 400–800* (Oxford, Oxford University Press).

Wijnendaele, J.W.P (2016) "Stilicho, Radagaisus and the So-Called 'Battles of Faesulae' (406CE)," *Journal of Late Antiquity* 9, pp. 267–284.

(2017) "The Early Career of Aëtius and the Murder of Felix (c. 425–430 CE)," *Historia: Zeitschrift für Alte Geschichte* 66.4, 468–482.

Wilcox, A. (2012) *The Gift of Correspondence in Classical Rome: Friendship in Cicero's Ad Familiares and Seneca's Moral Epistles* (Madison, University of Wisconsin Press).

Williams, J. (2014) "Letter Writing, Materiality, and Gifts in Late Antiquity: Some Perspectives on Material Culture," *Journal of Late Antiquity* 7, pp. 351–359.

Wilson, M. (1987) "Seneca's Epistles to Lucilius: A Revaluation," *Ramus* 16, pp. 102–121.

Wolff, É. (2012) "La description par Sidoine de son voyage à Rome (Lettres I, 5)," *Itineraria* 11, pp. 1–11.

(2014a) "Quelques jalons dans l'histoire de la reception de Sidoine Apollinaire," in *Décadence, "Decline and Fall" or "Other Antiquity"?*, M. Formisano and T. Fuhrer (eds) (Heidelberg, Universitätsverlag Winter), pp. 249–262.

(2014b) "Sidoine Apollinaire et la poésie épigraphique," in *Memoria poetica e poesia della memoria. La versificazione epigrafica dall'antichità all'umanesimo*, A. Pistellato (ed.) (Venice, Edizioni Ca'Foscari), pp. 207–218.

(2014c) "Sidoine Apollinaire lecteur de Martial," in *Présence de Sidoine Apollinaire*, R. Poignault and A. Stoehr-Monjou (eds) (Clermont-Ferrand, Centre de Recherches A. Piganiol – Présence de l'Antiquité), pp. 295–304.

(2015a) "La lettre VIII, 11 de Sidoine Apollinaire sur le rhéteur Lampridius," in *Caritatis scripta: Mélanges de littérature et de patristique offerts à Patrick Laurence, Collection des Études augustiniennes – Série Antiquité 199*, Aline Canellis et al. (eds) (Paris, Institut d'Études Augustiniennes), pp. 191–197.

(2015b) "Martial dans l'Antiquité tardive (IVe-VIe siècles)," in *Il calamo della memoria. Riuso di testi e mestiere letterario nella Tarda Antichità 6* (Collection of Papers Given at the 6th International Conference at Triest, 25–27 September

2014), L. Cristante and T. Mazzoli (eds) (Trieste, Edizioni Università di Trieste), pp. 81–100.

(2017) "Agir par lettres: le cas de Sidoine Apollinaire," in *Conseiller, diriger par lettre, Epistulae antiquae 9*, É. Gavoille and F. Guillaumont (eds) (Tours, Presses Universitaire François-Rabelais), pp. 71–83.

Wolfram, H. (1990) *Das Reich und die Germanen, Zwischen Antike und Mittelalter* (Berlin, Siedler).

Wood, I.N. (1992) "Continuity or Calamity: the Constraints of Literary Models," in *Fifth Century Gaul: A Crisis of Identitity?*, J. Drinkwater and H. Elton (eds) (Cambridge, Cambridge University Press), pp. 9–18.

Woolf, G. (1998) *Becoming Roman: The Origins of Provincial Civilization in Gaul* (Cambridge, Cambridge University Press).

Yates, J. (1843) *Textrinum Antiquorum: An Account of the Art of Weaving Among the Ancients, Part 1: On the Raw Materials Used for Weaving* (London, Taylor and Walton).

Zaliznjak, A.A and A.D Shmelev (2007) "Sociativity, Conjoining, Reciprocity, and the Latin Prefix *Com-*," in *Reciprocal Constructions*, V.P. Nedjalkov (ed.) (Amsterdam, John Benjamins), pp. 209–230.

Zecchini, G. (1985) "L'Imitatio Caesaris di Aezio," *Latomus* 44, pp. 124–142.

Zeller, J. (1905) "Das concilium der Septem provinciae in Arelate," *Westdeutsche Zeitschrift für Geschichte und Kunst* 24, pp. 1–19.

Ziolkowski, J. (1984) "Avatars of Ugliness in Medieval Literature," *The Modern Language Review* 79, pp. 1–20.

Zimmermann, F. (1914) "Des Claudianus Mamertus Schrift *De statu animae libri tres*," *Divus Thomas* 2, pp. 238–256, 333–368, 470–495.

Index Locorum

General Index

Aëtius, 3, 112, 120
Agricola, 81, 141
Agrippinus, 129, 135
Altman, J., 15n89, 18n4, 59n4, 60n12, 78n54, 136, 136n181, 139, 139n1, 169, 169n87, 178, 178n27
Alypia, 40, 61, 105, 107
Amantius, 167
Ambrose, 42n113, 50, 181
amicitia, 6, 8, 8n47, 25, 26, 31, 32, 35, 36, 40, 41, 49, 64, 67, 82, 88, 90, 96, 119, 125, 143, 153, 179
Anthemius, 5, 6n30, 40, 40n101, 50, 61, 63, 64n22, 67, 89, 108, 116, 174n15, 175n16
Aper, 49, 164
Apollinaris (grandfather), 2, 38, 70, 72
Apollinaris (son), 92
Apollinaris (uncle), 27, 74, 75, 115, 119, 157, 161
Arbogastes, 34
Arianism, 98, 101, 103
Arrius Antoninus, 177
Arvandus, 6, 10, 60, 66, 67, 77, 93n13, 98, 105, 141, 147, 152, 185
astrology, 98n34, 125
Attila, 3, 120
Augustine, 6, 13, 16, 35n77, 51, 55n174, 78, 139, 188
Ausonius, 40n105, 42n115
    allusions, 44
Auvergne, 8, 48, 95n23, 114, 167
Auxanius, 143, 147, 152
Avitus
    daughter, 3, see also Papianilla
    death, 1, 4, 23, 104, 112, 113, 114
    panegyric, 4, 39
    reign, 4, 39, 106, 113
    son, 7
Avitus (relative), 52
Avitus of Vienne, 188

Bakhtin, M., 68n32, 122
barbarians, 2, 4, 12, 19, 34, 39, 41, 47, 50, 95, 96, 100n44, 114, 132, 137, 167
Basilius, 100
baths, 28, 41, 56, 73, 75, 79, 89
Bourges, 56n177, 131n164, 141, 150
Brundisium, 67
Burgundians, 7, 12n70, 21, 34n72, 97n30, 115, 165n78

Campanianus, 67
Candidianus, 42
Censorius, 168
Christianity, 51, 52, 68, 100, 127
    churches, 62n14, 73, 129, 129n155, 132, 133, 135, 141, 148, 168
    Gallic Church, 100, 134
        controversy, 37, 86
        episcopal elections, 52, 130
        leadership, 6n35, 56, 118, 121, 126, 132, 133, 151
    heaven, 151, 156, 181
    in North Africa, 139
    martyrdom, 55n175, 127, 182
    scripture, 19, 51, 133
        allusions, 55, 132, 152
    values, 53, 55, 56, 126, 128, 129, 132, 135, 136, 160, 168
Cicero, 9n49, 15, 23n25, 24, 28n48, 50, 52, 59, 73, 147n28
Claudianus Mamertus, 37, 54, 58, 78, 86, 161, 178
Clausetia, 160
closure, 83n71, 87, 98, 170, 184
clothing, 62, 79, 103
Constantine III, 2, 22n21, 38
Constantius, 74, 119, 125, 138, 171, 174, 175, 177

Damocles, 23, 187
dating, 21, 60, 73, 76, 89, 106n74, 170, 174n15
diegesis, 140, 147, 165, 168
Domitius, 73, 79, 83, 89, 91, 150n42, 170

235